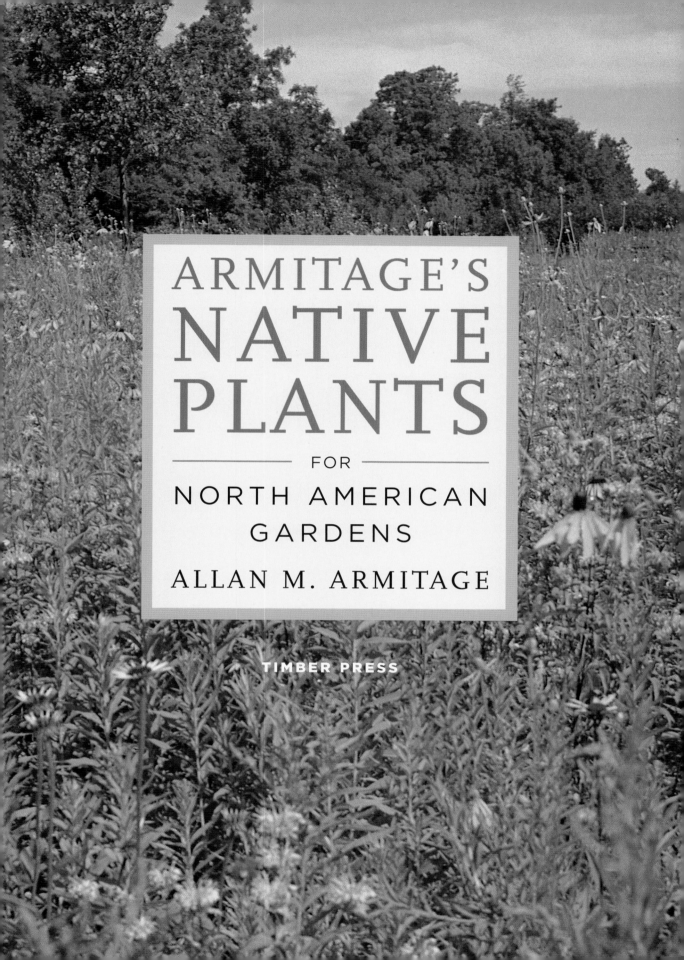

ARMITAGE'S NATIVE PLANTS

FOR

NORTH AMERICAN GARDENS

ALLAN M. ARMITAGE

TIMBER PRESS

All photographs, including the title-page image of the meadow at John and Yvonne Cunnington's home in Ontario, are by the author.

Published in 2006 by
Timber Press, Inc.
The Haseltine Building
133 S.W. Second Avenue, Suite 450
Portland, Oregon 97204-3527, U.S.A.

www.timberpress.com

For contact information regarding editorial, marketing, sales, and distribution in the United Kingdom, see www.timberpress.co.uk.

Reprinted 2006

Printed through Colorcraft Ltd., Hong Kong

Library of Congress Cataloging-in-Publication Data

Armitage, A. M. (Allan M.)
  Armitage's native plants for North American gardens / Allan M.
Armitage.
      p. cm.
  Includes bibliographical references.
  ISBN-13: 978-0-88192-760-3
  ISBN-10: 0-88192-760-0
  1. Native plants for cultivation—North America. 2. Native plant
gardening—North America. I. Title: Native plants for North American
gardens. II. Title.
  SB439.26.N7A76 2006
  625.9'517—dc22   2005022495

A catalog record for this book is also available from the British Library.

For my grandchildren,
Mary Grace, Drew, and Hampton.

To share time with them is the true definition of joy.

CONTENTS

PREFACE

On writing another native plant book

I walked to the library and drove to local bookstores to find books about native plants. From field guides to publications about the simple love of wildflowers, well-written and well-illustrated books were plentiful. Most were written by outdoor enthusiasts with far more knowledge than I, and most were written with a trail and backpack in mind, to satisfy the inquiring mind and help us better appreciate nature.

Now that is all well and good, and I too enjoy the thrill of walking a mountain path and coming across a colony of galax or blue cohosh. Makes me feel a little like Meriwether Lewis even though I recently breakfasted at Bob Evans. My problem is this: when I see such magnificent populations, I want them in my garden. I can't help it. It may be a genetic flaw, but that's the way it is. While I do enjoy hiking to those lovely drifts in the mountains, I would rather hike to my garden bench, mug of coffee in hand, and see such colonies beneath my beloved oaks.

This book is not written for extreme native plant enthusiasts. In fact, I suspect the right wing of the "Native Party" will not particularly like this book. Those purists are the ones who believe that all exotics are bad, and that all natives are good. Rather, it is written for my daughters, Laura and Heather, and their friends and gardening buddies, who would love to try some native plants but don't know where to start.

On what plants to include

The dilemma was not what plants to include in this book, but which to omit. Wonderful native plants are mentioned by botanists, native enthusiasts, and conservationists, but many are so difficult to find that I did not include them. Availability to mainstream gardeners became one of the main criteria for both inclusion and omission, based on my research for each genus. With this in mind, I omitted such taxa as *Ageratina aromatica* (small-leaved white snakeroot), the ditch-loving *Coreopsis nudata*, *Helenium vernale* (spring helenium), and on and on. Other plants begged to be included, but I couldn't find anyone selling them. Another criterion was potential for the future. Perhaps, with the native plant movement continuing to gain momentum, I can include many more in the next edition.

Certainly the question of availability became highly subjective. I included many taxa that will never see a garden center but can be found with a few clicks of the mouse. Laura and Heather will not spend days on a computer looking for a particular plant, but they will spend an hour or so. The list of available natives is greatly expanded: if true gardeners want a plant badly enough, they will find it.

Teaching and traveling are also wonderful ways to test availability. I use my garden and those of others in our community as living laboratories for teaching herbaceous plants. Of the hundreds of plants I teach, a significant portion are natives that these everyday gardeners have planted over the years, plants that have found their way into the garden community. And, without doubt, the more I travel, the more I see people embracing native plants for their gardens. That natives have been accepted by mainstream gardeners is now a given. Therefore, in this book you will notice that I have concentrated on natives that grow in gardens, not those that grow on the ridges of mountains or only by the stream bank.

On the inclusion of cultivars

Here is a quote from Prairie Moon Nursery, a fine native plant establishment (see "Sources and Resources"): "Many [cultivars] do not have the genetic variations of the plants they were developed from and can be aesthetically less pleasing than their wild relatives. Some have been selected to be larger and more aggressive and take over when planted in a mix with other native species." As a gardener, I don't happen to agree, but when have gardeners ever agreed on definitions of gardening? For me, cultivars are the gardeners' candy store. If you like purple coneflower, a dozen choices of that great native plant now await you. Should cultivars be called native? I don't know—should rap be called music? It is simply a matter of opinion. I believe garden-improved cultivars, both selections and hybrids, will only help mainstream gardeners further embrace the world of native plants.

On the difficulty of buying native plants

Although I tell myself that nobody will miss a shovelful, or that a subdivision will definitely be built right over those trout lilies in fifteen years, my conscience continues to win, and stewardship has prevailed over greed. But whenever and wherever I try to purchase those trout lilies, reality hits. Anyone who has ever viewed a hillside of trilliums quickly realizes that one plant just doesn't do it. I want to purchase at least ten, and I am willing to pay a reasonable price; however, the reality is that many of the native plants I desire simply are not there.

While more and more gardeners search the Internet and buy from mail-order sources, the paucity of native plants to be found on retail shelves is more than frustrating; this commercial scarcity of many wildflowers provides yet one more temptation to return to that colony with my trusty shovel.

Times are changing, thankfully. Good nurseries are making significant inroads against this problem, and to be sure, I don't blame commercial producers or retailers: it is as much a problem of market demand (in truth, there are simply not enough of us) as it is of production (many wildflowers are hard to domesticate—propagation and growing time are both issues). While crazy enthusiasts like you and me may lust for a pot of jack-in-the-pulpit, most weekend gardeners do not even notice its absence or even its presence—in their quest for hostas and geraniums. The dream of recreating a hillside of trilliums or a meadow of liatris rapidly morphs into hunting for three or four for the Armitage garden. Those of us who would like to recreate a population of mayapples can always try, but unless one empties the college fund, we often start with a colony of one. Time and patience, not brains or money, are the true necessities if wildflower bounty is wanted in the garden.

On our changing times

Certain areas appear to be way ahead of others in the use and appreciation of native plants. The heartland—including Kansas, Wisconsin, Missouri, Nebraska, Iowa, and Colorado—has worked hard to show people the beauty and utility of native grasses and wildflowers; natives are everywhere out there, and native nurseries in this region are leaders in the country (again, see "Sources and Resources"). The Southeast has also been a magnet for native enthusiasts, with well-established native plant conferences in Cullowhee and Gatlinburg, and the message is slowly filtering down. Every region is now more aware of natives, not just as part of our heritage, but much more importantly, as part of our gardens. There is absolutely nothing wrong with astilbes, petunias, or Japanese maples, and they should all be part of our gardens, but isn't it nice to see our own plants being mainstreamed and slowing the rapid franchising of America?

On marketing native plants

As native plant enthusiasts, we can rail at the shortsightedness of retailers and gardeners for using more oriental poppies than atamasco lilies and purple coneflowers. But let's be honest, how many of your neighbors even know that purple coneflower is a native? They are not stupid, they are simply uninformed, and it is everyone's job to do some informing. I am happy to report that at least three national programs to market native plants will be unveiled in 2006, proclaiming their presence with banners and otherwise informing gardeners that these beautiful plants are native to America. But the message that really needs getting across is that many of them make excellent garden plants. Gardeners are conservationists and proud Americans, but most of all they want the money they spend and the time they allocate to provide pleasure in their garden. We can get frustrated, or we can get moving.

On native plants and medicine

The histories of pharmacology and botany are intertwined. Plants and medicines are strongly linked and will be forever. Growing plants strictly for their ornamental value is a very recent event, reflecting our prosperity and confidence in modern medicine; however, a large and vibrant portion of the world continues to embrace herbal medicines. The holistic medicine movement has found its way to the corner pharmacy, where colorful vials of echinacea, saw palmetto, hypericum, and dozens of other plants are available for what ails us. And if you can't find what you are looking for there, check out the Internet, where almost anything can be ordered.

There is little doubt that ignoring the medicinal benefits of our native plants is no smarter than ignoring the importance of antibiotics created in the lab, and similarly, getting too carried away with what Native American Indians did may not be the smartest way to treat your child's illness. I am captivated by the ingenuity and brilliance of native peoples in using medicinal herbs, but I am equally enamored by the strides modern medicine has made. In writing this book, I have tried to incorporate some of this country's fascinating herbal history, but often, as in any story incorporating history, the facts may be a little embellished in the telling. Embrace the stories, embrace the healing powers, but do so with common sense.

On a garden of native plants

I have said it before and I say it again—I am not a fan of theme gardens. I love roses but can't stand the monotony of rose gardens. I enjoy annuals, but give me a shrub or two. Perennials are beautiful, but without some annuals and woody material, a perennial garden is gruesome. And words shall not appear in this book to describe what I think of daylily gardens, peony gardens, iris gardens, or herb gardens. I am not welcomed by many specialty plant groups.

Like many gardeners, I enjoy mixing natives with exotics; I am simply not capable of limiting myself to one or the other exclusively. Most gardeners are country blind, and that is a good thing. Our gardens and landscapes are richer for the diversity and assimilation. Some people prefer to celebrate only those plants which "belong" here, and they will talk you to death about why this is right. I like to celebrate plants that work in my garden, and I let the plants do the talking.

When I see a perfect miscanthus or a gorgeous scaevola, I will not feel guilty that I didn't plant buffalo grass or copper canyon daisy in its place. Does a chocoholic spurn Ghirardelli or Godiva because they aren't made in Hershey, Pennsylvania? There is sufficient diversity in native material to have all sorts of different plants, but why eliminate the rest of the world in a zeal for America? Good grief, we are gardeners, not Minutemen!

On the Internet

It is here, and it is here to stay. This is not the place to discuss the quality of plant material bought from the Web, or the quality of information there; but, if you try hard enough and persist long enough, you can probably find plants of big bluestem and indian pink on the Internet, and the situation will only continue to improve. As wonderful as this resource is, however, real shelves with real plants, and real people in real garden centers, will continue to be the principal means of attracting gardeners to native plants. That is not as big a problem as it appears; simply marketing the native plants already being sold at retail centers would go a long way to attracting interest in others.

On the fallacy of good guys vs bad guys

Two common misconceptions among gardeners are that if it is native, it cannot be invasive, and that only "exotics" are bad guys. How many times have I heard the names kudzu, privet, multiflora rose, lythrum, and honeysuckle used as an excuse to trash all nonnative plants? They are simply handrails, leaned on by those with an agenda. Some stories are horrific, true, but I will not grow a meadow garden because I have to, and I will not incorporate dogfennel because it is native. If I make a meadow, if I incorporate natives, it is because that is how I want to garden, not how I want to live.

I have had my dealings with people who believe that natives are the only way to garden, who would not have an exotic in their garden. I have no problem with them just like I have no problem with people's religious beliefs—just don't preach them at me or anyone else. What we don't need is the religious right in our garden. Makes you want to gag just thinking about it, doesn't it?

The way some people equate natives with godliness is scary. If you believed all they said, a native would never move, and all seeds would either fall by the roots or birds would happily transport the seeds where they are meant to be. One has only to look at a meadow or prairie to know that it would take one heck of a big flock of birds to create those large colonies of native flowers and grasses. Birds do a lot of pooping, but it would be a paltry meadow or grassland if the plants did not reseed themselves. If you are going to lecture me about natives behaving themselves, do so while you help me get rid of milkweed and northern sea oats. They must have missed that lesson.

On maintaining native plants

I am the first to tell you that my design skills are suspect, but incorporating a native into a plant design is no more difficult than incorporating any other plant. Their maintenance, however, is a different topic. Many of our natives have evolved large taproots for survival or small leaves to conserve water. Overwatering may be a problem with plants that are normally drought-tolerant, as many of our natives are. Realistically, many of our plants need tough love to look good in a garden setting. They do not want or need great handfuls of fertilizer, and they benefit from vigorous pruning when they begin to look weedy. And in the case of meadow gardens, talk with your gardening buddies and look into the benefits of burning. Of course, you might want to notify the local fire department as well.

On the meaning of "native"

This question is at the center of many a heated discussion. I listen, I opine, but I need something to wrap my arms around. A native to me is a plant that was in what we now call mainland America when the Europeans first arrived—a definition that is by necessity vague (I own up to my nebulous opinion, but I have neither the time nor the inclination to argue the fine points of European history). I also include cultivars—selections and hybrids—of native parentage. This is a gardening book, not one on political correctness.

Some people believe "native" means only their county, or their area of the state, or their region of the country. This book is national in scope, but I hope that those who wish to incorporate only their own regional plants will find the information provided under habitat helpful in making their choices. Let's share a cup of tea or a glass of wine and enjoy our national treasures, not argue over them.

A-to-Z GENERA

| *Aconitum* | monkshood, wolfsbane | Ranunculaceae |

I wish this wasn't the first entry in the book, as I debated long and hard whether to even include the genus. My dilemma stems not from the fact that aconitums are extremely poisonous (the term "wolfsbane" should be a hint), nor that the American species may not be as gardenworthy as the European or Asian forms, but that they are so difficult to purchase. It is the last limitation that bothers me most, because, my gardening friends, what good is anticipation without fulfilment? Unfortunately, this theme will resurface often. I have included some harder-to-find gems in the faint hope that demand will result in supply, and anticipation will be fulfilled.

All aconitums produce handsome divided leaves, bear flowers in summer to fall, and do better in the North than in the South. They arise from tubers; you need not test their poisonous properties by biting into one—that would likely be the last bite you took. All parts are poisonous, but the tubers have the highest concentration of aconite.

| *Aconitum reclinatum* | trailing wolfsbane |

Unlike most other species in the genus, this is a vining, sprawling plant, up to 10' in length, that needs to be grown through other plants in the garden. It looks great in the spring as the basal leaves emerge, but it can get a little wild as it loops its way here and there. In late spring or early summer, elongated white to cream-colored flowers are formed. Plants provide more of a curious journey than a destination, but they are fun to try. All aconitums are best grown in climates with cool nights; this one is way too weedy-looking in the South to even try it.

Aconitum reclinatum

Aconitum reclinatum

Habitat: In mountain woods from Virginia to West Virginia and south to north Georgia.

Hardiness: USDA Zones 4–7.

Garden site: Full sun to afternoon shade, moist. If plants dry out, they decline rapidly.

Garden maintenance: Cut plants back after they decline in late summer or fall. Provide ample moisture.

Aconitum uncinatum   southern monkshood

An upright grower, to about 3', with handsome lacy foliage and smooth stems. The violet to purple hooded flowers appear in late summer to fall. They can be good garden plants but often require support to stand up straight. The common name is a bit of a misnomer: they do far better in more northerly climes than in the South.

Habitat: In woods from Pennsylvania to Indiana and south to Georgia and Alabama.

Hardiness: USDA Zones 5–7.

Garden site: Full sun to afternoon shade, moist.

Garden maintenance: Maintain moisture to reduce the incidence of yellow leaves. Cut back plants after flowering.

Recommended propagation

Seed: Purchased or collected seeds should be sown in containers and placed in the refrigerator for about three months. Alternatively, place the seeds in a bag with moist sand or perlite and store in the fridge. Bring out the seeds and allow them to germinate at around 70F.

Cuttings: Terminal cuttings can be taken in late spring. Root in a 3:1 mixture of perlite:peat at around 70F.

Division: Small tubers can be removed and planted elsewhere. Slow but effective.

Etymology

Genus: From an ancient Latin word, *akoniton*, for poisonous plants.

Specific epithet: *reclinatum* ("bent backward"), in reference to the plant's trailing habit; *uncinatum* ("hooked at the end") describes the spurs on this species.

Common name: Monkshood refers to the shape of the flower; wolfsbane suggests its use as a poison bait for wolves.

Actaea   bugbane, baneberry   Ranunculaceae

The genus *Cimicifuga* (bugbane) has gone the way of the Lorax. Essentially, cimicifugas no longer exist and are now incorporated into *Actaea* (baneberry). There are many similarities among the plants, and I suppose this makes some taxonomic sense, but like the old song about Istanbul and Constantinople, I can't help wondering, "Why did *Cimicifuga* get the works?" I feel emptier with its demise.

Bugbanes have a large garden following, which goes to show how weird gardeners are—a following for a bugbane? All the fifteen or so species have a classic upright growth habit, good-looking foliage, and handsome, long-lasting white flowers. That some of them are North American is simply a bonus to those who cherish our natives. Plants produce a stout, cylindrical, knotty blackish rhizome, which has been used medicinally for years. All leaves are alternate and have one- to three-ternate segments and long petioles, similar to other members of the Ranunculaceae. The flowers generally open in the fall and are characterized by having small sepals and no petals. The sepals, which are often dispelled early, make it appear as if there is nothing at all to the flowers. In fact, it is the many stamens that give the flowers their fullness and beauty. Nearly all gardens that specialize in native plants include bugbanes; the wonderful Fletcher Steele garden in Naumkeag, Massachusetts, includes them by the dozen—an unforgettable sight. In general, patience is a good thing when planting bugbanes, but they are worth the wait. Don't expect them to look picture-perfect for at least two years. Plants are best in northern gardens (those below zone 6), although southern gardeners swear by them as much as at them.

The root of these plants, particularly that of black cohosh (*Actaea racemosa*), is used in America to treat many disorders, and can be found in pharmacies and through the Internet. In small doses, it eases children's diarrhea, and studies support its effectiveness in treating hot flashes in women. As a tincture it is taken as an antidote against poisoning, including rattlesnake bites. Roots are collected in the fall, after the fruit is formed and the leaves have died down, then cut into pieces and dried.

Actaea podocarpa   American bugbane

The leaflets of this species (formerly *Cimicifuga americana*) are almost round and heart-shaped at the base; each leaf has three to five serrated lobes. Plants can grow up to 6' in height, but in the garden, I seldom see these more than 4' tall. In the late summer and early fall, the white flowers stand erect on upright racemes, up to 2½' in length. The flowers have three to eight pistils, thus many seeds per fruit are formed (this is of little importance, except to help you determine if you actually have the bugbane you thought you did); the fruit, known as a follicle, is held on a short stem. Plants may be a little more heat-tolerant than *Actaea racemosa*, our other native species.

Habitat: In moist woods in the mountains of Pennsylvania to Tennessee and south to Georgia.
Hardiness: USDA Zones 3–7.
Garden site: A consistently moist, shaded site is best.
Garden maintenance: If plants dry out, the foliage quickly shrivels up and dies. The flower heads are best removed after flowering, allowing more energy to be stored in the rootstalk; this is more important in the southern end of the range.

Actaea podocarpa

Actaea racemosa   common bugbane, black snakeroot

Actaea racemosa (*Cimicifuga racemosa*) is the tallest and most breathtaking of our native actaeas, providing handsome foliage and 4–6' branching flower stems that sway in the late summer breeze. It and the Asian species *A. simplex* are the two most likely to be available in catalogs and garden centers. Depending on the area of the country in which you live, there is little to choose between them. The leaflets are ovate to oblong, pointed at the tips and generally triangular (cuneate) at the base. In the garden, black snakeroot generally towers over other woodland plants, its long wand-like racemes of white flowers making a spectacular sight in late summer. Put your nose in the flowers; you will find a slight fragrance, not at all overwhelming, but pleasant nevertheless. The individual flowers have only one pistil each, thus only one seed per flower will be formed—a good identification feature when trying to determine just which bugbane you are looking at. Plants may be a bit more cold hardy than *A. podocarpa*.

What used to be var. *cordifolia*, in which the leaf bases are heart-shaped, is now *Actaea cordifolia*. Plants are generally shorter and later to flower.

Habitat: In moist woods from Massachusetts to Ontario south to Georgia, Tennessee and west to Missouri.
Hardiness: USDA Zones (3)4–6.
Garden site: Consistently moist areas of partial shade. Plants need morning

sun but perform better with afternoon shade. Too much shade results in poor flowering.

Garden maintenance: Do not allow to dry out, or leaves will go crispy at the edges and simply look tired before their time. In the South, remove spent flowers.

Recommended propagation

Seed: Seeds should be brown before gathered from the plants. Place immediately in seed flats, and maintain at approximately 60F for about three months. After three months, place in a cold frame or area where temperatures are about 40F. Seeds should germinate in the spring. Flowering plants occur the second year.

Division: After sufficient years, division can be accomplished, but plants look better as they age, so I prefer to leave them alone.

Etymology

Genus: From the Greek, *aktea* ("elder"). *Cimicifuga* comes from the Latin *cimex* ("a bug") and *fugo* ("to drive away"); the European species *Cimicifuga foetida* was used as a bug repellent.

Specific epithet: *americana* ("of America"); *podocarpa* is from the Greek ("fruit on a foot"): the fruit are borne on a fleshy stalk; *racemosa* ("with flowers in racemes").

Common name: Black snakeroot is used to distinguish it from common snakeroot (*Aristolochia serpentaria*). The roots are somewhat black, and plants were reputedly a treatment for snakebites. Bugbane refers to the bug-repellent property of the original species, *A. foetida*.

Actaea racemosa

Adiantum   maidenhair fern   Adiantaceae

Ferns often get a bum deal in books on herbaceous plants; they are seldom thought of as perennials or annuals, but rather as, well, ferns—a bit like the lower castes in an old Indian society. Then again, there are fern crazies out there with entire gardens dedicated to these plants, and what a trip that is when you visit them! I have enjoyed the collection at the New York Botanical Garden, run by fern expert John Mickel, but let me also introduce you to the outstanding fern collection, beloved and constantly expanded by George Sanko, at the Native Plant Garden at tiny Georgia Perimeter College in Decatur, which ranks among the Top 40 in the world: www.gpc.edu/~ddonald/botgard/george3.htm.

Ferns have their own vocabulary and terminology, so displays of these plants are both an education and a wake-up call. I greatly enjoy these pteridophytes and am constantly discovering their tremendous diversity—so many ferns, from so many countries, yet our natives are also outstanding. Among the most popular groups are the maidenhair ferns, two species of which are readily found by the "normal" gardener; a third will require a little digging through catalogs and the Internet.

Adiantum capillus-veneris   southern maidenhair fern

This is an exceptional fern, but probably not as eye-catching as the northern form. Having said that, I have seen fabulous plants and colonies in the Birmingham Botanical Garden and everywhere on the southeastern coast. This is a better plant for gardeners in the Deep South, Gulf Coast, and the West Coast,

Adiantum capillus-veneris

but if you live in a more temperate area, where both species may be grown, you will likely have more success with the northern. Plants need limestone soils and should be kept consistently moist—not always an easy thing to do.

Habitat: On limey rocks often near waterfalls, widespread in tropical and semi-tropical areas of the world, including the southern United States.

Hardiness: USDA Zones 7–10.

Garden site: Shady, moist areas in basic soils.

Garden maintenance: If soils are acidic (less than pH 5.5), add dolomitic lime. Constant moisture helps in establishing the plants; try to position them by water features, if you have them, particularly those with splashing water, like waterfalls. Do not crowd plants; they will decline with various diseases if too dense.

Adiantum pedatum   northern maidenhair fern

At about 8" tall, this species is one of the daintiest of the native ferns and certainly the most popular of the maidenhairs. The thin black stems and horseshoe-shaped fronds are highly unusual, imparting a uniquely soft look to the shade garden, but this wimpy-looking appearance belies the toughness of the plant, which routinely bounces back from cold winters and warm summers, not to mention wind, rain, sleet, and snow. Plants spread by rhizomes (large colonies can occur within three to five years) and lend themselves to a fun demonstration: cut off a frond and plunge the foliage into water—amazingly, the frond remains dry.

Adiantum pedatum

I have seen some selections in botanical gardens and private collections, but availability in garden centers is almost nonexistent. There is considerable debate as to the identity of *Adiantum pedatum* var. *aleuticum*, with more upright fronds; most taxonomists believe it to be a separate species, *A. aleuticum*. Obviously, with a name like that, it displays outstanding cold tolerance. Other forms once associated with *A. pedatum* have been put into *A. aleuticum*. 'Subpumilum' (dwarf maidenhair) is only 3–6" tall and native to the coastal Northwest. Cute, but only hardy to about zone 5. 'Imbricatum' is intermediate in size and has blue-green foliage. Also cold hardy in zones 5–7. The taxonomic debate continues; if you can find these, try them, but I suspect the best garden performer will be the old-fashioned species itself, which is readily available. As to the more-difficult-to-find variants, a good means of procuring them are the several fern societies that offer spores.

Habitat: In rich shaded soil, often beneath moist overhangs, and in limestone-rich areas as far north as Alaska and northern Canada south to Louisiana and Georgia.
Hardiness: USDA Zones 2–7.
Garden site: Plants perform best in filtered light and well-drained, cool soil. This fern spreads fairly slowly. Shaded, moist conditions are important, but plants fall apart if planted in low-lying areas with poorly drained soils.
Garden maintenance: A fall application of dolomitic lime in acid soils is beneficial. Do not allow plants to become too crowded; disease will result.

Recommended propagation
Spores: Spores are formed on the back of the fronds. To collect them, cut off the fronds as the spore cases become almost black and place them in a bag. Keep the bag in a warm area, and the spores will be released. Sow the spores on moist soils. and cover with plastic or mist, as needed (the young plants are very sensitive to drying out). Transplant carefully to another

Adiantum pedatum

Adiantum aleuticum 'Subpumilum'

container to allow the sporelings to establish roots. Grow on until ready to plant outdoors.

Division: Plants are best divided in early spring or late fall, when they are dormant. Each piece should have a viable "eye" on the root system. Transplant and water in. If done during the summer, trim most of the fronds off the divided piece, transplant, and water well.

Etymology

Genus: From the Greek, *adiantos* ("dry, unwetted") for its water-repelling habit.

Specific epithet: *capillus-veneris* ("hair of Venus"); *pedatum* ("like a bird's foot"), referring to the divisions radiating from the same point.

Common name: Maidenhair alludes to the fineness and arrangement of the fronds.

Adlumia fungosa   **Allegheny fleece vine, climbing fumitory**   **Fumariaceae**

When I first read about this plant, I wanted to see it. I loved the way the name *Adlumia fungosa* ran off my tongue. Weird I know, but how many botanical names do you like to say? It turned out that it was a neat vine, whose beauty was in its refinement. The off-white flowers, with their light pink to purple coloring, are handsome up close but will never compete with *Clematis* for eyeball appeal. However, no apologies needed: visitors who see this plant in the garden are always intrigued (and always want a piece). Plants climb rapidly through hollies or other shrubs by their thin, twining stems and can reach 10–12' in a single season. The flowers resemble bleeding hearts (*Dicentra*) without the blood, and are in the same family; they form in the spring and continue blooming for four to six weeks.

Although their native dwelling extends to the South, plants have more vigor where night temperatures remain in the low seventies and below. I grow it in the Armitage garden because I enjoy it, but I have seen prettier specimens in the North.

Availability is mainly through seed vendors; plants occasionally may be found through specialty catalogs.

Habitat: New Brunswick to Ontario and Michigan, south to North Carolina and Tennessee.

Hardiness: USDA Zones 3–7.

Garden site: Partial shade, plants do poorly in full sun.

Garden maintenance: Sometimes vines need help climbing. The best site allows them to climb through shrubs or other plants; I use evergreen hollies as my trellis, but they can be trained onto fences and other structures. The fact is, plants look almost weedy in habit, but the flowers will have people claiming it, not taming it.

Recommended propagation

Seed: Plants often self-sow, and
seedlings can be removed and
placed elsewhere. Mature flowers
form a seed pod that is easily collected. Seeds are small and can be
planted in a prepared bed of fine
soil. It is likely that, as with bleeding
heart, a four- to six-week period of
cold is required before they will germinate. If seeds are to be stored,
collect them and place them in a
container with milled sphagnum
moss and keep them in an airtight
jar in the refrigerator. Plants require
eight to ten weeks before being big
enough to transplant.

Etymology

Genus: For Major John Adlum
(1759–1836), a native of
Pennsylvania and a well-known

Adlumia fungosa

grape breeder in his day. He was one of the first people to experiment with
grapes in America, and in 1819 introduced the Catawba grape to the
American market.

Specific epithet: *fungosa* ("resembling fungus"), perhaps in reference to the soft
(not to say spongy) flowers.

Common name: Allegheny fleece vine refers to the mountains where it is common; fumitory is the common name for the Fumariaceae family.

Agastache	giant hyssop	Lamiaceae

Many *Agastache* hybrids have been introduced recently, some from Asia, one or
two from Europe, but probably the greatest concentration of *Agastache* species
occurs in the southwestern United States. All have flowers rich in nectar, and all
are magnets to hummingbirds and butterflies. The leaves have a marvelous fragrance, and the flowers often smell pleasant as well. However, they are not for
everybody all the time. Especially the "all the time" part. They can look spectacular in the spring and early summer, and struggle later on. But I guess we can
say the same for most plants, can't we? Several fine, nonnative species and cultivars, such as the Asian *Agastache rugosa* and 'Blue Fortune' (an *A. rugosa*

hybrid), have been introduced to American gardeners, but we have plenty that call this country home from which to choose.

Agastache aurantiaca	golden hyssop

Golden hyssop is probably the brightest of the species, producing golden orange flowers through much of the season. Many species of hyssop are highly drought-tolerant; this one is not. It certainly does not require any more than average irrigation, but it is not one I would put in a xeric situation. The species itself is seldom seen in garden centers or mail-order catalogs, but it is a parent to many fine selections and hybrids, mostly the result of crosses between it and *Agastache coccinea*.

'Apricot Sprite' and 'Navajo Sunset' are stunning. 'Apricot Sprite' is about 2' tall and filled with vivid apricot flowers in the summer. 'Navajo Sunset' is taller, up to 3½', with many golden orange tubular flowers in the summer. Both are eye-catching, and both are attractive to butterflies and hummingbirds. Water and fertilize well. Zones 7–9.

'Coronado' is an upright grower with silvery aromatic leaves. The tubular yellow flowers are heavily stained with orange, and open in late summer. Plants grow about 2½' tall. I have seen this rated to be hardy as far north as zone 4 but more likely to zones 5–6.

'Just Peachy', introduced by High Country Gardens of Santa Fe, New Mexico, provides subtle shades of pink- and peach-colored flowers. The 2½' tall plants are perhaps hardy to zone 6.

'Shades of Orange' is another High Country Gardens introduction. Plants are about 2½' tall and produce many tubular blooms from peach to dark orange. Zones 6–10.

Agastache aurantiaca 'Apricot Sprite'

Agastache aurantiaca 'Navajo Sunset'

Habitat: Arizona to New Mexico, south into Texas and northern Mexico.
Hardiness: USDA Zones 6–10.
Garden site: Full sun, well-drained soils.
Garden maintenance: None, other than cutting back if needed in late spring to
   encourage branching.

Agastache cana   mosquito plant, Texas hummingbird plant

This is a handsome plant when grown well. The triangular foliage is blue-green,
and the striking late summer flowers are a pink-rose hue, easily visible across
the garden. The foliage is fragrant but not to the extent of *Agastache rupestris*.
Highly drought-tolerant.

‘Desert Sunrise’ is an excellent hybrid (*Agastache cana* × *A. rupestris*) and
grows to 4' tall and 2' wide. The flowers are a fascinating combination of orange,
pink, and lavender shades, rich in nectar for hummingbirds. This is by far the
best of the many agastaches planted at Powell Gardens, outside of Kansas City.
Zones 5–10.

‘Heather Queen’ is an erect grower with dark pink blooms in early summer.
Plants reach 30–36" in height. Zones 7–10.

‘Purple Pygmy’ is said to be a selection of *Agastache cana*, but I suspect it is a
hybrid. It grows only about 18" tall and bears attractive clusters of purple flower
spikes on compact plants.

Habitat: Western Texas to southern New Mexico.
Hardiness: USDA Zones 5–8.

Agastache cana

Garden site: Place in full sun and a dry, well-drained area. They do poorly in moist soils.

Garden maintenance: None.

Agastache foeniculum   anise hyssop

Plants have the fragrance of anise and generally bear many densely spaced lavender flowers on each upright stem. This is probably the most "national" of the species offered by nurseries, which is to say that more people from more areas have more success with plants with *Agastache foeniculum* in their parentage than with other hybrids. Stronger and more upright than *A. rupestris* or *A. cana*, plants are, in general, more cold-tolerant as well. They usually grow 2–3' tall. Cultivars of anise hyssop are successful as cut flowers and landscape plants.

'Alabaster' is a cream-colored form of the species.

'Golden Jubilee' has remarkable golden yellow foliage that contrasts well with the lavender-purple flowers. I recommend it highly.

Honey Bee series includes 'Honey Bee White' (an improvement on 'Alabaster', being more compact and a better white color) and 'Honey Bee Blue' (similar but with lavender flowers).

Licorice series includes 'Licorice Blue' and 'Licorice White', which produce lavender-blue and creamy white flowers, respectively. These may be hybrids with *Agastache urticifolia* (nettle hyssop).

Habitat: Dry woodlands and prairies from North Dakota to Kansas, west to Colorado.

Agastache foeniculum

Hardiness: USDA Zones 5–9.
Garden site: Full sun, good drainage.
Garden maintenance: Cut back to about 1' in the spring to allow for more
 branching; one cutback is sufficient.

Agastache rupestris   licorice mint, rock anise hyssop

This hyssop has slender, spreading branches and dozens of rose-orange tubular flowers. The late summer and fall flowers are quite beautiful, but it is the distinct smell of anise that arises when the narrow leaves are touched that makes me want it in my garden. Place it near a path where the foliage can be disturbed whenever someone walks by. This is also a can't-miss plant if attracting hummingbirds is important. I have grown this plant in the Southeast, but plants succumbed to afternoon rains and humidity after about five years. An excellent choice for a xeric garden.

I am not aware of any available selections of this species. 'Firebird' appears to be the result of a cross between it and *Agastache coccinea*. Plants are 2–3' tall and about 2' wide, and bear 12" inflorescences of orange-copper flowers from mid summer to late autumn.

Habitat: Mainly in the mountains of southwestern New Mexico, to central
 Arizona and south into northern Mexico.
Hardiness: USDA Zones 5–8.

*Agastache
rupestris*

Garden site: Place in full sun and a dry, well-drained area. Plants do poorly in moist soils.

Garden maintenance: Cut back in late spring if additional branching is needed.

Hybrids

The hybrids are in most cases more vigorous, more colorful, and better garden plants than the species. The parentage of many of the newer hybrids is not accurately known.

'Tutti-frutti' (*Agastache pallida* × *A. mexicana*), one of the older hybrids, has garnered both lavish praise and stinging criticism (much like writers of horticultural books). I have had trouble embracing it in the Southeast, seen it look good in Texas, and thought it was outstanding at Chanticleer in Wayne, Pennsylvania. Plants produce 12" long inflorescences of tubular raspberry-red flowers from mid summer to late fall, and grow 2½–3' tall and about 2' wide. The foliage is strongly scented. Zones 6–10.

Recommended propagation

Seed: Nearly all species and hybrids are raised from seed. It is a simple matter of sowing the seeds in a moist, fine mix and placing the container at 70–75F after gently watering them in. Seeds germinate in five to ten days.

Cuttings: Take one- to two-node terminal cuttings anytime from late spring to fall. A rooting powder is useful but not necessary. Place the cut end in a moist, fine mix and place the container at 70–75F. Rooting will occur in most taxa within two weeks.

Division: Only with large clumps. Cuttings are easier on the plant and usually more successful.

Agastache 'Tutti-frutti'

Etymology

Genus: William Stearn suggests the name comes from the Greek *agan* ("very much") and *stachys* ("ear of grain"), referring to the many flower spikes. According to L. H. Bailey, it comes from the Greek for "many-spiked," a similar nod to the many flowers produced.

Specific epithet: *aurantiaca* ("orange-colored") and *coccinea* ("scarlet") are obvious references to the flower color of the respective species; *foeniculum* ("fennel") refers to the fragrance of the foliage; *rupestris* ("rock-loving") suggests that plants need excellent drainage.

Common name: Hyssop refers to the fragrance of the foliage, similar to the true hyssop, *Hyssopus officinalis*. Common names that include anise or licorice also refer to the fragrance of various species.

Amsonia	**blue star flower**	**Apocynaceae**

Blue star flower is endemic to much of the United States. Various species are found from the Southeast to the Northwest, and several forms are available to gardeners as well—a direct result of their outstanding performance in gardens.

Amsonia hubrichtii	**narrow-leaf blue star**

This species is No. 1 in certain areas of the Midwest. Its charm lies in its soft, narrow, asparagus fern–like foliage, which is a light green most of the season. The flowers are light blue, even tending toward white. People love this plant because it grows vigorously, spreads out well, and turns golden in the fall. But let's not get too carried away with this fall color thing, especially in warm climates. Without doubt, they are more colorful in the North than in the South, but they certainly don't compete with a maple. Plants in general are not as exciting in the Armitage garden as in the Midwest or North; in my garden, they tend to

Amsonia hubrichtii

Amsonia hubrichtii

get a little too tall and floppy, but I still love the look of the foliage. Plants grow about 3' tall and equally wide.

Habitat: In fields and meadows in Arkansas, Oklahoma, and Missouri.
Hardiness: USDA Zones 5–9.
Garden site: Full sun in all areas of the country; plants do not tolerate shade well. Provide a dry site in the garden and irrigate as needed.
Garden maintenance: Plants may spread open in late summer and fall, which is more of a problem in times of high temperature and afternoon rain. Plants can be supported to remain upright if that bothers you. A spring cutback will help alleviate that problem.

Amsonia tabernaemontana   eastern blue star flower

Without doubt, this is the most common species, certainly in the eastern half of the country and well into the Midwest and West Coast as well. As a species, the 2½–3' tall plants are perfectly fine for gardens, providing lustrous green leaves with a white midrib and many light blue flowers for three to four weeks in early spring—one of the first plants to flower. The flowers are followed by long, narrow seed pods; even they have some ornamental value. The golden fall color is good, but not as good as in *Amsonia hubrichtii*. They are long-lived plants: I have not killed them in the fifteen years they have been growing in the Armitage garden. This is high on my list for best native perennial in the garden.

Plants perform well in areas of afternoon shade but will tolerate full sun in the northern part of their range. They tolerate shade but not well, and should receive at least four hours of light to be at their best in the garden. The species is easily found; its variants are much more difficult to track down.

'Blue Ice' is a dwarf form of the species, growing 18–24" tall. This is an excellent plant for the garden where something a little shorter is needed.

Amsonia tabernaemontana

Amsonia tabernaemontana, seed pods

Amsonia tabernaemontana 'Blue Ice'

Amsonia tabernaemontana var. montana

var. *montana* is another fine choice, also with a more dwarf habit, growing only about 2' tall.

var. *salicifolia* has thin leaves, like a willow (*Salix*) and many pale blue flowers.

Habitat: In moist woodlands and stream banks from Massachusetts to Kansas, south to Georgia and Texas.

Hardiness: USDA Zones 3–8.

Garden site: Full sun in the North and West, afternoon shade is tolerated in the South.

Garden maintenance: None, if placed in full sun. If in too much shade, some staking may be needed, but better to move it.

Other species for the garden

Amsonia ciliata is known for its more narrow leaves, which are somewhat hairy, and var. *filifolia* has narrower leaves yet. Plants grow 3–4' tall.

Amsonia illustris is native to central United States and is particularly well known and well used in Missouri, Kansas, and Oklahoma. The 2–4' tall plants have flowers similar to other amsonias but bear lustrous shiny leaves, somewhat

Amsonia tabernaemontana var. salicifolia

Amsonia ciliata

thicker than those of *A. tabernaemontana*. I find the two species very similar and can only really see a difference when they are grown side by side.

In the Southeast, I have had less garden success with *Amsonia illustris* than with others, but in the Midwest, the opposite appears to be true. Gardeners in other parts of the country may have had different experiences. Both *Amsonia ciliata* and *A. illustris* are available in nurseries in the central Plains states and through mail order, both are hardy to at least zone 5, and both require the same light conditions as *A. tabernaemontana*.

Recommended propagation

Seed: If collecting your own, check for mature seeds in August, or when the narrow fruits (follicles) change from green to yellow, then brown (fruits split along one side, and seeds can be lost if you forget to check). Seeds should be dried for a couple of days, then either immediately sown to containers or stored in the refrigerator. Germination is enhanced by cutting one end of each seed (stratification) and soaking them in water prior to sowing, or by storing the seeds for about three months at 40F before sowing.

Cuttings: Take a two- to three-node cutting in May or just before the flowers fade. They will root easily and be ready for transplanting four to six weeks later. Rooting hormone enhances rooting percentage and vigor but is not necessary for success. Cuttings taken later in the season are less successful.

Division: Divide an "eye" and associated roots in early spring as the new growth starts to emerge. Transplant immediately.

Etymology

Genus: For 18th-century Virginia physician Charles Amson.

Specific epithet: *ciliata* ("small hairs") refers to the small hairs around the leaf margins; *filifolia* ("thread-like leaves"); *hubrichtii* honors Leslie Hubricht, who found the plant in the early 1940s; *illustris* ("lustrous") is a reference to the shiny leaves; *tabernaemontana* is a mouthful and remembers Jakob Theodor von Bergzabern, a personal physician to the Count of Palatine in Heidelberg, Germany in the 16th century—at that time, latinizing one's name was not an unusual practice, and he changed his name to Tabernaemontana, after a mountain town near where he was born. Does this last make any sense? Of course not, but so the story goes. Jakob went on to write and illustrate botanical texts and died around 1590.

Common name: The flowers easily recall blue stars.

Andropogon	beard grass, bluestem	Poaceae

Beard grasses make up a large part of America's tallgrass prairie and are hugely important in our bio-history. Most bear handsome flowers (for grasses) and flat leaves that often turn color in the fall, and a couple are also excellent for showy seed heads during the winter. Once established, they are all extremely drought-tolerant and are favorites for reclamation purposes. Be careful when ordering seeds or plants by common name; the bluestems associated with this genus are often confused with little bluestem, *Schizachyrium scoparium* (which see).

Andropogon gerardii   big bluestem, turkey foot grass

This is a big plant, 4–7' tall, and therefore not suitable for most gardens. It is mostly seen as a windbreak, or along highways for erosion control; however, its reliable cold hardiness and drought tolerance have also made it a favorite for large landscapes and naturalizing areas, such as meadows. Rhizomes are short or absent in the Midwest, and plants are essentially clump-formers; in Texas, plants tend to be more rhizomatous. The leaves are blue-green, 12" long and about ½" wide, and softly hairy near the base. The flowers, which begin in mid summer, are held close to the axis of the two- to three-times branched inflorescences, which some people say resemble turkey feet. Flowers are followed by drooping seed heads. Both the seed heads and the flowers make useful cut stems for drying, and plants are gaining popularity as landscape plants for their quick growth and brilliant red foliage in late fall.

'Pawnee', somewhat shorter than the species at 4–5', is a welcome introduction to gardeners. Foliage is a little darker green and often takes on a handsome red tinge in the fall.

Habitat: Plants are of major importance in the central states; although they are assumed to be native only to the midwestern prairies and the eastern edge of the Great Plains, they occur over most of the United States.
Hardiness: USDA Zones 3–8.
Garden site: Normal soils, full sun.
Garden maintenance: Although deep-rooted and drought-tolerant, plants benefit from regular irrigation the first year. They will always look better if provided with a little care. Mow or cut back hard in winter or early spring.

Andropogon glomeratus   bushy bluestem

This large grass is not for everybody, but it is certainly impressive. Plants grow 5–6' in height and spread to about 3'. Even when not in flower, the flattened blue-green leaves provide a nice effect. The flower stems start to emerge in late summer to fall, carrying bushy inflorescences (thus the common name). After frost, the foliage has handsome fall and winter color, but the flower plumes can be even more eye-catching: they turn a copper-orange that persists for months. Flowers can also be cut and enjoyed indoors anytime.

Habitat: From New York to Kentucky, west to California, south to Texas and east to Florida.
Hardiness: USDA Zones 3–9.
Garden site: Full sun.
Garden maintenance: Cut back hard in the spring to allow new growth to emerge.

Andropogon saccharoides   silver beard grass

A bit of discussion is brewing here. Some taxonomists have relegated this species to *Bothriochloa* (boh-three-oh-KLOH-ah), which we will have to live with, even if we can't pronounce it. I think we can dispense with this argument for a while and simply enjoy the plant. A much smaller and more easily managed grass than *Andropogon gerardii*, this ornamental bunch grass is increasingly popular in native gardens and in xeric settings. It grows 2–3' tall and 2' wide, and its flower heads are white and fluffy from late summer into winter. The bright green leaves turn a handsome orange in the fall. Useful in the smaller garden but also in meadows or along driveways.

Habitat: Midwestern prairies into the Southwest.
Hardiness: USDA Zones (5)6–8.
Garden site: Any garden soil is appropriate. Full sun.
Garden maintenance: Irrigate to establish when young. Mow as needed.

Other species for the garden
Andropogon ternarius (split beard broom sedge) has fluffy silver inflorescences in the fall on 2–2½' tall plants—not as big as other members of the genus. The inflorescences are often but not always divided into threes. Handsome colorful foliage in the fall as well. Zones 6–9.

Who in their right mind would buy common broom sedge, *Andropogon virginicus*? It is a pioneer plant, seeding with abandon, and is listed as a weed in almost every state in which it occurs. However, there I was at a native plant conference in North Carolina, and two speakers, both excellent native enthusiasts, were going on and on about the foliage color in the winter—I was almost ill. Of course, they are right. As I constantly tell my students and must remind myself, "There is no such thing as a bad plant, only a bad use for a good one." No doubt its very tenacity, along with drought- and salt-tolerance, makes this weed especially good for meadows and reclamation. Still a lousy garden plant but popular for what it does best: colonize.

Recommended propagation
Seed: Collect or purchase seeds, and direct sow in the garden in the fall, or germinate in containers and put out in the spring.
Division: Divide grasses in the early spring.

Etymology

Genus: From the Greek, *aner* ("man") and *pogon* ("beard"), referring to the silky hairs on the flowers.

Specific epithet: *glomeratus* ("clustered"); *saccharoides* ("resembling sugar cane"); *ternarius* (composed of or arranged in threes); *virginicus* ("of Virginia").

Common name: Beard grass is a partial translation of the genus name; bluestem refers to the glaucous blue stems and foliage of *Andropogon gerardii*; silver beard grass hints at the silvery foliage of *A. saccharoides*; turkey foot grass is suggestive of the three-way divided flower spike.

Anemone	windflower	Ranunculaceae

All the world loves anemones, and our gardens are all the richer for species and cultivars from Asia and Europe. Outstanding breeding efforts have resulted in vigorous hybrids in many colors and sizes, and although there are anemones native to the United States, trying to find them in a garden center or catalog is a difficult task indeed. Compared with Japanese hybrids especially, no native anemone is even on the radar screen of availability.

Anemone canadensis	Canadian windflower

This is the only native anemone I can recommend to gardeners without hesitation, mainly because it is more readily available (relatively speaking) than other native anemones. Canadian windflower is only 1–2' tall and grows in partial shade in the Midwest or full sun in the North. Plants tolerate most soils, but they also enjoy consistent moisture, going dormant rapidly if drought conditions persist. The beautiful single white flowers consist of four to six sepals, each up to 1½" wide. They open in May in warmer climates to July in cool summers. The leaves are often lustrous green, divided into three to five lobes. Like all anemones, the flowers themselves are not persistent, but plants come back for many years. If sufficient plants are available, place them on about 1' spacing, so that a colony will quickly be established.

Specialty wildflower nurseries often carry plants of Canadian windflower (and occasionally others as well), and seed houses will offer seed. Availability is still limited, and I am not sure why.

Habitat: Common in woods and prairies. Plants are native from Labrador in the North, Massachusetts in the Northeast to Colorado and North Dakota in the West. They extend to about Maryland in the South.

Hardiness: USDA Zones 2–6.

Garden site: Partial shade; they do poorly in full sun.

Garden maintenance: None.

Anemone canadensis

Other species for the garden

Anemone cylindrica (western thimbleweed) and *A. quinquefolia* (wood anemone) are also excellent plants where cool temperatures and consistent moisture are the norm. Unfortunately, availability for the home gardener is poor.

Anemone virginiana (eastern thimbleweed) is excellent in northern climes, and with divided leaves, a creamy white flower, and a height of about 1½', it fits well into most gardens. Zones 2–7.

Recommended propagation

Seed: Several studies have been conducted specifically on the sowing of *Anemone cylindrica*. Seed heads need to be cleaned and chaff removed. Seeds should be damp stratified by mixing them with equal amounts of damp vermiculite and peat moss; keep the seed mixture in a plastic bag or container at 34–36F for three to four months. After the cold treatment, place mix in containers and germinate at 70–80F. Using this method, expect germination of approximately 75 percent in two to three weeks.

Cuttings: Root cuttings can be an effective means of propagation. Cut thick sections of root approximately 3–4" long from lifted plants; cut the top of the section straight across and the bottom at an angle (or vice versa—either way, you will always know which end is up even when the cat jumps on the table and knocks them off). Place root sections vertically (top up) in a moist, well-drained medium. Cover the tops of the root sections with a thin layer of sand or vermiculite and place in a cold frame or unheated greenhouse.

Division: This is the easiest method for *Anemone canadensis*. Divide in the spring, or after the plants have gone dormant.

Anemone virginiana

Etymology

Genus: A Greek legend tells us that Anemone was a beautiful nymph, and Boreas, the god of the north wind, was in love with her; she scorned his love and in anger, he transformed her into a flower (hence windflower). Or perhaps it is to do with the great sorrow for slain Adonis, who was gored by a boar, and from whose blood sprang the blood-red flowers of *Anemone coronaria*. More pragmatic writers believe the name is simply derived from the Greek word *anemos* ("wind"), as most flowers and seed heads sway in the wind.

Specific epithet: *canadensis* ("of Canada"), by which epithet early writers included the northeastern United States; *cylindrica* refers to the cylindrical fruit; *virginiana*, for England's Queen Elizabeth, the Virgin Queen; *quinquefolia* ("five leaflets")—actually the leaf is usually divided into only three segments, but the side segments are so deeply cut as to appear to be five.

Common name: Windflower has been explained; thimbleweed refers to the shape of the fruit. Remember thimbles? They have been disappearing rapidly as handsewing is less and less taken up by the MTV generation.

| *Anemonella thalictroides* | rue-anemone | Ranunculaceae |

This is the only species—small (less than 4" tall, not much wider) and ephemeral, but one that I look forward to every year. I wish I could obtain it in the hundreds: there is no such thing as having too many rue-anemones. Plants arise from small tubers in early spring. The 1" wide flowers, which consist of five to ten white sepals but no petals, arise on thin black stems and persist for only a few days. Perhaps it's this wispy countenance that beguiles me—surely there are far more colorful and enduring flowers to cherish. The leaves are divided into three, and each segment again divided into threes; the final segments are notched in the margin. Leaves range from a bronzy green in early spring to light green as the season progresses. Under warm, dry conditions, the foliage may turn purplish and then disappears, going into dormancy in the heat of summer and reappearing as soon as the snow melts. The species is far more available than the cultivars.

'Cameo' has double white to blush-pink flowers.

Don Jacobs of Eco Gardens in Decatur, Georgia, has selected 'Eco Atlas Double', 'Eco Pink', and 'Eco Starry Night', all significantly different from the species.

'Schoaf's Pink', the best-known cultivar, was discovered by Oscar Schoaf in Owatonna, Minnesota. Beautiful full rose-pink, almost purple double flowers characterize the selection, which is expensive and hard to find. I was offered one for $25.00, and as beautiful as it looked in its 4" pot, I declined. Probably not a smart decision.

Habitat: In woods from Maine to Minnesota in the North to Oklahoma and Florida in the South.
Hardiness: USDA Zones 4–8.
Garden site: Partial to heavy shade; they do poorly in full sun.
Garden maintenance: None. The difficulty is knowing where you planted them after they go dormant so you don't dig them up by mistake.

Recommended propagation
Seed: Seeds may be collected or purchased. For best results, collect the seeds as they ripen. This ripening is difficult to see: be sure to check periodically at the same time new flowers are appearing. Seeds appear to need a warm, moist period followed by a cold, moist period before germination will occur. Either store in moist sphagnum moss for at least eight weeks at room temperature followed by an additional eight weeks at 35–40F before sowing, or

Anemonella thalictroides

Anemonella thalictroides 'Cameo'

sow immediately and place the seed tray under similar conditions. Once the cold treatment has been satisfied, move the tray to 60–70F conditions.

Division: As plants mature, small tubers form beneath the soil. These may be divided as the plants are going dormant, or early in the spring as the plants appear. Not all tubers have viable "eyes," so take only the largest. This is the best way to propagate the cultivars.

Etymology

Genus: *Anemonella* ("little anemone"), for the obvious similarities of its flowers to *Anemone*; the suffix *-ella* means "little" or "looks like."

Anemonella thalictroides 'Schoaf's Pink'

Specific epithet: *thalictroides* refers to the similarity of the foliage to that of meadow rue, *Thalictrum*; the suffix *-oides* also means "looks like."

Common name: The flowers resemble those of *Anemone*, and the foliage is similar to that of rue (*Ruta*).

Antennaria	pussy-toes	Asteraceae

The most common form of pussy-toes in our gardens is the European *Antennaria dioica*, and a pretty plant it is. Many species are native to this country, particularly in the western United States, but only a handful have gained a measure of popularity among propagators and gardeners. The small flower heads are surrounded by dry, papery bracts, generally off-white or light pink in color—this is one of many genera with papery flowers, often referred to as everlastings. Plants are dioecious: some bear only staminate (male) flowers, while others bear pistillate (female) ones. In most species, however, even though the plants are dioecious, the pistillate plants can still produce viable seed without fertilization from the staminate plants. The gray-green leaves are usually woolly or silky, covered with fine white hairs. Leaves are mostly basal; those growing on the flower stems are much smaller. Plants spread well by runners that appear from the side of the plants. I enjoy pussy-toes in my garden: they are simple, they flower well and freely, and they make a handsome silvery appearance in the spring garden.

Antennaria plantaginifolia   ladies' tobacco

The foliage is the best part of this plant, especially if you like growing plants that look like the weeds you just dug out of the lawn. The large green basal leaves are smooth and have three to seven conspicuous veins; the stem leaves are much more narrow. The stems rise about 1' above the foliage and provide clusters of small whitish flower heads. They are quite floppy and can be a little too weed-like for some tastes.

Habitat: In dry woodlands or fields from Maine to Minnesota and south to Missouri and east to Georgia.
Hardiness: USDA Zones 3–7.
Garden site: A dry site is much preferable to a wet one. Full sun to afternoon shade.
Garden maintenance: Very little, plants may be cut back if they get too floppy.

Antennaria solitaria   solitary pussy-toes

I much prefer this plant to the previous species: it is shorter, has prettier foliage, and does not look like a weed. The 2–3" leaves are spoon-shaped and quite woolly and the runners are long and slender. The flowering stem can still be a bit floppy, but not as much, in my experience, as ladies' tobacco. The flower stem bears but one cluster of silvery flower heads. Plants are also drought-tolerant, surviving xeric conditions with ease, making them an excellent choice for the partially shaded dry area of the garden.

Habitat: In woods from Maryland and western Pennsylvania to Indiana and south to Louisiana, Alabama and Georgia.
Hardiness: USDA Zones 3–8.
Garden site: A dry site is much preferable to a wet one. Afternoon shade too is preferable. Application of a winter mulch is not recommended.
Garden maintenance: Very little. Plants may be cut back if they get too floppy.

Other species for the garden
Antennaria alpina is native to Nevada, Utah, and near the timberline in western Canada. Plants grow no more than 3" tall and spread slowly. They are highly desirable as ground covers between rocks and pathways. Few flowers are formed. The cultivar 'McClintock' may belong here. Zones 3–7.

Antennaria parlinii (Parlin's pussy-toes) is native from the central Plains states to the Southeast. Plants form mats of bright green foliage and sport spring flowers. About 12" tall.

Antennaria virginica (shale barren pussy-toes) is occasionally offered and provides silvery foliage and white flower heads. Native to a small area of the country, where it roots into rock crevices, this 15" tall ground cover may not fit the growing conditions in all gardens. Probably hardy in zones 4–7.

Recommended propagation
Seed: Seeds may be collected and sown in the late summer or spring. Clean off the down to reveal the seeds before sowing.
Cuttings: One- or two-node cuttings of the runners may be rooted easily.
Division: This is the easiest method for the mat-forming species.

Etymology
Genus: From the Latin, *antenna* ("the yard of a sailing ship"). The extended stamens were fancifully likened to the antennae of butterflies.
Specific epithet: *alpina* refers to the alpine regions where the species is found; *parlinii* is named for its discoverer, John Crawford Parlin (1863–1948); *plantaginifolia* refers to the leaves (*folia*), which resemble plantain (*Plantago*); *solitaria* describes the solitary flower cluster characteristic of the species; *virginica* ("of Virginia").
Common name: Pussy-toes equates the hairy, rounded flower heads with the toes of your favorite young feline. Ladies' tobacco is an enigma, as Harold Rickett writes in the wonderful *Wild Flowers of the United States*: "Why ladies' tobacco? I have no record of such a use, by ladies, gentlemen, or others." Shale barren refers to the habitat of *Antennaria virginica*; solitary pussy-toes describes the number of flower heads formed at one time.

Aquilegia	columbine	Ranunculaceae

Everyone loves columbines, and we definitely have our fair share from which to choose. Large-flowered hybrids dominate the garden market and for good reason: they are impressive, colorful, and, well, big. Many of our finest garden species are native to Asia and Europe; the hybrids may consist of up to four parents in their family trees. In the Armitage garden, I try them all, from diminutive cultivars to 3' tall hybrids, and not a one do I dislike; I have come to realize, regrettably, that I cannot plant every columbine out there, but I know that if I had to choose only one or two for my daughters, they would be hybrids. Still, we are awash in great natives and, for me, I can fall in love with species from the East, the West, and the Southwest. In the rush for size, let's not overlook our outstanding natives.

Aquilegia caerulea	Rocky Mountain columbine

This is an absolutely stunning plant. The people of Colorado believe they may have the prettiest mountains as well as the prettiest flower in the country. Just ask a Coloradan. It is one of the largest columbines in the genus, providing gor-

Aquilegia caerulea

geous long-spurred blue and white outward-facing flowers on 2–3' tall plants. Although it is better suited to cooler climes, we have grown plants in the Horticulture Gardens at the University of Georgia. Plants persisted for three years, and while there was not a Colorado-like riot of color, they caught the attention of all who walked by.

Plants are more common in the West than in the East but are available through mail-order companies throughout the country. Cultivars appear every now and then, but are seldom found at the consumer level. Rocky Mountain columbine is an important parent in many of the large-flowered hybrids, so with almost any columbine in your garden, you will have a piece of the Rockies.

'Remembrance' is a hybrid with *Aquilegia caerulea* as one of the parents. The flowers are violet-blue and white. Introduced by Plant Select, a cooperative program administered by the Denver Botanic Gardens and Colorado State University, in 2001, to honor the memory of the students and teacher of Columbine High School.

Habitat: At high elevations from central Idaho to southwestern Missouri and south to Arizona and New Mexico.

Hardiness: USDA Zones 3–7.

Garden site: Afternoon shade unless you are in the cool mountains; there, little shade is required.

Garden maintenance: Leaf miners can be a problem with this species as with all others. Simply cut back the disfigured foliage after plants have flowered; new healthy foliage will arise, and the miners will have gone.

Aquilegia canadensis   Canadian columbine

The most popular native species, although still not easy to buy, is the Canadian columbine. The nodding red and yellow flowers dominate my garden in the spring, providing a range of heights at 2–4' tall. They provide softness around coarsely textured ferns and shrubs, and the flowers are favorites of hummingbirds. The leaves are typical of most other columbines, and, yes, native or not, they too are afflicted with leaf miners in late spring. At least in the East, plants

44

Aquilegia canadensis and *Tiarella cordifolia*

reseed readily, and so my wallet is saved from having to buy more than a half-dozen. The seedlings are formed in late spring and early summer and can be moved to other parts of the garden as soon as they are ready to be handled. This plant has been recognized as a good garden plant as long as there have been gardens in this country—why, even Thomas Jefferson admired it at Monticello.

Many subtle color forms of the species may be found, ranging from deep rose to light pink. 'Corbett', one of my favorites, grows only 1–1½' tall and produces dozens of light yellow nodding flowers. It was found by two brothers, Andrew and Larry Clemens, in the late 1960s near the town of Corbett, Maryland. They shared seeds and plants with Richard Simon, an outstanding nurseryman and the owner of Bluemount Nurseries in nearby Monkton, who first offered this selection in 1992.

'Little Lanterns' is a dwarf form of the species, in the same red and yellow colors. 'Canyon Vista' appears to be similar to 'Little Lanterns' in all respects.

Aquilegia canadensis 'Corbett'

Aquilegia canadensis 'Little Lanterns'

Habitat: East in Newfoundland and Quebec, west to Manitoba, south into Florida and southwest to Texas.

Hardiness: USDA Zones (2)3–8.

Garden site: Partial shade; they do poorly in full sun.

Garden maintenance: Plants will get leaf miner visitation—entire families some years, just a few of the kids on others. Clean up debris (dead leaves and the like) around the plants in the fall to reduce subsequent populations. You can live with the damage or cut plants back almost to the ground immediately after flowering. New clean foliage will emerge and by that time, the miners will have completed their life cycle, and the leaves will remain unblemished. Burn the infected leaves. If you do cut plants back, seeds will not mature, which is a shame, because there is nothing more fun than collecting dozens of seeds and pretending you are Johnny Appleseed, tossing seeds all about the garden . . . well, maybe not—but tossing the seeds around certainly gives me pleasure and a few new plants as well, so I just put up with most of the leaf miner damage.

Aquilegia chrysantha	Texas columbine

The Texas columbine provides some of the brightest color on some of the largest flowers in the garden and is a parent to many long-spurred large-flowered hybrids. Large sunshine-bright yellow flowers with 3" long, tapering spurs make these plants favorites wherever they are planted. The outward- to upward-facing flowers are borne on 3–4' tall plants.

'Denver Gold' is a particularly showy selection and a 2001 winner in the Plant Select program, administered by the Denver Botanic Gardens and Colorado State University.

var. *hinckleyana* (*A. hinckleyana*; Hinckley's columbine) occurs only in the Big Bend area of Texas. Somewhat smaller in stature and flower size than the species, it is nevertheless an excellent plant if it can be found; it is usually sold as Texas Gold columbine.

The species is often available from seed, the variety and cultivars less so except through western mail-order sources. Since there appear to be so few differences among the plants mentioned here, find one and enjoy.

Habitat: In woods from western Texas to Arizona and south into Mexico.

Hardiness: USDA Zones 4–9.

Garden site: Partial shade, consistent moisture.

Garden maintenance: Leaf miners are also present on this group of plants (see *Aquilegia canadensis*). They are not as cold-tolerant as many other species; some winter protection is called for below zone 5.

Aquilegia chrysantha

Aquilegia chrysantha var. *hinckleyana*

Other species for the garden

Aquilegia formosa (Sitka columbine) is the western equivalent of the Canadian columbine. Those of us in the East wax poetic over the Canadian columbine, but in the West, this species is far more common. It is bigger, a little brighter, and even tougher. Plants are mixed up in the trade, and quite truthfully, unless a wild population has been identified and both species are grown side by side, they are difficult to tell apart. Native from the mountains in southern California, north to coastal Alaska, and east to Utah and Montana. Hardy in zones 4–7.

Hybrids

'Blazing Stars' columbine resulted when Texas garden historian Pam Puryear of Navasota, Texas, showed horticulturist Greg Grant a small family of hybrid offspring from a spontaneous cross of *Aquilegia chrysantha* var. *hinckleyana* and *A. canadensis*. Grant collected seeds and, with the help of Jerry Parsons of the Texas Agricultural Extension Service, produced many generations of seedlings. After about ten years, a new, stable columbine was born. Grant named the new columbine for his gardening friend Bernice Ikins of Bandara, Texas. Taxonomically, it is known as *A.* ×*puryearana*

Aquilegia formosa

'Bernice Ikins'. Plants retain the red and gold color of the Canadian columbine but bear significantly longer spurs and larger flowers. Hardy in zones 3–8.

Recommended propagation

Seed: Self-sown seedlings are the easiest and cheapest way to increase the population. If your garden does not produce many seedlings, gather the seed while the fruit capsules (follicles) are just turning dark. Place the seeds in sphagnum moss and keep them in the refrigerator until ready to be sown. Sow in pots or in a prepared bed in fall or early spring.

Division: Avoid, unless clumps are obviously in need of division.

Etymology

Genus: From the Latin, *aquila* ("eagle"), referring to the spurs (talons) and form of the petals.

Specific epithet: *caerulea* ("dark blue"); *canadensis* ("of Canada") was meant by early botanists to include northeastern United States; *chrysantha* ("golden"); *formosa* ("beautiful").

Common name: From the Latin, *columba* ("dove")—the five-spurred petals were thought to resemble as many doves.

Arisaema	Jack-in-the-pulpit	Araceae

The increasing popularity of this genus has brought many members from Asia and Europe into American gardens. However, there are at least two species of native Jacks in the Armitage garden that I would not be without, and all are reasonably easy to find in garden centers or catalogs.

Arisaema dracontium	green dragon

This is a must-have plant for the shade garden. *Arisaema triphyllum* is the common, classic native plant, but green dragon is the classiest. I love the way the stems come out of the ground like a spike, and how the leaves and flower appear like magic as it expands to its 3–4' height. The dark green leaf is 2½–3' long and divided into anywhere from five to fifteen segments. The flower is fun to show people, but the long skinny spadix looks like Jack got caught in a noodle factory and was stretched to form a long, narrow tail. The green spathe is not hooded as in common Jack but rather is open, disgorging its tail for weeks on end. Sounds gruesome, but you will love it.

Habitat: In woods from Quebec to Minnesota, south to Texas and east to Florida. Its habitat is similar to that of *Arisaema triphyllum*, but it is not nearly as common.

Arisaema dracontium   *Arisaema dracontium*

Hardiness: USDA Zones 4–8.

Garden site: Moist shade.

Garden maintenance: In some gardens, plants will need some support, particularly if heavy shade is the norm. They will not fall over, but some support helps their posture, and they simply look better.

Arisaema triphyllum   common Jack, indian turnip

Our common Jack is the most well known and probably the most variable of any available North American Jack. It grows from a tuber and emerges with a single trifoliate leaf (in three parts). The leaf is usually green, but patterns of variegation are not uncommon. The basal flower has the typical broad spathe (pulpit) and narrow spadix (Jack). The spathe is generally greenish to purple but can also be mauve or white, and may or may not be strikingly striped in maroon, at least at the base. It generally forms a "hood" and hides the spadix, which consists of separate male and female flowers. Some taxonomists have split the species into other species or variants based on the shape and segments of the leaf and the color and striping of the spathe, but I am a lumper and have elected to keep the variability within this interesting species. I have seen plants as tall as 3' in height, others less than 1' (12–15" is common). They truly are magnificent, especially when a stand of twenty or more are planted. Plants are often summer-dormant, crawling back beneath the soil in early to mid summer, depending on temperatures.

Gardeners should be able to locate started plants at better nurseries, and sometimes the small tubers may be purchased.

Habitat: In moist woods from New Brunswick to Quebec, west to Manitoba, and south to Kansas, Louisiana and east to Florida.

Hardiness: USDA Zones 4–8.

Arisaema triphyllum

Arisaema triphyllum

Garden site: Afternoon shade is essential, morning sun is beneficial; however, plants may also grow well in deep shade. Adequate moisture results in bigger, more persistent plants.

Garden maintenance: None.

Recommended propagation

Seed: The mature fruit on both species consists of a cluster of round red berries, each consisting of one to five seeds. The seed should be cleaned from the fruit; wear a pair of gloves because the plant contains calcium oxalate crystals, which can cause a skin rash and other uncomfortable burning. Sow the seeds in a moist seed tray, cover with plastic film, and place in the refrigerator or cooler for about three months. After the cold treatment has been completed, allow the seedlings to germinate where they are protected from squirrels, gophers, and other such playful varmints. Germination will occur within two to three weeks, but subsequent growth is slow. They will go dormant after the first leaf has emerged, at which time they can be potted up into larger containers and placed in a cold frame over the winter. Put in the garden the second spring.

Division: Additional corms will occur over time, and these can be separated and moved to other areas of the garden in early spring. Do so as plants go dormant.

Etymology

Genus: From the Greek, *aris* or *aron* ("Arum") and *haima* ("blood"), in reference to the red blotching on the spathe or leaves on some species. Others believe the name refers to the close familial relationship to *Arum*; at one time, plants in this genus were part of the genus *Arum*.

Specific epithet: *dracontium* ("like a dragon"), the long spadix resembles the tail of a dragon; *triphyllum* ("three-leafed").

Common name: Jack-in-the-pulpit has been explained (see *Arisaema triphyllum*). Indian turnip refers to the corm, which was palatable and eaten by Native Americans, but only after cooking. The whole plant, again, contains calcium oxalate, which causes awful pain and suffering; boiling removes the crystals.

Aruncus dioicus	**goatsbeard**	**Rosaceae**

Goatsbeard is represented by *Aruncus dioicus* only, but it is one of the most impressive native plants we can include in our gardens. They can grow 3–5' tall, and even when not in flower their bold appearance is remarkable. Plants are dioecious, meaning that some plants are male, others are female. All flowers consist of five small white petals; the males have fifteen to twenty stamens, the females two to four pistils. There is no particular advantage in garden performance, and you won't know which gender is in your garden until plants are in flower in late spring. The stately, billowy flowers are a tremendous source of nectar and pollen and are visited by droves of bees, beetles, and other associated winged and legged insects. In the garden, with sufficient moisture and well sited, they are 55-mph plants. They are at their best in the Midwest and North; they do poorly south of zone 6.

'Kneiffii' has deeply cut, almost fern-like foliage. Plants are not as tall as the species and the flowers are not as full or dramatic, but the leaves provide a graceful look to the plants.

'Zweiweltenkind' ('Child of Two Worlds') is a little shorter than the species.

Habitat: Pennsylvania to Indiana south to Arkansas, east to the mountains of North Carolina. It also occurs on the West Coast. It is interesting that references in America call it an American native, while authors in northern Europe and parts of Asia claim this species as one of their own. Neither seems to acknowledge the possibility of the other.

Hardiness: USDA Zones 3–7.

Garden site: Morning sun and afternoon shade is recommended. Keep plants consistently moist, or leaves will deteriorate badly.

Garden maintenance: Plants can be big, thus siting them correctly in the first place is important. Maintenance will be increased if planted in areas of warm summer nights. After many years, they may have to be divided. This is hard work because of the size of the roots—be careful. Find some young backs to help, or your back may have to be maintained.

Recommended propagation

Seed: Before gathering, wait for the thin fruit on female plants to turn from green to yellow with a tinge of red. The seeds are small and will need to be cleaned from the fruit. Sow the seeds on the surface of a prepared seed tray,

Aruncus dioicus

Aruncus dioicus 'Kneiffii'

then stratify at 40F for about three months. Place the stratified tray in conditions of light and 70–72F temperature for germination.

Division: Plants are difficult to divide "cleanly," and the attempt to do so can damage both the division and the dividee, although it can be accomplished. Mature plants would challenge the strength of Paul Bunyan himself.

Etymology

Genus: No particular story to tell here—simply, the genus name seems to be the classical name for these plants.

Specific epithet: *dioicus* ("dioecious"), having male and female flowers on separate plants.

Common name: Goatsbeard makes sense if you have seen enough goats. Big goats, mind you, but sensible enough.

Aruncus dioicus 'Zweiweltenkind'

| **Asarum** | **ginger** | **Aristolochiaceae** |

Gingers include some of the most fascinating plants in the garden. All flower very early in the spring, often before new spring foliage has arisen. I love teaching these plants to students and guests, because to truly appreciate them, you must go down on your hands and knees and get flower-to-eyeball. Some of my elderly visitors may still be there, I think, trying to get up.

All tolerate shade, even a lot of it, but morning sun is never a problem. Foliage is generally lustrous and somewhat heart-shaped, and all leaves appear directly from the root. Interest in this group is growing, as more exotic gingers, particularly the large-flowered forms from Asia, are introduced; I have grown over a dozen taxa, including natives of Asia, Europe, and the United States. The nonnative forms are terrific, but the townies needn't take a backseat to any of them.

| **Asarum arifolium** | **arrow-leaf ginger** |

The arrow-leaf ginger is one of the most common and useful gingers for the gardener. The arrowhead-shaped leaves are mottled and evergreen and beautiful in the spring and early summer; the winter foliage is not particularly attractive. At home, I remove the old leaves in early spring to enjoy the lush new growth, which would otherwise be hidden. The many tan-colored flower buds give rise to 1" wide brownish urn-shaped flowers in the spring. Plants are denizens of the mid to Deep South and not sufficiently cold hardy for most of the Midwest or Northeast.

Habitat: In woods from Virginia to Kentucky, south to Florida and Mississippi.
Hardiness: USDA Zones (4)5–8.
Garden site: Moist, shaded area. The thick leaves lose little moisture and help plants through periods of drought.
Garden maintenance: None.

Asarum arifolium, buds

Asarum arifolium

Asarum canadense   *Asarum canadense*, flower

Asarum canadense   Canadian ginger, deciduous wild ginger

Canadian ginger is one of the easiest and best gingers on the market. Each plant produces only two large green leaves, somewhat furry and heart-shaped, but over a few years, they can fill significant acreage. The small flowers, which consist of sepals only, are formed at ground level about the same time the leaves are being produced in the spring and can be viewed quite easily at that time. Later in the spring, even if flowers are still present, serious digging through the thick canopy is necessary to find them. Pollination is by beetles and ants, but the fleshy sepals persist so the seed capsules are effectively hidden. This is one of the few deciduous gingers that has become popular as a garden plant. Plants are grown from rhizomes, which, when crushed, have a strong aromatic smell of true ginger.

Habitat: In woods, from Quebec to Manitoba, south from eastern North Dakota to eastern Kansas and Oklahoma, east to Arkansas, Alabama and up into North Carolina.
Hardiness: USDA Zones 3–8.
Garden site: In moist shade. Morning sun is preferred for best growth, but plants can tolerate dense shade as well.
Garden maintenance: The only maintenance needed is to keep colony under control if it exceeds its boundaries. This is easily accomplished by lifting the offending plants.

Asarum shuttleworthii   Shuttleworth's ginger

Another Southeast native, this species bears handsome mottled rounded to heart-shaped (4" long) evergreen foliage that is rather aromatic. The 2" long flowers are vase-shaped and purple-brown with reddish purple spots inside. Plants spread slowly by rhizomes.

'Callaway', a dwarf form only 6" tall with exquisite mottled foliage, was found by Fred Galle in a garden in western Georgia; he brought it back to Callaway Gardens in Pine Mountain, Georgia, and observed its performance for several years before introducing it. Handsome and more readily available than the species—the only complaint is that it's an even slower grower.

'Carolina Silver' has arrowhead-shaped leaves marked with silver.

var. *harperi* (Harper's ginger) is native to central Alabama and normally has unmottled foliage.

'Velvet Queen' has rounded leaves bearing handsome silvery mottling. Larger flowers than the species.

Habitat: From Virginia to West Virginia south to Georgia and west to Alabama.
Hardiness: USDA Zones 5–8.
Garden site: Moist shade.
Garden maintenance: None, but since these are slow growers, planting more
   densely at the beginning will reduce the weeds that are sure to occur on
   uncovered soil.

Other species for the garden

Asarum caudatum is easily identified by the long narrow "tails" on the ends of the sepals. The evergreen leaves are heart-shaped and solid green, not mottled. Native from Washington State to western Montana, south to northeastern Oregon. This is really a fun plant to show children who like pulling the tail of their dog.

Asarum heterophyllum and *A. virginicum* (heartleaf) are native to the southeastern United States. Both usually have nonmottled evergreen foliage and are hardy to about zone 5.

Asarum shuttleworthii 'Callaway'

Asarum caudatum

Asarum heterophyllum (mottled form)

Recommended propagation

Seed: Although seeds can be purchased, germination is best if seeds are sown immediately upon collection. Seeds ripen approximately four to six weeks after the appearance of the first flowers. Seeds of all species require a cold treatment, which can effectively be given by sowing seeds in a container and placing it outdoors or in a cold frame. The container must be kept evenly moist while being subjected to the cold. Plunging the pot in compost to just below its rim helps keep the environment consistent. Alternatively, the seed tray can be held in the refrigerator or cooler for ten to twelve weeks at 35–40F. Once temperatures warm up, germination occurs in four to six weeks, depending on temperature.

Cuttings: Root cuttings are effective. Remove a small piece of the rhizome with a pair of leaves attached. Place the cutting in a container with 3:1 perlite:peat at 70–75F with consistent moisture.

Division: Plants should be divided in the fall, when they are going dormant.

Asarum virginicum

If sufficient moisture can be provided, early spring division is acceptable. Replant divisions immediately.

Etymology

Genus: Perhaps a translation of "wild ginger" from Latin or Greek, but the meaning is obscure.

Specific epithet: *arifolium* ("with leaves like an arum"), essentially in the shape of an arrowhead; *caudatum* ("with a tail"); *harperi*, after Roland Harper, a 1920s plant explorer of the southeastern United States, particularly Alabama and Georgia; *hetero* is from the Greek ("diverse") and *phyllum* from the Greek ("leaf"), thus *heterophyllum* tells us that the plant has different leaf shapes; *shuttleworthii*, for 19th-century writer Robert Shuttleworth; *virginianum* ("of Virginia").

Common name: The rhizomes and even the leaves of many asarums have an aroma of true ginger, but the intensity of fragrance differs from species to species and according to the sensitivity of one's nose.

Asclepias	milkweed, pleurisy root	Asclepiadaceae

A young man approached a farmer. "Excuse me, sir—I noticed you have some milkweed in the pasture. May I pick it so I can collect some milk?" The farmer laughed. "Be my guest, son, but you can't get milk from a milkweed plant." But the young man was persistent, and sure enough, in a few hours he returned, carrying two large buckets of milk. The next day the young man returned, having noticed honeysuckle all over the farm. "Son," the farmer smiled, "you can't get honey from a honeysuckle vine." But the young man was persistent, and sure enough, in a few hours he returned, carrying two large pails of sweet honey. The next day the young fellow returned. "Excuse me, sir, but I noticed goldenrod in the next field, and—" "Hold on, son, let me get my coat."

Milkweed has been the bane of farmers and the subject of jokes for years. It also provides unique floral features for the budding plant scientist. Biologists love studying its curious flower parts, in particular a cup-like structure called a corona between the petals and the stamens. The pollen occurs in a waxy mass, and great gobs of the stuff are carried off by pollinating insects. Most milkweeds are characterized by milky sap (although *Asclepias tuberosa* is almost devoid of it) and have flowers clustered together in an umbel (all flower stems coming from the same point of attachment, like an umbrella). I find it interesting that there is so much love for milkweed in this country—and I'll admit I have been slow to embrace these plants, many of which sure look like the old pasture weeds on the farm. But for true believers, there is no such thing as a bad milkweed, and companies like The Milkweed Farm in Virginia sell seeds of over two dozen kinds. Many species are found throughout the world; some of our most common, such as *A. curassavica* (bloodflower), are native to South America but have escaped in the Southeast. We have an abundance of our own native milkweeds in this country, some beautiful and highly ornamental, others weeds that reduce farm yields; most look far better in a meadow planting with other meadow plants than they do in the mixed garden. *Asclepias tuberosa* and perhaps *A. purpurascens* may be the exceptions, shining anywhere. All are excellent butterfly plants, attracting swallowtails, monarchs, American ladies, and hairstreaks. Unfortunately, they also appeal to aphids. Having any form of milkweed in the garden almost guarantees you'll be an aphid farmer as well.

Asclepias incarnata	swamp milkweed

This is but one of the dozens of native species in the country and one which has also captured the eye of propagators and nurseries. The plant is an upright grower with strong stems filled with milky sap. The reddish pink flowers occur in large clusters in early to mid summer. Leaves are narrow and pointed; the narrow seed pods, 3–4" long, occur in pairs and are filled with seeds that are ready to fly away.

'Cinderella' has handsome rose to pink flowers; 'Ice Ballet', a popular white-flowering selection, appears less weed-like, and 'Milk Maid' has smaller creamy white flowers as well. 'Soulmate' bears rose-purple clusters of flowers. All taxa have red-brown seeds with a silky tail within the seed pods.

Habitat: In moist soils from Maine west to Manitoba, south to New Mexico, and east to Florida.

Hardiness: USDA Zones 3–9.

Garden site: Plants prefer consistently moist soil, but they also perform well in average, well-drained gardens. Full sun.

Garden maintenance: None, although plants can look yellow and decrepit by late summer. Cut back if they are too much of an eyesore. Aphids will likely visit as well.

Asclepias incarnata 'Ice Ballet'

Asclepias purpurascens   purple milkweed

As a real skeptic of anything milkweed-ish, you can imagine how much I surprised myself by embracing this beautiful deep purple–flowered plant. It is still a milkweed, but the flowers catch your eye immediately on turning the corner. Plants are about 1' tall, and flower in late May to early June. Not as fragrant as *Asclepias syriaca*, but not bad either. Full sun, zones 4–7.

Asclepias sullivantii   smooth milkweed, Sullivant's milkweed, prairie milkweed

Asclepias purpurascens

Another of the many upright forms that looks much like *Asclepias syriaca* but is more ornamental and a bit more civilized. It is also better behaved than common milkweed because it does not run by rhizomes. Plants are often confused with common milkweed, but this plant has smooth stems, leaves, and seed pods, and the leaves have distinctive reddish midveins and a significant upward sweep. The pale to strongly pink-purple star-like flowers appear mostly in the upper leaf axils from late spring into summer. Flowers are a nectar source for many butterflies, and leaves are a food source for monarch butterfly larvae. Plants grow 2–4' tall, and when they mature, they produce handsome smooth seed pods that are quite useful in dried flower arrangements. It is excellent, as are most of these milkweeds, in a natural or butterfly garden, where its weed-like tendencies will be more or less ignored. The milky latex reputedly has a particularly high rubber content, and in the 1940s was investigated for usefulness in rubber production. Highly drought-tolerant.

Habitat: North to Minnesota, east to southern Ontario and Ohio, west to Nebraska, Kansas, and south to Oklahoma.
Hardiness: USDA Zones 4–7.
Garden site: Full sun.
Garden maintenance: Once established, it is best to leave plants undisturbed. Their deep taproots make transplanting difficult.

Asclepias tuberosa   butterfly weed

For many people, this is the most gardenworthy species out there. Botanists consider it to be a weed, but an outstanding weed to be sure. Like the middle orb of

Asclepias tuberosa

Asclepias tuberosa, seed pods

a stoplight, it begs you to slow down and take a look. And if you do, you will notice hairy alternate 3–4" long lance-like leaves and orange to brick-red flowers. The skinny fruit is 4–5" long and packed with seeds, which once open, fly away with the wind on their silky parachutes. The blooms are useful for cutting as well, especially so for their lack of milky sap. These 2' tall plants are recommended for dry areas in the garden, as they tolerate drought well.

Gay Butterflies Mix produces 2' tall plants with flowers from early to late summer in a wide range of colors, including gold, orange, red, and pink. No cultivars in single colors are available commercially, although occasionally seed identified as "red shades" or "orange shades" may be found. There is sufficient diversity in the species that selections could be made, but since vegetative propagation is difficult, maintaining the purity of the cultivar has proven to be a challenge.

Habitat: In open areas from New Hampshire to Minnesota and Colorado and south to Arizona, Texas, and Florida. Plants also extend to North Dakota and as far west as California.

Hardiness: USDA Zones 3–8.

Garden site: Full sun—this is a lover of wide-open spaces.

Garden maintenance: Very little, except when hordes of aphids appear, which they surely will. You can do nothing: after all, aphids need a home as well. If they bother you, spray them off with a garden hose. They will probably reappear, but maybe they will get confused and go to your neighbors'. Keep spraying until they stay away. Aphicides, in liquid or powder form, are another alternative.

Other species for the garden

The large green leaves and drooping white flowers of *Asclepias exaltata* (poke milkweed) have never really done much for me. They would probably be most at home in a meadow wildflower area; in my garden, they appear like weeds, and

I already have enough of those. Still, while I may swear at it, others swear by it, and if the flowers are studied closely, they are indeed quite beautiful. Plants grow 3–5' tall, and like most milkweeds attract a wide assortment of butterflies. Native from Maine to Minnesota, south to Iowa, Georgia and Kentucky. Hardy in zones 4–7.

I would never have *Asclepias syriaca* (common milkweed) in my garden; I have always viewed it as an agricultural pest. However, the further you get from the farm, the more the plant grows on you, especially if you stick your nose in the flower. You will be surprised at the wonderful honey scent. Although I will never be a bona-fide of this vigorous weed, others enjoy this 3–6' tall plant with its fragrant pink flowers, and it is also loved by butterflies. Plants spread aggressively by rhizomes; large colonies will likely appear within a few years. Removal may be necessary, but they have long taproots and will not take kindly to such efforts. Hardy in zones 3–7.

Recommended propagation

Seed: Gather seeds by extracting a mass from the fruit when they turn brown. Use one hand to hold the mass of seeds and the other to pull the down away. If seed is to be stored, place in the refrigerator in a sealed container. Purchased seed will already be cleaned of the silky down and should be stored in the refrigerator for approximately three months.

Fresh seeds do not require a cold treatment and can be sown immediately in the summer; I recommend sowing in small containers rather than seed flats, to better accommodate the long taproot that forms. Transplant carefully into the garden once plants are large enough to be handled. If sown indoors in the winter, an incandescent light should be burned above the pots for at

Asclepias syriaca

least six hours in the middle of the night to simulate long-day conditions. Otherwise, seedlings will turn yellow and languish.

Stem cuttings: Two- to three-inch terminal cuttings can be taken before flowering and stuck in a moist 3:1 mixture of perlite:peat and covered with a plastic tent and placed in warm area. Rooting should occur within six weeks; once green is visible, place in an area with long natural daylength or use incandescent lights as just described.

Root cuttings: Dig a mature plant, cut 2" sections of the taproot using a straight cut at the top of the section and an angled cut at the basal end (or vice versa—see *Anemone*—so long as you can remember which way is up). Place the sections vertically (top up) in a similar mix. Keep warm and moist. With luck and sufficient gentleness, the donor plant will survive this trauma.

Etymology

Genus: Plants were believed to have great medicinal powers, and thus were named for Asklepios, the Greek god of healing.

Specific epithet: *exaltata* ("very tall," "lofty"); *incarnata* ("flesh-colored") and *purpurascens* ("becoming purple"), in reference to the flower colors; *sullivantii*, for 19th-century American botanist William Starling Sullivant; *syriaca* ("of Syria")—the species was incorrectly thought to be native to that area; *tuberosa* refers to the swollen root.

Common name: Milkweed and butterfly weed refer to the milky sap so abundant in many of the species and the host of butterflies attracted to all the plants, respectively. Pleurisy root refers to the healing properties demonstrated by the dried roots of the genus; the roots cause a specific action on the lungs, assisting expectoration, subduing inflammation, and exerting a general mild tonic effect on the system, making it valuable in all chest complaints. It is of great use in pleurisy, mitigating the pain and relieving the difficulty of breathing. Smooth milkweed refers to the smooth leaves and seed pods, while poke milkweed refers to the fact that plants of *Asclepias exaltata* resemble the common pokeweed of the South.

Aster   Asteraceae

Asters are classic North American roadside and pasture plants, but they are also global, having nativities in Europe and Asia. Plants range 1–6' in height and are characterized by having alternate leaves and many flower heads in numerous colors. As beautiful as some of these weeds are to the botanist, they have a long way to go before they earn a place in the garden. Few native species have found a place in the mainstream garden, as selection and breeding of our endemic forms have resulted in sturdier, more compact cultivars in a variety of colors. How to choose asters for this book was an exercise in indecision; in the end,

I selected those I enjoy, either as straight species or as represented by their available cultivars. A look through catalogs proves you can be a lover of natives and still come away with something that doesn't look like a weed. Nearly all the names are changing, beware; see "Index of Botanical Names," where the latest word in nomenclature is given parenthetically, e.g., *Aster divaricatus* (*Eurybia divaricata*).

Aster carolinianus

Aster carolinianus   climbing aster

With 10–20" long grayish stems, this has to be among the largest, lankiest of the asters. It does not really climb—sprawling aster would be a better name. The leaves are elliptical, approximately 4" long. I wrapped a piece of 4' tall chicken wire fencing around the plant years ago, and stems poke through and over with gusto. Lovely pink flowers occur in late October, making it one of the latest in this large group. This is definitely one for the South, being hardy only to zone 7, but what a treat it is.

Habitat: In moist areas from North Carolina to Florida.
Hardiness: USDA Zones 7–9.
Garden site: Full sun, provide plenty of room.
Garden maintenance: They need something to climb through or must be tied, otherwise they romp around the ground like kudzu. I cut mine back to the top of its cylindrical girdle in the spring. Plants are somewhat evergreen and don't die back to the roots during the winter.

Aster divaricatus   white wood aster

I really enjoy this plant. People may disagree with me, arguing that there are far more colorful asters, and they would be right. I put this plant on the top of my list for its prostrate habit, ease of growing, and white flowers, which occur in mid to late summer, earlier than many other species. It seldom flowers in the fall unless constantly cut back. Other asters are more noticeable, but this species needs little maintenance and no staking and seems to have few disease or insect problems. It is easy to distinguish from other speices by its habit, its heart-shaped leaves, and its black zigzag stems.

Aster divaricatus

'Fiesta', selected in Waseca, Minnesota, has leaves heavily streaked in white; they sort of look like confetti has fallen on them. Flowers are light lavender.

'Raiche Form', found by Roger Raiche, bears larger white flowers than the type and wiry dark stems.

'Snow Heron' was a chance seedling from the garden of Heronswood Nursery in Washington State. The dark green leaves are splotched and streaked with white, and the flowers are white.

Habitat: In woods or shady roadsides north to Maine, west to Ohio, and south to Alabama and Georgia.

Hardiness: USDA Zones (3)4–8.

Garden site: This is one of the few asters that does not tolerate full sun. Place in dappled shade or afternoon shade, but allow for at least four hours of sun. Since they are prostrate, plants may be placed in the shade of larger plants, and they will grow up and out from that point.

Garden maintenance: The amount of maintenance depends on the amount of shade and heat in the garden. I recommend cutting the plants back to about 8" in late spring to increase branching. Additional cutting back will delay flowering.

Aster ericoides   heath aster

I worked with the heath aster for many years as a cut flower species and have come to admire its habit and floriferousness. Plants bear very small leaves (like heath and heather) and small flowers, and they are often overlooked in the wild. They can be over 3' tall, but in windy, dry areas, they may be less than 18" in height. Up

*Aster
ericoides
'Pink Star'*

to a hundred small flower heads with white-to-pink ray flowers and yellowish-to-purple disk flowers are produced. In the wild, many of the bottom and middle leaves abscise before flowering, which makes the plant look even more weedy; with selected cultivars, the appearance of this excellent wildflower is much improved, as are its chances of being more widely used in American gardens.

'Pink Star', one of my favorites, offers hundreds of 1" light pink flowers in late summer.

'Snowflurry', only 6–8" tall, is covered with small white flowers in late summer and into early fall. Excellent dwarf form, useful for rock gardens.

Habitat: Found throughout North Dakota, north to Manitoba and east to Maine, then southwest through the Great Plains to northern Mexico at elevations below 7500'. Native to most of the eastern United States except the extreme Southeast.

Hardiness: USDA Zones 3–7.

Garden site: Full sun, well-drained soils. Give plants some room, to reduce the incidence of rust and other foliar problems.

Garden maintenance: Cut back hard in late spring. Be on the lookout for rust—it knocked us for a loop in the Southeast.

Aster lateriflorus   calico aster

With a bit of looking, you can purchase this native plant. Plants grow about 3' tall with small bronzy green leaves and small (¼–½" wide) white or occasionally lavender flowers, often along one side of the flowering branch; its many stems have been described as stiff, arching, and often straggly. Unless you are

Aster lateriflorus 'Horizontalis'

Aster lateriflorus 'Prince'

an aster collector, after all is said and done, the species is rather forgettable. I am not saying it shouldn't be embraced if that is your thing, but the cultivars are so much more beautiful. Perhaps that's why the species is so difficult to find. Save yourself a good deal of grief by not planting any of them south of zone 6.

'Horizontalis' is the oldest offering and also best displays the horizontal habit of the species.

'Lady in Black' is relatively new and quite popular. Small white flowers with rounded centers of raspberry stamens open in late summer to fall. The small leaves are the kicker of course, being anywhere from light purple to inky black on many-branched stems. Plants are 2–3' tall. Both stem and flower color are enhanced by cool temperatures.

'Prince' is another older form but outstanding nevertheless. Leaves and stems are a rich black-purple, and white-pink flowers occur in late summer and fall. Terrific plants, growing 2–2½' tall. They prefer cool weather to strut their stuff, which is why I love all black-foliaged asters much more in Montreal than in Atlanta.

Habitat: Throughout the country except the extreme Southeast.
Hardiness: USDA Zones 3–7.
Garden site: Full sun, consistently moist.
Garden maintenance: These are spreading asters and need little cutting back
    or pruning. Do not cut back after 15 July, or frost may occur before
    flowers open.

Aster novae-angliae   **New England aster**

The New England aster—one of the most common roadside weeds in the East—has been tamed or hybridized into many cultivars. The species itself is highly variable, growing 1–8' tall, but may be distinguished from similar species by its sessile (no petiole) lanceolate leaves and the stalked glands on the bracts beneath

Aster novae-angliae 'Andenken an Alma Pötschke'   *Aster novae-angliae* 'English Countryside'

the flowers. Flower color is also variable, but commonly lavender to purple. Dozens of cultivars are available through nurseries and mail-order catalogs. Small cultivars are not uncommon in this species.

'Andenken an Alma Pötschke', one of the most popular cultivars, bears handsome pink flowers during the fall on 3–4' tall plants.

'Barr's Violet' grows about 4' tall and has deep violet-blue flowers in mid to late summer.

'English Countryside', found by Ann English of Athens, Georgia, is 3–5' tall with outstanding lavender-blue flowers in late fall. Possibly a hybrid with *Aster oblongifolius*.

'Harrington's Pink' bears light pink flowers and can reach up to 5' in height. Plants often need support. Discovered by Millard Harrington in Quebec.

'Hella Lacy', named by Allen Lacy for his wife, is an excellent 3–4' tall cultivar with violet-blue flowers.

'Honeysong Pink' bears rich pink daisy-like flowers with lemon-yellow disks. Flowers bloom in August and September on 3½' tall stems.

'Mt. Everest' is a good choice for white flowers and grows at least 3' tall.

'Purple Dome', a compact form, grows only 1½–2' tall and—at least in the first couple of years—remains a dome-shaped ball.

'Red Star' is a 15" plant with red flowers in fall.

'Violetta' has deep purple flowers but does not flower as heavily as some others. Plants are 3–5' tall.

Habitat: In meadows or roadsides east to Quebec, west to Alberta, south to the mountains of Colorado, Arkansas, Kentucky and North Carolina.

Hardiness: USDA Zones (3)4–8.

Garden site: Full sun. Do not crowd them too closely with other plants, although as some of these monsters grow, that is almost impossible. Good air circulation helps reduce incidence of foliar diseases.

Garden maintenance: Cutting back stems to about 1' several times a season is

Aster novae-angliae 'English Countryside'

Aster novae-angliae 'Harrington's Pink'

highly recommended for all asters, but particularly for the New England asters. You can cut back as late as 15 July and flowers will still occur. Otherwise, staking will be needed, or they will simply fall over other plants like a drunk at a cheap bar. Foliar fungicides are used to control rusts, powdery and downy mildews, and leaf spots, but if your plants get all these things, trash them and grow something a little less sickly. Plants may be cut to the ground after flowering if foliage begins to decline.

Aster novi-belgii   New York aster, Michaelmas daisy

Michaelmas daisies rival New England asters in color and diversity. They differ from *Aster novae-angliae* in having nearly smooth or only finely downy stems and smooth, sharply toothed leaves, but they are not easily distinguishable without a close look. They are generally shorter than New England asters and are easier to control in the garden. Since the species itself is listed at 1–4' tall, I suppose it would make sense to expect many selections to grow up to 4' in height, but just as many are less than 2' in height (many of the shorter forms are listed under *A.* ×*dumosus*). Michaelmas daisies are far more manageable and easier to enjoy than New England asters, especially when you don't have to pry them off the ground to stake them. To be honest, these do lack the laid-back look of the New England crowd, but they are all terrific.

'Alert' is 12–15" tall and bears deep crimson-red flowers in late summer. An excellent dwarf red aster.

'Blue Gown' flowers quite nicely in September with lavender-blue flowers on 30" tall plants.

'Climax' and 'White Climax' are among the taller of the Michaelmas daisies, growing 4' in warm climates and somewhat less in cooler summers. Large light blue or white flowers, respectively.

'Daniella' is a compact, late-blooming aster covered with small double flowers in early fall. Plants are only about 8" tall, but spread out twice the height.

Aster novi-belgii 'Blue Gown'   *Aster novi-belgii* 'Woods Pink'

'Heinz Richard' produces a dazzling show of pink frilled flowers on 15" stems from late summer through fall.

'Peter Harrison' is another fine short form, growing 14–16" tall, with a profusion of pink flowers in fall.

'Professor Anton Kippenberg' has certainly stood the test of time, being one of the first great short asters in gardens and continuing to be a favorite. Plants produce bright bluish flowers on a 10–14" tall plant in late September.

'Richness' has rich blue flowers on 2' tall stems, in late summer and early fall.

'Royal Opal' is 12–14" tall with icy blue flowers around a yellow eye.

'Snowball' bears dozens of white flowers on 15–18" round mounds in the fall.

'Woods Purple' and 'Woods Pink' are two of my favorites, growing only about 9" tall but smothered with flowers in early to late fall. No-brainers.

Habitat: From the coast of Newfoundland south into Georgia.
Hardiness: USDA Zones 3–7.
Garden site: Full sun, requirements similar to those of *Aster novae-angliae*.
Garden maintenance: Full sun. Even though they are generally short, cutting
    back, except for the obvious dwarf forms, is recommended. Many more
    stems and flowers will be your reward for seizing control.

Aster oblongifolius   aromatic aster

The aromatic aster, one of the last wildflowers to bloom, is loaded with blue-purple daisy-like flowers that persist into late October. When brushed lightly, the blue-green leaves release a fresh, hard-to-describe but pleasant fragrance. This aster grows from rhizomes (as do most asters) and will attain a height of 2–3' in the wild. Up to a dozen well-branched stems occur on a mature plant, and each holds narrow 1" long leaves. The flowers are violet to pink to blue, each being about 1" wide. This species is spectacular at the San Antonio Botanical Garden

*Aster
oblongifolius
'Raydon's
Favorite'*

and was declared a Plant of Merit by the Missouri Botanical Garden in 2003. Enough said.

'Fanny', occasionally offered as a selection (of various species, including this one), grows about 2' tall and twice as wide, and is covered with 1" lavender-blue flowers in the fall. A late bloomer, possibly a hybrid with New England aster. She was brought to the attention of gardeners by South Carolinian Ruth Knopf of Boone Hall Plantation, who received the aster from her maid Fanny, who had acquired it as a pass-along plant from her grandmother.

'Raydon's Favorite' is also one of mine, with large lavender flowers covering the plant in mid to late fall.

Habitat: Widely distributed from North Carolina in the East, west to
Pennsylvania to Wisconsin, over to North Dakota and Colorado at elevations up to 7000', south into Oklahoma and New Mexico and Texas.
Hardiness: USDA Zones 3–7.
Garden site: Full sun, well-drained soils.
Garden maintenance: Cut back hard once in late spring.

Other species for the garden

I could go on and on about asters. As species or as selections, there is something for everyone—but let's not get too carried away here, or this will turn into an aster book and that would be very boring. Suffice it to say that asters of every persuasion can be purchased if one looks hard enough. Here are a few others I enjoy that are not too difficult to find, but there are dozens more. Try them all, but don't become an aster collector: you will lose all your friends.

Aster azureus (sky-blue aster) is found all over the country but seems to be most loved in the Plains states. I include it because it has beautiful blue flowers with yellow centers, which butterflies love, and the blue-green foliage and dark stems add an additional pleasant dimension. No cultivars, normal brutal maintenance. Zones 4–8.

Aster fendleri (rock aster) is native from the Plains states to Texas and produces many rayed, cupped flowers of light lavender on 4–12" plants in late summer and fall. 'My Antonia' has glossy dark green leaves and clean white flowers with yellow centers in late summer and fall; plants are about 1' tall. A Great Plants for the Great Plains selection in 1999, this plant was discovered near Willa Cather's birthplace in Red Cloud, Nebraska, and named for her famous novel.

Aster laevis (smooth aster) has never performed particularly well in the UGA Horticulture Gardens; perhaps we have not sited it well, or perhaps we are a little warm for it. But others love it, and the raves have convinced me to include it here. The lanceolate leaves are smooth, and the flowers deep lavender to violet. 'Bluebird', the only cultivar offered, is distinguished by the large clusters of single violet-blue flowers with golden centers, each about 1" wide. Plants grow 3–3½' tall. Zones 3–7.

Aster umbellatus (flat-top aster) is a wonderful prolifically flowering white aster often seen along the side of the road. Left to its own devices, it may get 6' tall, but a ruthless cutback in late spring will result in manageable plants. Flowers in the fall for at least eight weeks. Insect- and disease-free, this overlooked plant should be brought home every now and then. Zones 3–7.

Recommended propagation

Seed: Not all seeds are viable, so sow heavily to ensure reasonable germination percentage. A cold treatment stimulates more germination in a shorter period of time but probably won't result in enhanced germination percentage overall.

Cuttings: Terminal stem cuttings are the propagation method of choice for the species and cultivars. Take cuttings before June for best results. Place three-node cuttings in containers of moist medium (3:1 perlite:peat) and keep moist. Roots will appear in three to four weeks. Keep them growing in containers, cut off any flower buds, then transplant to the garden in the fall.

Division: A simple and effective means of propagation. Cutting a pie-shaped wedge will provide enough new material and will not be missed by the mother plant. Best to do this in cool weather, such as early spring, but you can try it whenever the mood hits you as long as you water the transplants well.

Etymology

Genus: From the Latin, *aster* ("star"), in reference to the form of the flower.

Specific epithet: *azureus* ("azure"), referring to the sky-blue color of the flowers; *carolinianus* ("of the Carolinas"); *divaricatus* ("widely spreading"); *ericoides* ("resembling *Erica*"), because the slender branches and bracted leaves closely resemble those of heath (*Erica*); *fendleri*, for German botanist August

Fendler, who collected plants in North and Central America; *laterifolius*, from
lateri ("at the side") and *florus* ("of flowers"), the flowers are borne on only
one side of the stem; *laevis* ("smooth"), in reference to the leaves and stems;
novae-angliae ("of New England"), which was derived from Anglia
("England"); *novi-belgii* ("of New Belgium"), meaning a nativity of New York,
which state was established by Dutch settlers who named it for the Low
Countries of Belgium and The Netherlands; *oblongifolius* ("oblong-leaved");
umbellatus refers to the type of inflorescence, in this case an umbel.

Common name: Calico aster refers to the diverse colors of the disk florets
as they mature; aromatic aster exudes a pleasant odor when the leaves are
brushed; rock aster refers to the diminutive size and its habit of growing
between rocks; Michaelmas daisies flower near 29 September, the
Christian feast of St. Michael the Archangel, observed by Western
churches on 29 September and in the Eastern (Orthodox) Church on
8 November.

Astilbe biternata	false goatsbeard	Saxifragaceae

One of the most underutilized plants, native or not, in American gardening is
our own *Astilbe biternata*. Propagation of the species is not particularly common,
perhaps because dozens of colorful *Astilbe* hybrids are available everywhere. Our
poor old large-leaved native is not so blessed, being available in white only, and
not even a pure white. In fact, it looks more like an aruncus than an astilbe. I
have grown it in the Armitage garden for many years, and it has performed reasonably well but prefers cooler climes. I would be lying if I told you others
shared my delight in this plant, for compared to the reds, pinks, and pure whites
of the hybrids, it is easily overlooked. But the heck with them: it is my garden,
and this plant is always welcome—if I can find it for sale. That is the other problem: go into any retail outlet and ask for this, and you will most likely draw a
blank expression and the comment, "I didn't know there was a native astilbe."

Plants take a few years to become established. You will have more success in
zones 4–6 than in the South (above zone 7).

Habitat: In mountain woods from Virginia to Kentucky, south to Georgia and
Tennessee.
Hardiness: USDA Zones 4–7.
Garden site: Partial shade and moist soils
Garden maintenance: Maintain consistently moist soils. Remove spent flowers
for best return the next year.

Recommended propagation
Seed: Collect seeds from plants and allow them to dry for a few weeks. Sow in
moist, warm conditions. Germination is slow and inconsistent.

Division: Divide only if the clump is sufficiently large; this will take three to five years.

Etymology

Genus: From the Greek, *a* ("without") and *stilbe* ("brightness"), referring to the dull leaves on some species.

Specific epithet: *biternata* ("twice ternate"), referring to the leaves first being divided into three (ternate), then each of the three segments divided into three again.

Common name: Astilbes look much like *Aruncus*, goatsbeard.

Athyrium	lady fern	Athyriaceae

The genus is well represented, including the marvelous nonnative species, *Athyrium nipponicum* 'Pictum' (Japanese painted fern) and *A. otophorum* (auriculate lady fern). The lady fern, *A. filix-femina*, is native to many north temperate areas of the world, including the United States. It is probably one of the most variable, yet its ease of performance makes it a no-brainer for most gardeners. Several fancy forms of lady fern are now available, many the result of hybridizing with other species. The genus also contains *A. thelypteroides* (silver spleenwort), but it is more difficult to track down. All athyriums are deciduous.

Athyrium filix-femina	lady fern

Lady fern is the easiest of the native species to grow. Plants reach 18–36" in height; and although mostly green in color, they are often more handsome in the spring, when they can produce a flush of reddish growth. They grow in circular clusters and do not run, which easily differentiates them from the rambling *Dennstaedtia punctilobula* (hay scented fern), another fine native. In the Armitage garden, they are among the most visible, growing in deep shade and providing a handsome green background all summer. They are not, however, without problems. The stems are brittle and snap in winds or when squirrels run through them. And of course, they are toast when my yellow lab Hannah chases said squirrels.

The wide variability of the species contributes to the dozens of available selections with fancy, crested, or plumose fronds, or with a more dwarf habit. Unless you are into the distorted look, most are a heck of a lot more interesting than they are beautiful. You will find many at good garden centers and some of the more unusual cultivars through mail-order nurseries.

'Cristatum' has flat fan-like crests on the pinnae and the tips of the fronds.

Athyrium filix-femina

Athyrium filix-femina 'Cristatum'

'Fancy Fronds' is only 6–8" tall and has delicately dissected fronds with a small apical crest.

'Frizelliae' is sometimes called the tatting fern, because the unusual fronds resemble the loops and knots of tatting lace. Only 12–18" tall.

'Lady in Red', a New England Wild Flower Society introduction, grows 30–36" tall. The deep burgundy stems of this fern contrast wonderfully with the green fronds.

'Veroniae Cristatum' has triangular fronds that are crisped and crested.

'Victoriae' is difficult to describe, but here goes: the leaflets (pinnae) criss-cross each other and the crested tips of the fronds. Sounds weird, looks weird, is weird—give me the species any day.

Habitat: I consider all varieties of lady fern native to the United States, but some taxonomists argue that only *Athyrium angustum* (*A. filix-femina* var. *angustum*; northern lady fern) and *A. asplenioides* (*A. filix-femina* var. *asplenioides*; southern lady fern) are native to these shores. The northern lady fern grows throughout eastern Canada, the Northeast, and south to North Carolina. The southern lady fern is found throughout the Southeast in moist woods and swamp forests. Lady ferns, varieties included, are circumpolar, occurring on wet sites ranging from Alaska to Labrador and Greenland, through Saskatchewan, Nebraska, Missouri, Illinois, Ohio, West Virginia, and south to North Carolina.

Hardiness: USDA Zones 4–8.

Garden site: Plants do best in shady conditions with moist to wet soil.

Garden maintenance: Remove old fronds if they fall over and break or if they turn brown.

Athyrium pycnocarpon   glade fern, narrow-leaved spleenwort

Plants grow in circular clusters, five to six fronds from each rootstalk. They grow about 6' wide and up to 3' tall. The fronds are made up of undivided lance-shaped pinnae (leaflets) and resemble Christmas ferns in shape; they are a bright, light green in spring, deep green in summer, and bronze in early fall. These ferns are useful as ground covers as they will spread considerably, particularly in very moist, shady spots. The sori (fruit dots, where the spores are held) are long and narrow and lack the silver sheen of those of its close cousin, *Athyrium thelypteroides*.

Habitat: In basic moist soils in north and central North America.
Hardiness: USDA Zones 3–6.
Garden site: Consistently moist, shady areas. This will tolerate wetter conditions than silvery spleenwort.
Garden maintenance: Add some lime and maintain moisture to speed this fern's establishment in the shade garden.

Athyrium thelypteroides   silver glade fern, silvery spleenwort

This rather tall (up to 3') fern is not particularly eye-catching, but in northern gardens, it performs well. It looks similar to lady fern, but the margins of the pinnae are rounded, not cut. The fruit dots are prominent and silvery, thus its common name. The availability of spleenworts in general is poor through normal outlets—better to try plant societies and the Internet.

Habitat: In rich, moist well-drained woods from Nova Scotia to Montana, south to north Georgia mountains. Quite common.
Hardiness: USDA Zones 3–6.
Garden site: Moist, shady area.
Garden maintenance: None.

Recommended propagation

Spores: Sow spores on moist, prepared seed soil mix, and keep under plastic to retain humidity. Mist often when sporelings become visible. Transplant to an intermediate container as soon as they can be handled. Grow on until ready for transplant to the garden.
Division: Cut rhizomes when dormant, or in early spring when the fiddleheads are first visible. Dividing the crowns and replanting them level with the soil renews vigor.

Etymology

Genus: The derivation of the genus name is uncertain. Perhaps it comes from the Greek *a* ("without") and *qureos* or *thureos* ("shield"), referring to the spore cases being on the side only. Or it may have come from the Greek *athoros* ("good at breeding"), referring to the diverse forms of sori, or even from the Greek *athuros* ("spiritless"). I opt for unknown.

Specific epithet: From the Latin, *filix-femina* ("fern-feminine"); *pycnocarpon*, from the Greek *pycno* ("dense") and *carpon* ("fruited"), referring to the dense arrangement of spore cases; *thelypteroides*, from *thelypteris*, another type of lady fern, and *oides* ("resembling").

Common name: Lady fern is an anglicized version of the Latin epithet; glade fern refers to the small sunny openings in the forest where *Athyrium pycnocarpon* is usually found; spleenwort refers to the supposed medicinal value of some ferns (actually *Asplenium*) in treating ailments of that organ.

Baptisia	false indigo	Fabaceae

This great native genus boasts long-lasting plants in a handful of colors, all wonderfully suited for the garden. Plants provide colorful stems, handsome foliage, beautiful flowers, and interesting fruit to gardeners throughout most of the country. Gardeners in the know realize that the crummy-looking stick in a gallon container at the nursery can become a wonderful plant in a few years. Most plants take a minimum of three years to love, but they get better every year (to be honest, most will continue to look pretty awful each fall, when the stems and fruit wither and turn brown).

Baptisias are native from the East to the Midwest and can be enjoyed by anyone with a full-sun location. Like all members of the bean family, they produce flowers with the characteristic wing and keel petals and bean-like fruit. In most cases the leaves are divided into three segments. Another common feature are the small appendages on the petiole called stipules. The length of the stipules differs among species and aids in their identification. The nomenclature of this genus is very confused, with varieties and cultivars seemingly interchanged at random. Some taxonomists split the genus into numerous species; others lump two or three species as one. Read this at your own risk.

Baptisia alba	white indigo

I believe that at least in the East, this is the easiest and most handsome form of indigo available. The dark stems emerge like black asparagus and carry white flowers in early spring. The foliage is a little darker green than *Baptisia australis*, and plants are a little more shade-tolerant, although a sunny locale is still recommended. Plants can grow 3–4' tall in the garden.

Most of the many white forms of *Baptisia* are classified as separate species. The form of *B. alba* I am familiar with is var. *pendula*, often listed as *B. pendula*.

Baptisia alba

Baptisia alba, emerging shoots

Baptisia alba var. *pendula*, seed pods

The main difference appears to be its pendulous fruit (the fruit of the type is upright).

Habitat: From Virginia west to Tennessee and south to Florida.
Hardiness: USDA Zones 4–8.
Garden site: Full sun.
Garden maintenance: Remove desiccated brown branches as needed.

Baptisia australis   **false indigo**

Probably the most common species and certainly the most available. The deep blue to violet flowers emerge in the spring on green stems that can rise to heights of 3–4' and spreading almost as wide. The compound foliage is light green and reasonably handsome, and the subsequent oblong fruit provide further ornamental value. As with all baptisias, the taproots are deep, and plants should be moved only if absolutely necessary.

Baptisia australis

No cultivars are listed, but several hybrids (which see) involving this species have been developed. *Baptisia minor*, sometimes considered to be a variety (*B. australis* var. *minor*), is significantly shorter (1–2') but with flowers almost the same size; it occurs from Missouri to Texas and westward.

Baptisia minor

Habitat: In moist, open places from Pennsylvania to Indiana south to Georgia and Tennessee.

Hardiness: USDA Zones 3–8.

Garden site: Full sun, but needs to be irrigated in times of drought to maintain ornamental appearance.

Garden maintenance: Plants can look ragged in the fall, with significant early leaf drop. The dead stems should be cut to within about 18" of the soil.

Baptisia leucantha   **prairie false indigo**

Even though the blue-flowered *Baptisia australis* is the best known, the flowers of most baptisias are white or yellow. This is one of the many white-flowered baptisias, all of which are difficult to tell apart without some study. This species makes a handsome compact 3–4' tall shrub, with dark stems and dark green foliage. The flowers are white, sometimes with some purple markings, and occur on 2–3' long racemes in the spring. Probably the best habit of the white baptisias, but not necessarily the one with the most blooms.

Habitat: In open ground from Ohio to Minnesota and Nebraska, south to Mississippi and Texas.

Hardiness: USDA Zones 4–8.

Garden site: Full sun.

Garden maintenance: None. Clean up dead stems in winter or spring.

Baptisia sphaerocarpa   yellow indigo

A good deal of debate concerns the yellow-flowered forms of baptisia as well; therefore, when you purchase a yellow-flowered indigo, some surprises may await you. Plants sold as *Baptisia sphaerocarpa* are all quite beautiful, but the range of color is quite remarkable. Many taxonomists have lumped this species and *B. viridis* together, thus we see flowers ranging from soft pastel to bright butter-yellow. The differences between the two species was that *B. viridis* had lower leaves divided into three segments, the upper with two or sometimes one, whereas *B. sphaerocarpa* typically has all leaves divided into three. Plants tend not to turn brown when they wither in late fall. The other yellow species sometimes offered is *B. tinctoria* (which see), which is easily distinguished from *B. sphaerocarpa*.

Habitat: In open spaces from Texas and Louisiana, north to Missouri and Oklahoma.

Hardiness: USDA Zones 4–8.

Garden site: Full sun, consistent moisture.

Garden maintenance: Essentially none. Clean up dead stems in the winter or spring.

Other species for the garden

Baptisia bracteata (*B. leucophaea*; *B. bracteata* var. *leucophaea*)—the names keep changing for this handsome early-flowering indigo. Regardless, the leaf seg-

Baptisia sphaerocarpa (light yellow)   *Baptisia sphaerocarpa* (deep yellow)

Baptisia tinctoria

Baptisia 'Purple Smoke'

ments are up to 4" long and stipules (bracts) up to 1½" in length. The flowers are held in 8" long racemes and vary in color from off-white to cream. From Michigan to Minnesota and south to Kentucky, Louisiana, and Texas.

Baptisia tinctoria (rattle-weed), another yellow-flowered species, is distinct for its small (about ½" long) leaf segments, small flowers, and rounded fruit. It makes a handsome rounded shrub, and I have seen plants performing beautifully from Massachusetts to Georgia. This was cultivated as a source of yellow dye during colonial times. From Maine to Minnesota and south to Louisiana and Florida.

Hybrids

Plant breeders have become interested in this genus, and two wonderful hybrids are presently available with more on the way.

'Purple Smoke', a cross of the blue and white species, is a vigorous 3' tall plant with violet flowers. It has been flowering in the Horticulture Gardens at the University of Georgia for five years now and gets better every year. Outstanding.

'Carolina Moonlight' is newer than the former hybrid and bears light yellow flowers. I have not trialed it as long as 'Purple Smoke', but it too appears to be a winner.

Recommended propagation

Seed: Seed is the most common means of propagation. Collect the seeds when the pods darken and the seeds have expanded. Place the seeds in a refrigerator for at least six weeks; twelve weeks is even better. When ready to sow, soak the seeds overnight, then sow on moistened medium (3:1 perlite:peat works well) at about 75F. Plants grow slowly, requiring at least two years from seed to flower.

Division: The rootstalk is deep and tough, but it can be done. Dig deeply and make a clean cut using a sharp knife. This should be accomplished in the fall or early spring, only after two to three years' growth. Apply fungicide to the cut surfaces before replanting.

Etymology

Genus: From the Greek, *bapto* ("to dye"), in reference to the use of some
species for dyes.

Specific epithet: *alba* ("white"); *australis* ("southern"); *bracteata* ("having bracts");
leucantha ("white-flowered"); *leucophaea*, from *leuco* ("white") and *phaea*
("dusky, dark"), pertains to the off-white flowers; *sphaerocarpa*, from *sphaero*
("round") and *carpus* ("fruit"); *tinctoria* ("used in dyeing"); *viridis* ("green"),
in this case referring to the stem and leaf color.

Common name: The "false" is a reference to the plants' use as a substitute—
albeit not a great one—for the true indigo, *Indigofera*, of the West Indies.
In the mid 1700s, when *Indigofera* was in short supply, the English government contracted with farmers in Georgia and South Carolina to grow
Baptisia australis to supply a blue dye. The farming of baptisia was one of
the first recorded examples of agricultural subsidies in America.

Berlandiera lyrata	chocolate flower, green eyes	Asteraceae

Although we have managed to kill this plant with great efficiency in the trial
gardens at the University of Georgia, it deserves a far better fate—in fact, it was
a 2004 winner in the Plant Select program, administered by the Denver
Botanic Gardens and Colorado State University. It appears to perform well in
the western part of the country, particularly the Plains and Rocky Mountain
states, as well as the Southwest. Solitary quarter-sized daisies, yellow with a
dark center, are produced from mid to late summer. The ray flowers (usually
eight) are marked on their undersurface by lines of red, green, or maroon; they
are generally dropped in late afternoon, leaving behind only the green bracts
cupped around the center of the flower. The effect is like a daisy with a green
eye, thus its other common name. Plants often reseed where comfortable. The
foliage is interesting in that it is a dark, almost dusky green. Plants grow about
12" tall.

Habitat: From southwestern Kansas west to Colorado and south to northwest
New Mexico and east into Texas.
Hardiness: USDA Zones 5–8.
Garden site: Well-drained areas in full sun.
Garden maintenance: Deadheading, to enhance continued flowering, is all that
is needed.

Recommended propagation

Seed: Easy from seed.
Cuttings: Can be propagated from terminal cuttings.

Etymology

Genus: For J. L. Berlandier, a Belgian botanist who explored in Texas and
New Mexico.

Specific epithet: *lyrata* ("of lyrate form"), in this case the leaves have a broad,
rounded tip, and the lobed sides diminish in width toward the base (lyrate).

Common name: The chocolate-colored stamens give off a faint smell of chocolate, hence chocolate flower.

Bidens	fennel-leaved marigold, sticktights	Asteraceae

Bidens is a common basket and container plant, but the only species that has
enjoyed any garden presence, and that only through its cultivars, is *Bidens ferulifolia*. It barely made the native designation as it essentially resides in Mexico,
with a foot in southern Arizona and southern Texas. Another species, *B. cernua*,
is native to a good deal of this country. I can find no nurseries offering plants,
but seeds are reasonably available.

Bidens cernua   nodding beggarticks, nodding bur-marigold

This native plant pretty much remains a wildflower. Never have I seen it shine
in an American garden, although I admit to visiting but a minuscule percentage
of gardens around the country. Plants can grow to 6' in height but can be as
short as 1' in harsh climates. The flower heads start out erect, then become

Bidens cernua

slightly nodding or lean sideways. Plants begin to flower in late summer through the fall; they perform better in consistently moist areas but still do well in "normal" soil situations.

I saw it in its full glory in the Zurich Botanical Garden, of all places. I noticed this wonderful 3' tall upright plant with many 1" wide yellow daisy flowers, and indeed it was our native, nodding beggarticks. Perhaps cool nights agree with it. That garden vista alone persuaded me to include it; however, not to get too carried away, it is listed as an invasive weed in Nebraska, Wyoming, and other Great Plain states.

Habitat: In moist areas from New Brunswick to British Columbia, south to North Carolina, Oklahoma, New Mexico, and California. Also Eurasia.
Hardiness: It is an annual, overwinters through seed.
Garden site: Consistently moist area, full sun. It is a waterside plant.
Garden maintenance: Maintain irrigation when needed. They may require staking to remain upright, particularly in hot climates; if they get too gangly, cut back hard.

Bidens ferulifolia   **Apache beggarticks**

Plants are prostrate and bear yellow daisy flowers over small dissected leaves. The species itself is never used in gardens, but its wild tendencies have been tamed in the many cultivars that have emerged over the years. These brightly colored annuals are sometimes planted like sweet alyssum at the front of beds, but their most common use by far is in hanging baskets and mixed containers, where they add color all summer.

The cultivars are improvements over the species in that their flowers are larger, their stems are shorter, and they flower for a long period of time. Even though they are native to warm areas, they are at their best in areas where summer nights are relatively cool (West Coast, Northeast); they are also seeing more use in the Midwest and Southeast. All look essentially the same—golden yellow daisy-like flowers on divided foliage—but there are differences in performance.

'Gold Marie' is the oldest cultivar around but still available. It does not have the heat performance of the next two cultivars.

'Peter's Golden Carpet' flowered the longest and performed best in trials at the University of Georgia.

'Smiley' also performed well, but flowering began later and plants were not as vigorous as 'Peter's Golden Carpet'.

Habitat: Open fields in southern Arizona and southern Texas.
Hardiness: USDA Zones 10–11.
Garden site: Full sun. If planted in baskets, water frequently.
Garden maintenance: If stems get too long, cut them back.

Bidens ferulifolia 'Smiley'

Recommended propagation

Seed: For the species, collect seeds from flowers in summer; clean and sow immediately. Place seed trays in a warm, moist area. Misting is recommended.

Cuttings: Remove all flowers on two- to three-node cuttings.

Division: Possible with mature plants. Water in immediately.

Etymology

Genus: From the Latin, *bidens* ("with two points"), a reference to the prominent prongs on the seeds.

Specific epithet: From the Latin, *cernua* ("inclining the head"), hence nodding; *ferula* is the classic Latin name for fennel, *folia* ("leaf"), thus *ferulifolia* ("leaves resembling those of fennel").

Common name: The yellow flowers do indeed resemble marigolds; nodding refers to the tendency of mature flowers to droop; bur and sticktights refers to the seeds, which you'll find clinging to your clothing after walking through a stand of bidens in late summer or autumn.

Blephilia ciliata   Ohio horsemint, pagoda mint   Lamiaceae

I first saw this plant in the take-your-breath-away native garden of Ann Wakeman in Fulton, Missouri. If you looked in the dictionary for native plant passion, you would find Ann's name listed—I saw her garden in the offseason (you know, the "You should have been here two weeks ago" season), and it was still memorable. I asked her what the "monarda-looking" thing was, and she replied that it was Ohio horsemint, but that she much preferred the term "pagoda mint." The pale

Blephilia ciliata

lavender flowers with purple spots are in whorls, bringing to mind the roofs of a pagoda, and are at their best in early to mid June. The individual flowers are surrounded with oval, pointed bracts with hairy margins. I saw them again at the great Powell Gardens in Kingsville, Missouri, where they looked wonderful in a drift. Plants grow only 12–20" tall; all parts have a pleasant smell of mint but without the thug-like properties. They remain evergreen in the winter.

Habitat: Open woods, mostly edges of woods, in central and northern Missouri, Kansas, and Oklahoma.
Hardiness: USDA Zones 5–7.
Garden site: Full sun, adequate drainage.
Garden maintenance: Plants will reseed. If that is a problem, cut off flower heads before they go to seed.

Other species for the garden
Blephilia hirsuta (hairy horsemint) is similar except the leaves are hairy. It too is reasonably available.

Recommended propagation
Seed: Easy from seed that is collected in mid to late summer.

Etymology
Genus: From the Greek for "eyelashes," referring to the hairs on the bracts.
Specific epithet: *ciliata* ("fringed with hairs") for the bracts; *hirsuta* ("hairy") for the leaves.
Common name: I don't know where the term "horsemint" comes from. It is not a true mint, nor can I find what it has to do with horses.

| *Boltonia* | false aster | Asteraceae |

A few species—including *Boltonia caroliniana* and *B. decurrens*, neither of great ornamental value—are native to the United States, mostly from the Midwest to the East. Plants are denizens of pastures and ditches, where their small white flowers blend in well. They are often the mainstay of meadow, pasture, or wild-flower plantings, although they may be overlooked by all but the birds and butterflies they attract.

Boltonia asteroides

Here is a terrific late summer–, fall-flowering plant for the back of the garden. It behaves like an aster and should be treated similarly in the garden. Plants are 4–5' tall if left to their own devices and put on hundreds of small white flowers with a yellow cone in the middle. The leaves are small, with a nice blue-green luster. Few gardeners use the species itself, but a couple of varieties (var. *latisquama*, bigger, darker flowers, smaller leaves; var. *nana*, short but poor vigor) and two popular selections are easily available to gardeners.

'Snowbank' is by far the most widely used form of this native species. A New England Wild Flower Society introduction, it is similar to the type but more dwarf. Plants grow 3–3½' tall and are covered with small white flowers in late summer and early fall. Foliage is an obvious blue-green.

'Pink Beauty' is a poorer choice but useful if light pink flowers are needed. The plants are tall but often fall over, and the flowers, although bigger than those

Boltonia asteroides var. *latisquama*

Boltonia asteroides 'Snowbank'   *Boltonia asteroides* 'Pink Beauty'

of 'Snowbank', are fewer, resulting in a less interesting and less ornamental plant for the garden.

Habitat: From New York to Manitoba and North Dakota, south to Texas and Florida.
Hardiness: USDA Zones 4–8.
Garden site: Full sun. Prefers moist soils but will do fine with occasional irrigation.
Garden maintenance: A single cutback in May or June results in additional branching and a shorter plant. Be prepared to stake plants that are not in full sun.

Recommended propagation
Seed: Seeds are not often viable; if they are, germination occurs within two weeks.
Cuttings: Two- to three-node cuttings root in warm, moist conditions in one to two weeks. This is the main method of propagation for cultivars and species alike.
Division: After two to three years, plants can be divided.

Etymology
Genus: For James Bolton (1750–1799), a self-taught naturalist who achieved expertise in birds, butterflies, and plants, and illustrated natural history publications. He is best known for his work on mushrooms and other fungi in Britain.
Specific epithet: *asteroides* ("resembling *Aster*").

Bouteloua	grama grass	Poaceae

This prominent genus in the short grassland prairies of the Midwest consists of approximately fifty species, a couple of which have become popular in the native plant garden or in the low-maintenance landscape. Grama grasses are "love them or ignore them" type plants: if you find them functional and reasonably ornamental for a long period of time, then you will likely plant more, but they are also easy to pass by and not anywhere near as sexy as ornamental grasses like *Pennisetum* or *Panicum*. They are more curious than beautiful, being recognized for the ways in which the flowers are held on the stems, and are, in general, quite drought-tolerant, which in itself has led to increased garden use.

Bouteloua curtipendula   side-oats grama

Probably the tallest of the grama grasses, plants attain 2–3' in height but grow in tufts, spreading slowly by rhizomes. The small spikes of flowers with bright purple and orange flower parts are arranged in two rows along one side only of the rachis, thus providing its common name. Flowers and fruit occur from June through September in the Midwest. The purple-tinged flowers appear on arching stems above the blue-green foliage in early to mid summer; the color fades to tan as the seeds mature. The flowers do not shatter readily and are therefore useful for cut arrangements. The fruit is handsome, consisting of small oat-like seeds suspended on one side of the stem. Excellent for dry soils but will not persist in the face of competition from taller grasses. Plants are best used in mass plantings in naturalized areas, although their size also makes them useful companions to other perennials in the middle or back of the garden. The species is reasonably available by mail order, particularly in the Midwest and Canada.

Few cultivars for the garden have been selected; however, improved cultivars have been developed for reclamation. Of several cultivars evaluated at a mine site in the Southwest, 'Vaughn' ranked best for both stand density and vigor in all three study years, followed by 'El Reno'. 'Trailway' is being sold, but I cannot tell how it differs from the species; it may perhaps be a bit more vigorous.

Habitat: Mainly in the prairie states and provinces of United States and
   Canada, also in Central and South America. This is the state grass of Texas.
Hardiness: USDA Zones 2–7.
Garden site: Full sun. Plants seem to do a little better in higher pH soils and do
   poorly in hot, wet climates.
Garden maintenance: Little is needed. Cleaning up in the spring helps the
   plants look more ornamental as the growing season starts.

Bouteloua gracilis   blue grama, mosquito grass

An excellent, functional, low-growing grass, particularly useful for low-rainfall areas (it even substitutes for turf grass in desert areas like Las Vegas and Los

Angeles). Plants are tuft-formers, and although somewhat slow to establish, they are highly durable. Blue grama has been used to rehabilitate disturbed sites and to revegetate dry parts of the central Great Plains. The Blackfoot tribe used the number of spikes produced at each stalk to forecast the severity of the coming winter: one spike was mild, and three was severe.

The fine-textured leaves are narrow, light green, and 2–4" in length. They grow from the base of the plant, and can be twisted or curled. The leaf edges are either flat or rolled inward. The curved flowering spike is produced June through September, and the mature purplish flowers, which hang below the flowering stem, are held in two rows on one side only, looking like mosquitoes clinging to the plant (hence one of the common names). Each spike may hold up to sixty flowers. This is one of the main short grasses of the Great Plains, essentially forming rough sod and more than proved by the test of time. Use this species, and your garden will appear to be overrun with Great Plains mosquitoes, without the bites.

Habitat: From Wisconsin to Alberta, California and Texas, southward through Mexico into South America. It is found in all western states except Washington, Oregon, and Idaho.

Hardiness: USDA Zones 3–7.

Garden site: Full sun, preferably in a rock garden or perhaps the front of a garden bed. Plants are more curious than beautiful. They are moderately salt-tolerant and grow in any soil, but prefer a slightly acid pH.

Garden maintenance: Cut back spent flowers as needed.

Recommended propagation

Seed: Seed is available, and gramas can be direct sown into the garden site, or can be sown in containers for transplanting later.

Division: Divide crowns in early spring.

Etymology

Genus: For Claudio and Esteban Bouteloua, 19th-century Spanish brothers and gardeners; Claudio was a professor of agriculture in Madrid.

Specific epithet: *curtipendula* comes from *curtus* ("shortened") and *pendula* ("hanging"), referring to the flowers; *gracilis* ("graceful") pertains to the slender leaves.

Common name: From the Latin *grama* ("grass"); blue grama refers to the flower color when the spikes of *Bouteloua gracilis* first appear.

Buchloe dactyloides   **buffalo grass**   **Poaceae**

I first came across this warm-season grass a few years ago in an island setting at Powell Gardens in Kingsville, Missouri. The month was early March, and the

*Buchloe
dactyloides*

grass was still dormant, brown but not at all unattractive. Availability is still modest, but I see great potential for this species as a fine-looking drought-tolerant turf. It is already being used in landscapes in new subdivisions in Kansas and Missouri; I have not yet seen it in the East.

The best part is that it needs far less water and fertility than most other turf grasses; plants grow only 4–6" tall so seldom need mowing, and they are tough and resilient. Plants are tufted and stoloniferous, spreading well in heavy soils. Our common turf grasses, with their gluttonous consumption of water and fertilizer, have many detractors, but let's face it: people like lawns. This species provides an environmentally friendly alternative.

Cultivars that green up earlier and stay green longer are better choices for mainstream acceptance. One such garden-friendly cultivar is 'Legacy', developed at the University of Nebraska and designed for the rigors of turf. It was awarded the prestigious Green Plant Award by the Mail Order Gardening Association in 2001 as the year's outstanding new plant.

Habitat: Nebraska to Missouri.
Hardiness: USDA Zones 4–8.
Garden site: Plants do poorly in sandy soils, otherwise soil is not an issue.
  Full sun.
Garden maintenance: Once plants fill in, little maintenance appears to be
  needed. Patience is a must, however, as plants may not green up until
  mid spring.

Recommended propagation
Seed: The species can be propagated by seed; cultivars are vegetatively reproduced only.

Cuttings: Cuttings are propagated in plug flats. Plugs are planted directly into the turf site at a 1' spacing.

Division: As with any grass, a division of the turf may be cut and moved to fill in additional areas.

Etymology

Genus: A shortened form of *Bubalochloe*, said to be a rendition of the vernacular "buffalo grass."

Specific epithet: *dactyloides* ("resembling fingers"), referring to the habit of the foliage.

Common name: Same as the genus.

Callirhoe	wine cup	Malvaceae

These adaptable ground covers come equipped with a tuberous root highly suited to dry conditions. The low-growing plants have handsome flowers, generally rose, red, and purple, sometimes white. They are excellent in the West and Southwest, not as resilient in the East. Plants grow only 1–2' tall but, where they are comfortable, spread rapidly and flower for two to three months. Whether species or cultivar, no wine cup is particularly well-behaved in the garden; all require a placing that allows their long stems to hang over or out of something, so the flowers can be seen to advantage.

Callirhoe alcaeoides	pale poppy mallow

This little-known garden plant grows 6–9" tall and forms an attractive ground cover. The handsome 2½" wide flowers are generally white to rose with at least a tinge of pink, and no bracts are found beneath the flowers. These two characteristics help to differentiate it from the rose-wine to purple flowers of *Callirhoe involucrata*. The stems are roughly hairy, and the leaves are divided into narrow lobes.

'Logan Calhoun' differs from the species by having pure white cupped flowers on 8–12" plants, with a spread of 4'. It was named for its discoverer, who found it growing in the southern Great Plains.

Habitat: Illinois to Nebraska and south to Alabama and Texas.
Hardiness: USDA Zones 4–8.
Garden site: Sunny, well-drained. Plants perform well in containers or on the edges of raised banks.
Garden maintenance: Cut back when needed.

Callirhoe bushii   Bush's wine cup

Callirhoe bushii

I remember seeing this plant in gardens in the United Kingdom, and then in the Midwest, and wondering how it differed from *Callirhoe involucrata*. The flowers seemed to be the same shape, size, and color, and I wondered if the label was simply incorrect; however, when I finally planted the two side by side, I noted the larger, thicker leaves of this species and the more divided foliage of common wine cup. Bush's wine cup was taller and a little less aggressive, at least in the Southeast. Still not a great deal of difference, but this is an excellent plant to try, especially if you cannot find the common one. It is a highly drought-tolerant species, flowering throughout the summer regardless of abuse. Perhaps I was not the only one confused about the differences; plants have only recently been given species status, in the past being referred to as *C. involucrata* var. *bushii*.

Habitat: In dry areas of Arkansas, Missouri, Oklahoma, and Kansas.
Hardiness: USDA Zones 4–8.
Garden site: Full sun, well-drained soils.
Garden maintenance: Cut back when plants get lanky.

Callirhoe involucrata   common wine cup

The best and most popular species in the genus, and the most adaptable. Plants are cold hardy, long-lived, and extremely drought-tolerant. The wine-colored blooms, about the size of a half dollar, are formed at the ends of the many hairy stems. Beneath the flowers are three bracts (involucre) similar to the sepals. The flowers continue to open from late spring into the summer. The plant has received kudos from many areas; it was a 1999 winner in the Plant Select program, administered by the Denver Botanic Gardens and Colorado State University, and I have seen outstanding plants in gardens in Missouri, the lower Midwest, the mountain states, and into Texas. Unfortunately for me and other southeastern gardeners, however, it struggled and eventually succumbed to rain and humidity in the Horticulture Gardens at the University of Georgia. I keep trying! Several varieties have been cultivated, but I know of no cultivars.

var. *tenuissima* has extremely dissected leaves with pale lilac blooms with stripes of white in late spring. Plants tend to go summer-dormant. Probably zones 6–9.

Habitat: From North Dakota to Oklahoma and Texas, eastern Wyoming and eastern Colorado.
Hardiness: USDA Zones 4–8.
Garden site: Full sun, well-drained soils.
Garden maintenance: Cut back when plants get lanky.

Other species for the garden

Callirhoe digitata is more upright than others, standing 2½–3' tall with five- to seven-lobed leaves. The wine-colored flowers are held on long flower stems and lack the bracts seen in *C. involucrata*.

Callirhoe involucrata

Recommended propagation

Seed: The brown sickle-shaped seeds have a hard coat and should be scarified; this abrasion of the seed coat allows water and oxygen into the embryo. For small lots of seeds, placing them between two layers of coarse sandpaper and grinding them back and forth for a while is effective, or you can line an old coffee can with sandpaper and shake the heck out of them. After scarifying, place them in the seed flat or in a bag with moist peat moss and cool them at 40F for about three months. Bring them out and germinate them at 70F. About a year is required from sowing to flowering.
Cuttings: Take two- to three-node terminal cuttings before flower buds have appeared.
Division: Plants have a large taproot, which discourages division. Rather, transplant self-sown seedlings while still young to help distribute the plants.

Etymology

Genus: In Greek mythology, Callirhoe was the daughter of Achelous, the deity of the river by that name and ruler of all rivers.
Specific epithet: *alcaeoides* ("resembling *Alcea*," mallow); *bushii*, for botanist Benjamin Franklin Bush (1858–1937); *digitata* ("shaped like an open hand"), referring to the leaves; *involucrata* refers to the ring of bracts (involucre) at the base of the flowers.
Common name: Wine cup makes sense when you look at the flowers, both in color and shape.

Camassia	camas, indian hyacinth, quamash	Liliaceae

Most camassias are native to the Northwest, although one or two can be found in the eastern half of the country. They are all bulbs, and all have clusters of long, narrow basal leaves before the flowers emerge. The flowers are usually blue to violet and borne on long, unbranched racemes. A good deal of history is associated with the genus; bulbs of *Camassia quamash* were part of the diet of native Indians in the West and likewise sustained Lewis and Clark and their men as they traveled westward. All camassias make wonderful additions to the garden, particularly near streams or low areas where moisture is plentiful. They flower in the spring and persist for one to two weeks, depending on the onset of warm temperatures. Reasonably ornamental fruit follow; these contain black seeds, the size and shape of BBs. Plants will naturalize, particularly if you live in the High Sierras or other "camassia friendly country" in the Far West.

Camassia cusickii	Cusick's camas

The bulb of this species is probably the most vigorous and largest in the genus, weighing up to half a pound. Good grief, this behemoth can produce 2" wide strap-like leaves and flower stems carrying up to a hundred pale blue star-shaped

flowers. Many flowers open at once, meaning plants are a very colorful presence in the garden. The nutritional value of camassias is well known; however, if you have had too much to drink and decide to do a taste test of camassia bulbs, you might want to pour another scotch instead. Most sober gardeners contend that the bulbs smell bad and are not palatable, and the people at Pacific Rim Native Plant Nursery in Chilliwack, British Columbia, rate the taste from "blah to horrible."

'Zwanenburg' has larger deeper blue flowers.

Habitat: On steep, moist hillsides in eastern Oregon.
Hardiness: USDA Zones 3–8.
Garden site: Full sun, moist area (well drained, not swampy) needed for bulb development.
Garden maintenance: Remove yellowing leaves and spent flower heads, unless seed is needed.

Camassia cusickii

Camassia leichtlinii   great camas

The large spring flowers (up to 1" across) are radially symmetrical (those of *Camassia quamash* are slightly asymmetrical) and are light to deep blue-violet in color. Usually only three to five flowers are open on the raceme at once, and when they wither, they twist around the capsule before finally falling away. I like this as a garden plant because the plants are stout, seldom having problems with the elements; however, their native habitat is cool and moist, and heat and humidity limit their persistence in many gardens.

Good bulb catalogs may list a half-dozen cultivars, including a white form ('Alba') and one with violet flowers ('Atroviolacea'). 'Blue Danube' has dark blue blossoms (sometimes listed under *Camassia cusickii*), and 'Lady Eva Price' produces magnificent deep violet flowers. There are also double ('Plena') and semi-double ('Semi-plena') forms, but they are too ugly to be described. If I want double-flowered bulbs, I'll find some double tuberose. These are too nice to mess up.

Camassia leichtlinii 'Alba'

Habitat: On moist mountain meadows and hillsides from the northern Coast Ranges of California and the Sierra Nevada to western British Columbia.

Hardiness: USDA Zones 5–8.

Garden site: A cool, moist garden is best; good drainage with adequate summer moisture is a must. Full sun is preferred.

Garden maintenance: Remove the leaves when they yellow. Cut off spent flowers before they go to seed unless you are collecting seed for propagation.

Camassia leichtlinii 'Lady Eva Price'

Camassia leichtlinii 'Plena'

Camassia quamash

Camassia scilloides

Camassia quamash   common camas, quamash

This is the most common of the native camas and still one of the most beautiful. It is also famous for being the most palatable; however, most of us are going to find more tasty edibles and will purchase this for its shorter height (usually no more than 2½') and handsome deep blue to violet flowers. Again, as with *Camassia cusickii*, many flowers on the raceme are open at once.

'Orion' has deep blue flowers, and 'San Juan' bears almost purple blooms. Both are excellent garden plants.

Habitat: Moist meadows from the northern Coast Ranges of California to British Columbia, east to Montana, Wyoming, and Utah.
Hardiness: USDA Zones 4–7.
Garden site: Full sun, adequate summer moisture is needed.
Garden maintenance: Deadhead after flowering to direct energy to bulb for next year's growth.

Other species for the garden
Camassia scilloides (wild hyacinth, eastern camas) is not nearly as bold or handsome as the western forms. The leaves are grass-like and rather floppy, although the pale blue to lavender flowers, which are borne on a 1–2' tall stalk, are attractive. Sites in eastern gardens may mirror more closely the native range of this species, and quamash success may therefore be a little easier, if not as brilliant. Native to southern Ontario to Michigan and west to Wisconsin, and Kansas, and south to Texas and Georgia.

Recommended propagation
Seed: Ripe seed should be sown as soon as possible in a soil mix providing moisture and drainage.
Division: Mature bulbs produce offsets, which can be removed and placed in containers for growing on. Cultivars must be propagated from offsets.

Etymology

Genus: From the Indian name for the plant, *kamas*, a variant of *quamash*, possibly from the Nootka Chinook Indians in the western United States.

Specific epithet: *leichtlinii* honors German horticulturist Max Leichtlin (1831–1910), who introduced many plants into cultivation; *scilloides* notes the similarity to plants of the genus *Scilla*.

Common name: Camas is derived from the original genus name, *kamas*.

Campanula	bellflower, harebell	Campanulaceae

I include this genus because I enjoy bellflowers; however, the native campanulas would be far, far down on my list of favorites. Although they are not in my garden, I present here a tough rock garden form and another decent garden plant that is also useful as a cut flower.

Campanula americana	tall bellflower

Under cool conditions *Campanula americana* (*Campanulastrum americanum*) can be a stout plant, easily growing up to 5' tall without support. The lower leaves are ovate and pointed; the upper leaves are lanceolate and pointed at both ends. The pale blue flowers have a white ring in the center and, with their five lobes outspread, are more saucer- than bell-shaped. The flowers are striking: the style hangs outside them and curves up at the end. They are formed in the upper leaf axils and in many-flowered terminal inflorescences in summer. Plants are usually biennial; sometimes they flower the first year and can be treated as an annual. No cultivars are available, although the white-flowered var. *alba* is sometimes seen. And by the way, recent taxonomic studies have placed the plant in a new genus, *Campanulastrum*. Thought you might like to know.

Habitat: From southern Ontario to Minnesota and South Dakota and south to Florida, Alabama and Oklahoma.

Hardiness: USDA Zones 4–7.

Garden site: Full sun, well-drained soil. Plants do poorly in heat and high humidity. They are much better in zone 4 than in zone 7.

Garden maintenance: If plants flower the first year, remove spent flowers to allow for the return of the plant the second year; in general, two years is a normal growth cycle. As cuts, flowers have a vaselife of nearly a week. Bring them in and enjoy.

Campanula rotundifolia common harebell

Plants overwinter as small rosettes of round leaves but in the spring send out additional linear to lanceolate leaves that are not round at all. They stay low, at most about 1' tall, and bear upright flower buds that give rise to pendulous blue flowers. The flowers can be quite persistent and handsome in many areas of the North and West but usually look poor in the South. There is a great deal of variation in branching, stature, and leaf size.

'Alba' is a white form. 'Mingan' is a natural sport, found by the botanists of the Montreal Botanical Garden; flowers are medium blue, dark in spots. 'Purple Gem' has rich purple flowers.

Habitat: Native to England and much of North America, from Canada south to
    Pennsylvania, West Virginia, Illinois, Nebraska, Texas and California.
Hardiness: USDA Zones 3–6.
Garden site: Sunny location, good drainage—a rock garden or slope works well.
Garden maintenance: Plants can get weedy, in which case they are easily
    removed.

Recommended propagation
Seed: Easy from seed. Provide a period of cold, moist stratification to facilitate
    germination. Place seeds in a seed mix then place in the refrigerator for six
    to eight weeks prior to placing in a warm area for germination. The easiest
    way is to sow the seeds in the fall or place the seed tray in a cold frame dur-
    ing the winter.
Division: Divide as plants mature.

Etymology
Genus: From a diminutive of the Latin *campana* ("bell-shaped");
    Campanulastrum uses the prefix *astrum* to denote incomplete resemblance
    or inferiority to a campanula.
Specific epithet: *americana* ("of America"), meaning the first identification
    occurred in America; *rotundifolia* refers to the rounded basal leaves.
Common name: Harebell is tough to track down. The "bell" part refers to the
    flowers, certainly, and the best proposition I can find for the "hare" is that
    plants grow in places frequented by hares. Works for me.

Cardamine toothwort Brassicaceae

Not a lot of cardamines are offered; however, two or three are quite wonderful for the shaded garden. Until recently, these useful plants were listed under *Dentaria*, which may often still be the case. Whatever the name, this excellent group has been winning converts to the native plants bandwagon for years.

Toothworts bear handsome green leaves and upright, clean white flowers, which occur in late winter to early spring in the South (often before the leaf canopy of hardwoods fills in), and early to mid spring in the North. Seed pods, known as siliques, contain dark brown seeds that can easily be gathered for additional plants. Plants grow from rhizomes or small tubers and can make significant colonies if conditions are suitable. They go summer-dormant and may disappear as early as late spring if moisture is lacking. People are still debating the merits and sense of folding the genus *Dentaria* into *Cardamine* and hate the fact these beautiful native plants are now associated with a genus that contains hairy bittercress, *C. hirsuta*, one of the worst weeds in all creation.

Cardamine concatenata   pepper-root

Cardamine concatenata (*C. laciniata, Dentaria laciniata*) is perhaps not as common as common toothwort but is easily incorporated into the garden. In general, plants bear three whorled leaves, each with three segments. The toothed segments are often so deeply lobed that each leaf appears to have five parts. Flowers are similar to other toothworts, although pink forms sometimes are available. This species is also a little more heat-tolerant than common toothwort and may be a more useful choice for gardeners in the Deep South.

'Eco Flamingo' has flowers that are obviously pink, much more so than the species.

Habitat: Quebec to Minnesota and Nebraska, south to Florida, Louisiana, and eastern Kansas.
Hardiness: USDA Zones 3–7.
Garden site: Partial shade, moist and well-drained soils.
Garden maintenance: None. Occasional division may be needed.

Cardamine concatenata

*Cardamine
diphylla*

Cardamine diphylla   common toothwort

Cardamine diphylla (*Dentaria diphylla*) is the most common of the toothworts, growing throughout the United States and propagated routinely by nurseries. It is probably the most robust species in the genus, quickly forming large colonies in areas to its liking. Plants have two opposite leaves on the flowering stem, each leaf divided into three broad, toothed segments. The white to golden venation on each leaf is usually quite obvious, and this handsome foliage persists throughout the plant's life. White flowers, each with four petals, open in early spring. I have grown this in my southeastern garden, where it does reasonably well, but it performs more vigorously further north. Plants grow from a pockmarked rhizome. They need shaded, moist conditions to be at their best.

'Eco Cut Leaf' is more deeply divided than the species. 'Eco Moonlight' is a beautiful selection with unusually large, creamy white flowers. Eco Gardens is in Decatur, Georgia, and its owner, Don Jacobs, has developed many wonderful forms of native plants, *Cardamine* being just one of them.

Habitat: Quebec to Minnesota, south to Alabama and Georgia.
Hardiness: USDA Zones 3–7.
Garden site: Partial shade (morning sun is excellent) and moist conditions.
Garden maintenance: None. Plants can be divided occasionally if necessary.

Other species for the garden
Cardamine maxima (large toothwort) appears to be a hybrid with *C. diphylla*. Vigorous and handsome, it is well worth trying if you can find it for sale.

Cardamine diphylla 'Eco Moonlight'   *Cardamine diphylla* 'Eco Moonlight'

Recommended propagation

Seed: If conditions are poor, plants may go dormant before seeds mature; however, if seeds can be collected or purchased, this is an excellent means of propagation. Sow immediately; seedlings will likely not arise until the next spring.

Division: Dig up part of the colony and place it immediately where it is to be located. Divide in early spring, when the plants are vigorously growing, or wait until the fall (mark the colony as it will have disappeared).

Etymology

Genus: *Cardamine* comes from the Greek name for a plant of the cress family. *Dentaria* comes from the Latin *dens* ("tooth"), referring to the markings on the rhizome.

Specific epithet: *concatenata* ("linking together"), perhaps referring to the closely linked leaflets; *diphylla* ("two leaves"), *laciniata* ("divided into narrow segments"); *maxima* ("largest").

Common name: The suffix *-wort* refers to a supposed medicinal use, and the marks on the root, which look like they may have been made by teeth, suggested the plant might relieve toothache; pepper-root because the roots have a peppery taste: Native Americans pickled them, fermented them (to make them sweet), boiled them, and ate them raw with salt.

Caulophyllum thalictroides   **blue cohosh**   **Berberidaceae**

This interesting eastern native is probably better known for its medicinal value than its ornamental beauty. Plants are very much part of today's herbal medicine movement, mainly used to regulate menstruation. While they are beautiful in their own right, they are not going to reach out and grab you as you pass by. They grow 1–3' tall (the three-footer is a bit like a good fish story, 1–1½' is more common). The foliage is weird; in general, there is but one leaf near the top, almost

Caulophyllum thalictroides　　　　　*Caulophyllum thalictroides*

sessile and divided into three segments, and divided again into three, and again (triternate)—the overall effect is one of many leaves. The ultimate segments are small, somewhat round and notched, like leaves of meadow rue. There may be a biternate leaf near the base of the flower as well. Not so much the shape but the overall blue sheen of the leaves, particularly in early spring, makes the plant attractive. For this reason alone, it is worth growing. The ½" yellowish green flowers, which are formed in mid spring, are insignificant; however, they give rise to two beautiful metallic-blue fruits in late summer. The color of the foliage and the emergence of the fruit are what make gardeners come back for more. I have enjoyed plants in woodlands and in gardens mixed with ferns, mayapples, and Virginia bluebells.

Habitat: In moist woods from New Brunswick, west to Manitoba, south to Missouri and east to Alabama, Georgia, and South Carolina.
Hardiness: USDA Zones 3–7.
Garden site: Moist, shaded woodlands.
Garden maintenance: None to speak of, although occasional liming of the soils improves vigor. Plants are far more robust in cold-winter climates than in those with warm winters.

Recommended propagation
Seed: Quite difficult. Collect seeds in late summer; many may be immature or sterile. Clean the blue seed coat off the hard seeds using a blender, removing possible inhibitors and scarifying the seeds at the same time. Place the clean, scarified seeds in a prepared seed mix in the fall and put in a cold frame, allowing the seeds to go through cycles of varying temperatures. First-year seedlings should be 4–6" tall and may be transplanted directly to the garden.
Division: Division can be accomplished, but plants are slow growers. There is nothing prettier than a dense colony, so leave them alone—try the seeds again.

Etymology

Genus: From the Greek, *kaulos* ("stem") and *phyllon* ("leaf"), in reference to the large leaf attached to the stem.

Specific epithet: *thalictroides* ("resembling *Thalictrum*"), in reference to the leaf segments' resembling the foliage of meadow rue (*Thalictrum*).

Common name: Cohosh is a Native American word for the plant, and blue refers to the color of the stem and early foliage.

Centaurea	knapweed	Asteraceae

At first glance, centaureas appear thistle-like; but you will note, upon closer inspection, that they have few if any prickles and look more like bachelor's buttons or cornflowers. They are mostly native to Europe and have become highly aggressive weeds in many states. Spotted knapweed (*Centaurea maculosa*), a taprooted Eurasian perennial, is invading rangeland throughout the western United States and Canada, and is associated with reductions in biodiversity and wildlife and livestock forage, and increased soil erosion; *C. repens* (Russian knapweed) is another difficult and aggressive weed. Most of the centaureas we grow in the garden or see as roadside plants (bachelor's buttons, sweet sultan) are native to Europe and Asia and have simply found these shores to their liking; but there is a wonderful native species that deserves to be enjoyed by more gardeners.

Centaurea americana	shaving brush

The only gardenworthy native species is *Centaurea americana*, which is a useful garden annual and an outstanding cut flower. Plants grow 3–5' in height and produce smooth, entire lanceolate leaves and large (2–3" across) heads of rose to purple flowers. The bracts beneath the flowers look like overlapping shingles and are part of the ornamental value of this wonderful weed, which we grew as part of our cut flower research.

Centaurea americana, opening   *Centaurea americana* 'Jolly Joker'

'Aloha' has lilac-pink flowers and grows about 3' tall. 'Jolly Joker' bears 3" wide lavender flowers on 4' tall stems.

Habitat: Pastures and wastelands from Louisiana to Texas and Arizona, north to Missouri.
Hardiness: USDA Zones 10–11, plants should be considered annuals.
Garden site: Full sun.
Garden maintenance: Pinch plants when young to allow for better branching and shorter stature. Plants are susceptible to several fungal diseases: apply a broad spectrum fungicide in the spring and early summer. Flowers can be cut as soon as they open.

Recommended propagation
Seed: Easy. Sow seeds in a prepared seed mix, apply moisture and heat. Seed may be purchased or collected. Purchased seed will be more successful, as it is already cleaned.

Etymology
Genus: From the Greek, *kentauros* ("centaur"), the half-man, half-horse of Greek mythology.
Specific epithet: *americana* ("of America").
Common name: In some places, the plant was called hardhead, and knapweed is based on the same idea: "knap" is thought to be a form of "knop" or "knob" and—because of its solid, "hard" flower "heads," formed by the bracts, which lap over each other like tiles—knobweed became knapweed; shaving brush, because before the flower is fully open, it resembles an old-fashioned shaving brush.

Chamaelirium luteum	fairy wand, devil's bit	Melianthaceae

This is the only species in the genus, and although there are sexier plants around, I find it quite spectacular. It may be seen at the Atlanta History Center's Quarry Garden, which is lovingly maintained by Sue Vrooman—a walking encyclopedia who is happy to point out all the native treasures in her displays, including the fairy wands.

The 3–4' tall plants start out as rosettes from a tuberous rootstock, then send up narrow stems terminating in long racemes of hundreds of small white flowers that turn yellow as they age. Plants are male or female (dioecious). The males are shorter in stature but bear longer inflorescences, which tend to taper and bend over at the tip; the female inflorescence is shorter and consistently thick to the tip. For the fairy wand gardener, the sex of the child really does not matter, but if you are curious, check for pollen (and if it's there, it's a boy). Outstanding in drifts—it is not easy to find, but when you do, order a dozen.

Chamaelirium luteum

North American Indians harvested the root in the autumn and dried it for later use, mainly to alleviate the symptoms of menopause; it has since been studied as a possible natural remedy for menstrual problems and ovarian cysts.

Habitat: In moist areas from Massachusetts to Ontario and Michigan, south to Florida and west to Arkansas.

Hardiness: USDA Zones 4–8.

Garden site: Moist, shady areas are necessary for best flowering and perenniality.

Garden maintenance: Maintain consistent moisture levels. Removing spent flowers of female forms may extend longevity.

Recommended propagation

Seed: Fairly difficult. The small seeds do not store well and should therefore be sown in a cold frame in the fall. It is not easy to find seeds for sale; check specialty seed houses. Collecting them from established plants provides fresher seeds with a better chance of germinating. Plants may flower after about three years.

Division: Possible, but the beauty of the plant is in large clumps. If you must, divide carefully after three to four years in the ground.

Etymology

Genus: From the Greek, *chamai* ("dwarf") and *lirion* ("lily"), although it is not a lily nor particularly dwarf.

Specific epithet: *luteum* ("yellow")—perhaps Linnaeus studied only older flowers.

Common name: Fairy wand makes at least some sense, but devil's bit may be traced to superstitious folklore: the devil is supposed to have bitten off the rhizome.

Chasmanthium latifolium   northern sea oats   Poaceae

I get a kick out of people who argue the merits of native plants on their lack of invasive tendencies. While it is easier to name exotic thugs, we have a few of our own that wear invasiveness with pride, and this is one of them. That characteristic aside, this is a truly wonderful ornamental grass that provides three seasons of interest—something few plants, let alone grasses, can do. The broad foliage of this 3–4' tall plant is light green, smooth with an entire margin. In late summer, flattened spikelets appear in a one-sided inflorescence; they start out green and mature to bronze in the fall, when the seeds form, persisting through winter in milder climates. The seed heads make invaluable cut stems for drying or arranging with other summer flowers. Vigorous rhizomes help plants colonize an area, and the grass's roaming tendencies are furthered by reseeding, which results in many plants where you want them and an equal number where you don't. The seeds are mainly windblown; plants can be found fairly close to each other but far enough away to call them weeds. If filling in a sunny area is what you have in mind, you could do a lot worse than this grass. If temperatures are hot in the summer, plants have the impolite habit of falling over.

Habitat: Eastern United States down to Mexico.
Hardiness: USDA Zones 3–8.
Garden site: Full sun. Little else is needed.
Garden maintenance: Plants can be cut back in late spring with no harm; cut back in early summer, if toppling is a problem. Cut off seed heads as they are forming to reduce seedlings.

Recommended propagation
Seed: Plants tend to reseed. It is much easier to dig a seedling and place it where you want than to sow seeds yourself.
Division: This is the easiest and most efficient use of your time. Use a sharp shovel.

Chasmanthium latifolium

Etymology
Genus: An ancient Latin name for a plant.
Specific epithet: *latifolium* ("broad-leaved").
Common name: Plants resemble sea oats (*Uniola paniculata*).

Chelone	turtlehead	Scrophulariaceae

Turtleheads can be quite wonderful plants, and their deserved popularity is apparent by how readily available they are. Approximately six species of *Chelone* (rhymes with "baloney") have been described, all of which are native to the United States and Canada. Plants have opposite leaves, toothed and often shiny, depending on the species. The flowers are highly irregular, varying from rosy pink to white, and if you peer inside, you will notice some hairs (this beard is also a characteristic of a closely related genus, *Penstemon*). Plants are sought-after for their dark green foliage and their tendency to flower later in the season, begining in late summer and continuing into the fall. I have seen them look good from Madison, Wisconsin, to Athens, Georgia, so their range of success is not in dispute. All species can be attacked by caterpillars that disfigure the leaves; plants are particularly susceptible if stressed.

Chelone glabra	turtlehead

This is the smallest of the available turtleheads and one of the easiest to grow. Plants grow about 2' tall and produce opposite leaves. The toothed, broadly ovate to lanceolate leaves are either sessile or attached to the four-sided stem by short petioles. Flowers are often white, but can also be pink to purple. The beard inside the flower is white. This species was likely the one most used medicinally by the

Chelone glabra

native Indians; the Cherokee apparently used the plant to improve appetite, as well as to treat fevers and sores. A tea from the flowers was used as a gentle laxative.

Habitat: In moist areas from Newfoundland to Minnesota and south to Georgia, Alabama, and Missouri.
Hardiness: USDA Zones 3–7.
Garden site: Moist area with afternoon shade.
Garden maintenance: Maintain moisture.

Chelone lyonii   pink turtlehead

This species, mainly found at higher elevations in the eastern part of the country, is also readily available at retail outlets. The opposite ovate leaves have rounded bases and are attached to the four-sided stem with a 1–1½" long petiole. The leaves are shiny and extremely handsome. Flowers are rosy purple, with a yellow beard, and open in late July, remaining in bloom well into the fall.

Habitat: In open woods and moist areas in the Appalachian Mountains in North and South Carolina and Tennessee.
Hardiness: USDA Zones 3–7.
Garden site: Moist area with afternoon shade. The area need not be wet, but plants do not recover well if allowed to dry out.
Garden maintenance: Maintain moisture. This more-upland species may not do as well in hot, humid regions.

Chelone obliqua   rose turtlehead

Plants are similar to other turtleheads but have tapering leaf bases with short petioles or are often sessile. The lanceolate leaves are shallowly toothed and glossy green, and usually distinctly veined. The flowers are dark purple with white or yellow hairs making up the beard. They are as handsome as—and may flower even later than—other turtleheads.

'Alba' has white flowers; 'Bethelii' bears many deep rose flowers.

Habitat: Low-lying areas from Maryland to Illinois and Minnesota, south to Georgia, Mississippi and Arkansas.
Hardiness: USDA Zones 5–8.
Garden site: Moist area with afternoon shade.
Garden maintenance: Maintain moisture.

Recommended propagation
Seed: If harvesting ripe seeds, gather them when the capsules are brown.
A cold treatment of 40F for six weeks is recommended, followed by 70F

temperatures. Allow seeds to perceive light.

Cuttings: The easiest method is to take one- to two-node tip cuttings. Root in a moist medium at about 70F.

Etymology

Genus: Lots of stories out there. The one I like best is from Greek mythology: Chelone was a nymph who insulted the gods by ridiculing (or not attending) the marriage of Zeus to Hera. Not a good thing for Chelone to do—the gods punished her by turning her into a turtle. Perhaps the most sensible is that *chelone* is Greek for "tortoise," referring to the flowers.

Specific epithet: *glabra* ("smooth"), referring to the stems; *lyonii* commemorates John Lyon (1765–1814), a Scottish gardener who introduced

Chelone obliqua

many American plants to European gardens; *obliqua* ("lopsided"), although I am not sure to what part of the plant this is referring.

Common name: The flower is said to look like a turtle's head with a partly open mouth and a bearded lower lip. I have tried to see that turtle and it just doesn't work for me, but obviously it works for others.

Chrysogonum virginianum　　　　　　　　　　　　　　　　Asteraceae
green and gold, golden star, golden knee

Green and gold is a "doer"—gardeners in a large area of the country simply put this plant in the ground and get out of the way. The dark green leaves are opposite and ovate, with scalloped edges. The hairy flower stems rise 3–4" out of the basal foliage, and as plants multiply, a marvelous ground cover results. Only about five ray flowers are produced on the golden daisy flowers, a small number by yellow-daisy standards. Flowers are produced mainly in the spring, although a few may be formed later in the year as well.

The species is every bit as good as the named forms that are offered, classified by how they grow. Most spread by underground stems (selections of var. *virginianum*); some grow by strawberry-like runners (var. *australe*).

'Allen Bush' (var. *virginianum*), named for the excellent American plantsman, is similar to the species but offers uniformity of bloom and a longer flowering period.

'Eco Lacquered Spider' (var. *australe*) is unique among available selections and by far the fastest mover. Plants spread rapidly by many long (up to 3') spider-like runners, providing a dark green ground cover with typical golden flowers. The semi-evergreen foliage is so shiny, it appears to be lacquered. Probably hardy to zone 6. Selected by Don Jacobs of Decatur, Georgia.

'Pierre' (var. *virginianum*), named for Pierre Bennerup of Sunny Border Nurseries, was selected for its low habit and long bloom time.

Habitat: In woods from Pennsylvania and Ohio south to Louisiana and east to Florida.

Hardiness: USDA Zones 5–8.

Garden site: Best in partial shade and consistent moisture. In the North, full sun is appropriate if sufficient moisture is provided. Plants are excellent at holding down banks or along shaded paths.

Garden maintenance: If too much rain occurs, fungal diseases will occur in the middle of the clump. Spray or remove affected foliage. Similarly, powdery mildew can be a problem if the clump becomes overcrowded; divide the clump to enhance air circulation.

Recommended propagation

Seed: Collect seeds as flowers dry and clean any material which clings to them. Sow in containers, moisten, and store at 40F for about three months. Bring out to 70F; protect from rodents.

Chrysogonum
virginianum

Cuttings: A simple way to reproduce plants is to take one- to two-node cuttings of the runners (var. *australe*) in the spring.

Division: Easiest of all—simply cut and paste.

Etymology

Genus: From the Greek, *chrysos* ("gold") and *gone* ("joints"), in reference to the flowers' being borne at the nodes.

Specific epithet: *virginianum*, for England's Queen Elizabeth, the Virgin Queen.

Common name: All refer to the color, shape, or position (knee refers to node) of the flowers and/or the foliage.

Chrysopsis	golden aster	Asteraceae

Plants in this genus of yellow-flowered daisies blend into the summer landscape when times are good, hardly noticed, but they can be a godsend during seasons of drought. Fear of drought is not a good reason to include plants in your garden, however, and you may find tickseed and other yellow daisies more to your liking. Golden asters are not at all easy to find; seed sources may be your best bet. All plants bear yellow to golden flowers in summer and may continue to flower for much of the season.

Chrysopsis mariana Maryland golden aster, shaggy golden aster

Growing 18–24" tall, this plant can be extraordinarily handsome, or look like a sick puppy. It forms thick clumps, bearing narrow spatula-like leaves. The leaves and stems are sparsely covered with long grayish hairs (Bill Cullina, in *The New England Wild Flower Society Guide to Growing and Propagating Wildflowers of the United States and Canada*, compares them to "a man in the late stage of baldness"). Hardly makes me want to run out and buy the plant, but an apt description to be sure. Flowers appear in late summer or early fall and may bloom for six to eight weeks. Plants readily reseed.

Habitat: In rocky woods and open places from New York to Ohio and south to Texas and Florida.

Hardiness: USDA Zones 5–9.

Garden site: Full sun to afternoon shade, well-drained soils. Overwatering or boggy conditions will kill it in a minute.

Garden maintenance: Do not fertilize unless leaves look yellowish. Deadhead old flowers for longest bloom time, but do allow some to go to seed for future generations. At first hard frost, cut back to the ground.

Chrysopsis villosa	hairy golden aster

This species, also listed as *Heterotheca villosa*, is one of the western representatives of the genus. It is highly variable and wide-ranging; some authorities believe it to be a collection of interbreeding species. Whatever it is, when you slip this plant into the sunny garden, it will grow 1½–3' tall, and its leaves, which have undulating margins, will be covered with silvery gray hairs. The 1" wide flowers bloom from late summer to frost. In general, it is one of the most drought-tolerant daisies for the garden. If possible, choose the low-growing forms; they make better garden plants than the taller ones.

Habitat: In dry areas from Indiana to Minnesota and British Columbia south to Arizona, Texas and Missouri.
Hardiness: USDA Zones 3–8.
Garden site: Full sun, well-drained areas.
Garden maintenance: Deadhead for longest blooming period.

Other species for the garden
Chrysopsis falcata (*Pityopsis falcata*; sickle-leaved golden aster) is native to the northern Atlantic coastal plain and grows only 1' tall, a mound of silvery foliage. The 1" wide flowers begin in late summer or early fall. Zones 5–9.

Recommended propagation
Seed: Collect or purchase seeds; sow them in a seed container and cover. Place them in a cooler or refrigerator around 40F for about three months, or in a cold frame over the winter. Germination will occur readily at 70F.
Cuttings: One- to two-node cuttings root in late spring and summer.
Division: These plants have a long, deep root; division must be done carefully in early spring. Cuttings are safer.

Etymology
Genus: From the Greek, *chrysos* ("gold") and *opsis* ("appearance"), in reference to the flowers.
Specific epithet: *falcata* ("sickle-shaped"), referring to the leaves; *mariana* ("of Maryland"); *villosa* ("covered with soft hairs").
Common name: No explanations needed here: all refer to the specific epithet.

Claytonia	spring beauty	Portulacaceae

The genus consists of about fifteen species, and although most are native to western North America, others are endemic to South America, Australia, and New Zealand. Flowers are usually less than 1" wide and carried in a few- to many-flowered raceme. The flowers closely resemble the purslanes, but plants differ by growing from small corms. The most common spring beauty is the eastern species, *Claytonia virginica*, which is also the only one easily obtainable by gardeners; other species, such as *C. caroliniana* with its larger leaves and *C. lanceolata* from high elevations in the Northwest, have sufficient ornamental potential to be propagated commercially.

Claytonia virginica — Virginia spring beauty

When I come across a colony of these near the edge of the woods or hiking by a river, I must bend down to have a closer look. These 2–3" tall beauties are one of nature's Mona Lisa plants, always smiling but never grinning. In my garden, they establish reasonably well, but because they flower in the spring, the competition from other spring ephemerals forces me to look a lot harder for them (of course, that there remains about a foot of oak leaves over them may be another reason they are difficult to find). The opposite grass-like leaves are forgettable, but the striped portulaca-like flowers are beautiful, their pink stamens contrasting with the white stained pink petals. The five-petaled blossoms occur in many-flowered racemes, and even though they are less than 1" wide, they are visible for weeks. They are tough old birds, emerging through snow and colonizing the poorest of soils. One spring beauty simply does not do it—plant them in colonies and let them fill in. As they go dormant, the leaves turn yellow. If they must be moved or division of the colony is needed, this is the time to do it.

A true yellow form, f. *hammondiae*, has been reported, as has a more vigorous form, 'Robusta', which supposedly grows 2' tall, but both take superior sleuthing to find.

Habitat: In open areas from Newfoundland to Minnesota and south to Georgia, Alabama and Texas.
Hardiness: USDA Zones 3–8.

Claytonia virginica

Claytonia virginica

Garden site: Partial shade, well-drained soils: these are tough plants but water-logging is a sure way to kill them. Leave them alone, and they will colonize if the site is to their liking.

Garden maintenance: Fertilize sparingly; the addition of organic matter helps colonization.

Other species for the garden

Claytonia caroliniana (Carolina spring beauty) is similar but has larger leaves and distinct petioles, with sharper flower petals. It is said to be more heat-tolerant than *C. virginica*, but I don't consider plants as ornamental.

Recommended propagation

Seed: Seeds are slow and rather exacting as to germination requirements. If you are going to attempt to gather them, do so when the leaves are turning yellow after flowering. Allow the sown seeds to go through a summer, then a winter (a cold frame is useful for protection from critters and cold), and seedlings will emerge in the spring. Another year, at least, is required before plants flower. Allowing plants to self-seed is much easier.

Division: If division is needed, dig corms as leaves start to yellow. If foliage remains, it is easy to tell which way is up; otherwise, do your best to place the corms right way up.

Etymology

Genus: For John Clayton (1686–1773), one of the great early plant explorers in America, who came to Virginia from England in 1705.

Specific epithet: *caroliniana* ("of the Carolinas"); *virginica*, for England's Queen Elizabeth, the Virgin Queen.

Common name: This common name needs no explanation.

Clematis	virgin's bower, leather flower	Ranunculaceae

One can hardly avoid the incredibly exuberant *Clematis* hybrids. I too have been seduced by a few of them and am quite happy to be so smitten. Without doubt, subtlety is not one of their strong points, and many are far more colorful than our native forms. But I am also impressed with a few of our dozens of native clematis; unfortunately, few retailers are similarly affected. It is almost impossible to walk into your garden center and expect to walk out with one, but a few native clematis in particular are worth a diligent search.

The leaves of most clematis are pinnately divided; the petioles curl around any support to allow plants to climb. The flowers usually consist of four sepals, no petals, and numerous pistils. The pistils become the wonderful plumes of the seed heads; although the flowers are heralded as the main selling point, the seed heads on many clematis are as handsome and far more persistent than the flowers.

Clematis crispa swamp-leather vine, curl flower

This southeastern native bears bell-shaped blue to violet flowers on vigorous vines. The thin leaves are variable, ranging from three to seven pinnate segments which again may be divided in threes. The 1–2" long flowers open around late May or early June. They are solitary, nodding and flared open at the base, and the wavy or undulating recurved sepals end in almost colorless margins. The flowers are followed by good-looking but not spectacular seed heads, which are really more silky than feathery. Plants flower and fruit for months; they grow 6–8' tall but are also suitable for containers. I don't see this species, thought to be a parent of *Clematis* 'Betty Corning', as much as I would like—perhaps because its beauty is a little more subtle than the others I'll mention, and its lack of cold hardiness reduces its range.

Habitat: In wet places from Virginia, Tennessee and Florida, west to Texas and north to Missouri and Illinois.
Hardiness: USDA Zones 5–9.
Garden site: Moist areas suit it well, but normal soils are fine if well watered. Full sun.
Garden maintenance: Prune plants hard when needed. Maintain consistent moisture.

Clematis texensis Texas clematis

The species needs to be planted where the beautiful scarlet-red chalices can be admired up close. In areas where plants prosper, the flowers are borne singly or up to seven in a cluster; the sepals are about 1" long, with white woolly margins. In general, however, the species is shy of flowering, more of a collector's plant than a mainstream garden item. I have admired it growing at the beautiful garden of D. D. Martin in Courtland, Alabama, and have seen it in public gardens in the South. But for most of us, the hybrids (referred to as the Texensis Group) are more floriferous, more vigorous, and much more showy. All taxa bloom in the spring and grow 8–10' in a single season.

Members of the Texensis Group are characterized by vigorous growth, nodding flowers, and heat- and humidity-tolerance. My favorite and one of the most popular forms is 'Duchess of Albany', with its many rosy pink flowers, long bloom season, beautiful fruit, and ten-year longevity; it can also be used as a ground cover, scrambling over ugly junipers and forgotten cotoneasters. Others include 'Etoile Rose', with rosy red wide-open chalices; the pale 'Pagoda', with bell-shaped flowers shaped like a pagoda roof; 'Ladybird Johnson' with her deep red-purple tulip-shaped flowers; 'Princess Diana', who sports hot-raspberry tubular flowers; 'Sir Trevor Lawrence', with his wide-open red to pink flowers

Clematis texensis 'Duchess of Albany'

Clematis texensis 'Duchess of Albany', fruit

and golden leaves; and 'Gravetye Beauty', with its stunning wide-open red flowers. They are all reasonably easy to find, and—at least for my daughters—all are better garden plants than the species.

Habitat: Central and northeastern Texas.
Hardiness: USDA Zones 5–9.
Garden site: Full sun is necessary for best performance, but they do surprisingly well even in partial shade. Not as many flowers will be produced in shadier gardens, but they will grow vigorously and still not disappoint.
Garden maintenance: Place mulch at the base of the plant to provide shade and coolness to the roots. Plants flower on new wood, so they may be pruned to the ground in late fall or early spring. Pruning helps to keep the plant under control and stimulates new growth.

Clematis viorna	leather flower, vase vine

Vase vine belongs to a large group of clematis in the section Viorna, along with many other similar native clematis. This is one of the prettiest and most overlooked species in the genus. Plants easily climb 10' or more, with thin slightly hairy deep green leaves, divided into five to seven leaflets. The solitary 1" long vase-shaped flowers are pendulous and obviously thick and leathery; they are violet to purple outside and white on the inside, opening in the spring then giving way to handsome feathery fruit, about 1" long. This looks better growing through shrubs and other garden plants than on a trellis.

Clematis viorna

No cultivars are offered, but 'Odoriba' is thought to be a cross between this species and *Clematis crispa*. Plants grow 8–10' tall and bear rosy and white bell-shaped flowers with handsome green-yellow anthers in mid summer. Zones 5–9.

Clematis glaucophyllum, also called leather flower and another member of the section Viorna, is occasionally sold through mail-order sources. Plants bear solitary pink leathery bell-shaped flowers on vigorous vines. Zones 4–9.

Habitat: Along streams and woodland borders from Pennsylvania to Illinois, south to Texas and east to Georgia.

Hardiness: USDA Zones 4–7.

Garden site: Full sun to dappled shade.

Garden maintenance: Plants may be cut back hard when the vines become overgrown.

Clematis virginiana   virgin's bower, devil's darning needles

Plants provide an attractive semi-woody climbing vine suitable for landscape planting; they are best grown on a trellis or fence. This late-flowering (summer and fall) native is often confused with its European counterpart, *Clematis terniflora* (autumn clematis). While our native is not shy, it is not as vigorous, nor as invasive, as *C. terniflora*, which one loves for a couple of years and curses thereafter. The leaves of *C. virginiana* are generally divided into three toothed segments, and their petioles grasp onto anything in sight, resulting in 10' tall plants in a single season. The white flowers are small (sepals less than 1" long) but numerous; and plants are even more handsome when carrying the masses of feathery-tailed fruits that follow. They tend to do some reseeding, but not nearly to the extent of the European species.

Habitat: In moist areas from Quebec to Manitoba, south to Kansas, Louisiana, Mississippi, Alabama and east to Georgia.

Hardiness: USDA Zones 3–8.

Garden site: Full sun for most fruit effect.

Garden maintenance: Plants bloom on new wood and may be cut back hard in the spring. Provide root mulch.

Recommended propagation

Seed: Germination by seed is practiced mainly by seed breeders or individuals looking for new cultivars. Seeds should be sown when ripe, usually late summer or early fall, depending on taxon, and barely covered in a moist, fine, soilless mix. If a greenhouse is available, place the seeds in covered containers, so soil does not dry out; otherwise, place in a cold frame over the winter. Germination may take up to a year, depending on species or cultivar.

Cuttings: This, the most common method, is usually successful. Take a one-node internodal cutting from May to July. Remove one leaf, allowing one to remain. Apply rooting hormone on the cut end, and place in a 3:1 mixture of perlite:peat. Keep moist and warm (65–70F) and out of direct sunlight.

Division: Plants can be carefully divided in winter or early spring. Keep well watered after transplanting.

Etymology

Genus: From the Greek, *clema* ("tendril"); the Greek word *klematis* encompasses various climbing plants.

Specific epithet: crispa refers to the wavy (crispate) sepals; *texensis* ("of Texas"); *viorna* ("wine-red") refers to the flower color; *virginiana* ("of Virginia").

Common name: For the virgin in virgin's bower, see *Anemone*; a bower is a shelter (as in a garden) made of tree boughs or vines twined together—makes sense for this genus. Swamp-leather vine describes the texture and normal locale of *Clematis crispa*, while curl flower describes the shape of its flowers. Vase vine refers to the shape of the flowers of *C. viorna*. Devil's darning needles is a reference to *C. virginiana*'s long fruit.

| *Clintonia* | bluebead lily | Liliaceae |

These plants fill only a small niche in American gardens; however, I have included the genus because it is perfect for deeply shaded woodland areas, species occur in the East and the West, and once established, plants spread (albeit slowly) and persist for years. Plants produce handsome shiny leaves, lily-like flowers, and wonderful blue fruits, like small beads. They are extremely slow to mature, and most commercial growers can't afford the time for propagation and subsequent growth. Tissue-culture techniques may be the key—let's hope these plants will be easier for the gardener to find in the future.

Clintonia borealis   **bluebead lily**

This is a common understory plant in the higher ranges of the Appalachian Mountains and north into Canada, which suggests it is not highly recommended south of zone 5. The 1' tall plants produce two to five broad, oblong, glossy green basal leaves, about 12" in length and 4–5" wide. The green-yellow nodding flowers, which occur in five- to eight-flowered umbels in the spring, are not particularly exciting: the main attraction is the shiny blue pea-sized berries that follow in the fall. Many stories concern the plant's gastronomic and medicinal uses; for example, young leaves (older leaves turn bitter), said to taste like cucumber, are chopped and added to salads, or boiled for ten minutes and served with butter and seasonings. The plant contains diosgenin, an anti-inflammatory chemical from which progesterone is manufactured. Native Americans made a root tea from it, taken as a tonic and to aid in childbirth, and used it to treat injuries of various kinds, from bruises to burns and infections. According to Daniel Reed of 2bnthewild.com (see "Sources and Resources"), some tribes believed dogs gnawed on the plant's root to poison their teeth, and anyone they bit "would need to procure the same root to extract the poison." Must have been smart dogs back then.

Habitat: In rocky woods and high meadows from Labrador to Manitoba, south to Wisconsin and New England and down to the mountains of Georgia and Tennessee.

Hardiness: USDA Zones 2–6.

Garden site: A cool, moist, shaded site is best. Southern gardeners need not attempt to grow this species.

Garden maintenance: Other than removing woodland mulch in the spring, there is no maintenance on this slow grower. Plants will probably require an additional two years to flower once purchased.

Clintonia umbellulata   **speckled wood lily**

One of my favorite wildflowers—and eastern and lowland gardeners will more likely succeed with this than they will with the more alpine forms. Three to five shiny, fleshy leaves, about 10" long and 3" across and each "pleated" in the middle, arise in early spring. The flowers are among the most ornamental of the

Clintonia umbellulata   *Clintonia umbellulata*

genus. Dozens of small white flowers with purple spots form an umbel in spring and continue for three to four weeks, then give rise to black berries.

Habitat: In woods from the mountains of New York to eastern Ohio and south to Tennessee and Georgia.
Hardiness: USDA Zones 4–7.
Garden site: An area with dappled shade and consistent moisture is best.
Garden maintenance: Little is needed. They are slow growers.

Clintonia uniflora   one-flowered clintonia, bride's bonnet

This white-flowered clintonia is the western equivalent of *Clintonia borealis*, with similar habitat and requirements. Up to four long, narrow basal leaves occur, which are glossy and somewhat fleshy. Usually, a single white star-like flower with bright yellow stamens occurs in the spring, after which a single bright blue berry, containing up to fifteen black seeds, is formed. Plants are adapted to cool, damp, acid, well-aerated soils and dappled shade. Plants spread by underground rhizomes.

Common folklore has it that native Canadian groups used the berries to form a blue dye or stain, and the plants to heal wounds or injuries to the eyes. The berries are a favorite food of the ruffed grouse; but—further proof that humans are not birds—they are not particularly tasty to people and should be considered poisonous.

Habitat: In shady woods along the Sierra Nevada in California, north into British Columbia and Alaska, and east to Montana.
Hardiness: USDA Zones 2–6.
Garden site: A cool, moist, shaded site is best. Eastern or southern gardeners need not attempt to grow this species.
Garden maintenance: Other than removing woodland mulch in the spring, there is no maintenance on this slow grower. Plants will probably require an additional two years to flower once purchased.

Other species for the garden
Clintonia andrewsiana (red clintonia) is even more difficult to find and as difficult to establish; however, the red to rose-purple flowers, which occur above the shiny green leaves in spring, are magnificent. Later, bright mid-blue berries are formed. Native to the western mountains, with a range similar to *C. uniflora*. Zones 3–6.

Recommended propagation
Seed: Use at your own risk of getting old before you see any mature plants. Clean the pulp from the fruit, sow the seeds, and expect seedlings in one to two years. Plants may take up to seven years to flower.
Division: If you have sufficient material, divide in the spring and replant all sections immediately.

Etymology
Genus: For DeWitt Clinton (1769–1828), mayor of New York City in 1803 and the presidential candidate for the Peace Party in 1812 (he lost to James Madison); he was responsible for the construction of the Erie Canal and wrote several books on natural history.
Specific epithet: *andrewsiana* commemorates English botanical artist Henry C. Andrews (1799–1830); *borealis* ("of northern nativity"); *umbellulata* refers to the flowers being held in an umbel; *uniflora* ("one flower").
Common name: Bluebead lily refers to the blue fruit of the genus in general; bride's bonnet describes the solitary white flower of *Clintonia uniflora*; speckled wood lily refers to the dots on the flowers of *C. umbellulata*.

Conoclinium coelestinum   hardy ageratum   **Asteraceae**

I seldom see this plant in a formal garden, perhaps because people simply enjoy it in meadows and along the edge of woods, where it is so common. Or perhaps it is that plants resemble the bedding ageratums they just bought at K-Mart, and they don't need anything else that looks like that for the garden. Fair enough, but it is still a fine plant for gardeners, especially those with a looser sense of garden style, who enjoy plants that reseed to form free vistas of lavender. Plants have opposite leaves and flat-topped clusters of soft sky-blue to lavender flowers. They are rhizomatous and can spread like wildfire, so be careful where you plant them. Plants can look weedy when they flop over in rains or wind. The species used to be classified as *Eupatorium coelestinum*.

'Album' is a naturally occurring white-flowered form; 'Cori' and 'Wayside Variety' are both more compact and do not fall over as readily.

Habitat: In New Jersey to Illinois, south to Texas and Florida.
Hardiness: USDA Zones 4–9.
Garden site: In moist soils, full sun to afternoon shade.
Garden maintenance: They can fly—be prepared to divide and conquer.

Recommended propagation
Seed: Can be easily grown from seed.
Cuttings: Terminal cuttings are an effective means of propagation, especially the named varieties. The use of a rooting hormone is recommended.
Division: Divide as needed.

Etymology
Genus: From the Greek, *konos* ("cone") and *klino* ("to lean"), in reference to the conical receptacle beneath the ray flowers.
Specific epithet: *coelestinum* ("heavenly"), as in the sky-blue flowers.
Common name: Plants look like the annual ageratum (*Ageratum houstonianum*) but are far more cold hardy, hence hardy ageratum.

Conoclinium coelestinum

Conoclinium coelestinum 'Wayside Variety'

| *Coreopsis* | tickseed | Asteraceae |

Some native plant genera are so much a part of gardening that their nativity is never considered: the plants are so successfully mainstreamed we don't even think of them as natives. *Coreopsis* is one of these watershed genera, with plants so gardenesque, I have to remind people that they are "ours."

All are daisies, all are colorful, and all flower for a long time. Some are more versatile than others; some want more hand-holding; some suck up and spit out anything but the worst conditions. The genus allows the purest native-ite to grow the species and yet provides a plethora of cultivars for my daughters. Everyone is happy! In general, all *Coreopsis* species are drought-tolerant, with the possible exception of *C. verticillata*. This does not mean they don't benefit from irrigation, but that they come back from drought rapidly. In fact, all can be watered to death quite easily.

The state legislature of Florida designated the genus as its official wildflower in 1991, after the colorful flowers were used extensively in Florida's roadside plantings and highway beautification programs. This from the state of hanging chads. Gosh, if these plants can make even a government happy, they ought to be celebrated.

| *Coreopsis auriculata* | mouse-ear coreopsis |

Mouse-ear coreopsis has no particularly redeeming qualities. It bears yellow daisy flowers in the spring and early summer and grows about 2' tall; about eight ray flowers surround the golden disk. Most of the leaves are basal and have small ear-like lobes at the base. In short, there are too many other good yellow flowers to waste time on this.

But let me stop raining on the parade: its selection 'Nana' is outstanding and definitely a keeper. Plants are dwarf, only 6–9" tall, and they flower early and profusely. Flowers are similar to the species, except they are sterile and held on short stems.

Habitat: In woodlands and open spaces from Virginia to Kentucky, south to Louisiana and Florida.

Coreopsis auriculata

Hardiness: USDA Zones 4–9.

Garden site: Moist, protected site with all-day sun in the North, afternoon shade in the South.

Garden maintenance: You can deadhead spent flowers to keep the plants blooming, but they will stop flowering in early summer anyway. Maintain consistent moisture if possible. Plants are susceptible to foliar burn and foliar fungi; apply fungicide in early spring.

Coreopsis grandiflora   common tickseed

Plants occur in open places by roadsides or wherever the seeds have fallen; look for the 1–2" wide golden daisies. The species is no more susceptible to foliar problems, nor is it any longer lived than cultivars, so if you find it, in catalogs or online, enjoy it.

Most growers are producing named selections and hybrids for garden centers, making this the most common coreopsis sold. A new hybrid with both common tickseed and some threadleaf coreopsis in its bloodlines is 'Crème Brûlée', discovered growing in Lois Woodhull's garden on Long Island, New York. The flowers are a soft yellow, and plants stand about 3' tall. A little too early to gush over this introduction, but it appears to be a winner.

'Early Sunrise' is likely the most common cultivar out there, bearing many semi-double flowers and producing blooms the first year from seed. Other members of the genus require a winter to look good in flower. An All-America Selection (AAS) award winner in 1989.

'Flying Saucers' is compact (less than 2' tall) with solitary 2" wide yellow flowers that are sterile, making deadheading less of a concern. Plants bloom from late spring to late summer and sometimes well into fall.

'Robin', a relatively new hybrid, provides handsome red markings in the disk, which is surrounded by golden ray flowers.

Coreopsis 'Crème Brûlée'

Coreopsis grandiflora 'Sundance'

Coreopsis grandiflora 'Tequila Sunrise'

'Sundance' is positively covered with handsome semi-double flowers. A good performer in heat and humidity. Brought to American gardeners by Robbie Dupont of Dupont Nursery in Plaquemine, Louisiana.

'Sunray' is the best of the double-flowered forms, producing many blooms on a 2' tall plant.

'Tequila Sunrise' has fine orange flowers but is characterized by its variegated foliage, which is a creamy yellow with a hint of pink. It lacks the vigor of other tickseeds and probably will not be persistent for more than two good years. A handsome color combination nonetheless.

Habitat: In dry soils on roadsides and fields from Florida to New Mexico and north to Kansas and Georgia.

Hardiness: USDA Zones 4–9.

Garden site: Full sun, can tolerate morning shade.

Garden maintenance: Deadheading spent flowers is essential to keep the plants blooming through mid summer. If allowed to go to seed, flowering stops and plants tend to decline rapidly. Spent flowers tend to hang on to the plant and become diseased. Apply fungicide in early spring to reduce incidence of foliar disease.

Coreopsis integrifolia   Chipola River tickseed

I have always admired this southeastern native, probably because it stays 12–18" tall and flowers in the fall, when my garden needs some color. Certainly not as prolific a flowerer as some other species, but the entire leaves are ovate to heart-shaped and remain in good shape all season. The flowers are similar to other members of the genus, that is, yellow daisies with seven or eight ray flowers around a darker center. They spread by rhizomes but are not rapid colonizers. This is not a dry-soil species, being native to moist areas, but plants do fine under normal garden situations.

Habitat: In moist soils from Florida north to North Carolina.

Hardiness: USDA Zones 6–9.

Garden site: Full sun, moist area is best. Plants will tolerate "normal" moisture levels, but will be more productive if water is available.

Garden maintenance: Maintain moisture if possible. Deadhead in late summer if needed, but plants flower so late in the season that little deadheading is required.

Coreopsis palmata	**stiff tickseed**

Gardeners will have a difficult time finding plants for sale, as its eye-appeal in retail stores cannot compete with other better-known members of the genus. This species is gaining momentum, however, for its upright habit, full-bodied flowers, and tolerance of the driest sandy or rocky soils. The distinctively pale yellow ray flowers combine with the flat yellow centers to form 1–2" wide blossoms atop stiff, upright stems from late spring to mid summer. The stem leaves are sessile, and the upper half of each leaf is divided into three narrow sections, sort of resembling a palm leaf. No basal leaves are present. Plants spread by rhizomes; once established, sizeable colonies may result.

Habitat: Open areas from Canada to Oklahoma.

Coreopsis palmata

Hardiness: USDA Zones 3–8.

Garden site: Well-drained site in full sun.

Garden maintenance: Even though plants are drought-tolerant, irrigate to help establish plants. Once established, cut back if needed. In the garden, plants may move rapidly—be prepared to share with neighbors.

Coreopsis rosea	**rose tickseed, pink tickseed**

This is a beautiful plant when grown well, showing off dozens of rosy pink flowers on dainty 2' tall plants. They make a wonderful colony and complement other annuals and perennials well. They run by rhizomes and usually grow in dense clumps. The ½–1" wide flowers occur on short stems, and the yellow center disk is a nice contrast to the pink rays. The whorls of linear, narrow, light green leaves resemble those of threadleaf coreopsis, *Coreopsis verticillata*. Unlike most coreopsis, they are not tolerant of dry soils, nor are they particularly tolerant of heat. Stems sprawl and mat in hot and humid climates, especially after a rain, and under stress conditions, which occur from time to time in everyone's garden, they can look like bedraggled weeds. I have never seen these look catalog-good south of zone 6. A couple of selections (or hybrids, with at least some *C. rosea* in the bloodlines) have been introduced.

'American Dreams' (not to be confused with the next cultivar) may differ slightly from the species, but to my eyes, it is essentially the same. The advantage is that plants may be more available under this better name.

'Sweet Dreams', by contrast, is quite different and eye-catching. The bicolor red and white flowers, about 1½" wide, can cover the plant in late spring. Dramatic and the best performer, even in more southerly gardens (to zone 7).

Habitat: In damp soils from Nova Scotia to Tennessee and north Georgia.

Hardiness: USDA Zones 3–6.

Garden site: Moist soils, full sun.

Coreopsis rosea

Coreopsis rosea 'Sweet Dreams'

Garden maintenance: Deadhead if possible, but if the planting is successful, this will become too tedious a job. Cut the entire plant back to half its height if it appears to be getting unkempt. This will also encourage late summer flowering. Where successful, the planting may get to the point of being invasive. For both poor plantings and invasive ones, it is nice to know that plants are Roundup-sensitive.

Coreopsis tinctoria	plains tickseed

Bearing some of the flashiest, most wonderful flowers in the genus, this plant will certainly be used more as the trend toward native annuals continues. Its past is colorful, too; native Indians used it to make dyes, and it crossed the pond years ago to become a highly popular color splash in European gardens. A visit to Monet's garden in Giverny, France, besides being a feast for the eyes, will finally allow you to identify the source of all those vaporous colors in his garden paintings. In many areas of the country, this annual has escaped and colors meadows and roadways. It is also one of the most common seeds in meadow gardening but need not be overlooked by non-meadowers who want to add impressionistic points of color to their gardens.

Plants can grow 2–3' tall and produce many bright yellow flower heads with red centers for months on end. The diversity is amazing—seldom do flowers on two plants look the same. They can get tired and die in mid summer, faster the further south one gardens. Without doubt, however, seeds will germinate from those plants; expect the same differences in flower color and even plant height to result from a single seed package. Plants are still called *Calliopsis*, but that name is no longer valid.

'Limerock Ruby' produces dozens of 1–1½" wide ruby-red flowers and appears to be a hybrid involving *Coreopsis tinctoria*. Excellent dwarf habit and persistent flowering made this a popular plant when first introduced. But it is winter hardy

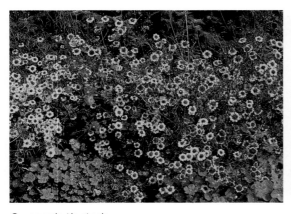

Coreopsis tinctoria

Coreopsis 'Limerock Ruby'

only in mild climates (perhaps zone 8 with confidence) and in the driest locations.

'Mardi Gras' is a selection of many-colored flowers.

'Nana' is a dwarf strain, perhaps more suitable for the gardener.

Habitat: In bottomland areas with ample moisture from Minnesota to Washington, south to California and east to Louisiana.

Hardiness: Annual.

Garden site: Plants do well on well-drained soils, and do not tolerate dry sites. Full sun, but will tolerate light shade.

Garden maintenance: Deadhead aggressively. Do not fertilize. Plants may be cut back in early summer to encourage persistence and reduce floppiness in warm weather.

Coreopsis tripteris   tall tickseed

This handsome member of the daisy family is most often used in naturalizing and meadow gardening; we don't see it too often in gardens because of its height and reseeding tendencies. Plants can grow up to 10' if well irrigated (4–6' tall is more common), and about half that size if under drought conditions. The leaves on the tall flower stems have a long (1") petiole and are divided into three small sections. The flowers are showy and large (1–2" wide), each with eight rounded yellow rays around a flat brown disk. Both the leaves and the flower heads have a faint smell of anise when crushed. Plants flower in mid to late summer and are

Coreopsis tripteris

Coreopsis tripteris

excellent for areas with poor, dry soils. Wherever it is planted, tall tickseed will reseed.

Habitat: In borders of woods and fields from southern Ontario to Wisconsin, south to Kansas, Louisiana, and Florida.
Hardiness: USDA Zones 2–8.
Garden site: Full sun, well-drained soils.
Garden maintenance: Deadhead religiously or plants can become a nuisance by reseeding. Irrigate infrequently to reduce height. Plants will flop over without support, particularly in rich moist soils, and wind will knock them over if they are not staked. Divide every two to three years.

Coreopsis verticillata	**threadleaf coreopsis**

If a poll was taken on the best coreopsis, opinions would be all over the map; however, I would venture to say that threadleaf coreopsis would be on the ballot. Plants grow 2–2½' tall in a rounded mound; foliage is always handsome and weatherproof, and the flowers are numerous most of the summer. The leaves are divided in three parts, and each segment is thin and thread-like. The foliage is beautiful as it is formed in the spring and provides an airy look all season long. Because the leaves are so thin, they lose little water and are excellent in dry conditions, much better than many other *Coreopsis* species. The native species is seldom seen for sale, having been superseded by many fine cultivars.

'Golden Gain' has performed particularly well in summer trials at UGA and is covered in single golden yellow flowers.

'Golden Showers' ('Grandiflora') has somewhat larger flowers than other cultivars but plants grow only 18–24" tall.

'Moonbeam' is still one of the premier cultivars for gardeners looking for a pastel creamy yellow flower color.

Coreopsis verticillata

Coreopsis verticillata 'Golden Gain'

'Zagreb' is about 2' tall and filled with flowers. It is the best performer when bright yellow flowers are needed on vigorous plants.

Habitat: In open woods from Florida to Alabama north to Maryland and
Arkansas.
Hardiness: USDA Zones 5–9.
Garden site: Dry, well-drained soils and full sun are best.
Garden maintenance: Deadheading plants is useful but difficult given the number of flowers which occur. Nor is it as important as with common tickseed. If plants become overgrown, cut them back in early to mid summer; they will return with vigor.

Other species for the garden

The only thing that limits our appreciation of the many species is their availability. So many taxa are now being produced, the commercial grower has trouble justifying additional ones that may sell in relatively small numbers; however, here are a few more for the coreopsis junkies out there.

Coreopsis helianthoides (*C. gladiata*; sunflower tickseed) is 2½–3½' tall and bears dozens of handsome golden flowers in the fall. Plants prefer moist areas but will do fine in irrigated gardens. Zones 7–9.

From the gardener's point of view, *Coreopsis lanceolata* (lanceleaf coreopsis) is essentially the same as *C. grandiflora*. It behaves the same in the landscape, is approximately the same size, and is native to many of the same areas. The plants are 1–2' tall with flowers over slender stems from spring to early summer. The 2–4" long narrow, hairy leaves are lance-shaped and occur as a basal rosette. Plants reseed well and escapees can often be seen along roadways and pastures; they are a common ingredient in meadow gardens. Several cultivars have been

*Coreopsis
verticillata*
'Moonbeam'

developed; 'Goldfink', a dwarf form with handsome yellow flowers and an orange eye, is probably still the best. Zones 3–8.

Coreopsis pubescens (downy coreopsis, star coreopsis) is becoming a little better known as more nurseries make it available. It blooms all season, like an annual, and like an annual is also short-lived. Plants grow 3–4' tall with golden yellow flowers and deep green leaves. Zones 5–9.

Recommended propagation

Seed: Many species are easily sown from seed, including most cultivars. Seeds need no particular cooling or pre-treatment. Sow in moist soil and maintain temperatures of 70–75F.

Cuttings: For selections and hybrids that don't come true from seed ('Tequila Sunrise', 'Limerock Ruby', and others), take one- to two-node cuttings in late spring or summer.

Division: Recommended for those species (e.g., *Coreopsis palmata*, *C. rosea*) that grow from rhizomes and fill in large areas. Divide in the spring.

Etymology

Genus: From the Greek, *koris* ("bug") and *opsis* ("like"), referring to the shape of the seeds.

Specific epithet: *auriculata* ("eared"), for the ear-shaped lobe on the leaves; *grandiflora* ("large-flowered"); *helianthoides* ("resembling *Helianthus*," sunflower); *integrifolia* ("with entire or uncut leaves"); *lanceolata* ("with lanceolate leaves"); *palmata* ("cut like the fingers on a hand"), referring to the three lobes on the leaves; *rosea* ("rose-like"), pertaining to rose-colored flowers; *tinctoria* ("used in dyeing"), the plants were a source of dye; *tripteris* ("three segments"), for the divided leaves; *verticillata* ("having whorls"), the leaves form a ring around the stem.

Common name: The seed looks like a bug or tick, hence tickseed; the Chipola River is a beautiful watershed in the panhandle of northern Florida and a habitat of *Coreopsis integrifolia*. Other common names refer to habit (stiff tickseed), habitat (plains tickseed), or color (rose tickseed).

| *Cornus canadensis* | bunchberry | Cornaceae |

Many fine native species occur in the genus, but nearly all have bark. While growing up in Canada, I lusted (a little too young to lust? perhaps a craving) after *Cornus florida* (flowering dogwood) and simply took this species for granted. Now that I reside in dogwood country, how I miss these little woodland plants. If you look closely at their base, you will notice that they are woody as well, so I suppose it might be a shrub, but a 4–8" one at best. Usually six leaves occur in a circle below the yellowish flowers, but the raison d'être for my missing the plants is the four beautiful white (sometimes pink) pointed bracts beneath the head of flowers.

These bracts persist for weeks and, as with dogwoods anywhere, are captivating when at their best. Each small flower has four minute sepals, four petals, and four stamens, and upon maturation forms a stone-red fruit. Plants are outstanding as a leave-alone wildflower at the edge of the woods, or in a shaded woodland garden.

There are no cultivars, but sufficient diversity exists in the species: flowers may range from white to yellow, and bracts from hot pink to clean white. Plants are notoriously difficult to find for sale; propagation is time-consuming, and it take a while to build up a reasonable population.

Habitat: In moist woods from the northern Coast Ranges of California through Oregon to Alaska, and all the way east.

Hardiness: USDA Zones 2–6.

Garden site: A moist area where they can be left to their own devices is best. If moisture can be maintained, they can tolerate considerable sun. They are terrific in shaded rock gardens where moisture can be supplied.

Garden maintenance: Too much shade and insufficient moisture result in non-flowering plants. A handsome colony will form, but few flowers will occur. Trying to grow these in the South is not worth the effort or the heartache.

Recommended propagation

Seed: Blend, mash, clean, and otherwise remove the pulp from the hard seeds in the fruit. Soak the fruit to assist in this messy chore. Place the seeds in a seed flat and leave outdoors in a cold frame, germination should begin next spring. Plants bloom the second or third year from sowing.

Division: A patch of bunchberries is too beautiful to divide, but if necessary dig when dormant in the winter or very early in the spring.

Etymology

Genus: From the Latin, *cornu* ("horn"), referring to the toughness of the wood.

Specific epithet: *canadensis* ("of Canada"), which epithet was also used by early writers to cover the northeastern United States.

Common name: For the "bunches of berries."

Cornus canadensis

Cornus canadensis, fruit

| *Corydalis sempervirens* | pale corydalis, rock harlequin | Fumariaceae |

I have always enjoyed plants in this genus, but I keep coming up short when I try to find some of our natives. They may not be as handsome or persistent as their Asian or European counterparts, but beauty is in the eyes of the beholder. All native species thrive in cool climates, and most prefer rocky, well-drained soils and reproduce from seeds and tubers. I am not sure there are any native forms I would run out and buy, but the one I would spend some money on is pale corydalis. Some people consider this a weed, and at times I have to agree. The slender plants can be up to 4' tall, although they may also grow no more than 12" tall. The blue-green foliage is the best part of the plant, looking a bit like the leaves of fern fronds, and handsome even when flowers are not present. The pale pink flowers have yellow tips and a single spur on the upper petal. They are sparsely produced during the summer and are only about 1" long; nevertheless, in areas of cool nights, they can make a handsome colony. They are most often found in climates with cold winters and cool summers. Plants will disappear rapidly in hot areas and may act as a biennial. Pale corydalis is a pioneer species, often found on dry soils of disturbed sites, frequently after fire. That is a bit of a dilemma for the gardener, who might watch this plant disappear over time for lack of fire. Probably not worth burning your house down over.

Habitat: From Newfoundland to Alaska, south to British Columbia, east to Montana, Minnesota, Tennessee, and Georgia.
Hardiness: USDA Zones 2–6.
Garden site: Poor soils, rock gardens, full sun in the North.
Garden maintenance: If even a third of its seeds germinate, the plant can get weedy.

Recommended propagation
Seed: Seed must be fresh and can be sown in place.

Etymology
Genus: From the Greek, *korudallis* ("crested lark"); the flowers have spurs like those of larks.
Specific epithet: From the Latin, *semper* ("always") and *virens* ("green").
Common name: Plants grow in barren areas, and the less-than-vibrant flowers are both "pale" and "painted," hence rock harlequin.

| *Crinum* | Florida swamp lily | Amaryllidaceae |

Crinums seem like such an All-American plant, well at least All-Southern one. Old homesteads in the South are repositories for perennial (zone 7) crinums planted throughout the last century, most tropical in origin, including the popular hybrids of *Crinum ×powellii*, whose parents are mainly South African. The native *C. americanum* can be obtained, however, and once planted grows 3' tall and produces large white flowers consisting of six narrow strap-like tepals and conspicuous extended stamens. Generally a single flower stalk bears three to four blooms. The flowers form periodically from spring to fall. Useful as a container plant where not hardy.

Habitat: In moist areas on the coast of Florida and Texas.
Hardiness: USDA Zones 8–10.
Garden site: Bright light, moist soils.
Garden maintenance: Moisture is needed for best performance.

Recommended propagation
Seed: Large seeds can be sown, expect about three years before maturity.
Division: Divide the bulb offsets in spring. This can be difficult digging.

Etymology
Genus: From the Greek, *krinon* ("lily").
Specific epithet: *americanum* ("of America").
Common name: Plants often grow in swamps.

Cynoglossum virginianum   **wild comfrey**   **Boraginaceae**

When I first moved to my home in north Georgia, I noticed these plants growing in my shaded back woodland. I had no idea what they were. However, after checking references and asking all the right people, I learned this was our native counterpart to the more popular European hound's tongue, *Cynoglossum officinale*. The plant is about 1½' tall and entirely covered with hairs. A half-dozen or so basal leaves clasp the stem, and from the middle of the rosette emerges a long flower stalk with two to three additional stem leaves in late spring. At the top is a loose inflorescence consisting of many small (less than ½" across) light blue flowers.

The plant was used medicinally by native Indians to treat a host of ailments; cancer, gonorrhea, and itching were all thought to be helped by drinking a tea made from the roots of the plant. In more recent times the leaves were smoked like tobacco. There is nothing particularly striking about the plant; however, it is unique, tolerates dry shade, and comes back year after year. It is difficult to locate, but I hope that as more gardeners discover it, plants will be more common.

Habitat: In open woodlands from Connecticut to Missouri and south to Texas and Florida.
Hardiness: USDA Zones 4–8.
Garden site: Shaded areas are best; the further north, the more sun is tolerated.
    Provide moisture as needed, but plants tolerate some drought.
Garden maintenance: None.

Recommended propagation

Seed: You'll find seeds in the nuts formed by the flowers. Plant the seeds in the summer or fall in a cold frame; seedlings will emerge next spring.

Etymology

Genus: From the Greek, *kyon* ("dog") and *glossa* ("tongue"), referring to the shape of the leaves.

Specific epithet: *virginianum* ("of Virginia").

Common name: The plant looks a little like comfrey, *Symphytum*.

Cypripedium	lady's slipper	Orchidaceae

I can think of two genera of native plants that everybody wants in their gardens, two genera that have been removed from the wild way too much, and two genera that usually die by the transplant shovel: *Trillium* and *Cypripedium*. And compared to travails of lady's slippers, trilliums have enjoyed a walk in the park.

People, including myself, love the pleated leaves, the slow-growing colonies, and the slipper-like perfection of these pink and yellow flowers. They are a great deal tougher than they appear, which is not to say I haven't lost my fair share. Sitting down beside a lady's slipper and probing around the leaves and flowers is an exercise in plant diversity and adaptability. And who needs to apologize for being curious? Botanically, plants have two pollen-bearing stamens near the opening of the "slipper"; but the third rudimentary stem bears no pollen, and that is the glistening shield-like object visible in the center of the flower. A single green bract, similar to but smaller than the foliage, stands behind each flower. The leaves are always pleated by conspicuous veins, which run from the base to the apex without branching.

My orchid thumb may have atrophied years ago, but I am happy to report that, with better availability and more accessible information, other people are finding slippery success. Lady's slippers are now routinely propagated through tissue culture, but these plants are expensive and in limited supply. Even so, buying such plants is not difficult and highlights your intelligence; digging them from the wild shows you are dumber than a rock. Not that you are guaranteed plants will thrive in your garden either way, but now instead of breaking the law (Minnesota's for one) to bring home plants that die, you can pay good money to do the same thing. And at least your friends will still talk to you.

Many well-respected nurseries feel that—as plants do not handle stress well and are susceptible to fungal attacks—lady's slipper orchids are best appreciated in the wild. Can't argue with that. Still, interest remains high among slipper aficionados, and entire Web sites and chat rooms help the addicted find these marvelous orchids and succeed with them in the garden. I visit every now and then to enjoy the cacophony of sound and spirit as diehard orchidites provide each other spiritual guidance. Isn't gardening great?

Cypripedium acaule, pink lady's slipper

One of the more common terrestrial orchids, and one that is easiest to find. It differs from other available forms in that the stem is essentially underground and generally bears two dark green leaves, which appear to grow out of the ground at the plant base. Plants may have several stems with one flower per stem; they generally grow 12–18" tall. The flower pouch is usually pink, although the color can be almost white to deep rose. Plants are widespread in

Cypripedium acaule

Canada (it is the provincial flower of Prince Edward Island) and abundant in the Northeast (it is the state wildflower of New Hampshire), and extend as far south as the Smoky Mountains. Cool weather and moist soils are highly beneficial.

Habitat: From Newfoundland to Alberta, south to Minnesota, Alabama and Georgia.
Hardiness: USDA Zones 3–6.
Garden site: In moist areas and partial shade.
Garden maintenance: Plants prefer filtered sun and acid soil; the addition of sulphur to reduce pH can be helpful. They tolerate dryer conditions than other species, but that does not mean they do not perform better with consistent moisture—simply, that a bog is not necessary.

Cypripedium pubescens   large yellow lady's slipper

The taxonomy of the yellow lady's slippers is more confused than the other species. Originally most of the yellow-flowered forms were *Cypripedium calceolus*, a species native to many areas of the world, and the forms var. *parviflorum* and var. *pubescens* were classified as American in provenance. Some still consider the American forms to be varieties; others have suggested they are separate species. While disagreement is still common, I opt to agree with Bill Cullina, of the New England Wild Flower Society, who treats them as separate species (*C. parviflorum*, *C. pubescens*). In any case, these are some of the most beautiful and in-demand plants—tissue culture became routine just in the nick of time.

*Cypripedium
pubescens*

This species is characterized by its green to slightly brown petals and sepals, and the yellow pouch with brown dots. They are big and bold, with as many as a dozen stems in a showy clump.

Habitat: From Nova Scotia to Maine, west to Minnesota and south to Missouri, Alabama and Georgia.
Hardiness: USDA Zones 4–8.
Garden site: Moist, acid to neutral soil.
Garden maintenance: None.

Cypripedium reginae   showy lady's slipper

With its pure white sepals and petals and pink to rose-colored pouch, this is among the most spectacular and beautiful of the lady's slippers and in 1962 was designated the state flower of Minnesota to boot. In general, plants produce five to seven pleated leaves and grow 2–3' in height, one of the taller forms. They are often found in moist, almost boggy conditions. The entire plant is hairy and has been known to cause dermatitis on those trying to dig it from the wild. Well deserved, may they itch for ages.

Habitat: In mossy swamps, bogs, and damp woodlands from Newfoundland to Manitoba, south to Missouri, east to the mountains of Tennessee and Georgia.
Hardiness: USDA Zones 3–8.
Garden site: It is pretty obvious from its habitat that plants will die if not provided with consistently moist, cool conditions.
Garden maintenance: Maintain the bog.

Cypripedium reginae

Other species for the garden
Cypripedium parviflorum (small yellow lady's slipper) is similar to *C. pubescens* but with smaller and brighter yellow flowers. Its petals are brownish with little green color, and its range extends a little further south. Equally beautiful.

Recommended propagation
Seed: Orchid seeds are extraordinarily small and lack sufficient food resources necessary for germination. In nature, orchid seeds have developed a symbiotic relationship with beneficial fungi known as mycorrhiza, which provide nutrition to the developing seed. It is an interesting relationship, one which is difficult to reproduce in the garden. The fungi are beneficial throughout the life of the plant but are essential in the early stages of development; therefore, purchasing mature plants could increase your chance of success.

Division: Clumps can be dug and divided in early spring. Each separated plantlet should have one to three fat, pointed buds.

Etymology

Genus: From the sandal or slipper (*pedium*) of Aphrodite, the goddess of love and beauty, who was born on the island of Cypress (*Cypri-*).

Specific epithet: *acaule* ("stemless," very short stems); *calceolus* (diminutive of "shoe"); *parviflorum*, from *parvi* ("small") and *florum* ("flowers"); *pubescens* ("downy"); *reginae* ("of the queen"), another reference to Aphrodite.

Common name: The large lip formed by the petals suggests a lady's slipper.

Darmera peltata

| *Darmera peltata* | umbrella plant | Saxifragaceae |

If your garden boasts a boggy area, where plants can be left to do their own thing, this may be a great plant for you. Before the leaves even emerge, 3' tall flower stems with many small pink flowers appear in early spring. These are bizarre enough, but then the large bristly leaves emerge from the roots just below the soil. The leaves are what makes the plant choice: they provide architectural sweetness in an otherwise wild area. They can be over 1' wide and are peltate (the petiole attaches at an indentation near the middle of the leaf). Give the plant room—its rhizomes will colonize (one reason it is used for stabilizing soils on marshy land). This is not a plant for all climates; in order to succeed, it needs moisture and cool temperatures. If it is happy, it will skip along with unbounded joy; if it is not, it will sit there, pouting, then disappear. Don't waste your money in the flatlands of the South.

'Nana', a dwarf form, is about half the size of the species and may be better for the less bold of heart.

Habitat: Along mountain streams in southwest Oregon to northern California.
Hardiness: USDA Zones 5–8.
Garden site: Moist stream beds, boggy conditions. If planted in areas that do not stay reasonably moist, plants will grow slowly, if at all. If allowed to get excessively dry, they will disappear.
Garden maintenance: If growing well, division every now and then may be necessary.

Recommended propagation
Seed: Sow seeds immediately; they seem to be short-lived. Once seedlings emerge, keep constantly moist.

Division: Divide the dormant rhizomes. They are tough, so be careful of your
  back.

Etymology
Genus: For 19th-century German horticulturist Karl Darmer.
Specific epithet: *peltata* refers to the peltate leaf attachment.
Common name: The peltate leaf, together with its shape, suggests an umbrella.

Delphinium — Ranunculaceae

I have seen some marvelous delphiniums in the West, the center of native delphiniums, and in the Smoky Mountains in the East. As potential plants for my
garden, however, these can't compete with the hybrids offered by nurseries,
mainly because I can't find most species for sale. That is the biggest problem in
gardenizing the native delphiniums: it is almost impossible to find more than a
half-dozen plants of more than one species, and impossible, therefore, to get a
handle on their garden performance.

The species are beautiful, but in a far more subtle way than the hybrids, and
subtlety has a place, doesn't it? Our natives tend to have leaves divided into three
or more finger-like segments. Flowers usually give way to three pods, which contain the black seeds.

All parts of the plants are poisonous, and several incidents of cattle poison-
ings have been reported in the West. Seeds might be worst of all on a per weight
basis. Don't add them to your bagel—poppy seeds are bad enough.

Delphinium exaltatum — tall larkspur

This is the most commonly offered native delphinium, and therefore it may
make it to gardens in Pointe-au-Pic in the Gaspé before most others. Plants are
vigorous and typically grow 4–6' tall, bearing loose terminal racemes of
gentian-blue flowers, each only about 1" long. The flowers consist of five
sepals, one of which has a distinctive spur, and small petals. Although the
flowers don't bloom until late summer or early fall, the palmately divided,
three- to five-lobed, deep green foliage is handsome nearly all season. Not only
that, the flowers persist for weeks. A terrific author and native plant expert,
Natalia Hamill of Lawrence, Kansas, gushes over this plant. If she likes it that
much, maybe we should be wondering why we spend so much money on
those English hybrids.

Habitat: In woods and rocky slopes in higher elevations from Pennsylvania to
  Ohio, south to Alabama and North Carolina.
Hardiness: USDA Zones 5–7.

Delphinium exaltatum

Delphinium tricorne

Garden site: Afternoon shade if gardening in the South; full sun can be tolerated further north. Alkaline soil is sometimes recommended.

Garden maintenance: Deadhead spent flowers if you wish the foliage to remain healthy; otherwise, allow seeds to fall and additional plants may occur.

Delphinium tricorne   dwarf larkspur

I occasionally see this sold by mail-order nurseries, so it might get into a few gardens yet. This is the antithesis of tall larkspur, growing only about 16" tall and bearing but a few blue to dark purple flowers in the spring. Regardless of its diminutive height and less than All-American flowering, they are handsome in their own right. Flowers fade quickly once they have been pollinated. Plants prefer a good deal of moisture, so they must be kept watered.

Habitat: In woods and rocky slopes from Pennsylvania to Minnesota and Nebraska, south to Oklahoma, Arkansas, Alabama, and Georgia.

Hardiness: USDA Zones 4–7.

Garden site: Full sun to partial shade, alkaline soils.

Garden maintenance: Deadheading the flowers allows for better foliage and perhaps an additional bloom or two.

Other species for the garden

Delphinium cardinale (scarlet larkspur) is native from central to Baja California. Plants bear vibrant scarlet flowers in tall, loose racemes in late summer. Because of the late flowering, the foliage is quite handsome for most of the season. Plants can reach up to 5' tall and are commonly used as a parent in making orange, red, and scarlet hybrids for the cut flower industry. Plants grow best in full sun and moist soils. An annual in most of the country.

Recommended propagation

Seed: Collect the seeds as the pods turn yellow; place in moist perlite or sand, or plant in containers or flats. Place in the refrigerator for about three months, after which time they will germinate at temperatures around 70F. They are slow to grow, particularly *Delphinium tricorne*.

Etymology

Genus: From the Greek *delphis* ("dolphin"), referring to the flower shape of annual larkspur.

Specific epithet: *cardinale* ("cardinal-red"); *exaltatum* ("very tall, lofty"); *tricorne* ("three horns") refers to the three pods, the ends of which curl outward like horns.

Common name: The spur on the back of the flower is presumably the lark's spur.

| *Deschampsia* | hairgrass | Poaceae |

Many countries claim hairgrass. Actually, the genus is circumpolar, meaning that it seems to be native everywhere, United States included. Of the fifty or so species, only two are grown to any extent in American gardens. They both have long, inrolled leaves, and these, along with their delicate flowers, make this a popular genus of grasses.

| *Deschampsia caespitosa* | tufted hairgrass |

Long, narrow, somewhat pleated leaves characterize these 3–4' tall plants. I have seen them growing beautifully in normal garden beds; they can also look spectacular in containers, with anything from trailing petunias to trailing vinca as companions. The flowers, which appear in spring to mid summer, are light and airy and occur in such numbers as to almost obscure the foliage. When well grown and well sited, this is one of the prettiest of all the ornamental grasses, but they are far

Deschampsia caespitosa 'Goldstaub'

prettier in the North than in the South, where they cringe at the thought of more heat and humidity. I love honesty in advertising: listen to this quote from Las Pilitas Nursery (see "Sources and Resources") in southern California: "[*Deschampsia caespitosa*] grows very poorly at lower elevations and looks like hell here at all times. If you live in a mountain meadow at 6000 ft. or in an awful climate like Vermont, this is a decent plant—if you live in LA we can sell you a plant that looks dead twelve months of the year." Needless to say, sales may be off at Las Pilitas, and obviously this grass is not particularly useful in the South. Plants do not spread, although some reseeding may occur; rather, they grow in tufts, which makes them excellent candidates for massing. Plants enjoy moist areas and tolerate partial shade.

Several cultivars have also become popular (seeing the need for translations, I wonder where they were bred?).

'Bronzeschleier' ('Bronze Veil') is 2–3' tall with bronze-yellow flowers.

'Goldschleier' ('Gold Veil'), 'Goldstaub' ('Gold Dust'), and 'Goldgehaenge' ('Golden Pendant') all have golden yellow inflorescences. The first two are only 1–2' tall. The latter is taller and later to flower.

'Schottland' ('Scotland') produces 2½' tall mounds of dark green leaves and airy flowers.

Habitat: Northern states from Vermont to the Dakotas, finding its way into the Northwest as well.

Hardiness: USDA Zones 4–7.

Garden site: Moist soils are preferable; afternoon shade in the southern range.

Garden maintenance: If sited well, little maintenance is required other than dividing after a few years.

Other species for the garden

Deschampsia flexuosa (crinkled hairgrass) is shorter (1–2' tall) and bears narrow wiry leaves and loose airy panicles of flowers with a purple tinge. Excellent in the North, poor in the South. A couple of cultivars are sold. 'Aurea' has bright yellow-green flower heads, and the colorfully named 'Muckenschwarm' ('Fly Swarm') really makes me want to run out and spend my money. Zones 4–7.

Recommended propagation

Seed: Seed is not difficult for the species.

Division: Divide cultivars and species when large enough to break apart.

Etymology

Genus: For Louis August Deschamps (1765–1842), a French naturalist and surgeon who investigated flora on the island of Java.

Specific epithet: *caespitosa* ("growing in dense clumps"); *flexuosa* ("zigzag"), in reference to the twisted flowers.

Common name: Hairgrass makes sense when the plant is in flower, but the foliage is hair-like as well.

Dicentra	bleeding heart	Fumariaceae

Bleeding heart is among the most popular non–daisy-flowered native plants to have penetrated mainstream gardening. From 6–8" tall ground covers to handsome garden plants, bleeding hearts can be found in large portions of the country, growing from rhizomes or small tubers. They possess rosettes of compound leaves (no stems) and nodding heart-shaped flowers, which appear, in some cases, to be bleeding. Love the plants, hate the name.

Dicentra canadensis	squirrel corn

I enjoy this small and wonderfully fascinating plant for the woodland garden, which grows from small, round, yellow tubers. It resembles *Dicentra cucullaria*

Dicentra canadensis

in leaves and stature, but the flowers are more heart-shaped (like those of *D. eximia*). Flowers have rounded rather than pointed spurs and are quite a clean white. Plants go summer-dormant, so don't worry about them when they disappear. I visited the wonderful Garden in the Woods in Framingham, Massachusetts, in early May, and the squirrel corn was spectacular—and that is saying a lot when you are talking about 8" plants. They are better suited for gardens in the Northeast and Canada than the South.

Habitat: In woods from Quebec to Minnesota, south to North Carolina, Tennessee and Missouri.

Hardiness: USDA Zones 3–7.

Garden site: Woodland setting, consistent moisture if possible. A good deal of sun results in more flowers; heavy shade produces few flowers.

Garden maintenance: None.

Dicentra cucullaria Dutchman's breeches

One of my favorite "I have to look hard to find it" plants is this little gem, which bears beautiful blue-green dissected leaves and grows no more than 9" tall, usually closer to 6". The leaves and flowers arise from a small tuber, and plants spread nicely along the woodland floor. Four to ten small creamy white flowers are held on one side of the inflorescence, each with two spurs pointing in the air. Plants bloom about a week after squirrel corn, and they too go summer-dormant, particularly in warm, dry summers.

Habitat: Moist, shady areas from Quebec to North Dakota, south to Kansas, Arkansas, and east to Alabama and Georgia.

Hardiness: USDA Zones 3–7.

Garden site: Shady, moist areas suit plants well. As with squirrel corn, a good deal of morning sun results in more flowers; flowers are few in heavy shade.

Garden maintenance: None.

Dicentra eximia fringed bleeding heart

Most plants offered by nurseries are selections of this species or hybrids with this as one of the parents. The 1½–2' tall species is handsome in its own right, and when conditions allow it to spread around, it is a welcome addition to the woodland garden. Up to ten compound basal leaves may be formed; these are deeply cut, providing a fern-like appearance to the plant. A dozen flowers or more, usually pink or rose, occasionally white, and with short, round spurs, are formed on the one-sided inflorescence in early spring. The inner petals extend

Dicentra eximia 'Alba'

Dicentra eximia 'Bountiful'

Dicentra 'Luxuriant'

below the outer petals, another visual difference between this and *Dicentra cucullaria*. Plants grow from an underground stem (rhizome) and spread well.

Many cultivars are offered; some of the more popular ones may be hybrids with *Dicentra formosa*. Here is but a handful worth trying.

'Adrian Bloom' had deep red flowers with blue-green leaves.

'Alba' is the white form of the species.

'Aurora' is a relatively new cultivar bearing white flowers.

'Baccharal' is an old favorite, with striking wine-colored flowers.

'Bountiful' has pink flowers.

'Coldham' produces blue-green leaves and burgundy flowers.

'Dolly Sods', from West Virginia, provides blue-green leaves with light pink flowers. Tony Avent of Plant Delights Nursery reports that this selection is one of the best bleeding hearts for hot and humid climates. I agree!

'Luxuriant' is an excellent cherry-red hybrid.

Habitat: In moist woods and mountains in New York, south and west to West Virginia, Tennessee and Georgia.
Hardiness: USDA Zones 3–9.
Garden site: Shady areas where moisture can be provided. Full morning sun is not a problem.
Garden maintenance: Little is needed. Plants can be cut back after flowering to reduce seed set, but that is not necessary. Remove unwanted seedlings if they become a problem.

Dicentra formosa   western fringed bleeding heart

This western species provides handsome deeply cut foliage and pendulous rose to pink (sometimes white) flowers. Up to ten flowers, each possessing an inner and outer set of petals, occur on a one-sided inflorescence in the spring. Plants are similar to *Dicentra eximia*, the most visible difference being that the inner petals hardly extend from the outer set in this species, but protrude significantly below in fringed bleeding heart. Plants are not tolerant of hot, humid conditions, and are not a good choice for southern or eastern gardens.

Several cultivars have been attributed to this species, such as 'Alba' (white flowers) and subsp. *oregana* (soft pink flowers), but many are hybrids with *Dicentra eximia*, which see.

Habitat: In moist woods from central California to British Columbia.
Hardiness: USDA Zones 4–7.
Garden site: Moist areas, or areas where irrigation can be used.
Garden maintenance: Little is necessary. Deadhead to remove spent flowers if the spirit moves you. Remove unwanted seedlings if they become a problem.

Recommended propagation

Seed: Black seeds are produced; these can be direct sown as soon as they are ripe. It is possible to buy seeds, but do not store them longer than necessary.
Division: The tuber types (*Dicentra canadensis* and *D. cucullaria*) can be dug when dormant and moved where needed. The other forms do not divide easily and are best seed-propagated.

Dicentra formosa subsp. *oregana*

Etymology

Genus: From the Greek, *dis* ("twice) and *kentron* ("spur").

Specific epithet: *canadensis* ("of Canada"), see *Cornus*; *cucullaria* ("hood-like"),
referring to the flowers, whose sides are slightly curved inward, resembling
a hood; *eximia* ("out of the ordinary," "distinguished"); *formosa* ("beautiful").

Common name: Bleeding heart refers to the shape of the flowers, not someone's state after a relationship's gone bad; squirrel corn describes the tubers.

Diphylleia cymosa	umbrella-leaf	Berberidaceae

Plants are closely related to our native mayapple but are much more difficult to
buy. They are also more fussy about where they will succeed, growing well in
cool, moist shade, usually by streams or flowing water. Plants bear two wonderfully large rounded leaves with five to seven toothed lobes. The leaves are peltate,
meaning the petiole attaches near the middle of the underside of the leaf, giving
them an umbrella look. They grow about 2' tall, although under optimal conditions, they may be up to 3' in height. In the spring, a dozen or so ½" wide white
flowers are held above the leaves on a long flower stem. All parts of the flower
are in sixes—six petals, six sepals, etc. In late summer, handsome blue berries,
each containing a plump seed, are formed, and these are made even more ornamental by the red stalks on which they are held. They are marvelous in northern
Quebec, and even though they will not do well in my Georgia garden, I hope
they become more available to others.

Habitat: In woods, usually by water, from Virginia to north Georgia.
Hardiness: USDA Zones 3–7.
Garden site: Cool, moist shade is best.
Garden maintenance: None.

Diphylleia cymosa

Diphylleia cymosa in fruit

Recommended propagation

Seed: Seeds must be fresh to germinate. Once the seed leaves emerge, apply weak doses of liquid fertilizer to enhance growth. Expect about two years before plants mature.

Etymology

Genus: From the Greek, *di* ("two") and *phyllon* ("leaf"), in reference to its two leaves.

Specific epithet: *cymosa* refers to the type of inflorescence (a cyme).

Common name: The way in which the leaves present themselves suggests an umbrella.

Disporum	fairy bells	Liliaceae

I must admit, I have an affinity for *Disporum sessile, D. flavens,* and the other Asian fairy bells that run through my garden, providing color and cover. However, a few with native roots provide more subtle ornamental value and are reasonably available as well. Treat them as you do Solomon's seal—that is, place them in areas of moist shade and allow them to fill in areas as they mature. Many fairy bells bring their flowers with them already formed when they arise in the spring; others open around the time the tree canopy is forming. A red berry, often containing a couple of seeds, is formed in late summer. None will knock your socks off, but all provide pleasure for the woodland gardener.

Disporum lanuginosum	yellow mandarin

The branched plants grow about 2' tall from rhizomes and bear attractive yellow flowers in early spring followed by orange to yellow berries. The flowers are long and somewhat tubular, occurring in one- to three-flowered inflorescences at the end of each stem. The plants are shiny above and slightly hairy beneath. Plant them in groups if possible, or they may get lost.

Habitat: In woods from New York to southern Ontario and south to Alabama and north Georgia.

Hardiness: USDA Zones 5–7.

Garden site: Moist shade.

Garden maintenance: None.

Disporum lanuginosum

Disporum maculatum

Disporum smithii

Disporum maculatum   spotted fairy bells

Heavily veined leaves provide much of the character for these nodding 2' tall plants. The flowers are whitish with small purple spots and occur singly or occasionally in pairs in late spring. Unfortunately, they often get lost in the foliage and are finished before you get your coffee in the morning. If you do happen to see the flowers before they fall, you will notice long white stamens sticking out of them. The plants themselves are handsome, as are the yellow fruits, and if planted in groups of five or more will add to the garden charm.

Habitat: In woods in eastern Ohio, south to Tennessee and Georgia.
Hardiness: USDA Zones 4–7.
Garden site: Moist shade.
Garden maintenance: None.

Other species for the garden

Disporum hookeri (creamy white bell-shaped flowers and red fruit) and *D. smithii* (greenish white flowers and beautiful orange fruit), both western species, are difficult to find in commerce but handsome if they can be established.

Recommended propagation

Seed: Sow seeds immediately as they mature (usually white in color), and germination should occur next spring. Small seedlings often occur around the plants, and these are the easiest means of increasing numbers.

Division: When the clump is big enough to divide, take a sharp spade and cut through the tangled roots in early fall. Transplant immediately.

Etymology

Genus: From the Greek, *dis* ("two") and *spora* ("seed"), referring to the two seeds in each fruit.

Specific epithet: *hookeri*, in honor of Sir Joseph Hooker; *lanuginosum* ("woolly"), referring to the underside of the leaf; *maculatum* ("spotted"), the flowers; *smithii*, in honor of English botanist J. E. Smith (1759–1828), the first president of the Linnean Society of London.

Common name: Fairy bells was inspired by the flowers of *Disporum hookeri*, which were thought to resemble the wings of a fairy; mandarin, from the color of mandarin robes, formal aristocratic garments of China.

Dodecatheon meadia	common shooting star	Primulaceae

No doubt this relative of primrose and cyclamen would be entirely forgettable were it not for its truly fascinating flowers. With the five petals pinned back, the flowers appear to be entering the Earth's atmosphere, and the common name is an apt description. The flowers are predominantly white to rose-colored, and sowing seeds generally provides a mixed colony. Plants flower in the spring, then the foliage disappears, occasionally leaving behind the red fruit. Dormancy occurs in late spring to summer, depending on temperatures and moisture, but plants return early in the spring. The popularity of shooting stars is mirrored by their decreased presence in the wild—way too many people have gathered far too many plants. That, combined with habitat loss, has made *Dodecatheon* endangered, imperiled, threatened, or protected in Florida, Louisiana, Minnesota, Michigan, Pennsylvania, and New York, and the list keeps growing.

The approximately fifteen species native to the United States are distributed almost everywhere, except perhaps the high Northeast. For the gardener, that there are so many is almost irrelevant; only two or three species are available as plants, although seeds can be obtained for others. One of the best seed sources is the North American Rock Garden Society (www.nargs.org).

Dodecatheon meadia

Dodecatheon meadia

Habitat: In open woods and meadows from Pennsylvania to Wisconsin, south to Texas and Georgia.

Hardiness: USDA Zones 4–7.

Garden site: These plants love moisture and will disappear rapidly under dry soil conditions. Moist shade is fine, even under canopies of high shade trees, but do not position plants at the base of the trees. Plants will go dormant soon after the canopy fills in. Plants also tolerate calciferous soils.

Garden maintenance: Add some dolomitic lime in the fall in highly acidic soils.

Dodecatheon pulchellum

Other species for the garden

The Far West is a hotbed for shooting stars, and gardeners there should try to find plants or seeds of *Dodecatheon alpinum*, with its toothed leaves and always white flowers; *D. clevelandii*, which probably bears the largest flowers in the genus; *D. hendersonii*, the first to bloom in most gardens; or *D. pulchellum*, with its rosy purple flowers. All are native to the West Coast, and all differ only slightly from the common shooting star. Flowers are generally pink to rose, although significant variability occurs. A few cultivars have been selected, but they tend to come and go. In the garden, they may interbreed and identification becomes fuzzy; however, as Bill Cullina of the New England Wild Flower Society states, "There is no such thing as an ugly shooting star."

Recommended propagation

Seed: Seeds are coffee-colored and should be sown as soon as they arrive or when collected. The problem is that they want to go dormant, so it is essential to maintain moisture. If dormancy occurs, then it simply takes more time to reach maturity.

Cuttings: Root cuttings provide additional plants.

Division: Mature clumps can be divided.

Etymology

Genus: From the Greek, *dodeka* ("twelve") and *theos* ("god"), in reference to the twelve principal Greek gods at the time. The name was given by the statesman Pliny the Elder, who died in the eruption of Vesuvius in 79 AD.

Specific epithet: *alpinum* ("alpine"); *clevelandii*, after lawyer Daniel Cleveland (1838–1929), an authority on ferns and a botanical collector in the San Diego area; *hendersonii*, after Louis Fourniquet Henderson (1853–1942), who traveled and collected in Washington and Oregon; *meadia*, after English physician Richard Mead (1673–1754); *pulchellum* ("pretty").

Common name: If you don't see the shooting star in these plants, you have been secluded too long. Get out, get busy, and enjoy the night.

Dryopteris	wood fern	Dryopteridaceae

This genus, more than any other fern group, may offer more members suitable for the gardener, providing the most diminutive to some of the largest plants for the shaded garden setting. Species are well represented in Asia and the Himalayas; however, we have a few beautiful species we can claim as our own. They grow from a stout rhizome and thus can spread readily; they usually have conspicuous scales on the stem bases as well as on the developing fronds (fiddleheads). They routinely hybridize, and gardens can sport all sorts of intermediates when more than one species is present. Most wood ferns should be grown in areas where moisture is plentiful and consistent. They can handle a good deal of sun if their roots are moist.

Dryopteris cristata   narrow swamp fern

An easily grown shade-loving fern, but it needs more than average moisture. Plants grow from rhizomes, which are clothed in light brown scales. The fronds are often described as ladder-like: the leaflets are widely spaced and almost ninety degrees to the stem, resembling the steps of a ladder. Plants have separate fertile fronds, which are longer and narrower than the sterile ones and grow straight up, while the

Dryopteris cristata 'The King'

sterile ones arch over. Only the sterile fronds are evergreen. 'The King' is a larger form of the species.

Habitat: Swamps and moist places from Newfoundland west to Saskatchewan, south to Montana, Arkansas and North Carolina.
Hardiness: USDA Zones 3–7.
Garden site: Although plants can grow in common garden sites, areas near a stream or other moist places are recommended. If moisture is plentiful, full sun is not a problem.
Garden maintenance: None.

Dryopteris filix-mas   male fern

If there is a lady fern (*Athyrium filix-femina*), it seems only fair that we males be represented as well. Although plants are native to the Northeast, Midwest, and West Coast, they are far more common in Europe than in the United States. Male fern is a favorite among fern people because it is relatively easy to grow and has a great variation in form. Similar to other wood ferns, the rhizome and the base of the stems are covered in furry brown scales. The numerous spore cases are held closer to the midvein than the margin, which is one way of distinguishing this fern from its close relative *Dryopteris marginalis*. Plants are upright and evergreen. Many cultivars are known, but only a few are easily located.

'Barnesii', probably one of the most distinctive, grows up to 4' tall and is quite narrow.

Dryopteris filix-mas   *Dryopteris filix-mas* 'Cristata Martindale'

'Cristata Martindale' has crested (flattened) pinnae on the fronds. Ugly as sin but popular nevertheless.

'Linearis' is about 3' tall, each frond bearing many slender pinnae, so slender that the spore cases stick out from the sides. This form has numerous subforms, such as 'Linearis Congesta', growing only 6–9" tall, and 'Linearis Cristata', with crests at the end of the slender pinnae. 'Linearis Polydactyla' is a particularly gruesome form with the tips of the fronds multi-forked. Seems prehistoric.

'Nana' is a dwarf form of the species.

Habitat: Cool, moist, rocky woods throughout the northern half of the country.
Hardiness: USDA Zones 4–8.
Garden site: Normal garden site will be sufficient. Moisture is recommended, but plants need not be in a swampy area. Provide some calcium if soil is highly acidic.
Garden maintenance: Crowns multiply readily, and dividing them will maintain the symmetrical look of the plant.

Dryopteris goldiana   giant wood fern

One of the biggest ferns in cultivation, this species often figures in the macho gardener's collection. Ferns bear large fronds, up to 4' in length and 1' wide, wider in the middle and then tapering abruptly to the tip. New fronds, which are covered in white and brown scales, are highly ornamental. The golden green fronds seem to tilt backward and can appear to cover significant space. The kidney-shaped spore cases are closer to the midveins than the margins. In the shaded Armitage garden, probably near its southern range, the fronds get big but break during summer rains and are not as attractive as they are further north. I still love them! Plants are deciduous in most of the country.

Habitat: Cool, moist woods from New Brunswick to Ontario, south to Iowa and South Carolina.

Hardiness: USDA Zones 3–7.

Garden site: Moist conditions are needed, otherwise fronds become brittle and easily break. The more moisture, the more sun the plants can take.

Garden maintenance: Remove old fronds, maintain moisture.

Dryopteris ludoviciana   southern wood fern

With glossy, dark green fronds and growing 2–3' tall, this is one of the most sought-after ferns in areas where summer temperatures are warm and winters are not too severe. I certainly seek it—unfortunately, I spend a lot of time seeking, as it is not easily found at retail. Only the upper third to half of the frond carries any spore cases (sori), and the fertile pinnae (leaflets) are much more narrow than the sterile ones. Although southern in habit, plants can be grown as far north as New York.

Habitat: North Carolina to Florida and Texas, including Louisiana.

Hardiness: USDA Zones 6–9.

Garden site: Consistently moist. Afternoon shade suits the plants well.

Garden maintenance: Remove the old fronds in the spring to enjoy the new croziers as they emerge.

Other species for the garden

Wood ferns encompass many native species and hybrids, and I would be remiss in not mentioning at least a couple of others.

Dryopteris ×*australis* is a hybrid between *D. celsa* and *D. ludoviciana*. Plants are big, bearing fronds up to 5' in length, the terminal one-quarter having

Dryopteris celsa

smaller fertile pinnae. An architectural plant, fine for southern gardeners. Probably hardy in zones 5–9.

Dryopteris celsa (log fern) is a natural hybrid between *D. goldiana* and *D. ludoviciana*. The 3–4' tall fronds are intermediate between the parents, wider than *D. ludoviciana* and more narrow than *D. goldiana*. The *D. ludoviciana* parentage allows southern gardeners to succeed with this one as well. Give plants plenty of moisture. Hardy in zones 5–9.

Dryopteris clintoniana (Clinton's wood fern) is a natural hybrid between *D. cristata* and *D. goldiana*, and inhabits the same swamps and wet woods in nature as does *D. cristata*. The ladder-like look is not present in this fern, but plants are totally evergreen. Difficult to locate but you will find they are excellent garden subjects if moisture is not a problem. Hardy to zone 4.

Dryopteris marginalis (marginal wood fern) is similar to *D. filix-mas* but bears the spore cases close to the margins rather than the midveins. Evergreen, sturdy, and an excellent addition to the shaded garden, particularly in the North. Hardy to zone 2.

Recommended propagation

Spores: Most ferns can be propagated by spores. Plants can produce hundreds of thousands of spores in a single season (one botanist estimated 52 million spores on one plant of *Dryopteris marginalis*). The life cycle of a fern is complicated, requiring two separate generations; however, many fern gardeners enjoy growing their own ferns from spores, either collected or obtained from fern societies. Expect a couple of years between sowing spores and putting plants in the garden.

Division: Many ferns form multiple crowns, and most wood ferns grow from rhizomes, which are easily divided and moved.

Etymology

Genus: From the Greek, *drys* ("oak") and *pteris* ("fern"), in reference to its woodland habitat.

Dryopteris marginalis (front)

Dryopteris marginalis (back)

Specific epithet: *australis* ("southern"); *clintoniana*, probably for Governor De Witt Clinton of New York (see *Clintonia*); *cristata* usually refers to crested leaves or pinnae, but none occur in this case—perhaps a case of mistaken identity; *filix-mas* ("masculine"); *goldiana*, for J. Goldie, a Scotsman who visited North America in 1817; *ludoviciana* ("of Louisiana"); *marginalis*, pertaining to margins—in this case, the spore cases are formed near the margins of the pinnae.

Common name: Most species are found in forested areas, hence wood fern; log ferns grow on rotted logs.

Echinacea   coneflower   Asteraceae

This has to be our most popular and well-known native genus, not only in American gardens but throughout the world. As garden plants, its members have few equals. The ray flowers provide the color, and the cone consists of purple to brown sterile flowers highlighted with prickly golden to orange-tipped scales. Most species (*Echinacea purpurea* is the exception) arise from a forked taproot and are quite long-lived. They tolerate full sun, return year after year, are havens for butterflies and honey bees, and, oh yes, they are beautiful. Coneflowers occur in nature in purple, white, and yellow, and hybridization continues to bring new and exciting cultivars to the marketplace. Selections in rose and orange are currently on the market, with reds and bicolors not far behind.

This also seems to have been a miracle plant, able to cure just about anything. Native Americans used *Echinacea* to treat snakebites, burns, toothaches, colds, sore throats, headaches, gonorrhea, mumps, tonsillitis, and smallpox (when mixed with puffball spores and skunk oil). With such recommendations, modern medicine could no longer ignore it. Echinacea tablets and tincture (mostly from *E. angustifolia*), now found in most pharmacies, have been shown to enhance the immune system, and to reduce the incidence of colds and flu.

Echinacea pallida   pale coneflower

Of all the coneflowers available to the gardener, this one likely elicits the most negative comments, not because it is difficult to grow, but because it seems to be missing half its petals (ray flowers). Like a tired old boxer, those that are there are droopy and skinny and rather washed out and pale. But that does not preclude a crazy gardener from wanting some of them in the garden; in fact, the sorry state of the flower probably evokes sympathy. Plants are 2–3' tall and rather narrow; they produce their flowers in early to mid summer. The ray flowers are up to 3" long but hang down, almost touching the stem. The cones, without

Echinacea pallida

Echinacea paradoxa

petals, are effective as fresh or dried flowers. In warmer areas, plants are not long-lived; perhaps three years is normal.

Habitat: In dry, open areas from Illinois to Minnesota and Montana, south to Texas and Georgia.
Hardiness: USDA Zones 4–8.
Garden site: Full sun, away from standing water.
Garden maintenance: None.

Echinacea paradoxa   yellow coneflower

This is a favorite of people new to the coneflower game, a paradox, "a yellow purple coneflower!" Plants are 2½–3' tall, with smooth, almost shiny 4–5" lanceolate leaves. The flowers are wonderfully fragrant and provide a large copper-brown cone, which is often visited by goldfinches and other birds as the flower dries in the garden in the late summer. The yellow ray flowers are narrow and droopy, a little wider than *Echinacea pallida*, but their bright yellow color is far more handsome. Many other yellow coneflowers are available, particularly in the genus *Rudbeckia*, but I still enjoy growing this, to have at least one paradox in my garden.

Habitat: In open sites in the Ozarks of Missouri and Arkansas.
Hardiness: USDA Zones 4–7.
Garden site: Full sun, dry to well-drained soils.
Garden maintenance: Removal of spent flowers may result in additional blooms. Propagate by dividing if the clump becomes too successful.

Echinacea purpurea   purple coneflower

Sure, there are other workhorses in the garden, but this is one of the Budweiser Clydesdales. Beautiful, temperamental at times, haughty but down-to-earth, and constantly photographed, purple coneflower has become all things to all people. So mainstream that most people do not know (or care) that it is a native plant, so interesting and rich in germplasm that the most recent round of cultivars is already turning the perennial market on its ear. The species is fine as is; no monkeying around is needed to enjoy it in the garden. Plants stand 3–4' tall, have dark green leaves, and produce many flowers with somewhat droopy purple ray flowers around a raised bronze disk. Bees, butterflies, and birds flock to this handsome plant, which blooms in late spring and summer. It is a dominant species in the prairies and should be so in any meadow planting. And, of course, it also holds its own in the garden, complementing its companions throughout the season. Many selections and hybrids are available, and more are coming along all the time.

'Alba', 'White Lustre', and 'White Swan' are all similar, bearing white ray flowers and coppery disks.

Big Sky series from ItSaul Plants in Atlanta includes 'Harvest Moon' (deep yellow with an orange cone), 'Sundown' (deeper orange and taller than 'Sunset'), 'Sunrise' (bright yellow, 2' tall), 'Sunset' (orange), and 'Twilight' (rose). All are pleasantly fragrant hybrids (likely with *Echinacea paradoxa*). Richard and Bobby Saul are two of the excellent plantsmen who are making our gardens richer.

'Kim's Knee High' is a dwarf form with handsome purple flowers; 'Kim's Mop Head' appears a little unruly, but then so was the hair of Kim Hawkes, the wonderful nurserywoman who selected it.

'Magnus' is supposed to have ray petals that stick out from the disk at right angles. In real life, that happens only some of the time. A good cultivar nevertheless.

'Orange Meadowbright' was the first of many introductions from the Chicago Botanic Garden, followed by 'Mango Meadowbright'. Other "to be named later" hybrids will soon appear.

Echinacea purpurea

Echinacea purpurea 'Kim's Knee High'

Echinacea purpurea 'Razzmatazz'

'Paranoia' bears stiff yellow flowers. It was selected by Plant Delights Nursery from a cross (*Echinacea paradoxa* × *E. purpurea*) made by Richard Saul.

'Razzmatazz' is an unbelievable double with fragrant flowers. I am not sure how good a plant it will be, but it certainly is different.

'Ruby Giant' has flowers that are significantly larger than those of other cultivars.

'Sparkler' is the first attempt at mottled foliage. We have a ways to go, but a variegated purple coneflower is not far off.

Habitat: In fields and prairies from Virginia to Pennsylvania and Iowa, south to Louisiana and Georgia.

Hardiness: USDA Zones 3–8.

Garden site: Full sun, well-drained soils.

Garden maintenance: Plants can be deadheaded to improve the overall appearance, but deadheading seldom results in additional flowers. With or without it, plants will continue flowering for weeks.

Echinacea simulata   glade coneflower

I first saw this plant in the garden of Arlen and Judy Allmon in Russellville, Missouri, and I couldn't for the life of me place it. It had the habit of *Echinacea pallida*, with its droopy thin ray flowers, but instead of the pale pink color, the flowers sported a vibrant purple hue that caught my eye. I surrounded it a couple of times, rubbing my chin professorially, before being told it was a glade

Echinacea simulata with *E. pallida*   *Echinacea tennesseensis*

coneflower. Where had I been? Why hadn't I seen this species? It just goes to show that we are never too old to learn—too old to remember perhaps, but never too old to learn.

Plants can be distinguished from pale coneflower by their yellow pollen and significantly richer color. They are about 3' tall, blooming at the same time as other coneflowers, and ought to be used far more often.

Habitat: Glades and open woodlands in the eastern and central Ozarks.
Hardiness: USDA Zones 4–7.
Garden site: As with other echinaceas.
Garden maintenance: None; however, too rich a soil or overfertilization will result in tall, spindly stems.

Other species for the garden

Echinacea angustifolia resembles purple coneflower but is much shorter (12–16" tall), and has more narrow leaves and ray flowers. It is sometimes grown as a garden plant but is best known as the principal source of herbal echinacea. The black roots yield most of the active ingredient.

Echinacea tennesseensis (Tennessee coneflower) is known to exist naturally only near Nashville and is on the Federal Endangered Species List. It is similar to *E. purpurea* but not as vigorous, about 2½' tall with narrow, rosy ray flowers and a shiny coppery disk. It has been somewhat homogenized through natural crossbreeding with *E. purpurea*, so obtaining the real thing commercially may present a problem. If you do, plant it away from other coneflowers if you wish to maintain genetic purity.

Recommended propagation

Seed: Seeds for many species and cultivars are easily purchased. Placing them in a warm (72F) area and keeping them moist should result in good germination. Seeds can be collected from the cone; wear gloves to avoid injury.
Division: Some species can be divided, but seed is the most prudent way to establish a good colony.

Etymology

Genus: From the Greek, *echinos* ("hedgehog"), in reference to the prickly scales on the cone.

Specific epithet: *angustifolia* ("narrow-leaved"); *pallida* ("pale"); *paradoxa* ("paradoxical"); *purpurea* ("tending to purple"); *simulata* ("resembling"), perhaps in reference to its similarity to pale coneflower; *tennesseensis* ("of Tennessee").

Common name: Coneflower comes from the raised "cone" of disk flowers.

Elymus hystrix	bottlebrush grass	Poaceae

This pasture grass, known for many years as *Hystrix patula*, is for the meadow gardener. It is not substantial enough to be considered an ornamental grass like switch grass (*Panicum virgatum*), and it certainly is not a turf species like buffalo grass (*Buchloe dactyloides*). The flowers are kind of cute, though, in a wild way, and they make the plant worth buying. They appear in a narrow, spiky formation and are somewhat bristly and translucent. The individual spikelets are held at almost ninety degrees to the flower stem, and really do resemble a bottlebrush. Flowers appear in early June and can rebloom in the fall, persisting into late fall. If picked when immature, they dry well and remain ornamental for a long time. The plants are erect, but the flat, pointed leaves are a little flimsy and bend over. Plants are best in part shade, and it may be better to have them as part of a mixed population so they can be supported by others.

Habitat: From Nova Scotia to North Dakota, south to Arkansas and east to Georgia.
Hardiness: USDA Zones 5–8.
Garden site: Partially shaded spot with reasonably good moisture.
Garden maintenance: None. Plants can be cut back if they start to decline.

Recommended propagation

Seed: This is the best way to propagate this grass.
Division: Divide in spring if clump is sufficiently large.

Etymology

Genus: From the Greek, *elemos* ("cereal").
Specific epithet: *hystrix* ("porcupine-like"), referring to the bristly flowers.
Common name: An excellent evocation of the flower formation.

Epilobium	willowherb	Onagraceae

This interesting genus consists of some beautiful plants, all native to West Coast and southwestern United States. The leaves are generally ovate with entire margins and an obvious midvein. The flowers have four petals and four sepals, and the reproductive parts (pistil and stamens) stick out from the blossoms. Flowers are held in a many-flowered raceme. In the past, the genus was associated with plants such as *Epilobium angustifolium* (fireweed) which multiplied rapidly and colonized disturbed areas, but recently the genus *Zauschneria* (California fuchsia) was lumped into it, and many of the disparaging statements about willowherbs have been softened.

Epilobium angustifolium   fireweed

Most species of the genus show invasive tendencies, but probably the most aggressive is *Epilobium angustifolium*. It grows from the Great Lakes of Canada to the California coast. Its astounding ability to colonize waste ground, particularly areas devastated by fire, provided its common name. Quite apropos when you realize that it was one of the first plants to return to areas devastated by the 1980 eruption of Mt. St. Helens. Since they spread so well, plants are well suited for use in meadows or other situations where their vigorous growth can be accommodated. The 3' tall plants are showy perennials, with handsome many-flowered inflorescences of pink to purple-pink in late summer and fall. After flowering, seeds are formed in long, thin pods. The alternate leaves are entire or sometimes have a slightly wavy margin. Plants are common in western United States; the Gaspé in Quebec too is ablaze with the stuff, as are roadsides in northern Europe. It never fails— American gardeners abroad exclaim about the beauty of a fiery patch of flowers to their European hosts, who look at them and say, "That's one of yours, wish you'd kept it."

Epilobium angustifolium 'Album'

Epilobium angustifolium with white valerian

165

'Album' bears white flowers with a green calyx. One of the many garden treasures at the marvelous Les Quatres Vents in Quebec, it is not common but quite beautiful if you can find it.

Habitat: The species is native throughout the world; however, in the United
  States it is found most often in disturbed soils in the central plains and the
  West Coast, from Alaska to California.
Hardiness: USDA Zones 3–8.
Garden site: Full sun.
Garden maintenance: Plants can get invasive; remove seed heads to reduce
  multiplication.

Epilobium californicum   California fuchsia

Unfortunately, here we have a taxonomic reshuffling that would seem nonsensical to anyone but a taxonomist. First, all the species of the "old" genus *Zauschneria* were lumped together into one species (*Zauschneria californica*), then the entire genus was folded into *Epilobium*. The name change has effectively confused both gardeners and growers, so it is not surprising that plants are still offered under *Zauschneria*. Plants that once belonged to *Zauschneria* were subshrubs (as are *Artemisia* and *Buddleja*), with flowers of fire engine red.

This 2' tall species consists of somewhat grayish, thread-like, narrow leaves and long, funnel-like, vermilion-red flowers in late summer and fall. The long, thin fruit is similar to fireweed, and when ripe, splits down one side and releases the small cottony seeds to the wind. The flowers are magnets for hummingbirds (another name for the plants is hummingbird's trumpet). A well-grown clump is as stunning as any red-flowered plant you can name. All plants do best in dry climes and do poorly in areas of high humidity and rainfall, unless exceedingly well drained. I have seen wonderful plants in Portland gardens, but always on slopes or in rock gardens. This is an outstanding selection for the West Coast, as well as gardens in Denver and other places with warm, dry climates. Plants are evergreen in mild winters but die back when temperatures dip below 20F.

Cistus Nursery on Sauvie Island, Oregon, offers a dozen selections and hybrids, all worth trying. 'Ghostly Red' has pure red flowers and fuzzy grey foliage; 'Glasnevin' has long tubular bright orange-red flowers and is the most popular offering; 'Solidarity Pink' has pale pink flowers.

var. *garrettii* (*Zauschneria garrettii*) is probably the hardiest form, tolerating low temperatures to zone 5. The 12" tall scarlet-flowered plants are best grown in rock gardens, where drainage can be controlled. The best is 'Orange Carpet', a 2001 winner from the Plant Select program, administered by the Denver Botanic Gardens and Colorado State University.

Epilobium californicum

var. *latifolium* (*Zauschneria latifolia*) is also herbaceous and tolerates zones 6–9, perhaps as low as zone 5. Scarlet flowers are formed atop 12–14" tall plants in summer. The leaves are much wider than the species. An excellent garden plant that should be more used.

Habitat: Limited to the West Coast, from southern California to southwest Oregon, and into Mexico.
Hardiness: USDA Zones 7–10.
Garden site: On a slope or rock garden, full sun.
Garden maintenance: Plants can be trimmed in the late fall and cut back hard in early spring after growth has begun.

Recommended propagation

Seed: Easy. Collect seeds as they split. Sow them in a seed germination mix and place in a moist, warm environment.
Cuttings: Terminal cuttings taken in late spring are usually successful. A propagation mix, such as 3:1 perlite: peat, works well.
Division: Clumps may be thinned out through division if they get too large.

Etymology

Genus: From the Greek, *epi* ("upon") and *lobos* ("a pod"), in reference to the petals' being carried atop the pod-like ovary; *Zauschneria* commemorates Johann Baptist Zauschner (1737–1799), a professor of natural history at the University of Prague.
Specific epithet: *angustifolium* ("narrow-leaved"); *californicum* ("of California"); *latifolium* ("having broad leaves").

Equisetum arvense

| ***Equisetum*** | horsetail, scouring rush | **Equisetaceae** |

Whenever a native plant obsessive spouts off about how gardens should contain no exotic plants, and how environmentally conscious gardeners should use native plants only, I wait until he's finished and simply say, "Horsetails!" Enough already—gardens would be boring indeed if we shut them to the outside world, and while most invasive plants are from elsewhere, nowhere is it written that natives cannot be troublesome. This one is troublesome with a capital T.

Horsetails are not ours alone: they are found almost everywhere in the world except Australia and New Zealand. The most common native species is probably *Equisetum arvense*, with its upright stems and obvious thin side branches, but *E. hyemale* and *E. scirpoides*, with reduced or no side branches, are sometimes available also. *Equisetum scirpoides* is shorter and less invasive; however, it too will move freely once established.

To grow horsetails is to grow history. Although they are common to some native landscapes, these are only a fraction of the populations of eras past. They were extraordinarily common 354 to 290 million years ago, during the Carboniferous Period, and along with their relatives were responsible for much of the coal reserves laid down during that time.

Horsetails produce strong, upright stems banded with dark circles at each node; the circles contain small amounts of silica. Even though some species produce a few side branches off the internodes, it is the stem that is considered to be ornamental, often used in flower arrangements as an exotic-looking filler. Horsetails are a fern ally and produce spores, not flowers. Of course, horsetail lovers know that to plant them is to jail them, and strong containers are the bars that bind. They are aggressive no matter where they are placed, but especially so if you plant them in a moist area. I love their look, and when you visit the Armitage garden, you will find them suitably corseted in a container in a water feature—so far so good.

Habitat: Throughout North America, more abundant in the North than in the South.
Hardiness: USDA Zones 1–10.
Garden site: In a strong container, or a pasture or field setting. Full sun to partial shade, moisture.
Garden maintenance: A strong back and lots of kids if it escapes. Otherwise, plant it and get out of the way.

Recommended propagation
Seed: Spores can be used but are not needed for the gardener.
Division: Easy.

Etymology
Genus: From the Latin, *equus* ("horse") and *seta* ("bristle").
Specific epithet: *arvense* ("growing in or pertaining to cultivated fields"); *hyemale* ("of winter"); *scirpoides* ("resembling a rush").
Common name: Horsetail is a nod to both the Latin root of the genus and its appearance; in the 17th century, the silica-laced plants were used to scour pewter, hence scouring rush.

| *Eragrostis elliottii* | blue love grass | Poaceae |

About 250 species of this genus can be found throughout the world, particularly in the tropics and in southern North America. Not much distinguishes our native species from similar ornamental species, but its common name makes for good magazine copy. The blue-green leaves are quite handsome, and the 3' tall flower stalks rise in mid to late spring, finally opening to a haze of silvery flowers from summer to fall. Plants are highly drought-tolerant.

'Wind Dancer'—an appropriate name for a delicate-looking grass whose flowers dance ceaselessly in the wind—is a recent selection that should allow American gardeners their first glimpse at this wonderful native. We have trialed it in containers, and it looks particularly good when combined with plants like verbena or bacopa falling over the edges.

Habitat: Native to the southeastern United States, including Texas, Louisiana, Mississippi, Georgia, Florida, and North and South Carolina.
Hardiness: USDA Zones 6–9.
Garden site: Full sun, good drainage.
Garden maintenance: None, but wet feet must be avoided. An excellent xerophyte.

*Eragrostis
elliottii
'Wind Dancer'*

Other species for the garden

The best of those sometimes offered is *Eragrostis spectabilis* (purple love grass). Plants bear light green foliage that turns to a nice bronze color in the fall. The flower stems appear in early summer, forming purplish seed heads in late summer. Both flowers and seed heads are useful for cut flowers.

Recommended propagation

Seed: Plants are easily raised from seed, 'Wind Dancer' included.
Division: Easily divided in the spring.

Etymology

Genus: Unknown.
Specific epithet: *elliottii* honors Stephen Elliott (1771–1830), a South Carolina botanist; *spectabilis* ("spectacular," "showy").
Common name: I have no idea why it is called love grass. Suggestions welcome!

Eryngium yuccifolium   **button eryngo**   **Apiaceae**

Gardeners who put this plant in their gardens enjoy the unusual, and love foliar texture and a good story. The genus is commonly used in gardens, but this is the only native species that enjoys a fair amount of acceptance. Plants produce a rosette of gray-green leaves from a thick taproot. After flowering, the rosette dies off, but new crowns are formed at the base, resulting in true perennial plants. The upright leaves are strap-like, and the margins are spiny, imparting a yucca-

Eryngium yuccifolium

Eryngium yuccifolium

like appearance and not a little pain. Plants may be up to 6' tall, but 3–4' is more common. The flowers are creamy white and occur in dense ball-like heads, not in umbels as do most other genera in the family. At the base of the flowers are undivided bracts, which are also sharp to the touch. Looking at the plant, you would think it comes from the deserts of Arizona rather than from open woodlands and prairies.

Habitat: From New Jersey to Minnesota south to Texas and Florida.
Hardiness: USDA Zones 5–9.
Garden site: Full sun, well-drained soils.
Garden maintenance: This is a large plant, so provide sufficient space. The deep taproot does not transplant well; site plants carefully, therefore, so that they can remain where planted.

Other species for the garden

Eryngium aquaticum (rattlesnake master) is a wonderful species for ponds or wet areas occasionally offered by nurseries, with a natural range from New Jersey down the Atlantic Coast and west to Mississippi. Plants differ from *E. yuccifolium* in that they are aquatic, with foliage more grass-like than that of *E. yuccifolium* and three-lobed bracts at the base of the flowers. The white or purple-tinged flowers are arranged in tight balls atop the 2–4' tall plants. Zones 5–9.

Recommended propagation
Seed: Easy from seed; purchase or collect your own when the flower heads have dried.

Etymology
Genus: From the Greek *eryngion*, for some sort of thistle.
Specific epithet: *aquaticum* ("growing in or near water"); *yuccifolium* ("leaves like a yucca").
Common name: Button eryngo is suggested by the arrangement of the flowers; rattlesnake master comes from the plant's supposed ability to cure snakebites, or perhaps to drive away rattlesnakes. There does not appear to be any justification for the snake stories.

Erythronium   **adder's tongue, trout lily**   **Liliaceae**

I have a difficult time getting my students excited about these plants, not because they lack beauty but simply because the flowers lack staying power. In the wild, I see magnificent colonies with many flowers, but in the Armitage garden, the colonies are slow to spread and flowers are never abundant. Whenever we gather as a class around a small clump in early spring, there are seldom more than one or two remaining. Rain (sometimes snow), wind, and time all take their toll, but I would never pass these by without pointing them out.

Ephemeral flowering is more common with the eastern native, *Erythronium americanum*, than with some of the western forms or hybrids. Such is life in the fast lane. I consider myself fortunate to be able to share even a few flowers with visitors. Species arise from corms, which are often available in the fall from bulb specialists. Plants that produce a pair of leaves usually flower, those that produce a single leaf will not.

Erythronium americanum   **yellow trout lily**

Shy of flowering they may be, but they are still a treat to see in the garden in very early spring (in the Armitage garden, flowering begins in early March) or progressively later as one goes north. North or south, it is one of the first flowers in the spring garden. These stemless plants push out one or two narrow pointed leaves, each painted with purple spots, looking like a kindergarten child got loose with a little paint. The nodding bright yellow flowers are about 1" across and appear soon after the leaves appear; the backs of the flowers are rose to pink. Each flower consists of six tepals (three petals and three sepals, almost identical

Erythronium americanum

Erythronium revolutum

except that three of the tepals are strongly curled back), and the pistil and rose-colored stamens stick out of the middle of the flower. They are easy to spot, but don't expect to see drifts of color—perhaps less than a dozen in a colony that seemingly could support twice that number. Plants were used in the past as an antibacterial agent, to reduce swelling, and to prevent conception.

There are no cultivars, but a white-flowered form, 'Alba', is occasionally offered. Most white-flowered trout lilies are *Erythronium albidum*, much more rare in the wild and even more so in retail; this species is more common in the Midwest than in the Atlantic states.

Habitat: In woods and meadows from Nova Scotia to Minnesota, south to
　　Alabama and Florida.
Hardiness: USDA Zones 3–8.
Garden site: Moist shade is best.
Garden maintenance: None. Since plants go dormant soon after flowering, it
　　may be useful to plant something else that comes up later to cover that
　　space (almost all other perennials emerge after these flowers are complete);
　　this is not important in the woodland garden.

Erythronium revolutum　　　　pink fawn lily

A handsome western species with wonderful foliage and many rose-pink flowers with flared back petals. This species, like others, flowers early and goes dormant later on. The foliage may be plain green but is often heavily mottled with dark brown to purple patterns. Two to four nodding flowers are produced per flowering stem; the yellow stamens stick out from the flower, contrasting nicely with its rose color. In the wonderful Dunn Gardens in Seattle, corms romp freely with hardy cyclamens, one dying back as the other arises—a useful combination for these early ephemerals.

Habitat: Moist, wooded areas from the northern Coast Ranges of California to
　　British Columbia.

Hardiness: USDA Zones 6–8.

Garden site: Plants prefer cool, shady areas, moist in spring and drier later in the summer.

Garden maintenance: Maintain consistent moisture, particularly in the spring.

Erythronium tuolumnense   Tuolumne lily, pagoda lily

Native to a small area of the Sierra Nevada in California, plants are much more showy than their eastern relative. Compared to *Erythronium americanum*, this is a monster, growing up to 1' tall. Usually two unspotted green leaves emerge in early spring, followed by one or two yellow, nodding lily-like flowers, each one having reflexed petals. Plants go dormant in late spring to early summer.

Many cultivars are available, each differing only slightly from the species. The most common is 'Pagoda', with pale yellow flowers and somewhat bronze foliage. Easily found and an outstanding form. In my Athens garden, plants flower after *Erythronium americanum* but are completed by mid March.

'Citronella' has gorgeous light yellow flowers, similar to 'Pagoda' but a little later to bloom.

'Kondo' has bright yellow flowers.

Habitat: In the western foothills of the central Sierra Nevada in California.

Hardiness: USDA Zones 5–8.

Garden site: Partial shade to full sun.

Garden maintenance: None.

Erythronium tuolumnense

Recommended propagation

Seed: Not easy, quite inconsistent. Sometimes seed germinates readily; other times it may take a year or so. Leave the seedlings undisturbed for a couple of years; they may take up to five years to flower.

Division: Divide corms when the clump is sufficiently full.

Etymology

Genus: From the Greek, *erythos* ("red"). Since there is no red in any of the species, it is thought the word actually described a different plant and was somehow attributed to this genus.

Specific epithet: *americanum* ("of America"); *revolutum* ("rolled backward"), a reference to the petals; *tuolumnense* ("of Tuolumne," a county in California).

Common name: Adder's tongue refers to the tongue-like shape of the flowering shoot as it rises up in spring; fawn lily relates to the mottled leaves, which call to mind Bambi; trout lily's mottled leaves recall the varied scale colors of some trout.

Eupatorium	Joe-Pye weed	Asteraceae

Travel almost any road in the northeastern United States or eastern provinces of Canada, and it is hard to miss the eupatoriums; do it in the fall, and it is almost impossible. Roadside weeds like *Eupatorium capillifolium* (dogfennel) should be honored as Great American Protectors: I have rejoiced as entire fields of scrap cars become covered with this towering white-flowered stuff, and oh, what an improvement! But what a pox recurs when the dogfennel dies back in the winter (I can only hope that the owners of these cesspools linger too long by the fennel and get covered as well). Other species further south, in the red states, are equally adept at covering whatever litter, trash, or assorted goodies mar the landscape.

Several species bear similar white flowers, but most are mauve to purple, washing over 4–7' tall plants. The combination of Joe-Pyes, goldenrod, and asters all flowering together gives fall color another meaning. Numerous medicinal benefits have been attributed to species of *Eupatorium*, from the healing of broken bones to the easing of kidney pain; boneset tea and tincture of hyssop were popular home remedies for colds, fevers, and insect bites, and pills and powders are now available at most homeopathic outlets.

Since the hardy ageratum was moved from this genus to *Conoclinium coelestinum*, the purple Joe-Pye weeds and white snakeroot (*Eupatorium rugosum*) are the only species in the genus worth inviting to the garden; however, other species are also useful for meadow gardens and attracting butterflies. All flowers in the genus consist of disk flowers only; there are no ray flowers.

Eupatorium purpureum subsp. *maculatum* 'Gateway'

Eupatorium purpureum

Eupatorium purpureum
Joe-Pye weed

Plants grow to 7' tall and bear flowers ranging from deep pink to mauve, maturing to purple. They are characterized by having whorls of three or five short-stalked, sharply toothed leaves surrounding dark burgundy stems. If you get bored, crush a leaf or two and enjoy the vanilla fragrance. Generally four to seven pink to mauve flowers per flower head occur, and up to ten heads are packed together to make an impressive 12–15" wide display. They are marvelous garden plants, providing architectural "bones" to the fall garden. Flowers are particularly appealing to butterflies, and the seed heads, while not overwhelmingly beautiful, are also attractive and persist well into winter.

'Gateway' belongs to subsp. *maculatum* (formerly *Eupatorium maculatum*). The subspecies generally has stems spotted with purple dots, and this selection of it is popular because it is shorter, only 4–5' tall. Not exactly a midget, but a better choice for smaller gardens. 'Carin', from North Creek Nurseries in Pennsylvania, is similar to 'Gateway' but with light pink flowers. 'Purple Bush', a recent introduction from Holland which I have not grown, is said to be more compact than 'Gateway' and with smaller flowers. Time will tell.

Habitat: Usually in moist areas (and now escaped to roadsides) from New Hampshire to Quebec to Minnesota, west to Nebraska and south to Oklahoma, Tennessee and Florida.

Hardiness: USDA Zones 3–8.

Garden site: Full sun. Plants are best sited in areas of consistent moisture; drying out reduces the stature as well as beauty. No sense in having a puny Joe-Pye weed.

Garden maintenance: It gets big and may need division or change of venue if it overgrows its original site. Removal of seed heads is not necessary but will reduce reseeding.

Eupatorium rugosum　　　　white snakeroot

This common roadside and pasture plant is characterized by opposite sharply serrated leaves and white flowers. They can also be particularly good garden plants, if given plenty of light and moisture. Plants contain barium sulphate and are toxic if eaten in quantity. Cows that graze on the plants produce poisonous milk; people who drink it contract milk sickness, which can be fatal. American Indians made a tea from the roots of plants and used it against diarrhea, painful urination, fevers, and kidney stones. The plant was also burned, and the smoke used to revive unconscious patients. Plants have recently been reclassified under *Ageratina altissima* but will still be found under *Eupatorium* in many catalogs.

The cultivar 'Chocolate', with chocolate-colored foliage and snow-white flowers, gives the species its garden credibility. The 2–4' tall plants do well in light shade, but the foliage is darker in sunny areas, and flowers more profusely. Introduced by Dick Lighty at Mt. Cuba, Delaware.

But beware—plants grow from aggressive rhizomes and can spread quickly, and both the species and the cultivar can reseed ruthlessly. Be equally so.

Habitat: In open areas from southeast North Dakota to Oklahoma.
Hardiness: USDA Zones 4–8.
Garden site: Full sun. Afternoon shade can be tolerated as you travel further south.
Garden maintenance: Cut back if plants get too leggy. If self-sowing is a problem, remove flower heads before they go to seed.

Eupatorium rugosum

Eupatorium rugosum 'Chocolate'

Other species for the garden

Eupatorium dubium (eastern Joe-Pye weed) is underused in American gardens. It has whorled leaves, which often have more than one main vein, and is the shortest of the Joe-Pye species, rarely exceeding 4'. On the endangered species list of Maine. Hardy in zones 3–8. The cultivar 'Little Joe' is similar to the species and should become quite popular.

Eupatorium fistulosum (hollow Joe-Pye weed) is occasionally used in the garden. Growing up to 8' tall and distinguished by its hollow stems, it is otherwise similar to *E. purpureum*. Every swallowtail butterfly for miles will visit the flowers. The 3–4' tall 'Bartered Bride', with whitish flowers, probably belongs here.

Eupatorium perfoliatum (boneset), with stems that appear to pierce each leaf, is particularly handsome in leaf. Late in the season, loose mounds of white flowers top the plants. Lucy Root of Essex Junction, Vermont, wrote me that she used this plant when she was a teenager, to ease the pain of fingers that had been pulled out of joint: "Cooking some leaves in boiling water for a few minutes made a very healing [infusion]. No wonder it is called boneset!"

Recommended propagation

Seed: Easy from seed. Collect or purchase seed; place in a moist, warm location.

Cuttings: Terminal cuttings (with one or two nodes only) root well and are the best means of propagation. Cuttings beneath the terminal growth may be hollow and will not root well.

Division: Mature plants can be divided.

Etymology

Genus: For Mithridates VI Eupator, the Greek king of Pontus and a lifelong enemy of Rome, who lived in Asia Minor from 132 to 63 BC.

Specific epithet: *dubium* ("doubtful"), perhaps because of its height or multiple midribs on the leaves; *fistulosum* ("hollow"); *maculatum* ("spotted"); *purpureum* ("tending to purple"); *rugosum* ("rugose"), in reference to the wrinkled leaves.

Common name: Joe-Pye weed is supposedly named for Joe Pye (or Jopi, or Zhopai), who, according to folklore, was a traveling Native American medicine man. He lived in New England around the time of the American Revolution and may have been from a tribe in Maine. He sold various herbal remedies to the colonists and apparently treated typhoid fever with the plant that bears his name; white snakeroot refers to the white flowers and the ability of the plant to treat snakebites.

Euphorbia   spurge   Euphorbiaceae

A huge genus of over 1600 species, populated with weeds and a few ornamentals—and even some of these have escaped to become difficult-to-eradicate weeds. From the poinsettia to the caper spurge, gardeners have been growing euphorbs for a long time. Most are native to other shores, and these overseas species are eminently prettier than most of ours. Of our native species, the most popular is *Euphorbia marginata*, but sometimes gardeners stumble onto and actually buy *E. corollata* and *E. cyathophora*.

Euphorbs are characterized by milky sap (keep it off your skin and out of your eyes) and weird flowers, which are limited either to pistils or stamens, never both. The flowers together are called a cyathium. In general, flowers are surrounded by white or colored bracts.

Euphorbia corollata   white spurge

Some people really love this plant, and I have seen it look good on occasion, but the occasions have been few and far between. There is nothing wrong with the plant; it is simply a little wimpy-looking for my taste. Plants grow about 3' tall and bear opposite entire leaves with thin stems. At the top of the plant, just below the flowers, is usually a whorl of five leaves. In late summer, five clean white bracts surround the small flowers. The foliage turns shades of orange in the fall, more so in the North than in the South. Seeding and a slow-creeping rhizome eventually combine to form decent stands.

Euphorbia corollata

Habitat: Roadsides and pastures from Massachusetts to Minnesota and Nebraska, south to Texas and Florida.
Hardiness: USDA Zones 3–9.
Garden site: Full sun, does well in dry locations.
Garden maintenance: None.

Euphorbia marginata   snow-on-the-mountain

This annual can be spectacular, providing pale green leaves with deep and irregular margins of white. The contrast is superb. Plants grow about 2½' tall and generally grow in a clump. The white flowers begin in early summer and are often lost in the foliage. This is one of my favorite large annuals; I have seen truly outstanding specimens, but I have seen some decrepit-looking ones as well.

The several available cultivars do not differ a great deal, but they have neat names. 'Mt. Kilimanjaro', 'Summer Icicle', and 'White Top' have various amounts of variegation on the topmost leaves.

Habitat: In open areas from Minnesota to Colorado and Montana, south to Texas.
Hardiness: USDA Zones 9–10.
Garden site: Full sun.
Garden maintenance: Pinch once in early summer to make the plants more bushy.

Other species for the garden
Euphorbia cyathophora (summer poinsettia) has erect 2–3' tall stems with linear to ovate leaves and obvious dentations. The bracts turn red as the flower matures. Seldom have I seen plants that made me want to purchase them for my garden. Zones 9–10.

Euphorbia marginata

Euphorbia cyathophora

Recommended propagation

Seed: The black seeds germinate well in warm, moist areas. Transplant carefully to reduce damage to the taproot.

Cuttings: Terminal cuttings root reasonably well. No rooting hormone is needed, but if you are going to use one, try a liquid form.

Etymology

Genus: For Euphorbus, physician to the king of Mauritania.

Specific epithet: *corollata* ("like a corolla"), referring to the white bracts that look so much like petals; *cyathophora*, referring to the cyathia (small flower-like cups); *marginata* ("margined").

Common name: Spurge comes from the Latin for "purge"—the milky juice of many species caused vomiting.

Filipendula rubra	queen of the prairie	Rosaceae

Many species in this genus are from Eurasia, but the queen is ours. Experience the majesty of this super-sized prairie species, and you are one step closer to sensory saturation. Plants are up to 7' in height, with large many-lobed leaves. The stem leaves are three- to five-lobed and alternate on the dark zigzag stems, while the larger terminal leaf is usually three-lobed; however, the leaves take a backseat when the deep pink flowers open in mid summer. The inflorescence, consisting of hundreds of flowers, can be knock-your-socks-off beautiful; it can also be awful if planted in too much shade, or if wind and drought have been

Filipendula rubra

consistently above average. After flowering, plants tend to decline somewhat but produce underground rhizomes that search out new territory. You must balance the beautiful with the not-so-beautiful if placing the queen in a formal garden, or allow her to naturalize in a more meadow-like setting.

Habitat: In moist meadows and prairies from Pennsylvania to Minnesota, south to Kentucky and Georgia.
Hardiness: USDA Zones 3–7.
Garden site: Moist, sunny area. Lots of room.
Garden maintenance: Plants can look poor after flowering. Maintain moisture to delay senescence of foliage. Plants are better in the meadow than in the garden.

Recommended propagation

Seed: Fairly easy from seed. Sow immediately to take advantage of late summer heat.
Cuttings: One- to two-node cuttings from new growth in early spring are often successful.
Division: Only to move wayward daughter plants.

Etymology

Genus: From the Latin, *filum* ("thread") and *pendulus* ("hanging"), referring to the threads that hang from the root tubers of *Filipendula vulgaris*, a European species.
Specific epithet: *rubrum* ("red").
Common name: Hard to argue with this one.

Gaillardia	blanket flower	Asteraceae

Blanket flowers have been in our gardens for eons, and their popularity only increases as more material is offered and additional breeding occurs. Although about thirty species are known, we use a paltry few. The perennials (best known for cultivars like 'Goblin') that have been so popular are hybrids between *Gaillardia aristata*, a perennial native, and *G. pulchella*, an annual native. Neither species is nearly as popular as the hybrids.

Gaillardia aestivalis	firewheel

I fell in love with this species when I first saw it in the Mercer Botanic Garden in Humble, Texas. The leaves are almost smooth, far less hairy than other more common species. The solitary flowers are held on long flower stems and continue all summer. A good deal of variability in ray flower color occurs, from deep

Gaillardia aestivalis var. *winkleri* 'Purple with Dark Center'

Gaillardia aestivalis var. *winkleri* 'White with Yellow Center'

purple to white to bicolors. As a bonus, the globe-like seed heads are very attractive and part of the charm.

var. *winkleri*, native to southern Texas, is highly variable. I would not have included this plant, which used to be impossible to buy; however, at the University of Georgia, we have made selections of it in four colors (with highly creative names) and expect to make them available soon.

Habitat: From Florida to Texas, northern Kansas and east to South Carolina.
Hardiness: USDA Zones 7–9. They have been perennial in Athens (zone 7b).
Garden site: Full sun, well-drained soil.
Garden maintenance: None.

Gaillardia aristata   perennial blanket flower

This perennial, a parent of the garden hybrids, is a handsome plant on its own. The leaves and stems are densely hairy, and the daisy flowers open in mid to late summer. Ray flowers are yellow or yellow with red on the base around a raised disk; the disk is initially flat but becomes more rounded as flowers mature. Plants are longer lived than the hybrids; they grow 2½–3' tall and can be a little leggy. There is nothing wrong with this plant (except for the height), if you can find it. It simply has been superseded by the hybrids.

All cultivars are hybrids known as *Gaillardia* ×*grandiflora*. Most are shorter and more compact, and flower for a long period of time.

'Baby Cole' is only about 6" tall, with 2–3" wide yellow and red flowers.

'Fanfare', popular since its 2003 introduction, is quite different. The ray flowers are not strap-like, as in most gaillardias, but trumpet-shaped.

'Goblin' has been around for years and is still an excellent choice. A dwarf form, 9–12" tall with red and yellow colors. 'Golden Goblin' is similar but with golden yellow flowers.

Gaillardia ×grandiflora 'Fanfare'

Gaillardia ×grandiflora 'Goblin'

'Summer Kiss' has handsome salmon to peach ray flowers. A little taller than the others, but an excellent color.

'Torchlight' is much like the species but more vigorous, and a better performer in the garden.

Habitat: In prairies and dry meadows from Washington State to northern Idaho to the Dakotas, south to Utah and eastern Colorado. They have escaped to coastal areas of the East and are often found on beaches.

Hardiness: USDA Zones 4–8.

Garden site: Full sun, well-drained soils. Dies quickly in wet soils.

Garden maintenance: Deadhead to enhance flowering time.

Gaillardia ×grandiflora 'Torchlight'

Gaillardia pulchella Torch series

Gaillardia pulchella   **annual blanket flower**

These self-sowing annuals tend to be highly variable; in a single population, the ray flowers tend to be all yellow, all red, or bicolor. The stems and leaves are very hairy, with ciliate margins. Plants grow about 2' tall, and flowers occur for much of the summer. Plants are most often seen as part of a wildflower or meadow mix.

Cultivars are a great improvement on the species. The Plumes series (in red and yellow) is good, but the Torch series (also in red and yellow) is even better. Both have much rounder and shaggier flowers than the species.

Habitat: In pastures and meadows in eastern and south central United States south to Mexico.
Hardiness: USDA Zones 8–10.
Garden site: Full sun, well-drained soils.
Garden maintenance: Remove spent flowers to increase flowering. Do not fertilize.

Recommended propagation
Seed: Easy from seed. Most cultivars are also available from seed.
Division: Occasionally done, but best from seed.

Etymology
Genus: Named in 1786 for French magistrate and patron of botany Gaillard de Charentonneau.
Specific epithet: *aestivalis* ("pertaining to summer"); *aristata* ("bearded," "hairy"); *pulchella* ("pretty").
Common name: Colored blankets have many colors, and so do these, hence blanket flower.

Galax urceolata

Galax urceolata, fall color

Galax urceolata	wandflower	Diaspensiaceae

You can buy this species from catalogs or occasionally from retail outlets, but seldom does it look as good as it does in nature. It forms marvelous dense populations in association with the rhododendron glades in the Smoky Mountains or in cool, moist environments, where the rhizomes can spread their wings. Not too many of us have such mountain glades or perfect conditions, however, so we struggle. This, I suppose, is true for many natives, but *Galax urceolata* seems more finicky about where it will succeed. That has been my experience with the few plants I have been able to secure; but I am a lowlander, and you may be more fortunate.

Plants arise from underground stems and spread well in cool, moist conditions and in soils that allow for a comfortable root run. The 2–6" wide round leaves are leathery and evergreen; in the fall, they have some brilliant red color, but in the winter they can be disfigured by frost, wind, and snow. I cut them off in the spring as new foliage begins to appear. Numerous small white flowers arise in late spring on 1½–2' tall leafless stems. The leaves are in great demand as bouquet fillers and have been harvested in western North Carolina for more than a hundred years to supply the national and international floral industry. These are beautiful plants once established, but because they are slow to propagate, they remain a rarity in gardens.

Habitat: Mainly in the mountains from Virginia to Kentucky, south to higher elevations of Alabama and Georgia.
Hardiness: USDA Zones 5–8.
Garden site: Areas of cool nights, moist soils, and shade.
Garden maintenance: I find that the old leaves can look bad in the spring, and I remove them (if I remember to do it).

Recommended propagation

Seed: Slow and difficult, requiring great patience. Seeds germinate in nature on mossy carpets; if you have such conditions, sow them there.

Cuttings: Cut roots into 1–2" sections in the spring before new growth starts and place on a perlite:peat medium; keep moist, and rooting will occur, albeit slowly. Stem cuttings are not recommended.

Division: Lift patches when sufficient population allows.

Etymology

Genus: From the Greek for "milk," possibly in allusion to the white flowers.

Specific epithet: *urceolata* ("urn-shaped").

Common name: The flowers are carried on a long, wand-like stem, hence wandflower.

Gaura	**beeblossom**	**Onagraceae**

From virtual obscurity to consistent presence in mainstream garden outlets, *Gaura* has certainly gained converts over the past decade. Its claim to fame is its members' long flowering period, their tolerance of both heat and cold, and the many ornamental cultivars that are now available.

Gaura lindheimeri	**whirling butterflies**

The long flowering period and cold tolerance of this southwestern native have surprised many landscapers and gardeners. In my opinion, the species is over-rated, and the time spent developing new cultivars may not pay off for the breeders; however, it can look good with its white flowers on long stems, waving in the wind just like butterflies a-whirling. The stems arise from the base and produce narrow alternate green leaves, which may be red, bronze, or speckled in the cultivars. Full sun and poor soils are all that is needed to make the plant look good most of the season. In the 1990s, cultivars were sparse, but in the early 2000s, a veritable explosion took place.

Gaura lindheimeri

Gaura lindheimeri 'Ballerina Blush'

Ballerina series, available in a blush and a pink, was bred for greenhouse production; plants are therefore short and compact, and they perform well in the garden.

'Blushing Butterflies', developed by Howard Bentley of Plant Growers Australia in Victoria, is a compact offspring of 'Siskiyou Pink'.

'Crimson Butterflies', another compact Bentley introduction, bears dark foliage and deep pink flowers.

'Dauphine' is an upright form that can grow 4–5' tall and equally wide. It is too big and unruly for most gardens but has been a useful parent in some of the hybrids.

'Karalee Petite Pink', with pink flowers, is one of the newer dwarf forms. Appears to hold its compact habit well. Other colors in the Karalee series are just around the corner.

'Passionate Pink', a cross between 'Siskiyou Pink' and 'Dauphine', has pink flowers and red to green foliage. As with all gauras, the leaves are redder in full sun than in shade. Height is about 2½'.

'Perky Pink' is a small cultivar with excellent pink flowers and a good compact habit. Suitable for containers.

'Pink Cloud' was developed by Leota Powell from 'Dauphine' and 'Siskiyou Pink'. Plants grow about 30" tall and are strong, upright, and covered in pink flowers.

'Pink Fountains', one of my favorites, displays compact habit and season-long flowering.

'Siskiyou Pink' is the only reason people ever noticed gaura. Introduced in 1994, this pink-flowering sport was the first cultivar to provide a different flower color and a less lanky habit. We can thank Baldassare Mineo of Siskiyou Rare Plant Nursery in Medford, Oregon, for his sharp eye.

'Whirling Butterflies', the very first selection in the genus, is supposedly a little more floriferous than the species and has whiter flowers. Narrow lance-

Gaura lindheimeri 'Pink Fountains'

Gaura lindheimeri 'Siskiyou Pink'

shaped leaves (1–3" long) are sometimes spotted with maroon. Maroon spotting is common on all gauras but not visible in dark-leaved cultivars.

Habitat: In open areas in southeastern Texas, Louisiana and Mexico.
Hardiness: USDA Zones (5)6–9.
Garden site: Full sun, preferably on the edge of a bank, where the floppy habit of some of the taxa can be used to advantage. Containers reduce vigor, which is a benefit.
Garden maintenance: Do not overfertilize; too much foliage will result, and plants will become leggy. Do not overwater for the same reason. In other words, don't "mother" these plants to death. After flowering, they may be cut back severely. Plants will rejuvenate, and flowers will reinitiate.

Other species for the garden
Gaura biennis has small white flowers on tall inflorescences; however, because it self-sows readily, it is often part of a wildflower mix. Hardy to zone 4.

Gaura coccinea (scarlet gaura) is a handsome small species, growing less than 2' tall, from Texas to California, and east to the Dakotas. The spreading narrow petals are white to pink, and the anthers are a brilliant red. Flowers mainly just before evening and is pollinated by moths. Hardy to zone 3.

Recommended propagation
Seed: Reasonably easy to grow from seed. Place in a seed tray; provide moisture and warmth (72–75F).
Cuttings: Take two- to three-node cuttings in the spring.

Etymology
Genus: From the Greek, *gauros* ("superb"), in reference to the flowers.
Specific epithet: *biennis* ("biennial"); *coccinea* ("scarlet"); *lindheimeri* honors Ferdinand Jacob Lindheimer (1801–1879), a German political exile who botanized extensively throughout Texas.
Common name: Bees like it, and the butterfly-like flowers appear to be whirling above the foliage.

Gentiana	gentian	Gentianaceae

I am not the one to be extolling the virtues of this genus. In fact, I have seldom—no, change that to *never* successfully established a gentian in any garden I have been associated with. Whether this is because of my horticultural inadequacies or the locale of the garden, or both, does not matter. Gentians and I have reached an agreement: I will no longer spend hard-earned money to buy them, and they will no longer be killed.

Gentians can be established in cool climates. If you live in such an area in the Pacific Northwest, Northeast, or Canada and have money to spend, give them a go. Otherwise, join me in admiring them from a distance and spend your money on plants that want to be with you as much as you want to be with them. This unrequited-love stuff is for the birds!

Many gentians are grown, but only a few natives are available and worthy of garden space.

Gentiana andrewsii   closed gentian, bottle gentian

One of the easiest, and pretty in its own way, even though the flowers don't really open. Plants grow 1½–2' tall and bear opposite dark green leaves, usually with one obvious vein and two others not quite as visible. In the summer, the 1½" long sessile dark blue flowers are borne terminally in three- to seven-flowered clusters, in the upper axils. The flowers look like pleated buds, some say pleated balloons, and remain closed, although you can open them from the top. Quite beautiful in groups, not much to talk about when grown as a single plant in the garden.

Habitat: In prairies from Quebec to Saskatchewan, south to Nebraska,
Arkansas and Georgia.
Hardiness: USDA Zones 3–7.
Garden site: Partial shade to full sun.
Garden maintenance: None, once established.

Other species for the garden
Gentiana clausa is similar to *G. andrewsii* but differs by having larger flowers and slight morphological differences in the flowers. Native from Maine to Minnesota, south to North Carolina.

*Gentiana
clausa*

Gentiana puberulenta (downy gentian) is occasionally offered through mail-order firms. The purple flowers open wide in the fall over stiff, serrated leaves. The stems are very slightly hairy or downy. Plants are about 15" tall and are native in well-drained areas from Kansas to North Dakota. They do best in dry soils.

Gentiana saponaria (soapwort gentian) is another bottle gentian, native to the Southeast, and tolerates heat as well as any species. The blue flowers open very slightly at the top. Does best in moist, rich soils.

Recommended propagation

Seed: Collect the seeds, sow in a coarse medium of 3:1 perlite:peat, and place in a sheltered area outdoors, such as in a cold frame. Germination will occur the following spring.

Division: If a fine colony is established, leave it alone.

Etymology

Genus: For Gentius, king of Illyria circa 500 BC, who is credited with discovering the medicinal value of *Gentiana lutea* (yellow gentian).

Specific epithet: *andrewsii* honors English botanical artist Henry C. Andrews (1799–1830); *clausa* ("closed"); *puberulenta* ("minutely downy"); *saponaria* refers to a similarity between the leaves of this plant and those of soapwort (*Saponaria*), although the person who thought this must have been smoking it rather than describing it. It is sheer coincidence that rubbing the leaves produces a soapy lather.

Common name: Looking at the closed, narrow flowers, both names make sense.

Gentianopsis crinita	fringed gentian	Gentianaceae

This is among the most sought-after of all gentian-related plants. Plants overwinter as a rosette and then grow 1–3' tall when in flower. The 2" wide flowers, bright blue with fringed petals, open in late summer to fall and are either solitary or borne severally at the top. Not easy to establish, but this most beautiful and interesting wildflower is well worth the try.

Habitat: Moist to wet places from Maine to Manitoba, south to Iowa, South Dakota and into the mountains of North Carolina.

Hardiness: USDA Zones 3–7.

Garden site: Open, moist areas.

Garden maintenance: Apply a little dolomitic lime every year. Maintain moisture.

Recommended propagation

Similar to *Gentiana*.

Etymology
Genus: From the Greek, *opsis* ("resembling"), that is, plants look like gentians.
Specific epithet: *crinita* ("having long, weak hairs"), referring to the fringes on the petals.
Common name: Obvious.

Geranium	cranesbill, heronsbill	Geraniaceae

I have admired this genus for years, studying the plants in England and Ireland as well as in the North and South of this country. The more I discovered, the more I realized how little I knew. Species occur all over the world, but most of the few that originate in North America are weeds and all are essentially ignored by horticulturists. The best of these natives is *Geranium maculatum*, but several western species hold some garden potential for geranium lovers as well.

Geranium maculatum	spotted cranesbill

Spotted cranesbill is not only the best but certainly one of the easiest native geraniums to establish in our gardens. Plants bear all the marks of a geranium—that is, palmate leaves, five-petaled flowers, and long, narrow fruit in the shape of a crane's bill—but the foliage is spotted, usually with yellow markings. All this plant needs to become mainstream is someone to champion it—and a few people to select more gardenesque cultivars.

Plants bear 1" wide, rose to pink flowers in spring; they grow up to 2' tall in heavy shade but are more compact in sunnier areas. This is one of the few shade-tolerant geraniums and is best planted with at least afternoon shade. Cool nights also help with vigor; in fact, some of the best specimens are at the North Carolina Arboretum in Asheville. Establishing a population is not diffi-

Geranium maculatum

Geranium maculatum

Geranium maculatum 'Espresso'

cult; plants reseed with ease and colonize quickly. A good amount of variability occurs within a population, and most available cultivars are based on this natural variability. White flowers are not uncommon (I see 'Alba' on the market), and bronze to purple foliage also occurs occasionally. The best selection I have seen is 'Espresso', which maintains a compact habit and excellent dark foliage all season.

Habitat: In woods and meadows from Maine to Manitoba, south to South Dakota, Arkansas, Tennessee and Georgia.
Hardiness: USDA Zones 3–8.
Garden site: Afternoon shade, or shade from a white pine or other open conifer. Full all-day sun is not recommended.
Garden maintenance: None.

Geranium richardsonii   wild white geranium

This mountain species does have its moments, and some people seem to enjoy it; that it is so hard to purchase has more to do, I suspect, with its common nature than any difficulty of propagation or production. Plants stand about 18" tall and bear white flowers with purple veins. The leaves can be up to 6" across and have three to seven palmate lobes; they also often have spots, similar to *Geranium maculatum*. It is quite cold-tolerant but struggles in areas of heat and humidity. Partial shade seems to suit it; consistent moisture is also a must.

Habitat: In light shade and moist areas of the Sierra Nevada, extending through much of western North America.
Hardiness: USDA Zones 2–7.

Geranium richardsonii

Geranium oreganum

Garden site: An area of afternoon shade is best, but if moisture is plentiful, full sun can be tolerated. A poor choice for the southern gardener.

Garden maintenance: Deadhead if needed.

Other species for the garden

Geranium oreganum (western geranium) has deep purple flowers in late spring to mid summer. Plants generally grow less than 2' tall.

Recommended propagation

Seed: Seeds can be collected, but be quick: when seeds are ripe, they are ejected and fall a long way from the plant. It is probably better to collect the fruit as it turns slightly yellow. Sow in a tray immediately, and place in a cold frame. Germination should be reasonably good in the spring, if not before.

Etymology

Genus: From the Greek, *geranos* ("crane"), an allusion to the shape of the fruit.

Specific epithet: *maculatum* ("spotted"); *oreganum* ("of Oregon"), but plants bearing this epithet could have originated in the old Oregon Territory of the Hudson's Bay Company, which included the states of both Washington and Oregon; *richardsonii* honors Sir John Richardson (1787–1865), a Scottish naturalist, meteorologist, doctor, cartographer, and Arctic explorer.

Common name: Cranesbill has been explained, and the same thing can be said of the fruit's resemblance to a heron's bill.

Geum	avens	Rosaceae

There are only a few herbaceous plants in the rose family, and fewer still that provide value for our gardens. The best known is lady's mantle (*Alchemilla*), which includes no natives, and the least known is *Geum*, whose native members are mostly overlooked. All avens bear five-petaled flowers and compound leaves, but in some species, it is the fruit that is most ornamental.

Geum rivale

Geum rivale

Geum rivale   water avens, indian chocolate

Geum rivale 'Album'

If you have a boggy area and live in the northern part of the continent, this is a terrific plant. Otherwise, save your money. Given that you have a chilly bog, you will enjoy the bell-shaped nodding bicolored (red and orange) flowers and bright green compound leaves. The leaves consist of seven to fourteen sharply toothed leaflets, the three at the end significantly larger than the others. Plants are generally less than 18" tall even when in flower; they are vigorous growers and can act as a ground cover if conditions are right. I have seen this species growing beautifully in the British Isles where winter temperatures are moderate, but with likewise moderate winters in Georgia I have had no success; however, in the chilly Laurentian Mountains outside Montreal, it grows wonderfully well, telling me it is the cool summers—not winter temperatures—that make the difference.

'Album' has white petals and rose sepals.

'Leonard's Variety' and 'Leonard's Double' have drooping mahogany-red flowers in single or double form, respectively. Both are vigorous growers.

'Lionel Cox' is 12" tall with primrose-yellow flowers and light green foliage.

Habitat: By streams and in bogs from Canada west to the Rocky Mountains, south to northern Washington and east through the Midwest and into the Northeast.
Hardiness: USDA Zones 3–7.
Garden site: Moist, sunny to afternoon-shade conditions are necessary.
Garden maintenance: None.

Geum triflorum   prairie smoke

This much-appreciated prairie plant is better adapted for garden use than *Geum rivale* as it does not require standing water to do well. In early spring, plants produce a cluster of two to three nodding flowers that are somewhat similar to those of *G. rivale*. The leaves consist of twenty-two to thirty wedge-shaped leaflets, and all are softly hairy. The most distinctive and ornamental part of the plant is its fruit, the long hairy plumes of which consist of 2" long flower styles. The feathery pink seed heads look like little puffs of smoke and sway in the breeze, a quite beautiful effect.

Plants require cool nights to look their best. They spread by rootstocks and grow less than 1' tall, making a unique ground cover. They thrive in poor, dry soil but will not complain if provided with richer, well-drained soils.

A cordial against the plague was made by boiling the roots in wine. Chewing of the root was also recommended for bad breath.

Habitat: Through the Cascades and Sierras, into Colorado, the Dakotas and into the Northeast.
Hardiness: USDA Zones 1–7.
Garden site: Moisture is useful, but gritty soils are best. Afternoon shade to full sun.
Garden maintenance: None.

Recommended propagation
Seed: Place sown seeds in a cold frame over winter; seeds germinate well after a cold period.
Division: As needed.

Etymology

Genus: No explanation known—simply a classic Latin name.

Specific epithet: *rivale* ("growing by streams"); *triflorum* ("three-flowered").

Common name: Avens is from the Latin *avencia*, *avantia*, or *avence*, all words of obscure origin; various spellings have been applied to the plant from very early times. Prairie smoke is an obvious reference to the fruit of *Geum triflorum*; indian chocolate refers to the thick brown root, which after being boiled apparently tastes like chocolate. Let me know.

Gillenia	indian physic, American ipecac	Rosaceae

I liked this genus when I first saw it overseas—and came back to find that one American species was all over the Smoky Mountains in north Georgia, and that native plant gardeners in the central Plains states had already embraced it. Its range is broad; it has already broken into mainstream gardening, and the two species that appear in our gardens share a rich medicinal tradition. Plants were used by Native Americans to treat respiratory disorders and as a powerful emetic; a tea made from them was employed as a laxative; and poultices were used for stings, swelling, and soreness.

Gillenia trifoliata	bowman's root

Gillenia trifoliata (*Porteranthus trifoliatus*) is an excellent informal plant with 1" wide white flowers often tinged with a little pink. Plants consist of wiry many-branched reddish stems. Leaves are alternate and in threes, each leaflet 2–3" long. At each node are small stipules, hardly leaf-like at all. Although they look good in our trials, they do better in the North than in the South and in afternoon shade; they can be grown in morning sun.

Habitat: From Ontario to Michigan, south to Kentucky, Alabama, and north Georgia.

Hardiness: USDA Zones 4–7.

Garden site: Full sun to afternoon shade. Consistent moisture is necessary for best garden performance.

Garden maintenance: None.

Other species for the garden

Gillenia stipulata (*Porteranthus stipulatus*), a more westerly native, is used more often in the Midwest and Plains states. A bit more heat-tolerant than *G. trifoliata*, it is further distinguished by having much larger leaf-like stipules (up to 1" long), narrower leaflets, and hairier stems; and the leaflets are deeply cut, giving it a more refined appearance. The two species are otherwise similar in

Gillenia trifoliata

Gillenia trifoliata

flower and habit. Native from New York to Illinois and Kansas, south to Texas and Georgia.

Recommended propagation
Seed: Easily grown from seed. A three-month cold treatment before sowing enhances speed and percentage of germination.

Etymology
Genus: For Arnold Gillen, a 17th-century German physician and botanist.
Specific epithet: *stipulata* ("with stipules"); *trifoliata* ("three-leaved").
Common name: Indian physic and American ipecac indicate a North American use for internal cleansing, not to say purging. Bowman's root is just another way to say that Indians (men who were known for using bows) used this plant (*American Journal of Pharmacy*, October 1898).

Helenium	sneezeweed	Asteraceae

All sneezeweeds are characterized by yellow ray flowers, usually with three or more lobes at the end, which helps distinguish them from sunflowers (*Helianthus*) and other similar daisies. Plants have a conspicuous disk, often brown or yellow. In general, they tend to be tall, although dwarfer, better-behaved cultivars have been bred. Of the thirty-five-plus species, three enjoy reasonable use in American gardens, and *Helenium autumnale* is particularly well known throughout the gardening world.

Helenium autumnale	dogtooth daisy

This is by far the most common species in gardens. In their native habitat, plants grow 3' tall and bear rough, serrated, alternate leaves, whose base runs

Helianthus angustifolius

Literally dozens of flowers are formed, each a clean gold color that stops people in their tracks. Plants will grow 6' tall in full sun and 8' in partial shade, so don't put them under trees. The taller they are, the more likely they are to topple when flowers start to form. They tolerate moist soils, but I have never seen this plant suffer if planted in "normal" soils.

'Gold Lace' is about 5' tall and is earlier to flower than the species.

'Mellow Yellow', a selection from Louisiana, bears softer yellow flowers and is 3–5' tall.

Habitat: In moist areas from Florida to Texas and north to Missouri and New York.
Hardiness: USDA Zones 5–9.
Garden site: Full sun, moist area is fine but not necessary.
Garden maintenance: I cut back plants in mid summer to help with branching and reduce mature height.

Helianthus annuus   **common sunflower**

If one was to select a one-stop shopping plant, this is it. As a garden plant, it provides ease of cultivation and a diversity of heights and eye-catching colors. As a commercial row crop, sunflowers are farmed for their oil and their seeds, which were used as a food source by native people long before the Europeans and are still a favorite snack of ballplayers. Commercially, they are among the most popular cut flowers in world markets, and breeders have concentrated on producing cultivars for long vase life. If that is not enough, not only have these sunny flowers been the subject many times over for great artists, but today adorn aprons

203

Helianthus annuus 'Sun Goddess'   *Helianthus annuus* 'Valentine'

and cutlery, coffee cups and even one of our state flags. Not bad for a plant that you can buy seeds for at K-Mart.

Plants grow rapidly and usually flower in early to mid summer. Provide full sun, and stake the larger ones. After flowering, the seeds in the disk start to form; while this is interesting, there is nothing ornamental about it. Don't be surprised when plants fall apart after flowering, as this is normal. If you want beauty in sunflowers all season, simply sow seeds at the base of the existing plants when they form a flower bud. By the time the elders lie down, the youngsters will be coming along fine.

Cultivars have been bred for color, height, improved vase life (pollenless flowers), and additional branching (rather than the single stem seen in older cultivars). I mention but a few of the many in various categories that I enjoy. Some are easier to find than others, but all will provide handsome color in most gardens.

Tall forms (exceeding 5'): These are excellent for cut flowers or the back of the border but often require staking.

'Chianti' bears 4" wide pollenless flowers on branched plants. The blooms are maroon and red, flecked with gold.

'Moonbright' has lemon-yellow flowers and a brown disk. Flowers are 6–7" across and don't produce pollen, which means they don't shed pollen, which makes them even better for cut flowers.

'Sunbeam' bears 5–6" wide golden yellow flowers around chartreuse-green disks. Pollenless and terrific.

'Sun Goddess' is a large single sunflower growing at least 5' in height.

'Sungold' ('Giant Sungold') is a terrific golden yellow double. I am not partial to double flowers, but I found this to be an excellent cultivar with strong stems and exquisite flowers. If you like double-flowered sunflowers, track this one down: it is worth the effort.

'Sunrich Lemon' and 'Sunrich Orange' are 5–6' tall single stem forms, extremely useful for cut flowers. The blooms are about 7" across and pollenless.

Intermediate forms (3–5'): Excellent for cut flowers or mid to back of the border.

'Floristan' has flowers 5–6" in diameter, with unique bicolored ray flowers, burgundy at the base and light yellow at the tips. The center is burgundy with gold stamens. Branched, about 5' tall. Quite an eyeful.

'Ikarus' is about 4' tall, similar to 'Valentine' but with slightly brighter yellow flowers.

'Monet' is a bit wild-looking, like the great garden of the man for which it is named. Single yellow flowers.

'Sonya' bears tangerine-orange 4" wide flowers with dark centers on 3–4' tall plants.

'Valentine' is well branched and seldom needs staking. The light yellow 6" wide rays surround a dark center. My favorite intermediate.

Short forms (under 3'): Excellent for containers or interplanted in the garden.

'Big Smile' is about 2½' tall with 5–6" wide single golden yellow flowers. Disks are burgundy.

'Music Box' is a mixture of yellow to mahogany colors on 2–3' tall plants. Multi-branched with many flowers.

'Sunspot' is a dwarf form of the Van Gogh sunflower, growing 2–3' tall. Flowers are yellow and up to 6" wide.

'Teddy Bear' bears 3–5" wide yellow double flowers. A cute name and a nice combination of double flowers and dwarf habit.

Habitat: In fields and prairies from the Great Plains of Saskatchewan to Texas.
Hardiness: Annual.
Garden site: Full sun.
Garden maintenance: Provide support for the taller ones (and even the intermediates in windy areas). The best method is to plant a group of half a dozen or more; they will support each other. If seeds are not needed, cut plants back after flowering; they will look a little better for a little longer. The best practice, however, is to have new seedlings growing at the base or ready to plant in place so that you can simply remove any plant that starts to look decrepit. Plants contract mildew and other foliar diseases; apply a fungicide if this bothers you.

Helianthus argophyllus   silver-leaf sunflower

This is one of my favorite sunflowers and should be in more gardens. It is often sold as 'Silver Leaf' and bears broad, hairy, silver-gray foliage. Quite outstanding in containers and in the garden, contrasting well with other green plant material. Plants are well branched and grow to about 4' in height. The flowers are normal sunflower-yellow and about 4" across, but it is one of the few sunflowers—

Helianthus argophyllus

Helianthus debilis

perhaps the only one—that looks just as good without flowers as with them. Help me out: I am tired of being the only person extolling the virtues of this species.

Habitat: In sunny fields in Texas, but has become established in much of the Southeast.
Hardiness: Annual.
Garden site: Full sun, good drainage. Equally at home in large containers or in the ground.
Garden maintenance: In times of heavy rains, water can collect on the hairy foliage, and fungal leaf spots can occur. As with *H. annuus*, it falls apart after flowering, but also as with common sunflower, it is easily replaced with the next round of seedlings: sow in stages.

Helianthus debilis   cucumber-leaved sunflower

I include this sunflower because I enjoy it. It too is an annual, but it differs from *Helianthus annuus* by having more branches at the base and more slender stems. Plants are hairy throughout, and the branches are often mottled with purple or white. Not the strongest plant in the garden, but still quite handsome. Flowers are generally 2–4" across.

'Italian White', the best-known form, bears ivory-white to light-primrose 4" wide flowers. The rays contrast well with the dark center. Plants grow 5–7' tall.

Habitat: In southeastern Texas, mostly, and eastward.

Hardiness: Annual.

Garden site: Full sun.

Garden maintenance: Stems can be weak and might need some support. Be wary of powdery mildew if sited in insufficient sun. Cut back after flowering.

Helianthus giganteus   **giant sunflower**

The name truly fits, and just like in the class photo where the big kids are in the back and your son is in the front, this is one of the big kids. While height can be intimidating, it is also rather awesome that a plant, any plant, could grow up to 10' in a single season. You could get out your chaise longe, mix up a few pitchers of margaritas, and watch the sunflowers grow. Beats the heck out of watching the grass grow.

The leaves are lanceolate, and for a plant this size, the flowers are quite small (2–2½" across). Flowers occur in very late summer or fall. One of the problems I have had in the UGA Horticulture Gardens is that even though the stems are stout, the plant will likely be ready to topple by the time it starts to flower in the fall. We place it at a corner of a fence and tie it up when it is only about 4' tall, then again later on. The other problem we have (and perhaps this is a southern problem) is that the bottom leaves decline by late summer, leaving lots of hairy, most unattractive legs. We solve this by planting shrubs or other plants at its feet. This is obviously not a plant for every garden—or one for the lazy gardener. Suffice it to say, I do not grow this at home.

Helianthus giganteus 'Sheila's Sunshine'

'Sheila's Sunshine' has soft yellow flowers and is prettier than the species. Still big, but glorious in flower.

Habitat: From Maine to Alberta, south to Colorado, Mississippi and east to Florida.
Hardiness: USDA Zones 5–9.
Garden site: Full sun. Placing it near a fence or other structure to support it is not a bad idea—they don't sell bamboo stakes long enough.
Garden maintenance: As above. Fertilize in mid summer to reduce yellowing of bottom leaves. In late fall, cut back to the ground.

Helianthus maximiliani   Maximilian's sunflower

This is a favorite son of the Southwest gardener—tough, rugged, and able to withstand abuse. I remember my colleague John Dole pointing out its merits as a drought-tolerant garden plant and its potential as a commercial cut flower. It is another giant to be sure, growing 7–8' tall, with raspy stems and many alternate, pointed 5–8" long lanceolate leaves held by winged petioles. The leaves are often folded lengthwise, a characteristic seldom seen in other sunflowers. The fall flowers are handsome not only for their yellow disks and rays but also because they are held close to the stem, in a spike-like arrangement, making a very showy display in the garden and in the vase.

'Santa Fe' is relatively compact (that is, it may grow to only the low end of its 6–8' range!) but is an earlier flowerer. A better selection for the gardener, courtesy of High Country Gardens in Santa Fe, New Mexico.

Habitat: In open spaces east of the Rocky Mountains from southern Canada to Texas.
Hardiness: USDA Zones 4–9.
Garden site: Full sun.
Garden maintenance: Cut back in early summer to maintain a semblance of height control. Support may be necessary.

Helianthus occidentalis   western sunflower

This interesting sunflower exists in the spring as a rosette of long-stalked leaves; then in late spring, an almost leafless flower stem arises, and in early summer an orange-yellow sunflower with a yellow disk appears. The flower stem contains a few leaves, but they are much reduced and resemble bracts more than leaves. Plants can be 6–8' tall. This is a good garden plant and highly valued for prairie and meadow plantings.

Habitat: Minnesota to Ohio, south to Florida and Texas.
Hardiness: USDA Zones 4–9.
Garden site: Full sun.
Garden maintenance: Cut stem back after flowering if plants start to decline.

Helianthus salicifolius   **willow sunflower**

This is probably the prettiest of all the sunflowers and is certainly the most hand-some as far as foliage goes. The leaves are narrow and willowy, and as the plant grows, a seeming umbrella of leaves forms at the top. The flowers, which appear in the fall, are similar to those of *Helianthus angustifolius*. Without maintenance, plants can easily reach 6' tall, then fall over with the weight of the flowers. If cut back once or twice until late June, the height can be controlled, and the plant will look spectacular even when not in flower. Probably my favorite perennial sun-flower (certainly the one with the best foliage), and one that I would recommend most strongly for the South and Midwest.

Habitat: From Nebraska to Oklahoma and Missouri and in eastern Colorado.
Hardiness: USDA Zones 4–8.
Garden site: Full sun. In shade, the plants stretch and fall over on the first
    windy day.
Garden maintenance: Cut back at least once before late June.

Other species for the garden
At least a dozen other species, for sale on the Internet and through mail-order firms, may be appropriate for your locale. Here are a few that have merit.

Helianthus hirsutus (woodland sunflower) is worth a try because it tolerates partially shaded sites better than most other sunflowers. Stems are hairy and can still be quite tall. Zones 3–8.

Helianthus salicifolius

Helianthus hirsutus

Helianthus mollis (downy sunflower) bears hairy gray-green leaves, and its butter-yellow flowers open in late summer and fall. Although some sources say it is well behaved and moves slowly, I am still a little cautious. Zones 4–8.

Helianthus ×*multiflorus* is a well-known cross between *H. annuus* and *H. decapetalus* (thinleaf sunflower), native to central and southeastern United States. Plants are 4–5' tall, with opposite coarse leaves, each 4–5" long. The foliage declines rapidly after flowering in warm, humid gardens, which can become a bit of a problem, at least in the South, but in general these are excellent garden plants, and many good cultivars have been selected. Flowers are always yellow to orange, and may be single or double. Zones 4–8.

Helianthus pauciflorus (*H. rigidus*; stiff sunflower) has a long taproot, which allows it to compete with prairie and meadow grasses. Plants grow 2–3' in height and have rigid stems but few flowers. The ray flowers are yellow; the center, red-purple, seldom yellow. Zones 4–8.

Helianthus simulans (tall narrow-leaved sunflower) is similar to but taller than *H. angustifolius*, up to 8' in height. A good backdrop plant in full sun for those with large garden spaces. Flowers consist of golden rays and a darker disk. Zones 6–9.

Helianthus tomentosus (*H. resinosus*; hairy sunflower) grows 5–7' tall and provides light to golden yellow flowers with a row of bracts behind them that can also be quite ornamental. Useful for cut flowers or in a sunny spot in the garden. Zones 5–9.

Recommended propagation

Seed: The annual forms (*Helianthus annuus, H. argophyllus, H. debilis*) are easily grown from seed; sow in the ground where plants are desired. The perennial forms can be propagated from seed or vegetatively.

Cuttings: Many perennial sunflowers can be rooted from terminal cuttings in the spring or summer.

Division: Tuberous-rooted forms like *Helianthus angustifolius* or *H. mollis* can be separated, but this is not a clean or gentle task.

Etymology

Genus: From the Greek, *helios* ("sun") and *anthos* ("flower").

Specific epithet: angustifolius ("narrow-leaved"); annuus ("annual"); argophyllus ("silvery leaves"); debilis ("weak," "frail"); decapetalus ("with ten petals"); giganteus ("unusually tall or large"); hirsutus ("hairy"); mollis ("soft," "with soft hairs"); occidentalis ("western"); pauciflorus ("few-flowered"); rigidis ("rigid"); salicifolius ("willow-leaved"); simulans ("resembling"), likely referring to its resemblance to *Helianthus angustifolius*; tomentosus ("densely woolly").

Common name: Sunflower is obvious, I hope.

Heliopsis helianthoides subsp. *scabra* 'Goldgreenheart'

Heliopsis helianthoides   oxeye, false sunflower   Asteraceae

This has always been a favorite perennial for the garden, native or not. The stiff stems, the opposite dark green foliage, the flowers, which seem to be a cross between rudbeckias and sunflowers—all are first-rate. Both the dome-shaped disk and the ray flowers are yellow to golden. Excellent for the garden or the meadow.

Two subspecies occur, the most common being subsp. *scabra*, the western form, with coarse leaves a bit like sandpaper and a bushy habit. Subspecies *helianthoides*, the eastern form, has less sandpapery foliage, thinner stems, and a more open habit. Subspecies *scabra* has yielded a number of fine cultivars. The best and most popular is 'Summer Sun', a 2–3' tall plant with large bright yellow flowers. Very heat-tolerant. 'Goldgreenheart' too is interesting, with yellow double flowers surrounding a green center. Catches your eye like a car wreck.

Habitat: subsp. *scabra* is native from North Dakota to southeastern Colorado and Oklahoma, subsp. *helianthoides* from Ontario to Florida and west to Mississippi.
Hardiness: USDA Zones 3–9.
Garden site: Full sun, well-drained soils. Does not like "wet feet."
Garden maintenance: Cut back after flowering if plants start to decline.

Recommended propagation
Seed: The species and many cultivars are best propagated from seed.
Cuttings: Terminal cuttings are effective.

Etymology

Genus: From the Greek, *helios* ("sun") and *opsis* ("resembling"), an allusion to the yellow flower heads.

Specific epithet: *helianthoides* ("resembling *Helianthus*"), *scabra* ("rough").

Common name: The disk resembles the eye of an ox. Hard to believe, I know.

Hepatica	liverwort	Ranunculaceae

Some of my favorite wildflowers reside in this genus, which consists of species from all over the world. *Hepatica acutiloba* (sharp-lobed liverwort) and *H. americana* (round-lobed liverwort) flower after snowmelt or even, in some cases, when what remains of the last $%# winter storm is still on the ground. They both bear light blue to almost white flowers but can sport deep blue flowers as well. The three-lobed leathery leaves differ only in their shape, and while they hang on, they must, in all fairness, be called deciduous. In general, they are far happier in the North than in the South; my zone-7 garden in Athens is about as far south as they wish to travel. If I had not seen what they really should look like, I would be pleased as Punch, but unfortunately, my eyes have seen the glory of hepaticas elsewhere. Who says travel is all good?

Hepatica acutiloba	sharp-lobed liverwort

The lobes are sharp, and the flowers are quite variable, from lightest blue to the occasional pink, and not uncommonly white. Plants flower in very early spring and hang on for two to three weeks, depending on temperatures. The colored parts of

Hepatica acutiloba

the flowers are sepals; beneath the sepals are short-stalked rounded bracts (involucres). The tips of the leaves are pointed. Plants are less than 8" tall, so they must be placed somewhere where they can be seen. Outstanding for moist, shady areas.

Habitat: In wooded areas from Maine to Minnesota and south to Missouri, Alabama and north Georgia.
Hardiness: USDA Zones 3–8.
Garden site: Moist shade is best.
Garden maintenance: Plants seem to respond to a basic pH, so an application of limestone every fall may help garden performance.

Hepatica americana	round-lobed liverwort

A few technical differences occur between the two species, but the easiest way to differentiate this from *Hepatica acutiloba* is simply to look at the tips of the leaves, which are rounded rather than acute. Plants may be a little smaller, and the flowers tend toward darker shades of blue.

Habitat: In wooded areas from Nova Scotia to Manitoba, south to Missouri and down to north Florida.
Hardiness: USDA Zones 3–8.
Garden site: Moist, dappled to full shade. Lime does not appear to enhance garden performance.
Garden maintenance: None.

Recommended propagation
Seed: Seeds should be sown in the spring and placed in a cold frame or other protected area until the following spring.
Division: Can be done in early spring if necessary, but don't mess up a good clump.

Etymology
Genus: From the Greek, *hepar* ("liver").
Specific epithet: *acutiloba* ("sharply pointed lobes"); *americana* ("of America").
Common name: *wort* translates as "supposed medicinal use for." It was believed (according to the 17th-century Doctrine of Signatures) that because the color and shape of the leaves resembled the liver, plants were good for ailments of that organ. Didn't work worth a flip.

Hepatica americana

Heuchera   alumroot   **Saxifragaceae**

The alumroots have been bred to within an inch of their lives, and most of the dark-leaved or spectacularly flowering hybrids have been crossed to such a degree that species delineation is blurred. This is not a concern for most gardeners, but for native plant enthusiasts—well, the line must be drawn somewhere. Many native alumroots originate in the West; these are generally represented in gardens by hybrids and are seldom used themselves. All but *Heuchera sanguinea* (coral bells) are grown for the foliage, although hybrids with both deep bronze leaves and striking red or pink flowers have recently been developed.

In general, full to partial shade is tolerated, and plants are quite adaptable to dry conditions. This is not to say they are at their best in drought, simply that they survive drought situations well.

Heuchera americana   **American alumroot**

This wonderful variable species ranges over a wide territory and has stood the test of time and the test of gardeners without hybridization. The foliage is held in a basal rosette and consists of rounded to triangular leaves, with broad rounded teeth; leaves are generally light green with veins of white, silver, or purple. The flowering stem arises in early spring and is usually leafless. The flowers are not for the gardener who is looking for flashy color; they are small, subtle, and light chartreuse. The stamens are the most obvious part of the flower, protruding visibly beyond it.

'Green Spice' is among the several fine cultivars introduced in the last decade. Plants bear silvery green leaves interwoven with purple veins; the margins are a little deeper green. This is very close to both 'Eco-Improved', from Don Jacobs of Eco Gardens, Decatur, Georgia, and to 'Dale's Strain', named for Dale Hendricks of North Creek Nurseries in Pennsylvania, which has even darker venation (a good bit of variability exists with this selection, thus the term "strain").

This species, along with burgundy-colored forms of *Heuchera villosa* and the western *H. micrantha*, has yielded a dizzying display of bronze- to purple-leaved hybrids. In general, the flowers are similar to those of American alumroot and not particularly memorable. There are too many to describe here, but a few of my favorites are 'Amethyst Mist', 'Can Can', 'Chocolate Ruffles', 'Chocolate Veil', 'Obsidian', 'Velvet Night', and the plant that started it all, 'Palace Purple'. Chartreuse and tan-colored leaves can be found on 'Amber Waves', 'Crème Brûlée', and 'Lime Rickey'. May the choices never end!

Additional cultivars, incorporating *Heuchera sanguinea* as a parent, sport excellent red to pink flowers over handsome bronzey foliage; these hybrids include 'Cherries Jubilee', 'Hollywood', 'Sunset', and 'Tango'.

Heuchera americana 'Dale's Strain'

Heuchera 'Chocolate Veil'

Habitat: In woods from Connecticut to Ontario and Michigan, south through Kansas to Arkansas and east to Alabama and Georgia.
Hardiness: USDA Zones 3–8.
Garden site: Shaded area with consistent moisture.
Garden maintenance: None, unless you wish to remove the spent flowers, which is not necessary.

Heuchera 'Sunset'

Heuchera sanguinea   coral bells

Although coral bells are among the Top Ten in perennial popularity, this southwestern species hardly registers with gardeners. When it is grown, it is for the bell-shaped bright red to crimson flowers, in which the petals and stamens are shorter than the sepals; the leaves are kidney-shaped to rounded, heart-shaped at the base and usually serrated as well. While the species is handsome enough, it has been like a racehorse put out to stud, and studly it has been. As with other heucheras, purity of species is not a high priority in the breeding and retailing of coral bells, and cultivars by the dozens have come from this stable.

The most common forms, 'Alba' (white flowers), 'Rosea' (rose-pink flowers), and 'Splendens' (rich red flowers), are generally listed as selections. The rest are hybrids with *Heuchera americana* (*H.* ×*brizoides*), *H. micrantha*, and perhaps *H. cylindrica*. These mixes added vigor and cold hardiness to a relatively weak and short-lived plant, and the resulting hybrids are better garden plants than the species. Still, those grown primarily for the brilliance of their flowers rather than

Heuchera sanguinea 'Alba'

their foliage retain a good percentage of *H. sanguinea* in their DNA, including many with fine rose to red flowers, such as 'Canyon Pink', 'Firefly', 'Fireglow', 'Huntsman', and 'Oakington Jewel'. White flowers can be found on 'June Bride' and 'White Cloud'.

Heuchera sanguinea 'Rosea'

'Raspberry Regal', a terrific cut flower form, grows to 3' in height.

'Snow Angel', with creamy white marbled leaves, brightens shady gardens; spikes of pinkish red bells rise above the variegated foliage in early spring. Better for drier areas of the country. A winner in 2003 from the Plant Select program, administered by the Denver Botanic Gardens and Colorado State University.

'Vesuvius' is fabulous, with the best combination of purple leaves and colorful flowers.

Habitat: In rocky outcrops at high altitudes in Arizona and New Mexico, running into Mexico.
Hardiness: USDA Zones 6–9 for species, 4–7 for hybrids.
Garden site: Partial shade and consistent moisture. Avoid afternoon sun.

Heuchera
'Vesuvius'

Garden maintenance: Heucheras have a tendency to "heave" in the winter, that is, lift themselves out of the soil; this leaves an exposed crown, which often results in a short-lived plant. I replace soil around the crown in early spring, which seems to increase longevity.

Heuchera villosa   hairy alumroot

Although variability is common in this species, it easy to distinguish from others. First of all the leaves are deeply lobed and light green, and have sharply pointed, rather than rounded, lobes. Petioles and flower stems are hairy, as are the leaves themselves, but less so. Lastly, the white flowers appear significantly later than other alumroots, sometimes not until late summer and fall.

'Autumn Bride', which has enjoyed a good deal of popularity, has large light green leaves and white flowers in late summer and fall. The excessively fuzzy leaves suggest it may be a selection of var. *macrorrhiza*. I have not had much luck with this plant in the Horticulture Gardens in Athens, where the hot and humid days make the plants languish during the summer. People at the Aldridge Gardens in Birmingham, however, say it is terrific. Must be me.

'Purpurea' is the prettiest of the forms of hairy alumroot, having wonderful purple foliage. The petioles are hairy, but the leaves much less so than 'Autumn Bride'. Ditto on the heat and humidity, though—but boy, where it is beautiful, it really shines.

Habitat: On wooded slopes and rock outcrops from Virginia to Missouri and south to Arkansas, Alabama and Georgia.
Hardiness: USDA Zones 6–9.

Heuchera villosa

Heuchera villosa 'Autumn Bride'

Heuchera villosa 'Purpurea'

Heuchera micrantha

Garden site: Partial shade, morning sun is fine, but full afternoon sun causes tired-looking foliage by early summer.

Garden maintenance: Choose the site well and provide consistent moisture.

Other species for the garden

Heuchera micrantha (small-flowered alumroot) is native to the West Coast and bears leaf blades that are longer than wide and shallowly lobed. The flowers are held on a long flower stem, and if the plant is well grown, numerous stems will be produced, making a fine show. The off-white petals are twice as long as the sepals, and while they make a reasonable display, in most gardens, particularly those in the East, they are not going to take anyone's breath away. The plant is a fine, subtle addition to the shaded garden, however, and has been an important parent of the hybrids.

Heuchera richardsonii (Richardson's alumroot) has three to four basal leaves, much like those of geranium; about ten to twenty yellowish to purple flowers, which essentially remain closed, occur on the flower stem. Hardy to zone 3—plants may be a better choice than *H. americana* for northern and midwestern gardeners.

Recommended propagation

Seed: Collect the black seeds, and sow after four to six weeks of cold stratification at 40F.

Division: Divide clump in early spring or early fall.

Etymology

Genus: For Johann Heinrich von Heucher (1677–1747), a professor of medicine at Wittenberg, Germany.

Specific epithet: *americana* ("of America"); *micrantha* ("small-flowered"); *richardsonii* for its discoverer, Sir John Richardson, a naturalist and explorer from Scotland; *sanguinea* ("blood-red"); *villosa* ("covered with soft hairs").

Common name: Alumroot suggests its healing, astringent properties; coral bells describes the flowers.

Hibiscus	mallow	Malvaceae

Like orchids and bougainvillea, hibiscus can transport us to an exotic tropical world—hammocks on the beach, palms swaying in the breeze, all that. Ah. In America, you can also find heavenly blooms, but your feet may be mired in a swamp rather than the white sands of Pago Pago. Some of our most wonderful species are called swamp hibiscus and swamp rose. Who says swamps can't be beautiful? The hybridization of ornamental hibiscus has utilized our native forms, mainly *Hibiscus moscheutos* (rose-mallow), resulting in incredible dinner-plate flowers for the garden.

Members of the genus are easy to identify: just look for a column in the middle of the flower, consisting of both male and female floral parts. The column is obvious, often sticking far out of the five-petaled flower. In general, small bracts (the epicalyx) may be found beneath the green sepals. The shape, number, and size of the bracts are helpful in distinguishing between members of the mallow family. Most hibiscus, whether species or hybrids, are large and require ample space to be at their best. All are quite slow to start growing in the spring—a little patience is a must for hibiscus lovers. Unfortunately, as much as we love them, so do the Japanese beetles. If these voracious pests are part of the garden landscape, be wary of planting too many members of this family. Even Japanese beetles need to eat, but you don't need to be providing the food.

Hibiscus coccineus	swamp hibiscus

Always a favorite among native plant enthusiasts, and a favorite among gardeners who do not need to have the biggest and the newest. Not that this plant is a shrinking violet: it generally grows 4–6' tall and sports five-petaled scarlet

Hibiscus coccineus

flowers 4–6" across. The fruit that follows is also reasonably ornamental and persists late into the year. Three to five unbranched stems arise from the base of the plant, and unless it is pruned at about 2' high, it will not branch out. The leaves are deeply divided and handsome in their own right, but, oh those flowers. Most of us put a plant or two in the middle or back of the garden, but not too far away, otherwise we won't enjoy the bees, the butterflies, and the hummingbirds that are constantly visiting. The upright nonbranching habit also makes this a useful see-through plant, so putting it in the front is not as bad as it sounds. The common name reflects its native habitat. If you have a wet area, this is a keeper; however, plants do not need a swamp to do well.

Habitat: In swamps near the coast of Florida to Alabama and Georgia.
Hardiness: USDA Zones 6–9.
Garden site: Full sun. If a wet area is available, this is a no-brainer. Soil moisture is useful but not necessary.
Garden maintenance: Plants lose leaves in the fall, and they can easily be cut back at that time or during early spring. Japanese beetles can be a problem.

Hibiscus grandiflorus	velvet mallow

Even though I obtained it from a botanical garden as *Hibiscus lasiocarpus* (hairy hibiscus), I believe (after a fair amount of sleuthing) the plant I am in love with is the velvet mallow, or a hybrid with lots of velvet in its blood. It is one of the finest plants we grow in the Horticulture Gardens at the University of Georgia. Every year plants laden with three-lobed gray-green velvet-hairy leaves draw the attention of passers-by. When I walk people by the plant, I tell them to touch and feel the leaves, and inevitably the comment is "Lamb's ears on a shrub." I mention the leaves because the plant does not flower until late in the season, but it simply does not matter. That is a strong statement when it comes to hibiscus plants, which are known for their large colorful flowers—and leaves only insofar as they are beetle food.

There is nothing wrong with the flowers—they are large, pink, and quite beautiful. Many other plants can boast similar floral beauty, but none have the combination of foliage and floral beauty this plant possesses. Plants grow 4–7' tall in a single season, emerging far more quickly than most other species (they are already 2' tall by the time others are just stirring); and unlike their cousin *Hibiscus coccineus*, they are not see-through plants. If the height is a little unsettling, place it in a large container; the root compression will result in a smaller, more manageable plant. As with many other hibiscus, plants do not branch particularly well. Last, but certainly not least, this species is not as attractive to beetles as are many of the hybrids.

Hibiscus grandiflorus

Habitat: In moist areas from southern Indiana to Missouri south to Texas and east to Florida.

Hardiness: USDA Zones 5–9.

Garden site: Full sun. Moist soils are beneficial, but plants will grow well in "normal" soils.

Garden maintenance: Cut back in late spring to encourage branching or if height is a problem. And even though you can expect relatively little damage from them with this species, be vigilant for Japanese beetles in summer.

Hibiscus laevis　　　halberd-leaved mallow

Another big mallow, this species (formerly known as *Hibiscus militaris*) can grow 8' tall, although 4–6' is more common. The long, almost sharp terminal lobe of the three-lobed upper leaves distinguishes this species from others, and the lack of significant hairs or pubescence is also unusual. The large 5–6" wide flowers are usually white with a dark center, but pale pink flowers are not at all rare; they generally open in summer and fall. An excellent plant for the back of the garden, or even better if a wet area needs a few plants.

Habitat: In wet areas from New York to Nebraska, south to Texas and east to Florida.

Hardiness: USDA Zones 4–8.

Garden site: Full sun, in areas where moisture is either abundant or which can be irrigated.

Garden maintenance: Be wary of Japanese beetles. Cut down to the ground after the first hard frost.

Hibiscus moscheutos 'Disco Pink'

Hibiscus moscheutos 'Old Yella'

Hibiscus moscheutos　　rose-mallow

When I think of rose-mallow, the first thing that comes to mind is how I wonder each spring if they are alive or dead. The horticulturist in me knows they are sufficiently cold hardy, but the gardener remembers the ice storms or the sudden drop in temperature that past February, and cannot help but worry—until the plants finally shuck off their lethargy and poke through the soil when I'm not looking.

The flowers are up to 8" across, usually of a light rose color, and bloom in late summer and fall. The leaves are often three- to five-lobed but can also be ovate to lanceolate in shape; they are green on top, lighter green and hairy beneath. When all is said and done, it is doubtful you will find the species itself when you walk into a box store or even an independent garden center. This is not necessarily a bad thing (unless you are a hard-core native-ite), as breeding and selection have resulted in an incredible diversity of selections and hybrids, all richer than the parents. Sounds like my kids—I hope the same is true for yours.

Hybrids of *Hibiscus moscheutos* were first developed in the early 1900s, often with *H. coccineus*, *H. laevis*, and others featured in the parentage. Many fine hybrids are now easily found; a few of my favorites follow.

'Anne Arundel' grows 4–5' tall with pink flowers. The foliage is more deeply cut than most of the other cultivars.

'Blue River II' bears clear white flowers with no eye, up to 10" across. The deep green foliage bears a hint of blue.

Disco series is still eye-popping. 'Disco Belle', 'Disco Pink', and 'Disco White' are all F_I seed-propagated strains popular for their compact habits and large flowers.

'Kopper King' has handsome pink flowers and dark foliage. Plants can reach 5' in height.

'Lady Baltimore' and 'Lord Baltimore' are old-fashioned but still popular. They form deep pink slightly ruffled flowers with red centers and crimson-red ruffled flowers, respectively. Plants generally grow 4–6' tall.

'Old Yella' is a 3–5' tall shrub whose quite pale yellow flowers have a red throat. Not nearly as yellow as the name implies.

Other species for the garden

Many other species hibiscus can be found with a little effort at home or on the Internet. Don't overlook *Hibiscus lasiocarpus* (hairy hibiscus), at 6' tall with handsome foliage, or *H. palustris* (swamp rose), with wonderful 6" pink flowers. Both are hardy in zones 5–8, sometimes lower if moisture is present around the roots.

Recommended propagation

Seed: If seeds are fresh, they will likely need storage until they ripen. Many people feel stratification benefits germination. Place the seeds between sandpaper and grind them together for about thirty seconds, then soak overnight and sow the next day.

Cuttings: Terminal cuttings root reasonably easily.

Etymology

Genus: From the Greek for "mallow."

Specific epithet: *laevis* ("smooth"), *militaris* ("pertaining to soldiers"), *moscheutos* ("musky").

Common name: A halberd is a 15th- and 16th-century weapon with a steel spike and an ax-like blade mounted on the end of a long shaft; the upper leaves of *Hibiscus laevis* reminded early taxonomists of that shape (this also explains the original name, *H. militaris*).

Hydrastis canadensis	golden seal, yellowroot	Ranunculaceae

The medicinal value of this species, mainly for treating problems with the mucous membranes, has been recognized for centuries. As early as 1905 the U.S. Department of Agriculture drew attention to its wanton harvesting, and this combined with deforestation in the eastern United States resulted in its being officially recognized as an endangered species by the Convention on International Trade in Endangered Species (CITES). I hate to sound so maudlin, so let me quickly mention that plants also make handsome garden additions and can be purchased from reputable nurseries, that is, those who propagate rather than dig. The 1½–2' tall plants are characterized by two deeply five- to seven-lobed, rounded leaves near the top, above which is a green-white flower with no petals, only three sepals. They fall away as soon as the flower opens, and all that remains are the numerous, prominent stamens and pistils. It looks better than I describe it.

Hydrastis canadensis

In the late summer, the dozen or more pistils become dark red berries and look somewhat like raspberries sitting on the top of the leaves; each berry contains one or two shiny black seeds. The fruit are wonderful to the eye but only briefly, as they are often eaten by squirrels and other mucus-impaired critters. The knotty and twisted roots are yellow, and were used as a dye.

Habitat: In woods from Vermont to Minnesota and Nebraska and south to Arkansas, Georgia and Alabama.

Hardiness: USDA Zones 3–6.

Garden site: Moist, cool, shaded areas suit the plant best. Coolness is the key—don't waste money trying to grow plants south of zone 6.

Garden maintenance: Do not allow plants to dry out, especially when first planted. If allowed to dry out, premature dormancy will occur. Plants respond well to light applications of a complete fertilizer in spring and, if conditions are to their liking, will slowly but steadily form colonies.

Recommended propagation

Seed: Use fresh seeds; collect them as the fruit turns red, otherwise the squirrels will beat you to it. Plant the cleaned black seeds in a flat, and protect from marauders. Don't expect anything until the next spring; transplantable size will occur in the second spring.

Division: Only when the colony is well established, carefully divide just as plants are emerging in the spring.

Etymology

Genus: From the Greek *hydor* ("water").

Specific epithet: *canadensis* ("of Canada"), see *Cornus*.

Common name: Golden seal and yellowroot both refer to the color of the rhizome; the "seal" refers to the appearance of the gnarly roots.

Hydrophyllum   **waterleaf**   **Hydrophyllaceae**

I have tried waterleaf in my garden: it is quite lovely one year, then disappears the next. I read that it is easy to grow, but like all wildflowers, it is easy to grow only if the garden environment is close to that of its origins. I am missing something, but if you have a woodland area, it does make a handsome addition, with large maple-like (*Hydrophyllum canadense*) or spotted (*H. virginianum*) leaves. Plants can self-seed, and additional colonies can be established.

Hydrophyllum canadense   **maple-leaved waterleaf**

This species, with by far the biggest leaves of the genus, has an apt common name: plants may actually be confused at first with a maple seedling. Try not to tell anybody you have done this, however, or your reputation as a gardener will be in tatters. The shallowly lobed leaves are occasionally splotched, but often are not. Each lobe terminates in a few sharp points. In early spring, the light blue flowers, which are held in groups (cymes), are usually found below the leaves. Plants make nice colonies where sited properly.

Habitat: In damp woods from Vermont to Ontario and Michigan, south to Missouri and east to Alabama and Georgia.
Hardiness: USDA Zones 4–7.
Garden site: Light shade in a moist area is best, but they tolerate some dryness as well.
Garden maintenance: None, other than occasional irrigation.

Hydrophyllum canadense

Hydrophyllum virginianum   eastern waterleaf

The main difference between this and *Hydrophyllum canadense* is that the leaves are pinnately divided (like a feather) usually into five segments, each leaf bearing obvious white splotches in the spring; these markings fade in the summer. The pale to deep violet flowers are handsome in the spring.

var. *atranthum* is darker flowered but, like all the waterleaves, is difficult to find retail.

Habitat: In moist woods from Quebec to Manitoba and south to Kansas, Arkansas, and east to Alabama.
Hardiness: USDA Zones 3–6.
Garden site: Similar to the previous species.
Garden maintenance: None.

Other species for the garden

Hydrophyllum appendiculatum (woollen breeches) is native to the Midwest and also has maple-like leaves, but they are far more hairy than those of *H. canadense*. Flowers are also pale blue but are held above the leaves, rather than below. All in all, a better garden plant. Zones 3–7.

Other fine species include *Hydrophyllum tenuipes* (Pacific waterleaf), with greenish white flowers, and *H. occidentale* (western waterleaf) with long leaves and bluish flowers, both native to the Northwest. They are worth tracking down for purchase.

Recommended propagation

Seed: Collect seeds as plants begin to decline, and sow immediately. Germination will be erratic, but seedlings should be numerous by the next spring.
Division: Only in the sense that random seedlings can be moved to make additional colonies.

Etymology

Genus: From the Greek, *hydor* ("water") and *phyllum* ("leaf"), noting that the leaves of some species contain a good deal of water.
Specific epithet: *appendiculatum* ("with appendages"), from the tiny reflexed appendages between the sepals; *canadense* ("of Canada"), see *Cornus*; *occidentale* ("western"); *tenuipes* ("narrow stalk"); *virginianum* ("of Virginia").
Common name: Most are straightforward. The woollen part of woollen breeches (*Hydrophyllum appendiculatum*) refers to the densely hairy leaves; not sure about the breeches.

Hymenocallis caroliniana

Hymenocallis caroliniana	spider-lily	Amaryllidaceae

Hymenocallis caroliniana (formerly *H. occidentalis*) is the only available species, but that is all that is needed: this has to be one of the most eye-catching of all bulbs when the flowers are open. Its lack of cold hardiness limits its popularity, but it should be used much more as a garden plant where hardiness is not an issue. Flowers are sweetly fragrant and characterized by the obvious white cup-like structure (the corona, like a daffodil's), from which the stamens arise. Under the corona are six long, narrow, and often twisted perianth (sepals and petals) segments, like the legs of a spider minus two. Up to six flowers occur on the flowering stem. Like other tender bulbs, they can be dug and stored over the winter; containers with bulbs can simply be moved to a frost-free area.

Habitat: In bogs, meadows, and streams from Florida to Louisiana and north to Missouri, Kentucky and Georgia.

Hardiness: USDA Zones 7–10.

Garden site: A sunny site is best. Moisture is useful but plants do well in "normal" soils.

Garden maintenance: None, except winter protection. They are frost-tender.

Recommended propagation

Seed: Easy from seed, but expect three years before bulbs are mature enough to flower.

Division: Any offsets that occur can be lifted and transplanted.

Etymology

Genus: From the Greek, *hymen* ("membrane") and *kallos* ("beautiful"), in reference to the corona.

227

Specific epithet: *caroliniana* ("of the Carolinas").

Common name: The spidery appearance can be traced to both the long stamens and the thin, elongated perianth segments.

Hypoxis hirsuta	yellow star grass	Amaryllidaceae

I think this is a neat plant, one which has only recently been discovered by growers. Unfortunately, it is small in stature, sometimes getting lost among other plants, and the leaves are kind of grassy—not exactly endearing to most gardeners. If we are honest, however, it merely joins the dozens of plants that turn people on because of their cuteness, not their eye-power. Given its diminutive size, it is hard to believe this species is so closely related to spider lilies and atamasco lilies.

Plants are only 4–9" tall and produce two to four flowers, on and off, on long stems much of the summer. The narrow hairy leaves are usually 12–15" (but can be up to 24") in length. The flowers are made up of six brilliant yellow tepals (three sepals and three petals). Plants self-seed as well as produce offsets from the bulb-like corm, eventually producing nice-sized colonies if left undisturbed. They are excellent for small areas, like rock gardens or small containers. Again, nothing to call home about, but a fun plant nevertheless.

Habitat: In open woodlands from Maine to Manitoba, south to Texas and Florida.

Hardiness: USDA Zones 3–9.

Garden site: Full sun to partial shade, good drainage.

Garden maintenance: None.

Hypoxis hirsuta

Recommended propagation

Seed: Fresh seeds should be sown and stratified (cool, moist treatment) for eight
to ten weeks in a cold frame or cooler. Plants take two to three years to flower.
Division: Divide corms when the colony reaches an adequate size.

Etymology

Genus: From the Greek, *hypo* ("under") and *oxys* ("sharp")—an old name that
was transferred to the genus. It makes no sense at all.
Specific epithet: *hirsuta* ("hairy").
Common name: The flowers are shaped like stars.

| *Impatiens* | jewelweed, touch-me-not | Balsaminaceae |

I often mention this genus to those who believe that only exotic species become
invasive. That it is one of our own allows some to overlook its wandering
tendencies. The bedding and New Guinea impatiens of gardens have arisen from
tropical countries, but our two native species are more at home in colder climates.
Great drifts of these "weeds" can be found in the northern states and Canadian
provinces wherever moisture and shade are abundant. They are still annuals in that
they don't survive the cold; however, their boisterous and plentiful seed dispersal
ensures that plants will return. They are useless as garden plants in the South.

The question that should be asked is this: are native impatiens good garden
plants? Their aggressive nature says no, unless a shady stream bank or boggy
area is available. They are handsome in leaf and flower and tolerate more sun
than given credit for. They thrive in deep shade, but flowering will be minimal.
On the other hand, having your own pharmacy nearby may be a blessing: rubbing the leaves of impatiens on affected areas is said to reduce the itching
caused by poison ivy (it apparently counteracts the chemicals that cause irrita-
tion), and a poultice from the plant is a folk remedy for bruises, burns, cuts,
eczema, insect bites, sores, sprains, warts, and ringworm.

| *Impatiens capensis* | jewelweed |

This is probably the most common species, providing 3–4' tall plants with orange
flowers, often with reddish brown markings. Several color forms may appear in
the same seed-propagated colony. Flowers occur throughout the season. In the
garden, cutting them back in early spring and again about two to three weeks
later makes for better-behaved plants, but they are still going to be weedy.

Habitat: In damp areas from Newfoundland to Saskatchewan, south to
Oklahoma and east to Alabama and South Carolina.
Hardiness: Annual.

Garden site: Moist shade.

Garden maintenance: Cut back if trying to keep them civilized. Since they
flower throughout the season, it is impossible to deadhead and remove fruit
before it ripens.

Other species for the garden

Impatiens pallida (yellow jewelweed) is a little taller and bears lovely yellow
flowers. Similar in habit, with the same roaming tendencies.

Recommended propagation

Seed: Easy, but best to let Mother Nature do it.

Cuttings: Can be done, but unless a particularly exotic form or color appears,
why?

Division: The seedlings can be spread out, but do not divide plants.

Etymology

Genus: "impatient," an allusion to the violent seed dispersal.

Specific epithet: *capensis* ("of the Cape of Good Hope"), obviously incorrectly
identified. Unfortunately, the International Rules of Nomenclature say the
name cannot be changed to make more sense; *pallida* ("pale").

Common name: The flowers hang from the plant much like a jewel from a
necklace, hence jewelweed; touch-me-not instructs people not to touch the
mature fruit capsule, otherwise, look out! Great fun to disobey.

Iris   **Iridaceae**

The popularity of the iris is as strong as ever, but limiting a garden to native
irises makes no sense at all. With beautiful Siberian, Japanese, Japanese roof,
yellow flag, and bearded irises out there, why would you look only at American
species? I hope, however, that you would not fail to include some of our natives,
as they don't take a backseat to any of those just mentioned.

Gardening with irises allows gardening in all sorts of environments, from
mild Mediterranean climates (Douglas iris, Oregon iris) to sunny wetlands
(Louisiana iris, southern blue flag) to shady woodlands (crested iris) to simple
border gardens. All irises are characterized by three falls (the segments hanging
down or sticking out) and three upright standards (the segments sticking up).
The falls are usually the showier parts, often with yellow or white streaks. The
size, color, and presence or absence of hairs (beard) or raised tissue (crest) on
the falls also help in identifying the species in the garden. All native irises arise
from rhizomes; the bulbous species are native elsewhere. Unfortunately, there
are many more irises in the wild than there are available to the gardener.

Slugs and iris borers are a threat as is mosaic virus, which causes streaking
in leaves. In the fall, cut back all leaves and discard them.

Iris brevicaulis and others   Louisiana iris

Louisiana irises are unique in form and exhibit a broad color range, not least of which are the coppers and reds used in the extensive breeding of this group. The common name was coined by John James Audubon; he used what he referred to as a Louisiana iris in the background of his painting of the Purula Warbler. Most taxonomists believe that five species make up the group of plants we call Louisiana iris; they all belong to the series Hexagonae (Louisiana irises) of sub-section Apogon (beardless irises) of section Spathula (rhizomatous irises). Other familiar types like Japanese, Siberian, and spuria irises belong to different series in the same section and subsection; little cross breeding between the series occurs. Louisiana irises are found in south central Louisiana and the Gulf Coast marsh areas from Texas to Florida. By far the greatest concentration, however, is in the state of Louisiana.

All are tolerant of water; most grow in bogs, but all can also be grown in "normal" soils with reasonable irrigation when needed.

Iris brevicaulis (lamance iris) is not a particularly good garden plant because the flowers tend to lie on the ground or at least be covered by the foliage. The deep blue to purple flowers have yellow markings and are produced on zigzag stems. A decent choice if short plants are desired.

Iris fulva (copper iris), an important parent of many of the hybrids, has to be one of the most beautiful irises in the genus. Striking copper-colored flowers rise up to 5' in height and open so wide as to look like a tabletop. Plants spread rapidly, and a colony of copper iris is a sight to see. Tolerates full sun and moist feet.

I have grown *Iris hexagona* (dixie iris) for many years in the Armitage garden and absolutely love it, though never are the flowers as numerous as I would like. Plants grow 4–5' tall and have handsome dark green leaves and deep violet flowers with yellow markings; huge six-sided pods eventually form, their weight such that they are impossible for the stems to carry. Lack of flowering at home can be attributed to the fact that I have too much shade and not enough water to allow them to thrive. Perhaps this is just as well, as they can become aggressive if conditions are to their liking. The similar but even larger *I. giganticaerulea* is truly a giant, bearing larger flowers (up to 6" across) and stouter plants.

Iris nelsonii (Nelson's iris), another fine garden plant, is similar in color to but more intense than *I. fulva*. It appears to be of hybrid origin, mainly from *I. fulva* and *I. giganticaerulea*. It combines the flower form and color of the former with the vigor and height of the latter. Unfortunately, it is difficult to obtain and is quickly reaching endangered status.

Many selections and hybrids of Louisiana iris are available, and should be used far more—their northern limits may surprise many gardeners (there are Louisiana iris enthusiasts in Rochester, New York). 'Mrs. Ira Nelson' is only one of the dozens of marvelous Louisiana hybrids; all are essentially the result of crosses (natural and man-made) between the different species discussed here.

231

Iris 'Mrs. Ira Nelson'

Iris hexagona

The breeding of hybrids ensures that the species—which are rapidly losing their habitat to expansion and may well be known in the future only as parents—will always be with us.

Habitat: *Iris brevicaulis*, mainly in south Louisiana but also in Arkansas, Missouri, Illinois and Ohio; *I. fulva* occurs in stream beds and marshes mainly in south Louisiana but also in Arkansas, Missouri and Ohio; *I. giganticaerulea* occurs only in coastal Louisiana; *I. hexagona*, swamps and streams in the coastal plain in Florida and South Carolina and Georgia; *I. nelsonii* occurs only in coastal Louisiana.

Hardiness: USDA Zones 5–9, depending on parentage. The Northwest seems to have the most problems with these irises, and it may be too cold in the Northeast. In northern areas, heavy snow cover seems to be essential to their success.

Garden site: Full sun, moist soils. "Normal" irrigation is fine, but performance will not be what it is when plants are provided with abundant water. In these days of water restrictions, choosing a naturally wet area is more sensible than trying to provide sufficient irrigation.

Garden maintenance: Cut back to the ground in the fall, and remove all foliage.

Iris cristata   **crested iris**

One of the finest dwarf irises for the garden, the crested iris thrives in partial shade in the South or nearly full sun in the North. In early spring, the blue and yellow flowers appear from the previous year's growth, and although they seldom knock you over with numbers, they will make you stop and take a second look. Plants are seldom more than 6" tall when in flower, but the leaves will eventually expand to about 1'. They will be lost if interplanted with larger

Iris cristata

species, but when planted on the edge of a path or in a moist, shaded area, they will not be overlooked—in fact, they can take over if conditions are to their liking. Plants spread by aboveground rhizomes, which are easily seen in the spring as they start to grow. They are part of the crested iris group of irises: the crest of tissue is easily visible on their falls.

'Alba', a form with white and yellow flowers, is generally listed as a cultivar. 'Eco Bluebird' bears darker blue blooms and seems to be even more vigorous than the species. 'Edgar Anderson' is light blue; 'Shenandoah Sky' has dark blue flowers; 'Vein Mountain' has blue to violet flowers.

Habitat: In rich woods from Maryland to Missouri and south to Arkansas, Mississippi and Georgia.

Hardiness: USDA Zones 3–8.

Garden site: Partial shade (with about three hours of sun) and rich soil are best.

Garden maintenance: Fertilize in the spring as growth begins. No other work required.

Iris cristata 'Alba'

Iris prismatica   slender blue flag

Where comfortable, this blue flag can naturalize and form large populations. Plants produce flat, almost grass-like leaves and grow only 1½–2' in height. The flowers are violet to blue with yellow markings and are produced on zigzag stems in early summer. The fruit is distinctly three-sided and helps in separating this from other blue flags.

Habitat: Wet areas from New Brunswick, Nova Scotia to Pennsylvania and
  south to North Carolina and Georgia.
Hardiness: USDA Zones 3–7.
Garden site: Full sun to partial shade, moist soils.
Garden maintenance: Maintain moisture. Cut back and remove foliage in the
  fall.

Iris verna   dwarf iris

The dwarf iris is just that, although not really any shorter than the crested iris. The flowers are also lavender to dark blue with yellow markings on the falls, and both flower in early spring. But that is where the similarities end. It is easy to tell the flowers apart because those of *Iris verna* are beardless and crestless, and appear well before the foliage expands; and its leaves are much thicker and deeper green (prettier actually). It is much less of a mover than crested iris, so it is not nearly as popular or available, perhaps because it has more stringent soil requirements than other irises. I consider it handsome but slow.

Iris verna

Habitat: In sandy and peaty places and pine barrens of Maryland to Virginia, south to Mississippi and Florida.

Hardiness: USDA Zones 4–8.

Garden site: Plants need a moist area, and one with no more than four hours of sun. Soils should be rich in organic matter and have a low pH.

Garden maintenance: None.

Iris versicolor   northern blue flag

A lot of blue flag irises are similar to each other, differing in habitat and only minor features. Small differences exist between this species and *Iris virginica*; in fact, they are lumped together by some authors, separated by others. This large northern species does best in wet areas or as a pond plant, and bears long-stemmed blue flowers with yellow markings, often many to a stem. Plants have wide, blue-green foliage that is as handsome as any species; they are vigorous and can easily attain 4' in height. These were very common on stream banks and lakesides, but unfortunately, they are increasingly replaced by *I. pseudacorus* (yellow flag iris), an even more vigorous foreigner.

'Mysterious Monique' has purple and yellow flowers (with that name, it will be a big seller); 'Party Line' and 'Versicle' are 2' tall plants with reddish to purple and white flowers, respectively.

Habitat: Shores, swamps, and wet meadows from Newfoundland to Manitoba, south to Minnesota and east to Virginia.

Hardiness: USDA Zones 4–8.

Garden site: Wet areas, full sun.

Garden maintenance: Maintain moisture. Cut back and remove foliage in the fall.

Iris versicolor

Iris virginica

Iris douglasiana 'Ice Blue'

Iris virginica   southern blue flag

A wonderful garden plant, but this species will grow in 6" of water and needs consistent moisture to be at its best. The light lavender flowers, with yellow markings on the falls, are similar to those of *Iris versicolor* but are carried on shorter, unbranched stems. New growth in the spring is usually tinged with burgundy. Plants can become 3–4' tall, and colonize a wet area in a few years.

Habitat: In shallow water and wet areas from Florida to Texas, and north to Virginia.
Hardiness: USDA Zones 5–9.
Garden site: Full sun, moist soils.
Garden maintenance: Maintain moisture. Cut back and remove foliage in the fall.

Other species for the garden

Nearly every native iris can work in the garden, but finding them can be a chore. Western gardeners do well with *Iris douglasiana* (Douglas iris) and *I. tenax* (Oregon iris) and their cultivars, such as *I. douglasiana* 'Ice Blue'; both these California irises are around 1' tall, with handsome flowers and a clumping habit, but they generally do poorly in hot-and-cold climates. *Iris setosa* is a good choice for far northern gardeners, hardy to at least zone 3. The standards of the violet-blue flowers are so reduced that flowers appear to have only three petals. Plants are 8–12" tall.

Recommended propagation

Seed: The pods of the wetland species can be impressively large, and the seeds are also big. Seeds of the wetland types require a cold period to germinate; seeds of *Iris cristata* and other woodland types need to be sown when fresh.
Division: Division is by far the easiest method of propagation. Best done in early summer.

Iris tenax

Iris setosa

Etymology

Genus: For Iris, the Greek goddess of the rainbow.

Specific epithet: *brevicaulis* ("short-stemmed"); *cristata* ("crested"); *douglasiana* commemorates David Douglas (1798–1834), a Scotsman who introduced many Pacific Coast plants to England; *fulva* ("tawny orange"); *hexagona* ("six-angled"), referring to the fruit; *giganticaerulea* ("giant blue"), perfect for a large plant with blue flowers; *nelsonii* commemorates Ira S. Nelson (1911–1965), an early director of the Society for Louisiana Irises; *prismatica* ("shaped like a prism"), referring to the flat leaves separated by a small angle; *setosa* ("bristly"), likely an allusion to the bristle-like standards; *tenax* ("strong," "tough," "matted"); *verna* ("of the spring"); *versicolor* ("variously colored"); *virginica* ("of Virginia").

Common name: I believe they all make sense.

Isopyrum biternatum	false rue-anemone	Ranunculaceae

I have always been enamored of rue-anemone (*Anemonella*) but was never able to purchase any of its cousin, false rue-anemone, to try in my garden. Of the thirty or so species only *Isopyrum biternatum* is being sold in reasonable numbers. The flowers, flowering time, growth habit, and ideal siting are all similar to those of *Anemonella*, but they can be distinguished with a little effort. *Isopyrum* is usually taller (9–15") and its leaves are alternate up the stem as well as basal, while those of *Anemonella* are basal only. There are differences in fruit as well, *Isopyrum* bearing a follicle, *Anemonella* an achene. Both prefer damp shade, and both go summer-dormant.

False rue-anemone has one- to three-ternate leaves, the last segment being two- to three-lobed. The leaves are much like corydalis and are quite handsome in their own right. White flowers are produced in the early spring. The drier the

Isopyrum biternatum

conditions, the poorer they will do and the faster they will go into dormancy. I have seen wonderful colonies in the Garden in the Woods in Framingham, Massachusetts, which—when compared to my Georgia experience—suggests that plants are better suited for cooler climates.

Some taxonomists have changed the name to *Enemion biternatum*.

Habitat: Ontario to Minnesota, south to Florida and Texas.
Hardiness: USDA Zones 3–7.
Garden site: Shady area with rich, moist soils.
Garden maintenance: None.

Other species for the garden

Isopyrum hallii (*Enemion hallii*) is a Northwest native growing 2' tall. Flowers are white tinged with pink.

Recommended propagation

Seed: As with *Anemonella*.
Division: Divide in early spring as plants emerge.

Etymology

Genus: From the Greek, *isos* ("equal") and *pyros* ("grain"). The fruit somewhat resembles grains of wheat.
Specific epithet: *biternatum* ("twice ternate"), referring to the leaves first being divided into three (ternate), then each of the three segments divided into three again.
Common name: Plants resemble rue-anemone, but are not the real thing.

Jeffersonia diphylla

Jeffersonia diphylla   **twinleaf**   **Berberidaceae**

This is a great plant, although not quite as adaptable as the third president was. In fact, I wish that something bigger, stronger, and stouter were commemorating him. Still, there he sits, wonderfully comfortable in some areas of the country, languishing in others. The 1" wide white flower is useful only because it produces seeds, and even that is amazing when you realize it only stays on the plant for a couple of days and opens in very early spring, when frosts are plentiful and pollinators are not.

It is the leaves that are so fascinating and why people like myself pay extraordinary amounts of money for the plant. Each blue-green leaf looks like it is paired with its identical twin, small when they emerge and enlarging after the plant flowers. The other neat thing about this plant is that you get to watch the lidded seed capsule mature; it slowly opens, sort of like a shy garbage can, finally emptying its cargo of ripening seeds into the cold, cruel world. Ants get to disperse them. I think you have to be there!

Plants tend to grow better in more basic soils, so I add a little crushed limestone (some people place a piece of limestone) at the base. My colony of one is thriving, but I don't think my heat and humidity is doing a lot for the future of Thomas's namesake.

Habitat: In woods from New York and southern Ontario west to Wisconsin
    and Iowa, south to northern Alabama and east to Maryland.
Hardiness: USDA Zones 4–7.
Garden site: Moist but not wet soils, along with shade in the summer.
Garden maintenance: Add dolomitic lime in the fall if soils are acid.

Recommended propagation
Seed: About two years of fluctuating temperatures are needed to establish seedlings. Sow immediately and protect from digging animals. With any luck, seedlings will self-sow.
Division: Very difficult; try it in early fall.

Etymology
Genus: For the third president of the United States.
Specific epithet: *diphylla* ("two leaves").
Common name: One of the more sensible common names out there.

Liatris	blazing star	Asteraceae

From an overlooked weed to a high-class imported cut flower, from an ignored native plant to the backbone of native plant gardens and meadows, liatris has seen it all. Nearly everywhere I go in my travels to find gardens incorporating native plants, gayfeather is just behind purple coneflower and tickseed in popularity. Its purple flower spikes work well in any garden and provide meadows a flick of color that moves the eye past the daisies. Plants persist for years, and gardeners have discovered that the cut stems are perfect for floral arrangements and bouquets. The spikes consist of dozens of small daisy flowers, consisting of disk flowers only, with bracts beneath. They open from the top to the bottom, a most unique deployment. Not long ago, you were lucky to be able to choose between two species; however, the genus is now a darling of native nurseries, and six or seven species are readily available to the gardener. They are sometimes difficult to tell apart; often, you must look at the number of flowers and their density, as well as the bracts beneath the flowers. Flowering occurs in mid summer in the Midwest, earlier in the Southeast. From earliest to latest, expect a sequence of *Liatris spicata*, *L. pycnostachya*, *L. scariosa*, *L. squarrosa*, *L. aspera*, and *L. mucronata*, with a good deal of overlapping. Plants arise from corms, so a good bulb catalog will often be an excellent source.

Liatris scariosa 'White Spires'

Liatris aspera	rough blazing star

This is one of the several "button" types of blazing star, also known as plumose forms. The flowers are rounded and not nearly as dense as *Liatris spicata* or *L. pycnostachya*, appearing as "buttons" on the stem. They are simply a different look, not better or worse; some call them cute. The flowering stem carries from twenty to forty flowers, usually sessile. The bottom leaves have petioles, the upper ones are sessile, and all are somewhat raspy and rough compared to other stiff-leaf forms. Plants can get tall (taller than 3') in rich soils and fall over, making quite a mess in the garden. I really like the button types, and if height is not a problem, then this is a terrific plant.

Habitat: In dry soils from Ontario to North Dakota, south to Texas and east to Florida.
Hardiness: USDA Zones 3–9.
Garden site: Full sun; shade results in even taller plants.
Garden maintenance: None.

Liatris microcephala	small-headed blazing star

As a gardener, it is good to have a choice. As big as plants like *Liatris pycnostachya* and *L. spicata* are, this is the opposite. These dainty plants are only about 2' tall, with small lavender flowers in late summer and fall. They tolerate drought and poor soil and will even grow in a little shade. The leaves are grasslike and disappear once the plant begins to flower. An exceptionally good plant around rocks and in the rock garden—it is an easy plant to love if that is the kind of area you are working with, but it is not something you would choose for a meadow or a mixed garden.

Habitat: Sandstone and dry barren outcrops from Georgia to Alabama to Kentucky and North Carolina.
Hardiness: USDA Zones 5–8.
Garden site: Full sun. Keep away from aggressive plants.
Garden maintenance: None.

Liatris pycnostachya	gayfeather

This is the liatris commonly seen in prairies and meadows of the Midwest, often by the thousands if the area has been left undisturbed. It is similar to *Liatris spicata* but larger in every way. One can tell the two apart by height if they are growing side by side; otherwise, look at the bracts beneath the flowers. In this one, they are pointed (even somewhat sharp to the touch) and reflexed a little; in

Liatris pycnostachya

Liatris pycnostachya

L. spicata, they are round or blunt, often with a purple margin. In the Plains states, in the northeast and Canada, this is the species of choice; however, in warm climates, the plant can simply be too tall for garden settings and ends up falling over or bent around itself like a grotesque purple pretzel. Some people find that enchanting; I like a little more decorum in my gayfeathers. The leaves are narrow and crowded up the stem. If a meadow is in your plans, this is the species that gives the most bang for the buck. If a bit of formality is in the cards, and if temperatures are typically warm for a time, you might want to try some of the others.

Habitat: In prairies and meadows, from Indiana to North Dakota, south to Texas and west to Mississippi.
Hardiness: USDA Zones 3–9.
Garden site: Full sun, consistent moisture is indeed helpful, but not necessary.
Garden maintenance: None.

Liatris spicata Kansas gayfeather

This has long been the most readily available and therefore the most popular species for meadows or gardens. The dozen or more flowers are held densely on the flower stem (it is often called the dense blazing star); when early summer arrives, they make gorgeous rose-purple accents in the garden. While plants can grow up to 4' in height, 2–3' is normal in most gardens. The foliage on this species, as with most others, is grass-like and not particularly memorable. The

Liatris spicata

Liatris spicata 'Kobold'

Liatris spicata
'Floristan
White'

habitat of this species is quite different from the others: it originates from moist areas, whereas all others are prairie species.

A white form, 'Floristan White' (which is just a fancy name for var. *alba*), is also available. 'Kobold', more dwarf than the species, is the most popular garden form.

Habitat: In marshy places from New York to Ontario, west to Wisconsin, and south to the Gulf states.

Hardiness: USDA Zones 3–9.

Garden site: Full sun. Plants tolerate more moisture than others and can be placed in a wet area, although swampy areas are not necessary.

Garden maintenance: None.

Liatris squarrosa	scaly blazing star

Another plumose form of liatris, scaly blazing star produces 2–3' tall plants with up to sixty flowers per stem! The flowers have small stems and are spread along the flower stem, like fuzzy balls on a stick. Often the stems are slightly hairy, and the leaves are rigid and often spotted. A unique plant for the garden.

Habitat: In dry fields from Delaware to South Dakota, south to Texas and east to Florida.

Hardiness: USDA Zones 5–9.

Garden site: Full sun; do not fertilize heavily.

Garden maintenance: None.

Other species for the garden

Many blazing stars are appropriate for the perennial garden and particularly for meadow plantings. All attract butterflies and hummingbirds.

Liatris acidota (sharp blazing star) is more subtle, not as showy or tall (2–3') as some of the others. Flowers are dark lavender. More southerly in provenance, likely hardy in zones 7–9.

Liatris ligulistylis is a big plant, up to 3' tall, with many large purple flowers per stem. Tolerates moist conditions well. Zones 4–8.

Liatris mucronata (narrow-leaf gayfeather, bottlebrush blazing star) produces tight clusters of ½" wide purple flower heads. The plant is about 2½' tall; the leaves are less than ¼" wide. Zones 6–9.

Liatris punctata (dotted blazing star) is native to the western part of the country and needs dry conditions to do well. Plants grow from a deep taproot rather

Liatris ligulistylis

than a corm. Another short plant (1½' tall), it is best in rock gardens or screes, where drainage is sharp. Zones 4–8.

Recommended propagation

Seed: Many species are sold as seed, and this is the easiest way to increase your collection. Sow in trays and place outdoors in a cold frame or other area where cold can be provided. Plants may bloom the next season.

Division: Separate the corms in late fall or winter. Many plants can be purchased as dry corms.

Etymology

Genus: Derivation unknown.

Specific epithet: *acidota*, from *akis* ("a point"), referring to the pointed bracts beneath the flowers; *aspera* ("rough"); *ligulistylis* ("strap-like styles"), the style is quite narrow in this species; *microcephala* ("small headed"); *mucronata* ("pointed"), referring to bracts beneath the flowers; *punctata* ("spotted"), referring to the stem; *pycnostachya*, from the Greek, *pyknos* ("dense") and *stachys* ("ear of grain"), referring to the dense flower spikes; *spicata* ("spike bearing"), *squarrosa* ("with parts spreading or recurved at the ends"), referring to the shape of the bracts.

Common name: Blazing star makes sense when you see hundreds of these plants in the prairie. Gayfeather is also appropriate, as the feather-like flowers in some of the species do make one happy.

Lilium	lily	Liliaceae

Of the hundreds of named lilies offered by bulb specialists, few are native to this country. In fact, few are native to any country: they've been hybridized in greenhouses and labs in the search for the "perfect" lily. Since one man's ceiling is another man's floor, we need not worry about perfection or perception, rather, let's simply find one that works in our own gardens. At least twenty species are native to this country, and if you search hard enough, you might find a handful that can be purchased, mainly from mail-order sources.

All lilies have three petals and three sepals, but because they look alike, they are referred to as tepals. Most of our natives tend to have pendulous flowers with reflexed tepals, and whorled leaves; all with this arrangement of flowers and foliage are known as turk's cap lilies. Cold hardiness is seldom an issue; most bulbs require at least six weeks of cold (about 40F) to produce flowers, thus fall planting is recommended.

Lily beetles can be a problem as can be disease. The most serious disease is lily mosaic virus, which is carried from plant to plant by aphids. Symptoms vary; in general, irregular yellow streaks or mottling appear on the leaves, many of which become twisted and distorted.

Lilium canadense   Canada lily, field lily, meadow lily

When I am asked to recommend the lily I most admire, regardless of provenance or hybridization, this without fail is my answer. Plants rise 4–7' in height and can bear ten to twenty flowers in summer. Since they are stem rooters, they generally are sufficiently strong to stand on their own. The flowers may be yellow, orange, or even red often with dark spots within, although yellow to yellow-orange is most common. The tepals are spread out but not reflexed, resulting in a trumpet shape. The leaves are mostly in whorls.

Perhaps one of the reasons it is tops on my list is that in north Georgia, I cannot grow it. I have searched and found bulbs, I have done all I can, but alas and alack, no luck for me. Plants do not perform well in high summer temperatures (hmm—Canada. Lily. Oh, now I get it). It is beautiful in gardens in the Northeast and absolutely gorgeous in the Gaspé Peninsula of Quebec, where it returns year after year. Bulbs are small and require some protection from moles and voles.

Habitat: In moist, open ground from Quebec to Minnesota, south to Virginia and Alabama.

Hardiness: USDA Zones 3–7.

Garden site: Full sun in a consistently moist area.

Garden maintenance: Be wary of moles and voles; caging the bulbs may be necessary if they are a concern. Aphids can be a problem. Do not allow to dry out, particularly when plants are emerging. Be sure sufficient soil is around the base of the stem to allow stem rooting. Staking will be necessary if temperatures remain high.

Lilium canadense

Lilium michauxii   Carolina lily, Michaux's lily

This beautiful species grows 2–3' tall and bears one to four orange-red nodding flowers, characterized by highly reflexed, spotted tepals and long, extended stamens. Flowering generally occurs in mid to late summer. Plants are stem rooters and can spread through underground stolons. The thick leaves are whorled and are broader in the upper half. An excellent choice for southern gardeners, but they are still more comfortable in the mountains than on the flatlands. Not particularly easy to locate, but worth the effort.

Habitat: In dry woods and open mountain slopes from Virginia and West
   Virginia, south to Louisiana and Florida.
Hardiness: USDA Zones 5–7.
Garden site: Full sun to partial shade.
Garden maintenance: See *Lilium canadense*.

Lilium philadelphicum   wood lily

The wood lily provides showy clusters of one to five erect (reminiscent of the Asian hybrids) blooms in mid summer; flowers are usually reddish orange with many darker spots at the base. The tepals are not attached to each other in a tube, a look so familiar in other lilies, but rather taper at the base into slender legs. The stems are whorled and can grow up to 3' in height, but not usually more than 1½' in gardens. Plants are stoloniferous, and if conditions are to their liking, a nice colony will occur.

Plants may be found over a wide area of the country, but I seldom see them for sale or in gardens. That is changing: several sources now offer nursery-grown bulbs, and I expect more gardeners who enjoy a challenge to try these native lilies.

Habitat: In woods and clearings from Maine to Ontario, south to Maryland,
   Kentucky and east to North Carolina.
Hardiness: USDA Zones 3–8.
Garden site: Full sun, although late afternoon shade will be beneficial. Good
   drainage is essential; however, do not allow to dry out.
Garden maintenance: Remove spent stalk and foliage in the fall.

Lilium superbum   turk's cap lily

To those tireless souls who trek up mountains and through woods in the eastern part of the country, the turk's cap lily is a familiar sight. Plants can tower over their admirers, easily growing 7' and carrying twenty to thirty strongly reflexed

Lilium michiganense

flowers; they are orange with maroon spots and usually with a streak of green at the base. The pistil and red stamens are obvious parts of the bloom, as the retreating tepals seem to want nothing to do with them. The leaves are whorled and scattered about the stem, each leaf bearing three to seven veins. This is one of the easier lilies to find and cultivate. In mid summer, it dominates the garden.

Habitat: In moist meadows and woods from Massachusetts and New York to New Hampshire, south to north Alabama and Georgia.

Hardiness: USDA Zones 4–8.

Garden site: Full sun, in a consistently moist area. Plants tolerate afternoon shade, particularly further south.

Garden maintenance: Remove old stems and foliage in the fall. Irrigate when needed.

Other species for the garden

Lilium columbianum (Oregon lily) and *L. washingtonianum* (shasta lily) are both native to the West Coast and excellent garden subjects, the former growing 2–3' tall with yellow-orange turk's cap flowers, the latter 2–4' tall with fragrant pink to purple flowers. Both require cool nights to do well and can be exquisite for gardeners with cool nights and warm days.

    Lilium michiganense (Michigan lily) is similar to *L. superbum* but bears dark orange flowers earlier than *L. superbum*.

Recommended propagation

Seed: Seed is a useful, but slow, method to increase hard-to-find lilies. Keep collected seeds indoors for three months, then sow and place in a cold area (cold frame, cold greenhouse, refrigerator). Count on germination the first year but an additional three to five years to see a mature plant.

Scales: Remove some scales from the bulb in the fall; plant as a cutting. They will mature twice as fast as seed, but still require two to three years.

Etymology

Genus: From the Latin, similar to the Greek *leiron* ("lily").

Specific epithet: *canadense* ("of Canada"), see *Cornus*; *columbianum* ("of British Columbia or the Columbia River"); *michauxii*, for French botanist André

Michaux (1746–1803), who traveled extensively in the Southeast and wrote about plants he encountered on his journeys; *michiganense* ("of Michigan"); *philadelphicum* ("of Philadelphia"); *superbum* ("superb"); *washingtonianum* ("of Washington State").

Common name: Turk's cap refers to the shape of a special turban worn by sultans of Turkey.

Lobelia   Campanulaceae

What a magnificent group of plants. From the dwarf electric-blue species edging garden beds and clambering out of baskets to the red-flowered monsters of river banks and streams, lobelias are nothing short of spectacular. Of the hundreds of identified species, about a dozen are native to North America, but only two of these are readily available from nurseries and garden centers; however, some excellent hybrids incorporating germplasm from native species are also sold.

All our native species are upright, bearing alternate leaves and long spikes of bright flowers. Three petals make up the lower "lip" of the flower, and two others form the upper lip.

Lobelia cardinalis   cardinal flower

I was asked by an Australian friend if there was one plant that everyone here would rally around as "America's native plant." After all, the Aussies have their eucalyptus, the Kiwis have their pohutukawa—what do we have that everyone

Lobelia cardinalis

knows? The American elm comes to mind, although I doubt that many people could recognize one, and so does the cardinal flower. Hikers and canoeists who see stands of cardinal flower are always amazed at the beauty and eye-popping intensity of color, and usually know it is "theirs."

Plants are short-lived perennials, although if placed in a moist, sunny area, they come back for many years. In the spring, they appear as a dark green rosette of leaves, and push up a flower stalk in early to mid summer. Seeds are abundant, and seedlings will often appear. Plants are found in moist areas, and gardeners often have little luck trying to simulate similar conditions in a garden.

The species itself is usually scarlet, although other hues of red to pink may occur; cultivars go by names like 'Alba' or 'Rosea' or something more creative like "rose-pink over white." They are handsome, grow well, and make a nice change from the scarlet of the species. 'Shrimp Salad', with handsome salmon-pink flowers, appears to be a straight selection of the species, but most cultivars offered are hybrids with *Lobelia siphilitica* (which see) and others.

Habitat: In wet soils along streams, swamps, and wet woods from Quebec to Minnesota, south to Texas and east to Florida.

Hardiness: USDA Zones 2–8.

Garden site: Consistently moist soils are necessary for best performance; even short-term dryness adversely affects growth. Full sun is best in moist soils, but partial shade is tolerated, particularly if soils dry out. Foliar diseases will occur on plants positioned in dry soils and full sun.

Garden maintenance: Maintain moisture. Keep soils mounded up around stem to aid in subsequent plant generations.

Lobelia siphilitica	giant blue lobelia

As with other upright lobelias, plants overwinter as stout rosettes and then, when you turn your back, plants erupt with long stems of alternate lanceolate leaves and dozens of flower buds that open to large blue to violet flowers. The three pointed petals that make up the lower lip are marked with white; the upper petals are teeth-like. Plants are quite beautiful, and relatively easy to grow, tolerating drier areas than their red cousin, *Lobelia cardinalis*.

'Alba' is a white-flowered variety of the species. The many hybrids between giant blue lobelia and cardinal flower are fine plants with excellent performance and good winter hardiness; however, consistent moisture is necessary to perform their best. We can thank North Carolina lobelia guru Thurman Maness for many of these outstanding plants. All are vegetatively propagated.

'Cranberry Crown' is about 2' tall with cranberry flowers; 'Cranberry Crush' is similar in color but at only about 18" tall is better for the front of the garden.

Lobelia siphilitica

Speaking of dwarf forms, try 'Grape Knee-Hi' from plantsman Dan Heims of Terra Nova Nurseries. Plants are only 12–15" tall with purple flowers.

'Pink Flamingo' has rosy pink flowers in mid summer.

'Purple Towers' has dark flowers on 4–5' tall plants and is truly outstanding interplanted among companions with lighter foliage.

'Rose Beacon' grows 2–3' tall and bears bright rosy pink flowers.

'Ruby Slippers' also bears dark, almost ruby-red flowers, on 3' tall plants.

'Wildwood Splendor' produces large lavender flowers.

Several hybrids are also produced from seed, and although I am not sure of the parentage, they seem to be winter hardy to zone 5, perhaps 4. The best is the Compliment series, with flowers in pink, purple, red, and scarlet.

Habitat: In wet areas and moist woods from Maine to Manitoba, south to Texas and east to Alabama and North Carolina.

Hardiness: USDA Zones 3–9.

Garden site: Full sun if consistent moisture can be provided. Plants tolerate "normal" garden sites, but irrigation is highly recommended.

Garden maintenance: If your plants are in dry soil and full sun, watch them for foliar diseases.

Lobelia splendens red lobelia

This fabulous plant (considered by some to be synonymous with *Lobelia fulgens*) has flowers of even a brighter red than those of *L. cardinalis,* and usually with darker, almost wine-colored leaves in the spring and summer. It is fabulous, but its southwestern provenance limits its perenniality, and plants (including

Lobelia ×speciosa

Lobelia ×speciosa 'Bee's Flame'

hybrids with red lobelia as a parent) are short-lived in the garden. A brilliant life to be sure, but alas, a short one. Flowers are generally blood-red, and leaves are longer and more narrow than those of *L. cardinalis*. The species is seldom sold but has been used extensively as a parent for some brilliant hybrids incorporating *L. cardinalis* and *L. siphilitica*. Such hybrids (often listed as *L. ×speciosa*) usually have purplish foliage and often very dark, brilliant red flowers. If winter hardiness is a priority, stay away from lobelias with bronze foliage; the mix of parents has made these hybrids tougher, but cold hardiness is still suspect. And if you know that, then really, so what? Even if they are only annuals, they beat the heck out of marigolds.

Hybrids (*Lobelia ×speciosa*) include 'Bee's Flame', 'Dark Crusader', 'Illumination', 'Queen Victoria', and 'Russian Princess'. All are brilliantly eye-catching, and hardiness may be sufficient, depending on your location.

Habitat: In moist areas in Mexico and Texas.
Hardiness: USDA Zones 7–9.
Garden site: As with other lobelias, moisture is always beneficial. Full sun only
   if a moist area is available, or if irrigation is incorporated.
Garden maintenance: See *Lobelia cardinalis*.

Other species for the garden
Lobelia spicata (spiked lobelia) is occasionally offered by mail-order nurseries. The lobed flowers vary from light blue to almost white and are densely held on

thin flower stalks. They are somewhat orchid-like from a distance. Not a plant to knock your socks off, but a nice touch to the garden nevertheless.

Recommended propagation
Seed: Seed is relatively easy, and many selections and hybrids are available from seed. The seeds are small; sow on the top on the soil mix to be sure they receive light, and place them in a warm area. Plants will germinate readily and can be placed in the garden the first year.

Cuttings: Take one- to two-node terminal cuttings by early summer. Root and plant in the garden in plenty of time for rosettes to be formed before winter.

Division: Sometimes colonies can be divided, but individual plants seldom make sufficient offsets to divide.

Etymology
Genus: For Mathias de l'Obel (1538–1616), a Flemish botanist and physician to James I of England.

Specific epithet: *cardinalis* ("cardinal-red"); *siphilitica*, in reference to its supposed use by American Indians as a cure for syphilis (but no reference appears in 18th- or 19th-century medical texts—wouldn't it be nice if taxonomists found a way to change the name of this secret remedy and leave us poor gardeners with our chrysanthemums and cimicifugas?); *speciosa* ("showy"); *spicata* ("spiked"); *splendens* ("splendid").

Common name: All make sense.

Lupinus	lupine	Fabaceae

North America is one of the world's great epicenters for lupines. Of the 200 or so species, the great majority are native to the continent, with British Columbia, California, Colorado, and Texas being particularly well known for their lupineness. In their native habitats, lupines are generally found in dry, stony soils. Their nitrogen-fixing properties have made them a cover-crop candidate to enhance the soil, but this same ability to adapt to poor soils, coupled with their self-seeding tendencies, has essentially made them weeds in areas of the West Coast, British Isles, New Zealand, and southern Europe, much to the envy of lupine-envious travelers.

Few species have been domesticated, although Texas researchers have been working with *Lupinus texensis* and *L. hartwegii* to make them more garden-friendly. Interestingly, it took Englishman George Russell, a hybridizer from Yorkshire, to popularize lupines. His Russell hybrids (as they are known), first introduced in 1937, resulted mainly from crossing *L. polyphyllus* from the West Coast with Mediterranean and South American species. These became the lupines of choice in horticulture for their many colors and forms—and because growers could easily raise them from seed. They remain the most popular lupines, chiefly because they are still the only lupines available to the main-stream gardener.

Although it is difficult to locate started plants of many lupines, even in the western states (where lupine cultivation is comparatively easy), seed for a surprising number of species is available on the Internet. In the eastern half of the country, where native lupines are few and far between, lupine envy rears up every now and then; but as more gardeners discover the eastern native *Lupinus perennis*, lupines are becoming less of an oddity even in that part of the world. Alas, those who live in warmer areas of the country will never perennialize lupines, but putting them out in the garden in the fall allows for early spring bloom.

Lupinus perennis	sundial lupine, wild lupine

One of the easier lupines to establish in gardens, and one which, if soils are sandy and well-drained, will vigorously reseed. That it is "easier to establish" than many others does not make it a no-brainer, as plants may still succumb to wet feet, heat, and high humidity. The wonderfully fragrant flowers are generally blue to violet, but occasionally color breaks will occur and other hues will appear. The leaves are divided into seven to eleven segments. Do not be surprised if after flowering plants appear to fall apart and die; some will disappear, some will go dormant, but if they are growing well, many seedlings will turn up, often at a fair distance from the mother plants.

Suzy Bales, a good gardening friend and superb garden writer, finds that sundial lupines do wonderfully well in her Long Island garden, where they reseed abundantly in both her wood-chipped paths and the raised beds of her vegetable

Lupinus perennis

garden, where she originally planted them. "Why would anyone struggle with Russell lupines when you can grow these with so little effort?" After seeing her plants, I have become a born-again lupian and am trying sundial lupines in the Horticulture Gardens in Athens, Georgia, as well as my own. Here's hoping.

This species is also the sole host for the Karner blue butterfly. Bill Cullina of the New England Wild Flower Society warns that natural hybridization of the sundial lupine with other species, especially *Lupinus polyphyllus* (Washington lupine), has meant that "the butterfly's food is being hybridized out of existence in some areas." It's particularly tough going on the coast of Maine.

Habitat: In fields and on sandhills from Maine to Minnesota, south to Louisiana and Florida.
Hardiness: USDA Zones 4–7.
Garden site: Full sun in the north, afternoon shade if successful in the South. Good drainage is necessary.
Garden maintenance: Essentially, the climate and garden conditions will determine long term success. Allow plants to reseed and move seedlings early in the spring if necessary.

Lupinus texensis   **Texas bluebonnet**

The official state flower of Texas is *Lupinus subcarnosus*, which is restricted to a small area near the Gulf and may be the least handsome of the bluebonnets. Of the at least four other species of Texas bluebonnets, *L. texensis* is the best known, seen growing as a familiar annual along roadsides and in uncultivated pastures. Plants are 6–18" tall, depending on soil conditions and climate, and produce some of the first prairie wildflowers to appear in the spring. Even if you live in Texas, however, they are not easy to grow and take time to establish. Like all lupines, this bluebonnet requires sandy soil. As lovely as it may be in your garden, don't expect the natural splendor Texas enjoys.

The plants generally have five light green, velvety leaflets and carry as many as fifty fragrant blue flowers per stem. The flower buds have silver silk-like hairs, and the leaf segments are hairy on both sides. The tip of the flower stem is conspicuously white, one of the easiest ways to recognize the plant. The white tips are the signal for bees that the plants are loaded with pollen. After pollination, the tips turn red (this same phenomenon occurs in *Lupinus perennis*).

Habitat: In prairies and open meadows north to Oklahoma, throughout Texas, east to Louisiana and Florida.
Hardiness: Annual.
Garden site: Don't even bother trying these unless you can mimic their natural habitat reasonably closely: full sun and sandy, well-drained soils are best.
Garden maintenance: None—they will do well or die.

Other species for the garden

Lupinus diffusus (Oak Ridge lupine) and *L. villosus* (lady lupine) are unifoliate lupines (that is, they have simple leaves with no leaflets). They occur in sandy areas in the southeastern United States. Flowers are blue to lilac and purple, and leaves are generally quite hairy. Strikingly beautiful, but extremely difficult to establish in the garden and almost impossible to locate in commerce.

Lupinus succulentus (arroyo lupine) is native to California. Plants are deeply rooted and can grow up to 3' tall. More tolerant of heavy soils than other western species. Likely hardy in zones 7–10.

Recommended propagation

Seed: The seed coat needs "sanding" or scarifying before it will germinate. Sow in situ. Allowing mature plants to release their seeds is easier, as winter satisfies the scarification requirement.

Etymology

Genus: From the Latin, *lupus* ("wolf"). Early botanists erroneously believed that plants destroyed the fertility of the soil.

Specific epithet: *diffusus* ("spreading, diffuse"); *perennis* ("perennial"); *succulentus* ("fleshy, juicy"); *texensis* ("of Texas"); *villosus* ("covered with soft hairs").

Common name: *arroyo* means "canyon" in Spanish, a common habitat for the arroyo lupine.

Lysichiton americanum   American skunk cabbage   Araceae

Does anyone really plant skunk cabbage? The very name suggests there may be a reason most sane gardeners stay away from it, but then again, "sane gardeners" may itself be an oxymoron. Susan and I were guests at the Long Island home of Carol Large, and sure enough in the wet areas of her fabulous garden were oodles of these cabbages, as pleasant as could be. True, they do have a musky aroma, but nothing like that of that other skunk cabbage, *Symplocarpus foetidus*, another denizen of the American swamp.

The flowers are typical jack-in-the-pulpit inflorescences, consisting of a green spadix and a large bright yellow spathe (pulpit); they emerge in early spring and can be seen from the next town over. The narrow leaves, somewhat blue-green and 3' long, emerge soon after. These are big plants, and can romp around with gusto. They are sometimes confused with *Lysichiton camtschatcense*, an Asian species, and *Symplocarpus foetidus*, which also reside in boggy areas (and are stinky enough to earn the title of skunk cabbage); however, *L. camtschatcense* has a white spathe, and *S. foetidus* opens its squat purple-spotted flowers even earlier than *L. americanum*.

Habitat: In swampy places from northen California to Alaska and east to Montana.

Lysichiton americanum   *Lysichiton americanum*

Hardiness: USDA Zones 4–7.

Garden site: Full sun. A boggy area that remains wet consistently throughout the year is best. If the site dries out for an extended period of time, plants will go dormant quickly.

Garden maintenance: None. Do you really want to go into a swamp to deadhead?

Recommended propagation

Seed: Seeds mature in the fall, and to collect them means you are a great plantsperson. You probably smell a little, but great nevertheless. The seeds have to be separated from the fruit, which is not an easy or pleasant experience. Plant the seeds, allow them to germinate, and place in a cold area over the winter. They may be ready to plant in about a year after sowing.

Etymology

Genus: From the Greek, *lysis* ("loosening") and *chiton* ("cloak"), referring to the manner in which the spadix falls away from the spathe as the fruits start to mature.

Specific epithet: *americanus* ("of America").

Common name: Skunk cabbage comes from the large cabbage-like leaves, which have a musky odor, as well as to the prominent veins on the underside of the leaves.

Maianthemum canadense   **Canada mayflower**   **Liliaceae**

These low growers cover vast areas of woodland in the north and northeastern part of the country and are a common spring flower in eastern Canada. They resemble dwarf false Solomon's seals (in fact, *Smilacina*, which see, has been taxonomically annexed into this genus by many). Plants are usually evergreen

Maianthemum canadense

Maianthemum canadense, fruit

and colonize the woodland with abandon. Immature plants consist of no more than a single waxy green leaf and far outnumber those in flower. Mature plants consist of a single, long, stalked leaf, which disappears as the thin raceme of clean white flowers begins to extend. On the raceme are two small, clasping, heart-shaped leaves. The flowers have to be viewed up-close-and-personal to be appreciated. The four stamens stick out in all directions, making each flower look like a carnivorous sundew (*Drosera*). The plant reaches no more than 4" (half that height is not uncommon), but don't let its diminutive stature fool you: plants can romp through a shaded garden in no time. The small creeping rhizome moves through the top inch or so of soil, and new plants arise all over the place. If fruits mature before being eaten by birds and other wildlife, they start off a mottled brown and eventually turn dark red.

If a woodland is part of your garden, these plants will perform well, with no maintenance and no complaints. Plants are best in the North and do poorly in warm, humid climates.

Habitat: In moist woods from Labrador to Manitoba south to South Dakota and east to Maryland and the mountains of western North Carolina.
Hardiness: USDA Zones 3–7.
Garden site: A woodland site is best; conditions of dry, hot sun are a waste of time and plants.
Garden maintenance: None.

Other species for the garden
Maianthemum dilatatum (false lily-of-the-valley) is the western equivalent of the eastern form. Leaves and flowers are bigger, but the plant's habit and preferred environment are similar. Native from northern California to British Columbia and Alaska and east to Idaho. Zones 4–7.

Maianthemum dilatatum

Recommended propagation

Seed: Usually the fruit yield three white seeds, which can be sown immediately and planted out in the ground the next spring.

Division: By far the easiest method—get out your shovel.

Etymology

Genus: From the Greek, *maios* ("May") and *anthemon* ("flower").

Specific epithet: *canadense* ("of Canada"), see *Cornus*; *dilatatum* ("spread out").

Common name: Plants look like real lily-of-the-valley (*Convallaria majalis*), hence false lily-of-the-valley. Mayflower makes sense for the obvious reason, although flowers may occur as soon as early April.

Marshallia grandiflora **Barbara's buttons** **Asteraceae**

I have always enjoyed this small member of the daisy family, so I was happy to find that a recent computer search quickly netted several companies that sell nursery-raised plants and others selling seeds. Of the approximately ten species in the genus, this is one worth getting excited about.

Plants may grow up to 3' tall but are generally 12–18" in height. The narrow basal leaves are 4–6" long, and the stem leaves are shorter and sessile. The foliage stays healthy most of the season, particularly if nights are cool; however, while the leaves are pleasant enough, it is the exploding head of mauve to purple flowers at the top of the stems that catches your eye. The flowers consist only of disk flowers, and they look a little like incomplete bachelor's buttons. Cute, but not as showy—lovely, if not stunning. They work well in a shady, moist area but can grow well elsewhere if provided with consistent irrigation.

Habitat: In woodlands and bogs from Pennsylvania to Kentucky and North Carolina.
Hardiness: USDA Zones 5–9.
Garden site: Full sun to partial shade.
Garden maintenance: None.

Recommended propagation
Seed: Easy to germinate at 68–72F.
Division: Can be divided carefully.

Etymology
Genus: For American plant explorer Humphrey Marshall (1722–1801).
Specific epithet: *grandiflora* ("large-flowered").
Common name: The flowers look like buttons, but I need help in tracing Barbara.

Mertensia virginica	Virginia bluebells	Boraginaceae

At least seven species are native to this country, but the only one easily obtainable is *Mertensia virginica*. One of the no-brainers for gardeners who want to show off native plants, Virginia bluebells have it all. They are wonderfully cold hardy: the pink buds emerge in very early spring, often before the smooth light green leaves. As the weather warms up, the pink buds, which are coiled like a helix, open to a cluster of azure-blue flowers in the shape of narrow bells. They flower for weeks, getting further and further away from the leaves. Colonies increase rapidly in size, mainly through seedlings but also through creeping rhizomes.

Nearly all members of the borage family (*Anchuza* and *Pulmonaria* are others) have hairy, almost sandpaper-like leaves and stems. This is an exception, with leaves and stems baby-bottom smooth. Summer dormancy can be a problem; as things heat up, leaves turn yellow and no mantras or prayers can reverse the trend. If the colonies become large, a similarly large hole in the garden will remain. Regardless, this species is a favorite and deservedly so. Plants light up the edges of my garden paths in March and April, and when they go dormant, there are so many other things to look at that they are hardly missed.

var. *alba*, with white flowers, can occasionally be found, but what's the point?

Habitat: In woods and moist meadows from New York to Ontario, west to Minnesota south to Kansas, east to Alabama and South Carolina.
Hardiness: USDA Zones 3–8.
Garden site: Place in partial to heavy shade and where moisture can be provided. They are best in deciduous rather than coniferous shade.
Garden maintenance: None while plants are growing, but they should be sited where other plants can hide the area they leave vacant when they go dor-

Mertensia virginica

Mertensia paniculata

mant. Planting annuals in the freed-up area is an alternative, or if you are lazy like me, simply throw some ornamental mulch over the area.

Other species for the garden
Mertensia paniculata (northern bluebells) is native through most of Canada and dips into the northern states. Plants are about 1' tall and are similar to Virginia bluebells but with broader leaves and smaller flowers.

Recommended propagation
Seed: Sow seed as soon as possible in containers outside. Cold stratification appears to be useful. Plant seedlings in the garden before temperatures warm up, and keep well watered, or they will go into premature dormancy.
Division: Dig roots after dormancy. Cut them apart and allow them to cure for a week or so in an area of dappled shade, so the cut surfaces do not rot.

Etymology
Genus: For Franz Carl Mertens (1764–1831), a professor of botany in Bremen, Germany.
Specific epithet: *paniculata* ("with flowers arranged in panicles"); *virginica* ("of Virginia").
Common name: Bluebells refer to the shape and color of the flowers.

Mitella diphylla	miterwort, bishop's cap	Saxifragaceae

This is much more a functional plant than a beautiful one, serving as a small green ground cover in partial to heavily shaded conditions. At first glance, the 12–18" tall plant is rather boring, consisting of a couple of opposite basal leaves, each in the shape of a maple leaf and with long petioles, and a pair of stalkless leaves on the flowering stem. Even when in flower, which occurs in early to mid

*Mitella
diphylla*

spring, it is easy to walk by without a second look. But if your old body allows you to bend over and really look at the small flowers, you will find them intriguing. The petals are cut at the edge, and the fringed margins give the flowers a true lacy appearance. The fruit is black.

Plants are closely related to the eastern foamflower (*Tiarella*) and the western fringe cup (*Tellima*), both of which see; and all benefit from the same growing conditions. Plants are more at home in the North than in the South.

Habitat: In woods from Quebec to Minnesota and to Missouri, Tennessee and South Carolina.
Hardiness: USDA Zones 3–7.
Garden site: Partially shaded with consistent moisture is best.
Garden maintenance: None.

Recommended propagation
Seed: Seeds can be collected or purchased and may be sown directly in late summer or fall, or sown into seed trays and placed in a cold frame.

Etymology
Genus: From the Greek, *mitra* ("cap"), in reference to the form of the young fruit.
Specific epithet: *diphylla* ("two leaves").
Common name: The two halves of the pistil form a two-beaked pod, resembling the miter or bishop's cap.

Monarda   beebalm   Lamiaceae

Along with tickseeds, coneflowers, whirling butterflies, and gayfeathers, bee-balms have been mainstreamed for years (and no one can deny that creativity is alive and well in the naming of plants!). Plants bear dense whorls of long, narrow flowers, each markedly two-lipped and with two stamens, and surrounded by bracts of white, pink, or light purple. In some species, like *Monarda didyma*, flowers are mainly at the top of the stem, but one or two species produce whorls of flowers up and down the stem. About sixteen annuals and perennials are known, all from North America.

Beebalms have some bad reputations to overcome, mainly their susceptibility to powdery mildew and their tendency to be invasive in garden situations. Let's be fair: not all species and cultivars are equally thug-ish or disease-riddled. And let's not forget that all beebalms are pleasantly fragrant and attract swarms of butterflies and hummingbirds. By the same token, don't believe everything you read, especially when it was written by someone selling plants.

Monarda bartlettii   Bartlett's beebalm

I have grown this species for only three years, but so far nearly everything about it tells me it is a winner. There are few references and fewer sources, but as more people try it, both of those will increase. Plants are upright, growing 2½–3' tall, and the magenta to rose-colored flowers somewhat resemble those of *Monarda didyma*.

The plant is quite beautiful and eye-catching in flower, but so are many other beebalms. No, the reasons I so enjoy this plant are that I have seen little mildew on it (other than on the lower leaves after flowering), and it has remained a clump, getting bigger each year but not roaming with anywhere near the vigor of *Monarda didyma* and its cultivars. I no longer plant *M. didyma*, knowing that in two years I will be removing great quantities of it, but I actually divide this species and give it to friends, with nary a guilty thought. It's one drawback may be its relative lack of hardiness, probably growing only to zone 7.

Monarda bartlettii

Habitat: Southwestern United States.

Hardiness: USDA Zones (6)7–9.

Garden site: Plants do well in full sun.

Garden maintenance: Although I sing its praises, it is still a beebalm. Watch for mildew and aggressiveness.

Monarda citriodora　　　　lemon beebalm

It is easy to distinguish this species from *Monarda didyma*. Its whorls of flowers are much further apart, resulting in obvious groupings on the flowering stem, not just at the top. The bracts around the flowers have many soft hairs (in fact, the whole stem is hairy) and are tapered to long, sharp points. The flowers are usually pink, occasionally white, and dotted with purple. Finally, these plants are far less cold hardy, perhaps returning in zone 7.

Habitat: In prairies and plains from Missouri to Nebraska and south to New Mexico, Texas and Alabama.

Hardiness: USDA Zones (7)8–10.

Garden site: Plants do well in full sun but may flower longer with afternoon shade.

Garden maintenance: Susceptible to mildew, but less so than *Monarda didyma*. Plants will reseed; flowers should be removed before fruit occurs if seedlings are not wanted.

Monarda citriodora

Monarda didyma
common beebalm, Oswego tea

This is the species that all the fuss is about. Although gardeners grouse about the plant, it is nothing if not beautiful. The scarlet flowers, which are densely arranged at the top of the flowering stems, are favorites of hummingbirds and butterflies. In the wild, plants grow 1–2' tall and are often seen in partially shaded conditions. Seldom is disease a problem in the wild, but this species has earned an awful reputation for fungal diseases when domesticated. Perhaps, as with garden phlox, the intense breeding for additional colors and sizes has reduced its natural resistance to disease.

Monarda didyma 'Croftway Pink' and *M. d.* 'Raspberry Wine' with rudbeckias

I love common beebalm for its sagey fragrant leaves and its prolific flowering in summer. I have seen colonies with intense colors that simply draw me to them like a magnet: in the wonderful Music Garden on the shore of Lake Ontario in Toronto, both dwarf and taller cultivars easily compete for attention with coneflowers and grasses. What I don't love, however, is the romping tendency of the plants. A single innocently planted pot can quickly morph into an aggressive colony, hurdling whatever is in its path. While that is not what I want in my garden, they may be perfect for a filler in an area that can handle such fluidity.

Many cultivars have been bred, not only for additional flower colors and habit, but also for powdery mildew resistance. I wish I could believe all the claims in the catalogs; even those with the cleanest claims must be tried in your own garden to be believed.

'Adam' bears cerise flowers, is more compact, and withstands dry conditions better than other cultivars.

'Beauty of Cobham' stands about 3' tall with pale pink flowers.

'Blaustrumpf'('Blue Stocking') carries violet-blue blossoms. One of my favorite blues, appears to be robust and more heat- and drought-tolerant than many others.

'Cambridge Scarlet', introduced in the early 1900s, bears flaming scarlet flowers on 3' stems over vigorous plants. Still popular but increasingly superseded by selections that are more mildew-resistant.

'Cherokee', one of several new hybrids bearing Indian names, has rose-pink flowers on 3' stems.

'Comanche' bears darker pink flowers with tan centers.

Monarda didyma 'Petite Delight'

'Croftway Pink', introduced in 1932, is still popular. Plants bear rosy pink flowers that blend quietly into the garden. Not mildew-resistant.

'Gardenview Scarlet', introduced by Henry Ross of Gardenview Park outside Cleveland, Ohio, has for the most part lived up to its highly mildew-resistant reputation; however, monarda is monarda.

'Jacob Cline', from well-respected plantsman Don Cline, is grown by several nurseries who feel it is among the most mildew-resistant of the available cultivars. The flowers are large and deep red.

'Marshall's Delight' is named for former Agriculture Canada breeder Henry M. Marshall. It was developed in Morden, Manitoba, from a cross between 'Cambridge Scarlet' and *M. fistulosa* var. *menthifolia*. Plants bear rich pink flowers on relatively mildew-free plants.

'Melissa' is a pink-flowered selection 3–4' tall.

'Panorama' is a seed-propagated strain of 3' tall plants of mixed colors.

'Petite Delight' is highly popular for its dwarf habit and fine rosy pink flowers.

'Prairie Fire' has lilac-red flowers.

'Prairie Night' is a handsome old (1955) cultivar with rosy red blooms.

'Raspberry Wine' bears clear wine-red flowers over dark green foliage.

'Sioux' is one of the few white-flowered forms available. The flowers are slightly tinged with pink.

'Squaw' is relatively mildew-resistant with deep red flowers.

'Vintage Wine' erupts with many red-purple flowers in mid summer.

'Violet Queen' has deep purple flowers. I have trouble seeing a significant difference between this color and flowers described as lilac-blue or violet-blue ('Blaustrumpf'). Probably just me.

Habitat: In woods and thickets from New York to Michigan and south to the mountains of Tennessee and North Carolina.

Hardiness: USDA Zones 3–8.

Garden site: Plants do well in full sun, but afternoon shade may result in longer flowering times.

Garden maintenance: Cultivars may be highly susceptible to mildew, especially in humid conditions and cool nights; start using fungicides early in the season if mildew is a problem. More than likely, and certainly in warmer climes, daughter clumps will have to be removed unless the garden area can handle them. Removing makes even more sense for disease control: the closer the plants are together, the greater the chance for mildew.

Monarda fistulosa	**wild bergamot**

This common eastern native is usually unbranched, and stems are softly hairy, at least in the upper parts of the plant. Plants are 2–3' tall; the serrated lanceolate leaves are pleasantly scented, and the flowers are generally lilac to pink. The flowers are densely whorled and generally occur only at the terminal of the stems, as in *Monarda didyma*. Plants grow from creeping rhizomes and are clump-formers. They tolerate warm conditions but are cold hardy into the northern states, and appear to be less susceptible to mildew than *M. didyma*.

Habitat: Throughout most of United States, north to Canada and south into Mexico.
Hardiness: USDA Zones 3–8.
Garden site: Full sun.
Garden maintenance: Cut back after flowering. Plants will spread, so be prepared to remove clumps if they become overcrowded.

Other species for the garden
Monarda punctata (spotted horsemint) is tremendously variable; at least six subspecies have been described. In general, the tips of the greenish bracts around the flowers are colored pink to lilac, and the flowers themselves, which occur as whorls at the top as well as beneath the terminal, are somewhat chartreuse with purple dots. If we were still in the '60s, I would say they are groovy. Fortunately, time moves on. The western subspecies are quite hairy; the eastern one, relatively smooth. Whatever the form, they are handsome and worth a try in the garden. Zones 4–8.

Recommended propagation
Seed: Easy enough, although seeds need significant cleaning if you collect them from the plant.
Cuttings: Terminal cuttings are easy to root. Take enough stem so that the bases are not hollow.
Division: Division is the easiest way: dig, move, and get out of the way.

Etymology
Genus: For medical botanist Nicholas Monardes (1493–1588), of Seville, Spain, who in the late 1500s wrote about the flora of America in *Joyfull Newes Out of the Newe Founde Worlde*.
Specific epithet: *citriodora* ("lemon-scented") as in the leaves; *didyma* ("twin," "in pairs"); *fistulosa* ("hollow") as in the stems; *punctata* ("spotted") as in the flowers.

Common name: Beebalm apparently comes from the folk use of the flowers, which, when pounded into a poultice, eased the pain of bee stings.

Bergamot comes from the scent of the foliage, which resembles that of the small, bitter Italian orange, *Citrus aurantium* subsp. *bergamia*, the source of oil of bergamot used in aromatherapy, perfumes, and cosmetics; these citrus plants are grown almost exclusively in southern Italy and are used to flavor Earl Grey tea. Oswego tea was coined by John Bartram (1699–1777), the father of American botany, who discovered Indians and white settlers near Oswego, New York, making tea from the leaves; it became a popular tea substitute in New England following the Boston Tea Party.

Muhlenbergia capillaris	**pink muhly**	**Poaceae**

When I was asked by *Fine Gardening* magazine to name a great ornamental grass for the South, I pored over my extensive knowledge of grasses ("let's see, miscanthus grass—hmm, oh yeah, miscanthus grass—wait, I've got it: miscanthus grass") for about a millisecond before I settled on muhly grass. Not one of the ubiquitous miscanthus grasses could budge me from my choice.

The muhly that has become so popular, for so many good reasons, is *Muhlenbergia capillaris*, although a number of other species are used, mainly in the Far West and Southwest. It is a good thing that nurserypeople discovered it because it is endangered in Connecticut, Maryland, and New Jersey, and in Ohio and Pennsylvania it is extirpated. Leave it to the federal government to choose a word that, no matter how appropriate, sounds like someone spitting.

Plants are handsome if not dramatic in the landscape during the spring and summer. The blue-green needle-like foliage arches over the 2–2½' tall mounds, and while they may not be a topic of conversation, they edge paths nicely and make reasonable displays. In the late summer and early fall, however, the conversation and the drama begin. The flower stalks begin as a light mist; then, within a week, they get fuller and taller, and pinker. A pink-flowering grass does not sound particularly ornamental, but the clouds of color come alive and make whatever they are near fade into the background. As a onesie, it will be ignored. They are much better planted in large drifts of ten to twenty plants; then the clouds of pink become eye-popping. Definitely not a grass to put in the median, as accidents will happen. Some people describe them as purple, others as reddish purple—whatever, they are magnificent. All the muhlies are extraordinarily brilliant when backlit in late afternoon and dusk.

'Regal Mist' is offered, but I have not seen it and so do not know how it differs from the species.

Habitat: In open area from Massachusetts west to Illinois, south to Texas and east to Florida.

Muhlenbergia capillaris

Hardiness: USDA Zones 7–10.

Garden site: Full sun, good drainage. In shade, the plants will be limp and flowering, poor.

Garden maintenance: Some people find that shearing them in the spring to about 8" high makes for stronger plants the next year. Unfortunately, they have been known to make a fine meal for rabbits.

Other species for the garden

Muhlenbergia lindheimeri (Lindheimer's muhly grass) is native to Texas and is the largest member of the family, easily growing to 4' or more. Silvery flower plumes rise above the foliage. 'Autumn Glow' bears cream-yellow to tan flowers.

Muhlenbergia rigens (stiff muhly grass) is occasionally offered by specialists, particularly nurseries in the Southwest. The gray-green foliage grows on 18" tall plants, which produce stiff silvery flower heads above the mounds. In groups, they are handsome but not nearly as ornamental as pink muhly; but they are fast-growing, drought-tolerant, and long-lived. Plants were used for making baskets by the Indians of California.

Recommended propagation

Seed: Plants are propagated from seed.

Division: Muhlies are bunch grasses and don't divide well until they are large enough to cut up without causing damage.

Etymology

Genus: For Henry Muhlenberg (1753–1815), a Lutheran minister and botanist from Pennsylvania.

Specific epithet: *capillaris* ("resembling hair"); *lindheimeri* honors Ferdinand Jacob Lindheimer (1801–1879), a German political exile who botanized in Texas; *rigens* ("rigid," "stiff").

Common name: Straightforward and sensible.

*Nassella
tenuissima*

Nassella tenuissima   **feather grass, silky thread grass**   **Poaceae**

Dummy that I am, I had been admiring this grass for years and never realized it was one of ours. But what else is new? Not only didn't I know it was a native, but I didn't realize it had undergone a name change. I knew it as *Stipa tenuissima*, but I must say, I like the new name for this great plant just fine. Plants are clump growers and will not spread all over the place; they grow no more than 2' tall and produce abundant clouds of silvery flowers that hang gracefully over thin foliage. The flowers are soft and are fun to run your fingers through. This is a terrific plant for containers as well as an exceptional softener for the garden.

Habitat: In open areas in Texas and New Mexico.
Hardiness: USDA Zones 6–10.
Garden site: Full sun to afternoon shade. Good drainage.
Garden maintenance: None.

Recommended propagation
Seed: Plants grow readily from seed.
Division: Can be divided, but they are slow growers.

Etymology
Genus: Perhaps from the Latin, *nassa* ("narrow-necked basket"), referring to the shape of the florets on some species.
Specific epithet: *tenuissima* ("very slender"), referring to the flowers.
Common name: The terms "feather" and "silky thread" refer to the flowers.

Nemophila   Hydrophyllaceae

Two species of these western natives are reasonably easy to find (at least, it is easy to find seeds from specialty seed catalogs). They do well with cool nights, warm days, and lack of rainfall—meaning you will see gorgeous stands in southern California most of the year, but in much of the country (such as in my garden in Athens), they excite everyone for about a month in early spring, then kick their legs up and roll over dead. But what a great month it is!

Nemophila maculata   five spot

I love this plant in flower, and the long leaves, with their many lobes, are in themselves quite handsome. Each of the five white petals bears a black spot, thus accounting for its common name. Plants are lanky, about 9" tall, but beautiful when the 1–2" wide flowers are in their prime. Unfortunately their prime time is short indeed in most of the country. Remember that month, and buy some seeds for next year.

Habitat: On the western slopes of the Sierra Nevada.
Hardiness: USDA Zones 8–11.
Garden site: Full sun in the North. Partial shade will prolong longevity.
Garden maintenance: None. Remove when dead.

Nemophila maculata

Nemophila menziesii

Nemophila menziesii 'Occulata'

Nemophila menziesii baby blue eyes

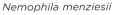

The 9–12" tall plants in bloom are knock-you-out beautiful, bearing baby-blue chalice-shaped flowers with white centers. The leaves are divided into nine to eleven toothed segments and can be almost covered by flowers in the spring. Great in northern and far western climes.

'Occulata' has very pale, almost white flowers with a dark purple center that stretches the sense of the word.

Habitat: In the Coast Ranges and foothills of the Sierra Nevada.
Hardiness: USDA Zones 8–11.
Garden site: Full sun in the North. Partial shade will prolong longevity.
Garden maintenance: None. Remove when dead.

Recommended propagation
Seed: Plants are easily raised from seed.
Cuttings: Two- to three-node cuttings may be taken in late spring.

Etymology
Genus: From the Greek, *nemos* ("wooded pasture," "glade") and *phileo* ("to love"), in reference to the habitat of some species.
Specific epithet: *maculata* ("spotted"); *menziesii*, for Scottish naval surgeon and botanist Archibald Menzies (1754–1842), who accompanied Vancouver on his voyage of Pacific exploration from 1790 to 1795.
Common name: Both refer to the flowers.

Oenothera	**evening primrose, sundrops**	**Onagraceae**

Flowers of *Oenothera* consist of four colorful petals and four sepals, which are pushed down from the flower when they open. Most species are native to this country, but many are simply weeds or thugs, with an "I dare you to plant me" attitude and—regardless of their origin—are not often welcome in the garden. Some species (*O. speciosa*, for one) are seductively beautiful, and for the first year or so, true love exists. Then, like a bad movie sequel, they are everywhere, and love quickly goes south. But a few species are more or less civilized and should be invited in from the wild. I find it interesting that many native plant nurseries offer only one or two, but perennial plant growers offer many more. Now there's a switch.

Oenothera caespitosa	**tufted evening primrose**

Not as common or as easily located in nurseries as some of the other species, these are nonetheless truly lovely plants with handsome silvery foliage, only about 8" tall and 12" wide. They bear beautiful white flowers, 3" wide, which fade to pink, and stay open but one day; the flowers bloom in the evening but are at their best in early morning (getting the worm is not the only reason to be an early bird). But don't let the small stature fool you: these plants have a big heart and possible nomadic tendencies. They are more of a menace in cool climes than warm; some people in the East do not find them particularly aggressive, but gardeners in the North and West see them move with lightning speed. Judging by the comments at www.em.ca/garden/home.html ("Who would imagine such a harmless-looking little plant could be such a monster?"), it sounds like lousy soil and containers are the key to success in Saskatchewan.

Habitat: From the prairies of Canada, east to North Dakota, west to the Pacific Coast and as far south as Texas.
Hardiness: USDA Zones 4–7.
Garden site: Full sun.
Garden maintenance: None, but see comments on *Oenothera speciosa*. Do not fertilize.

Oenothera fruticosa	**common sundrops**

This is among the most frequently seen sundrops in gardens around the world, mainly because plants are handsome and flowers are open during the day. The bright yellow flowers, which are often toothed, are held in clusters and are about 1½–2" across. The seed capsule is shaped like a club at the top and tapers to a

Oenothera fruticosa subsp. *glauca* 'Sonnenwende'

slender stalk, helping to distinguish this species from others. The species itself is not often offered, but its many cultivars are well worth trying in the sunny garden. But beware: although plants are not as quickly aggressive as *Oenothera speciosa*, they will run over time.

'Erica Robin' produces bright yellow flowers on willowy stems. The leaves often bear red spots.

'Fyrverkeri' ('Fireworks') is about 18" tall with red stems and buds that open to bright yellow flowers. Quite excellent.

subsp. *glauca* (at one time called *Oenothera tetragona* and *O. youngii*) differs by having broader, grayer leaves and smoother stems and leaves than the species. Many cultivars belong under this subspecies, including 'Sonnenwende' ('Solstice'), which is 18–24" tall with yellow flowers in mid summer.

'Hoheslicht' ('Highlight') is only about 1' tall with yellow flowers.

'Lady Brookeborough' bears dozens of bright yellow flowers.

'Yellow River' is 18" tall with 2" wide yellow flowers and mahogany leaves in the fall.

Habitat: From New England to Michigan, south to Missouri and Oklahoma and east to Florida.

Hardiness: USDA Zones 4–8.

Garden site: Full sun, well-drained soils.

Garden maintenance: None. Do not fertilize. If they get too aggressive, they should be passed over the fence to your neighbor.

Oenothera macrocarpa

Oenothera 'Lemon Silver'

Oenothera macrocarpa   Missouri evening primrose

This species (also known as *Oenothera missouriensis*) stands out from other common forms for its large flowers on relatively small plants. It is a favorite among gardeners because it is colorful and easily available; however; it requires excellent drainage and often succumbs to winter moisture if drainage is not what it ought to be. A great deal of variability occurs in the wild, but most domesticated plants have lanceolate leaves (usually somewhat silvery, in a basal rosette) and seldom grow more than 1' tall. An excellent late spring– and summer-flowering plant, always welcome but seldom long-lived, and best in a sunny rock garden.

'Greencourt Lemon' has gray-green foliage and pale yellow 3" wide flowers.

'Lemon Silver' has handsome silvery leaves and lemon-yellow flowers. Some taxonomists believe this to be a cultivar of *Oenothera macrocarpa* subsp. *fremontii*, which subspecies is treated by still others as a separate species, *O. fremontii*.

Habitat: On rocky hillsides, prairies, and roadsides from Nebraska to
   Oklahoma.
Hardiness: USDA Zones 4–7.
Garden site: Full sun, well-drained areas are essential. Do not fertilize.
Garden maintenance: None.

Oenothera speciosa   showy evening primrose

One of the prettiest wildflowers around, the four-petaled white to pink flowers are perfectly beautiful. The foliage consists of small, deeply toothed, narrow leaves. Plants flower in the spring and summer and move around at their pleasure. A wonderful choice for gardens where aggressive behavior is welcome but a bad choice for your mother's patio. They are fine in meadows where other

Oenothera speciosa

Oenothera speciosa 'Siskiyou'

equally aggressive taxa keep it in check; on the other hand, plants seldom grow more than 1' tall, which can be a problem in the meadow, where taller plants may cast too much shade.

Although the wild species opens white then turns pink, most domesticated plants open pink ('Rosea') and stay that way. The flowers are borne in the axils of the upper leaves, which are almost always smooth and somewhat sharply lobed.

'Siskiyou' has pink flowers and a bit more compact habit. This sometimes appears incorrectly as a selection of *Oenothera berlandieri*.

Habitat: In grasslands from Kansas to Oklahoma.
Hardiness: USDA Zones 5–8.
Garden site: Full sun is vital.
Garden maintenance: None, except its removal when it has eaten up sufficient acreage. Do not fertilize.

Other species for the garden
Oenothera biennis grows 3–6', too tall and rangy for more civilized areas, but its beauty will always earn it a place in the meadow garden.

Oenothera pilosella is a hairy 2' tall plant with lance-like foliage and yellow flowers. The petals are more or less heart-shaped and obviously veined. Hardy to zone 4.

Recommended propagation
Seed: Easy from seed.
Cuttings: Take tip cuttings in the spring or early summer.
Division: The running forms are easily divided any time.

Etymology
Genus: The word is derived from Greek roots that have nothing to do with the plant.
Specific epithet: *berlandieri*, for Belgian botanist J. L. Berlandier, who explored

Oenothera biennis   *Onoclea sensibilis*

Texas and New Mexico; *biennis* ("biennial"); *caespitosa* ("growing in dense clumps"); *fruticosa* ("shrubby," "bushy"); *macrocarpa* ("large-fruited"); *pilosella* ("covered with long soft hairs"); *speciosa* ("showy"); *tetragona* ("four-angled"), referring to the seeds.

Common name: Evening primrose refers to species that open in the late afternoon and evening; sundrops, to those that open during the day. The names are now used interchangeably, no matter the species.

Onoclea sensibilis   **sensitive fern**   **Dryopteridaceae**

A wonderful running fern that can cover garden areas in no time flat. Plants are among the easiest ferns to grow, and if provided with consistently moist conditions and afternoon shade, they will happily gobble ground. This very un-fern-like fern is easily distinguished from most others by the winged leaflets near the top of the frond. The fruit is on its own stalk, and the spore cases are contained in bead-like cases, almost like small brown grapes. When the fern dies back, only these fertile stems remain. The coppery red fiddleheads are massed in the spring, just waiting to explode. Plants are similar to the netted chain fern, *Woodwardia areolata* (which see), and are easily confused.

Habitat: Throughout North America.

Hardiness: USDA Zones 3–8.

Garden site: Shaded area with consistent moisture. The more moisture, as in a swamp, the more sun the plants can tolerate.

Garden maintenance: None, except that plants may need to be thinned out. They can be invasive.

Recommended propagation

Seed: Spores can be sown.

Division: Divide any time—this is the easiest means of propagation.

Etymology

Genus: Derivation unknown.

Specific epithet: *sensibilis* ("sensitive"). Plants are highly sensitive to cold and are among the first plants to go dormant after a mild frost.

Common name: Sensible, I think.

Osmunda   Osmundaceae

Some of the prettiest, largest, and weirdest ferns are found in this genus of about twelve species. They are deeply rooted, grow in moist, shady areas, and are richly hued as they die off in the fall. The spore cases are held either on separate fertile fronds or in the middle of a sterile frond. The three ferns described here are favorites among fern-ites, and all enjoy a wide growing range.

Osmunda cinnamomea   cinnamon fern

One of this country's most beloved ferns, there is little about it that can be improved. Whether it is popping up all over the shaded woodland or in your own garden, it is magnificent. The large fiddleheads are showy, with silver-white hairs that turn a rust color as they unfurl. If you haven't enjoyed the taste of fiddleheads, cinnamon fern is a good one to try. Fiddleheads are up to 8" in length and can be collected in the spring, then steamed or boiled; they are bit like potatoes: you need to add copious amounts of butter or salt to really enjoy them. We used to do this in the Laurentian Mountains in Quebec, where there were so many ferns in glades and woodlands, we never made a dent; however, if you

Osmunda cinnamomea fiddleheads emerging through epimedium

Osmunda cinnamomea

leave those poor heads alone, they become stately light green fronds with pointed leaflets (pinnae), up to 4' tall and 6–12" wide.

Plants form handsome symmetrical clumps and make useful specimens in the garden throughout the season; but perhaps their best time is in the spring, when the spore-carrying stems, which look like cinnamon sticks, are in their glory, splitting the new foliage as they emerge. The basal part of all the stems is covered in cinnamon-brown hairs, which are particularly distinctive in the spring. In the fall, the fronds turn yellow then bronze. These ferns don't run like *Onoclea sensibilis*, so they will never be a nuisance.

Habitat: Newfoundland to Ontario into Wisconsin east to Maine, south to Florida and west to Texas.

Hardiness: USDA Zones 3–8.

Garden site: Part shade in moist soil. If they are constantly wet, they can tolerate much more sun. They are best in the North, and reasonable south of zone 7.

Garden maintenance: Very little maintenance is required, except if they become too numerous and need to be moved. It is a good idea to leave the dead fronds over winter to protect the crown.

Osmunda claytoniana   interrupted fern

The creator of this plant must have been called away in the middle of the job, then forgot he missed a bit—it is that wacky. On the other hand, it could be a poster child for evolution, as no one would create such a plant (would they?). Actually, it is just a fern, and from a distance looks like many others. It is not until you look at some of the longer fronds, where the sterile portion is interrupted by fertile spore cases, that you notice the weirdness. The fertile leaflets are dark brown to almost black in the spring and turn cinnamon-brown when they mature. The top of the interrupted frond consists of blunt leaflets (pinnae), and plants can grow 4–5' tall. In a mature plant, some of the fronds are totally sterile (not interrupted) and distinctly curve outward. Those that are interrupted are more erect and taller. In heavy shade, all fronds may be sterile. Plants have a creeping rootstalk, and where conditions are to their liking, they can quickly fill in an area. In the garden, they are more interesting than beautiful, and of the three species of *Osmunda* discussed here, this

Osmunda claytoniana·

would be my third choice. It is a poor choice for areas with hot summers where night temperatures remain elevated.

Habitat: From Labrador to Ontario and Minnesota south to Arkansas and east to Georgia.
Hardiness: USDA Zones 3–7.
Garden site: Partial shade and moisture.
Garden maintenance: Little, unless plants start roaming too much.

Osmunda regalis	royal fern

Plants are native to much of the world, including North America, but we certainly cannot call dibs on it. When growing well, it is one of the largest (up to 6' tall) and most spectacular of our native plants. I have always admired these plants along stream banks, a spot that suggests one of the necessities for their success is rich and consistently wet soil. The widely spaced leaflets are divided and then are divided again; plants are easily recognized by this locust-tree appearance, a decidedly un-fernlike look. The spore cases are held in fertile leaflets at the terminals of the fronds, which start dark green and mature to a brownish color; this characteristic makes it easily distinguishable from the other species in the genus. In warmer areas, I haven't seen anything that can compare with the likes of those that appear in the United Kingdom or the West Coast of this country—except in Donna Lambert's garden in Athens, Georgia, where the "fern-lady" has wrought her magic once more. They are marvelous there, which allows me to teach it to my students without wandering far from home.

Osmunda regalis

Habitat: Throughout most of the eastern states as far west as Kansas and south into Texas and east to Florida.
Hardiness: USDA Zones 4–7.
Garden site: Consistent moisture, partial shade.
Garden maintenance: None.

Recommended propagation
Seed: Spores can be gathered and sown when they are fresh.
Division: Divide with sharp shovel or chain saw.

Etymology
Genus: Either for the Saxon god Osmunder the Waterman, who hid his family from danger in a clump of these ferns; or for the Scandinavian writer Asmund (c. 1025), who helped prepare the way for the Swedish acceptance of Christianity; or—the one I like best—derivation unknown.
Specific epithet: *cinnamomea* ("like cinnamon"), that is to say, brown; *claytoniana* honors John Clayton (1686–1773), see *Claytonia*; *regalis* ("royal"), in other words, of outstanding merit.
Common name: The fertile leaflets are the color of cinnamon, hence cinnamon fern. Interrupted fern is so called because its brown, fertile leaflets "interrupt" the green, sterile leaflets on the larger fronds. Royal fern is indeed of outstanding merit.

Pachysandra procumbens   Allegheny spurge   Buxaceae

Oh, such a great plant, but the victim of the American mentality of one-stop shopping, instant landscapes, and hurry-up offences. In its natural habitat, this ground cover does its thing in relative obscurity, and time is of little importance. The white flowers are tinged with purple and are quite fragrant, if you can find them. They are held in tight spikes in the leaf axils in an interesting way: the upper flowers of the spike are male (notice the fat stamens), and the lower flowers are female. As intriguing as this might be to at least one-half of one percent of you, plants are best admired for their large blue-green leaves, which are often mottled with white, much more than for their blooms. The new green foliage emerges upright in the spring and remains taller than the old foliage for months, finally settling down later in the season. As the foliage matures, the mottling becomes more obvious.

Unfortunately (or perhaps luckily), the plant will never be adopted by landscapers because it is simply too slow to compete with its Japanese cousin, *Pachysandra terminalis*. But that it is a slow grower is a poor excuse for gardeners to ignore it—not everything needs to be like English ivy. If placed in a shaded area, Allegheny spurge will compete well with other interlopers, but it will not double in size for a few years (one of the best plantings is at the North Carolina

Pachysandra procumbens

Arboretum in Asheville, where the cool nights and warm days result in magnificent stands). Enjoy its beauty (it beats Japanese spurge hands down), and be happy in the knowledge that you won't have to remove it any time soon.

Habitat: In woods from Kentucky to Louisiana and Florida.
Hardiness: USDA Zones 5–9.
Garden site: Shaded, moist areas are best.
Garden maintenance: If plants are evergreen, the foliage probably looks ratty in early spring. I remove the old foliage so I can enjoy the new leaves emerging. Removal (or nonremoval) of the old leaves does not affect the health of the plant.

Recommended propagation

Seed: The ripe seeds will be found where the spikes meet the leaf axils, as that is where the female flowers are located. In mid summer the seeds should be black. They can be sown immediately.
Cuttings: Try to get a leaf with a small amount of root attached, and treat it like a cutting.
Division: If the clump is sufficiently large, divide and transplant.

Etymology

Genus: From the Greek, *pachys* ("thick") and *andros* (to do with stamens); the filaments are thickened.
Specific epithet: *procumbens* ("prostrate").
Common name: This species is native to parts of the Allegheny Mountains, which themselves form the western part of the Appalachians.

Panicum virgatum	switch grass	Poaceae

The grass craze—one of the best to hit gardening in years—goes on and on. While ornamental grasses are not new, the leaders in the grass sweepstakes do change. The miscanthus grasses are still extraordinarily popular, but some of the bloom is off the rose, and other grasses are stepping in. Among the best of the new ornamental players is *Panicum*. Like *Miscanthus*, the genus contains culti-

Panicum virgatum　　　　　　　　　　　　*Panicum virgatum* 'Cloud Nine'

vars with handsome foliage, good winter color, and fine flowers and foliage that work in much of the country.

Of the more than 450 species in the genus, it is quite amazing really to think only one enjoys significant popularity in gardens. *Panicum virgatum* has rather flimsy leaves and open panicles of straw to rosy-colored flowers in late summer and fall. I hate people telling me I have to use a native plant, but I have no problem recommending this one at all, and this is the native grass landscapers and city planners choose when nativity is a must. Numerous selections of it have been released; most have been relatively trouble-free, but not all is perfect: in 2003, Mary Hirshfeld of Cornell Plantations in Ithaca, New York, reported a rust on the blue-leaved variants.

'Cloud Nine' is an outstanding cultivar, sporting bluish foliage that turns a handsome gold in the winter. In the fall, the flowers come out whitish and turn reddish as they mature. Plants are big, growing easily to 8' when in flower, but they stand up well by themselves. I love their haystack look in winter.

'Dallas Blues' is about 5' tall, but it makes an impressive fountain-like display of good blue-green foliage. The flowers are reddish purple. The foliage turns a coppery color in the winter. A nice cultivar, but it can flop badly.

'Haense Herms' is similar to the species but is a little more compact and has a red-orange tint in the fall.

'Heavy Metal' may be the best known of the blue-leaved cultivars. Plants grow upright to about 5' tall when in flower. The opening flowers have a pinkish hue.

'Northwind' is a selection from Northwind Perennial Farm in Wisconsin. Plants are upright and narrow with wide, green foliage and narrow plumes of flowers. The leaves and flower plumes turn a muted golden color in winter.

'Rotbraun' ('Red Bronze') carries rosy plumes of flowers in late summer, and its foliage too turns reddish in the fall.

'Shenandoah' is supposedly the reddest of the group; however, I have yet to be impressed. Some nurseries claim it is as red as bloodgrass (*Imperata*), but

Panicum virgatum 'Dallas Blues'

Panicum virgatum 'Haense Herms' in winter

imperata grass is a dog in 95 percent of the gardens I see it in, so that does little for me. 'Shenandoah' does have a hint of burgundy-red to its foliage, but it is redder in the fall. Plants are only about 4' tall when in flower, and that is a plus.

Habitat: Widely distributed throughout Canada and the United States, except in the coastal states and provinces of the West.
Hardiness: USDA Zones 3–9.
Garden site: Full sun.
Garden maintenance: Self-sowing can be a problem; if so, cut back before seeds occur. In any case, cut back hard in late winter or early spring.

Other species for the garden

Panicum amarum (bitter switch grass) is a beach grass often used for stabilizing dunes. 'Dewey Blue', selected by plantsman Rick Darke of Pennsylvania, is a clump-former with good blue foliage and light beige plumes of flowers in late summer. Plants grow 3–4' in height and are useful for xeric gardens. Zones 3–9.

Recommended propagation

Seed: Species often self-sow, as do some of the selections. Sow seeds in trays and allow to overwinter in a cold frame.
Division: Divide at any time, preferably when the plants are becoming active in the spring.

Etymology

Genus: From the Latin for "millet."
Specific epithet: amarum ("bitter"); *virgatum* ("twiggy").
Common name: The twiggy leaves were used in switches and brooms, hence switch grass.

Parthenium integrifolium
wild quinine, American feverfew
Asteraceae

Parthenium integrifolium

This is truly a wonderful garden plant, and that it is native over a wide range makes it even better. Some people feel this is best suited for the meadow garden, but I have really appreciated it in Ontario (plants are far better performers in northern gardens than in southern) and have seen wonderful clumps in gardens in Kansas and Missouri and in the Native Plant Garden at Georgia Perimeter College.

Plants stand 4–5' tall and form large clumps when they mature. The toothed, coarsely hairy leaves are aromatic, which is a plus, and the white flowers topping the foliage are terrific for three to four weeks in June and July. They are held in large flat-topped clusters up to 10" wide and essentially consist of disks, surrounded by five very tiny ray flowers. The flowers can also be picked and dried for indoor use. A word of caution here: plants have been reported to cause contact dermatitis in sensitive individuals.

Habitat: From New York west to Minnesota, south to Texas and east to Georgia.
Hardiness: USDA Zones 3–7.
Garden site: Full sun.
Garden maintenance: Remove dead flowers to keep plants looking good.

Recommended propagation
Seed: Easily raised by seed.

Etymology
Genus: From the Greek for "maiden," but the significance is unknown.
Specific epithet: *integrifolium* ("with entire or uncut leaves"), which also makes no sense since the leaves are definitely not entire.
Common name: Plants were used as a diuretic by Native Americans and also to reduce fevers, which last helps explain both American feverfew and wild quinine.

| *Penstemon* | beardtongue | Scrophulariaceae |

The United States is awash in native penstemons, although certain regions of the country are more awash than others. Most species are native to cool, moist mountain areas of the West or on hot, dry plains and deserts, but eastern forms, dwarf forms, upright types, and all sorts of colors may be found in the genus. It is easy to get hooked on penstemons, and people in the American Penstemon Society (http://www.biosci.ohio-state.edu/~awolfe/Penstemon/Penstemon.html) are kabobed, bringing in more converts every day.

I see penstemons by the cartload in gardens in Europe and quite a few on the West Coast of this country, but in the Southeast and Northeast, I stumble across only three or four of them. The Midwest and Plains states are leaders in the use of penstemons, but even there, growers and retailers are having a rough go of it. There are about 250 species, many of them ornamental, so I find it difficult to understand our lack of appreciation of this plant group. And I find it even more incomprehensible given the fact that at least 95 percent of them are from America. Just as with other natives like phlox, liatris, and solidago, plants had to go to England and the Continent to become popular and well bred, but in the case of penstemon, only a few have come back home. To be fair, many species are suitable only to very specific garden locales. Drainage is a consideration when gardening with many penstemons; *Penstemon cardinalis*, *P. eatonii*, and *P. palmeri*, for instance, are absolutely stunning but are not recommended for areas that receive more than 18" of rain a year. Most western species abhor wet feet, as I discovered viewing a number of forms in the Phoenix Botanical Garden. The eastern penstemons too are often found on rocky outcrops, underlining their similar need for well-drained soils, but *P. calycosus*, *P. digitalis*, *P. hirsutus*, *P. smallii*, and other eastern species are all more adaptable to heat and humidity than their western cousins, though they may not be as colorful as some of the more xeric forms. Midwestern species such as *P. cobaea*, *P. pallidus*, and *P. tubiflorus* are intermediate in their fussiness and are well worth trying wherever one gardens. Still and all, what with greater awareness by the gardener, better availability by the grower, and some excellent interspecific breeding, the day of the penstemon is dawning.

The presence of five stamens accounts for the name of the genus; the one that is sterile (the tongue) accounts for the first part of the common name. Sometimes the sterile stamen is tufted or hairy (the beard), sometimes it is not, a help in distinguishing species. Awareness of the nativity (east, west, desert) provides some useful information about placement in the garden and soil requirements. The eastern forms generally have less demanding soil and drainage needs than western and southwestern forms.

All are wonderful for attracting butterflies, and many, particularly the brighter-flowered forms, attract their fair share of hummingbirds as well.

Penstemon cobaea

Penstemon cobaea   **showy beardtongue**

I have run across this species in many gardens in the Midwest. One of the best uses was at Powell Gardens outside Kansas City, where it was combined with coneflowers and other natives and provided a nice contrast to the bright yellow daisies. Plants are only 1–2' tall and generally bear bluish white flowers with purple lines on the inside of the petal lobes in late spring. They are almost 2" long, quite large relative to the height of the plant, and are conspicuous in the garden when open. These should be cultivated far more than they are.

Habitat: On prairies and bluffs from Nebraska to Oklahoma, occasionally in eastern Texas and western Louisiana.
Hardiness: USDA Zones 3–7.
Garden site: Full sun, good drainage.
Garden maintenance: Removing the spent flowers helps leaves maintain their good looks.

Penstemon digitalis   **smooth white penstemon**

This is probably the most common species in gardens: it works well in most places in the country and the selection of 'Husker Red' and its subsequent promotion put it on every gardener's list. The species itself is about 3' tall, with smooth dark green lanceolate leaves. The white flowers are 1–1¼" long, often with purple lines on the lower side; they are obviously five-petaled and showy and are at their best in spring to early summer.

Penstemon digitalis 'Husker Red'

'Husker Red', developed at the University of Nebraska, differs by having maroon to purplish foliage. The foliage is best in a cool spring but fades significantly, to dark green, in warm summers; however, it brought the entire genus out of oblivion in America, and for that it is invaluable.

'Rachel's Dance' is a recent introduction with white tubular flowers spotting a bit of pink. Plants grow about 1½' tall.

Habitat: In meadows, plains, and open woods from Maine to South Dakota and Oklahoma, south to Virginia, Alabama and Florida.
Hardiness: USDA Zones 4–8.
Garden site: Full sun, good drainage, but this is a species that seems to be compatible with most gardens in the country.
Garden maintenance: Remove spent flowers to help leaves maintain their good looks.

Penstemon grandiflorus   large-flowered beardtongue

The pink to lavender flowers are almost 2" long, competing with *Penstemon cobaea* for the largest flowers in the genus. The upper two petals are curled back somewhat, and the lower three petals make a large "pouting" mouth. The leaves, a little different from many others in that they have a blue-green tint, are handsome in their own right; they are smooth, and the base of each clasps the stem. The 2–3' tall plants are beautiful in flower and remain so for about four weeks. As with other western forms, low precipitation and good drainage are musts.

'Prairie Jewel' has large white, lavender, rose-pink, and purple-violet flowers, which arise from handsome silver rosettes in the late spring. A selection in 2000 from the Plant Select program, administered by the Denver Botanic Gardens and Colorado State University.

'Prairie Snow' has wonderful white flowers on 2–3' tall plants. From Dale Lindgren of the University of Nebraska.

'War Axe' is a mix of colors, including pink, maroon, red, and purple.

Habitat: On dry, sandy soils from North Dakota to eastern Wyoming and Oklahoma.
Hardiness: USDA Zones 3–7.
Garden site: Full sun, well-drained soils.
Garden maintenance: Deadhead to encourage more flowers. Maintain good drainage.

*Penstemon
hirsutus
'Pygmaeus'*

Penstemon hirsutus   hairy beardtongue

One of the hardiest and one of the easier penstemons to grow—plants grow in Saskatchewan gardens as well as those in Virginia. Although native to rocky outcrops, they tolerate heavier soils than the western natives. Plants can grow up to 3' tall, but the common dwarf form is less than 1' in height. The foliage is thinly covered with short hairs, and the stems bear a fine whitish down. The tubular flowers range from rich to light lavender, sometimes fading almost to white. There is nothing spectacular about the plant, but it is a worker, and flowers for a long period of time.

'Pygmaeus', a dwarf form growing only 6–12" tall, is a great addition to rock gardens or well-drained places in the front of the garden.

Habitat: In dry or rocky soils from Quebec to Wisconsin and south to Tennessee and Virginia.
Hardiness: USDA Zones 3–7.
Garden site: Full sun, well-drained soils. Plants do poorly in wet soils. Site them in a high area or where drainage is good.
Garden maintenance: Deadhead spent flowers. Do not fertilize, or plants will get lanky.

Penstemon pallidus   pale beardtongue

Plants are similar to *Penstemon digitalis*, but the stems are hairy rather than smooth. More eastern in their habitat, plants are quite suited to some of the heat and humidity found in those states. The 1" long flowers are off-white with purple stripes inside and are held well above the toothed foliage. Numerous flower stems branch off the main stem, and at each division of the inflorescence may be found a small pair of green, somewhat hairy bracts. The flowers themselves are held in whorls on the flower stem. Handsome, but not as showy as *P. digitalis*.

Habitat: In old fields from Maine to Kansas, south to Arkansas and Georgia.
Hardiness: USDA Zones 3–8.
Garden site: Full sun, but this species is more tolerant of afternoon shade and moist soils. It does well in harsh, even brutal conditions.
Garden maintenance: Remove spent flowers.

Penstemon pinifolius pine-leaf penstemon

I have always enjoyed this plant's combination of narrow foliage and 1" long orange-scarlet tubular flowers. When the plant is covered with flowers in spring, it is attractive to butterflies and hummingbirds and hordes of people. The 1–2' tall plants bloom for about six weeks in early to mid summer, and as they mature they become woody, making a little shrublet. Plants can look spectacular, but they can also look somewhat weedy when not in flower. Hardiness is debatable; they appear to be hardy to zone 4 or 5, but they perform better in warmer climates. Good drainage is a must.

'Compactum', a more dwarf form of the species, flowers a week or two earlier.

'Mersae Yellow' has soft yellow flowers. Quite unusual.

'Shades of Mango' is really interesting in that the flowers start out yellowish (like a mango?) and change to scarlet as they mature. A cross between 'Mersae Yellow' and the species.

Habitat: In rocky soils in southeastern Arizona, southwestern New Mexico and into Mexico.

Penstemon pinifolius

Hardiness: USDA Zones 4–9.
Garden site: Well-drained soils are essential, full sun.
Garden maintenance: None.

Penstemon smallii   Small's penstemon

Although most of the beardtongues are from the West, the eastern part of the country can boast a few pretty ones as well, and this is probably the most ornamental species east of the Mississippi. Plants are relatively short, only 18–24" tall, and they grow in clumps. Flowers appear in late spring; they are about 1½" long and are pink with a white throat, an interesting and handsome combination.

This species will not knock your socks off, but its bicolored flowers, its dark green, purple-veined, toothed leaves, and its tolerance to partial shade make it a winner. Plants attract butterflies in abundance and occasionally a few hummingbirds as well. The drawback is that plants are typically short-lived. Allowing them to reseed is the best guarantee of longevity. In my Athens garden, they come and go, and seldom do populations hang about for more than a couple of years—probably a casualty of winter wetness in my heavy soils; however, when they are there, I do enjoy them.

Habitat: Mountain slopes and bluffs in western North and South Carolina, eastern Tennessee and into Georgia.
Hardiness: USDA Zones 5–8.
Garden site: Well-drained soils are essential. Full sun is tolerated in the northern range, but partial shade is useful further south.
Garden maintenance: Removal of spent flowers is practiced by some gardeners, and this may help in longevity, but allowing plants to reseed is probably the best way to keep the populations healthy.

Penstemon smallii

Penstemon strictus   Rocky Mountain beardtongue

To see a stand of Rocky Mountain penstemon in flower is a sight indeed. They grow up to 3' in height and are covered in 1–2" long blue-violet tubular flowers in early summer. Plants are highly variable, but the flowers are generally held in a one-sided raceme, unlike most other species. The opposite leaves vary, from quite narrow to lanceolate. I like these in the garden because they have an erect, full stature and fit in well with other perennials and small shrubs. They are better in the West than in the East: moisture and humidity are not particularly to their liking.

Habitat: Gravelly slopes from Wyoming to Utah and Colorado.
Hardiness: USDA Zones 4–7.
Garden site: Well-drained soils, full sun.
Garden maintenance: Deadhead spent flowers; keep plants away from wet areas.

Other species for the garden

There are so many native species, and finally enough available choices, compared to five years ago. Here are a few more with potential; not trying out a plant or two is now officially inexcusable.

Penstemon australis (Eustis Lake beardtongue) is a Southeast native, growing from the panhandle of Florida into Virginia. The species has fuzzy stems and can grow to 3' in height, bearing red-purple flowers. A dwarfer form (15–18") with mauve flowers tipped with white is also offered and is a better garden plant.

Penstemon calycosus (long sepal beardtongue), an eastern species, is a little shorter than *P. digitalis* and produces light violet or violet-pink flowers with long sepals, hence the common name. Worth trying in the garden.

Penstemon gracilis (slender beardtongue) is one of the hardiest penstemons, likely to zone 2. The tubular flowers are a soft lilac with some yellow on the inside. Plants are 12–15" tall.

Penstemon heterophyllus (foothill penstemon) is native to the dry hills of the Coast Range of California. The large lilac-blue to deep blue flowers are truly beautiful, and butterflies flock to them. Hardy to zone 7 at best. 'Züriblau' has

Penstemon strictus

Penstemon calycosus

Penstemon heterophyllus

many 1–1¼" long flowers in various shades of blue. A true xeric plant, it must be sited in a dry spot and is not suitable for most eastern gardens.

Penstemon virgatus (*P. unilateralis*; stiff beardtongue) has tall (up to 5') stems sporting bluish flowers. The small flowers are held close to the stem, giving it the appearance of a wand, hence its other common name, wandbloom penstemon. It is too tall and lanky for most gardens, but 'Blue Buckle' is only about 15" tall. Attracts butterflies and hummingbirds.

Hybrids

Many *Penstemon* hybrids—in all sorts of parental combinations but commonly including *P. barbatus*, *P. campanulatus*, *P. cobaea*, or *P. hirsutus*—are now available to gardeners. Most are hardy in zones 4–7.

'Alice Hindley' is a vigorous, upright grower, at least 2' tall, and is best sited in the middle of the garden. Its narrow lavender flowers are white on the inside.

'Blackbird' bears raspberry-red flowers for most of the summer and fall. Plants are about 2½' tall.

'Coral Kissed' produces many large white flowers from interesting salmon-colored buds. Mature height is 2–2½'.

'Elfin Pink' has salmon-pink spikes of tubular flowers on 12–18" tall plants. The foliage remains glossy green most of the season. Deadhead for continued bloom.

'Evelyn' is about 18" tall with many 1" long flowers of pale pink borne over very bushy plants. It appears to be a little more cold hardy than most.

'Garnet' has dozens of large, 1½–2" long wine-colored flowers that open in late summer and fall. Only moderately hardy in the United States, likely having *Penstemon hartwegii* or *P. campanulatus* in its parentage.

'Hidcote Pink', from the famous English garden by that name, bears soft salmon-pink flowers with white throats.

Penstemon 'Evelyn'

Penstemon 'Garnet'

'Pikes Peak Purple' has dozens of violet-purple flowers and blooms for months. Hybridized by Bruce Myers using Southwest American and Mexican parents, it is often listed as *Penstemon* ×*mexicali*. Mature height is about 18". A 1999 selection from the Plant Select program, administered by the Denver Botanic Gardens and Colorado State University.

'Prairie Dusk' bears rose-purple flowers in spring and continues all summer if deadheaded. Plants grow about 15" tall.

'Prairie Splendor' has white, rose, lavender, and pink flowers and is about 2' tall. Plants are vigorous and are useful for the middle of the garden.

'Raven' carries its large dark burgundy tubular flowers for much of the season. The 2–2½' tall plants have dark green foliage and red stems.

'Redrocks' bears many bright cherry-rose flowers with a white throat most of the season. Also hybridized by Bruce Myers, and another 1999 selection from the Plant Select program, administered by the Denver Botanic Gardens and Colorado State University.

'Schoenholzeri' ('Ruby') has pendulous ruby-red flowers, each with a white throat and stripes of red.

'Thorn' has handsome foliage and upright flowering stems to about 2' in height. The white flowers are stained with coral-red color, making for an interesting two-toned bloom.

Recommended propagation

Seed: Most penstemon seeds benefit from a cold treatment, either outdoors or in a refrigerator or cooler at 35–40F. Seeds also appear to require light for germination, so sow them on the top of the soil, and cover with a thin layer of coarse vermiculite.

Cuttings: Terminal cuttings root well; use rooting hormone and place in a warm spot.

Division: If rosettes multiply, division is easy.

Penstemon 'Hidcote Pink'

Penstemon 'Schoenholzeri'

Etymology

Genus: From the Greek, *penta* ("five") and *stemon* ("stamen"), referring to the five stamens.

Specific epithet: *australis* ("southern"); *barbatus* ("bearded"); *calycosus*, from the Greek *kalyx* ("calyx") and *cosus* ("long"); *campanulatus* ("bell-shaped"), referring to the flowers; *cobaea*, for Bernardo Cobo (1572–1659), a Jesuit naturalist in Mexico and Peru; *digitalis* ("foxglove-like"); *gracilis* ("graceful"); *grandiflorus* ("large-flowered"); *heterophyllus* ("with diverse leaves"); *hirsutus* ("hairy"); *pallidus* ("pale"); *pinifolius* ("with leaves like a pine"); *strictus* ("erect," "upright"); *virgatus* ("twiggy").

Common name: The common names refer to a habitat (e.g., Rocky Mountain) or characteristic (hairy, smooth) unique to that species.

Phacelia	scorpion weed	Hydrophyllaceae

What in the world is a scorpion weed? Sounds dangerous! I have enough bugs and critters without bringing in any more. Actually, plants are about as dangerous as a marigold, and a heck of a lot more rewarding. They produce handsome blue to mauve flowers on short plants and act as wonderful ground covers in shaded areas. There are about 150 species, most considered weeds and most native to western United States, but only a couple that you can find for the garden.

Phacelia bipinnatifida

Phacelia bipinnatifida   **fern-leaf phacelia**

This may be the easiest species to find in nurseries and one of the easiest to grow. Leaves are pinnately divided, and the leaf segments are pinnately lobed. Plants usually stand erect and are about 1' tall. The 1" wide flowers are light blue, often with white centers and protruding stamens. They arise from coiled buds (like a scorpion's tail) that straighten out as the flowers open. Phacelias are hard to tell apart; on this one, look for the divided leaves and the hairy sepals beneath the petals.

This woodland plant is beautifully displayed at Chanticleer in Wayne, Pennsylvania. It thrives in moist shade. Plants are biennials, but reseeding is generally sufficient to maintain the garden population.

Habitat: In woods from Virginia to Illinois and Iowa, south to Arkansas, and east to Alabama and Georgia.

Hardiness: USDA Zones 5–9.

Garden site: Moist shade is best, although morning sun will benefit flowering and growth.

Garden maintenance: None. Seedlings can be moved as needed.

Phacelia campanularia   **California bluebell**

The most common of the western species, especially California, and it makes sense that plants are better suited to gardens in that area of the country than to eastern gardens. It is a handsome plant with campanula-like gentian-blue flowers and lobed to toothed, ovate to elliptical leaves. Plants grow only 1' tall and

Phacelia purshii

spread by rhizomes and seeds. Treat as an annual in most areas of the country. Seeds can be sown directly to the ground in early spring.

Habitat: In desert and dry areas in southern California and Baja California.
Hardiness: USDA Zones 9–11.
Garden site: Dry soils, full sun to afternoon shade.
Garden maintenance: None.

Other species for the garden

Phacelia purshii (Miami mist) is offered every now and then. Its light blue flowers are characterized by highly fringed petals, and it makes a beautiful 15–18" tall plant. Native in woodlands from Michigan to Georgia. Hardy in zones 3–8.

Phacelia tanacetifolia (tansy-leaf phacelia), native in Arizona and southern California, has highly divided, almost fern-like leaves on 2–4' tall plants. Flowers are purple-blue. Needs dry, sunny conditions. Zones 7–11.

Recommended propagation

Seed: Plants grow readily from seed. For annual species, sow seeds in the early spring directly to prepared ground. For perennial species, do the same, or seeds can be sown in the summer and seedlings planted out the following spring.

Etymology

Genus: From the Greek, *phakelos* ("bundle"), for the bunched flowers of the original species.
Specific epithet: *bipinnatifida* ("almost [-*ifida*] twice-pinnate"), a reference to the lobes on the leaf segments; *campanularia* ("bell-shaped"); *purshii*, for

Frederick Traugott Pursh (1744–1820), a German horticulturist and writer who explored in the United States; *tanacetifolia* ("tansy-leaved").

Common name: California bluebell speaks to both habitat and flower shape; scorpion weed comes from the scorpion tail arrangement of the buds. Miami mist is a lovely name, but I can't find its origin.

Phlox — Polemoniaceae

It is difficult to find a genus that provides so many excellent plants for the gardener. Not only is it firmly fixed in the hearts and minds of native plant lovers, it has earned its place in gardens all over the world. Before I could champion a relatively poorly known native in this book, I first had to search high and low for sources (and many, finally, were omitted for lack of availability). Not so with this group. A half-dozen species and hundreds of cultivars are readily available, wherever you garden; and if you are not interested in selections and hybrids, there is still sufficient beauty in the species alone to make your garden beam with color.

Powdery mildew can be a problem on all species, the severity depending on locale. The low-growing forms like *Phlox divaricata* and *P. subulata* are sometimes tainted but not nearly to the extent of the upright forms like *P. ×arendsii*, *P. maculata*, and *P. paniculata*. Medium-height species such as *P. glaberrima* and *P. pilosa* are only slightly susceptible.

All species are characterized by opposite entire leaves, five-petaled flowers, and a long corolla tube. One of the characteristics of the genus is that the petals can easily be pulled away from the sepals. I use this trick to teach students why it is a phlox and not a dianthus (for example). Try it, it works! Bloom time is from early spring to mid summer, depending on the species. They range in size from 9–12" tall to those up to 3' in height. Choose your candy, and have a blast.

Phlox divaricata — woodland phlox

If you have some shade, and plants are compatible with the heat and cold common to your area, run out and buy some woodland phlox. The long, thin leaves with entire margins are always healthy; the plentiful blue to mauve flowers provide color from the time the snow melts through most of the spring. The five petals are nearly always notched, and usually elusively fragrant, resulting in another common name, wild sweet William. Plants grow 12–15" tall and fill in by reseeding. For many gardeners, the flower color of the species is just fine, but it is nice to have a choice, which the many available cultivars offer.

'Blue Elf' is only about 6" tall with mauve-blue flowers in the spring.

'Blue Moon' produces fragrant, dark blue flowers. An introduction from Garden in the Woods, Framingham, Massachusetts.

Phlox divaricata 'Louisiana Purple'   *Phlox divaricata* 'May Breeze'

'Clouds of Perfume' performs well nearly everywhere I have seen it. The silver-blue blooms do make a marvelous 18–22" tall cloud, but I can't say I have detected much perfume. Excellent name, nonetheless.

'Dirigo Ice' is smothered in icy blue, almost white flowers. Plants are 12–18" tall in flower. Neat color, great plant.

'Fuller's White' is an outstanding white-flowered cultivar, one which comes back true from seed. Found by Henry and Sally Fuller of Connecticut.

'Loddon Grove Blue' is a low-grower with lilac-blue flowers. Sometimes listed as 'London Grove Blue'.

'Louisiana Purple' is one of the most prolifically flowering and vigorous phlox I have grown. Excellent, but can get out of bounds.

'May Breeze' bears dozens of fragrant pale blue, almost white flowers. One of my favorites.

'Montrose Tricolor' is a newer introduction from Nancy Goodwin of Montrose Nursery, North Carolina. Plants have three colors on the foliage (pink, white, and green) and produce lavender-blue flowers. Hardly subtle and calming, but it certainly is interesting.

'Plum Perfect' has light purple flowers with a dark purple eye.

Habitat: In fields and woods from Quebec to Minnesota and south to Texas and east to Florida.

Hardiness: USDA Zones 3–8.

Garden site: Woodland settings are best; however, morning sun enhances flowering and reduces lankiness.

Garden maintenance: Spent flowers can be cut back if desired, but little else in the way of maintenance is required.

Phlox drummondii Drummond's phlox

The leaves of this annual phlox are opposite and narrow, and the flowers, mostly rose-red in the wild, are held in clusters above the foliage. Paradoxically, although the species is native to Texas and the Southeast, plants perform far better in Canada and the Northeast than in southern gardens. They are usually purchased from seed; however, recent breeding efforts have resulted in more colors, and some of the newer cultivars, like the Intensia series, show a positive contempt for rain, heat, and humidity—a nice advance for the southern gardener.

Phlox drummondii '21st Century Rose Star'

Astoria series consists of separate colors on 9–12" plants. They perform well but are not quite as tolerant of weather abuse as the Intensia series.

'Crème Brûlée' is a mixture of pastel colors, including subtle shades of pink, peach, and salmon.

Intensia series provides plants in a half-dozen colors. They have performed well from Colorado to Athens, Georgia.

'Phlox of Sheep'—is this not a great name?—is another mix, this one with flower colors more vibrant and less subtle than 'Crème Brûlée'.

'Silver Blossom' is a mix of pinks, pastels, and mauve flowers.

21st Century series consists of selections in several colors. All plants are compact.

Habitat: From Texas to Florida and north to the Carolinas.
Hardiness: Annual.
Garden site: In the North, full sun. In the South, some afternoon shade will prolong flowering.
Garden maintenance: Some early fertilization helps establishment of the plants. Deadhead when possible.

Phlox glaberrima　　　　　　　　smooth phlox

Many species of low- to medium-size phlox look alike when you walk around the garden. This is particularly true of the pink-flowered species, like this and *Phlox pilosa*, and the pink forms of *P. stolonifera*. In reality, many differences in flowers and habit distinguish one from the other. Smooth phlox is just that, which makes it quite unusual in the genus. It is also taller than the others mentioned, easily growing 3' in height. Its pointed, glossy dark green leaves are long (4–5") and narrow and seldom have disease problems, and in spring, the sheer numbers of rosy pink blossoms weigh the stems down. Cut plants back after flowering, and additional flowers will occur. Plants tolerate some afternoon shade but perform better in sunny areas.

This is a workhorse in the garden, and although it is a clump-former, it can also spread and cover some ground, not quite up to the standard set by *Phlox pilosa* (the most vigorous spreader, in my opinion) but no shrinking violet either. Several cultivars are available, but none are significantly different from the species.

Phlox glaberrima subsp. *triflora*

'Anita Kistler' has pink flowers with a hint of a white center.

'Morris Berd' also has pink flowers but with a white center more distinct than the previous cultivar. It flowers later than the species and may have some *Phlox paniculata* in its parentage.

subsp. *triflora*, with flowers in threes, is the shortest and, for me, the best performer of the available selections. It sucks up heat and humidity.

Habitat: In moist woods and thickets from Ohio to Wisconsin, south to east Texas and east to Florida.

Hardiness: USDA Zones 4–8.

Garden site: Moist soils are necessary for best performance, although drying out every now and then will not be a problem. In the South, a little afternoon shade appears to be useful; full sun in the North is fine as long as sufficient moisture is available. Stress (from drying out, or shade, or crowding) can result in mildew.

Garden maintenance: Cut back after flowering for additional bloom. Thin where needed to reduce incidence of powdery mildew.

Phlox maculata   spotted phlox

The spotted phlox is fairly easy to identify, with its strong upright habit and the reddish spots on the stems. Plants stand 2–3' tall and typically produce fragrant red-purple flowers. They have been mixed up in the trade and sold as *Phlox carolina*, but the latter has thicker leaves and unspotted stems. As with most phlox, the species is not as easy to find as many of the cultivars.

'Alpha' is part of a series that also includes 'Delta' and 'Omega'. They all stand 2½–3' tall and flower in early summer. Flowers are lilac-pink, white, and light pink with a darker eye, respectively. Quite handsome in flower, but I have not

Phlox maculata 'Alpha'

Phlox maculata 'Natascha'

been impressed with their mildew resistance, at least in our trials in north Georgia.

'Natascha' is wonderfully striking. With her star-patterned white and raspberry-pink flowers, she is not for all tastes, but she is also pleasantly fragrant and quite mildew resistant.

'Rosalinde' is about 2½' tall with deep pink flowers and reddish stems. Good resistance to mildew.

Habitat: In meadows from Quebec to Minnesota, south to Arkansas,
  Mississippi, Georgia and east to North Carolina.
Hardiness: USDA Zones 3–8.
Garden site: Full sun.
Garden maintenance: Avoid overcrowding to reduce potential mildew problems.
  Deadhead spent flowers.

Phlox paniculata   garden phlox, summer phlox

By far the most popular of the cultivated phlox, dozens and dozens of cultivars have been introduced over the last fifty years, many still in commerce. Much of the original breeding of summer phlox essentially ignored the problem of powdery mildew susceptibility, while modern breeders assail us with claims of mildew resistance. I have always found it interesting that stands of wild *Phlox paniculata* hardly display any susceptibility to the disease, and in trials of summer phlox at the University of Georgia, I always include a plant or two of the unadulterated species as a control. There is absolutely nothing wrong with planting the species: 95 percent of your disease problems will disappear, especially if you don't water plants all the time. The plants are 3–4' tall, with handsome leathery leaves and magenta-red flowers in summer. Gardeners, however, must experiment with different colors and must try the newest plants on the market; only a few of my favorites of the many are included here.

'Danielle' has handsome white flowers and grew a little over 4' tall in the trials at the University of Georgia. Plants flowered for eighteen weeks!

'David', selected from a stand of native plants for its resistance to mildew, bears white flowers on 2–3' tall stems. In general, plants are excellent and have lived up to their billing, but I have seen mildew cover them as well. Still, one of the best whites out there, and the 2002 Perennial Plant of the Year.

Phlox paniculata 'Robert Poore'

'David's Lavender', with lavender flowers, was new in 2005 and should be a winner. From ItSaul Plants in Atlanta.

'Delta Snow', a selection from the fine state of Mississippi, bears fragrant white flowers with a purple eye. A vigorous plant, 3–4' tall, with good resistance to mildew.

'Eden's Smile' appears to be an excellent plant, with good clear pink flowers on 2½–3' tall plants.

'Jeana' has many, many pink flowers on 3–4' tall plants. The leaves are moderately mildew resistant.

'Katherine' is 2–3' tall and bears lavender flowers with a white eye. Good mildew resistance.

'Laura' has many lavender flowers with a white center and dark eye. Plants stand about 2½' tall. I have not evaluated mildew resistance, but reports appear favorable.

'Nicky' is simply big and colorful. Plants grow 3–4' tall and bear rich magenta-purple flowers. Appears to have good mildew resistance.

'Red Riding Hood' has pink-red flowers on a 2' tall plant.

'Robert Poore', another selection from Mississippi, is a large vigorous phlox with rosy red to magenta flowers. Planted side by side with the species, flowers are fairly similar, but the color is more iridescent. Plants may not be quite as cold hardy as other cultivars (perhaps to zone 4), but they are the least susceptible to mildew of them all. I recommend it strongly.

Habitat: In open woods from New York west to Iowa and Kansas, south to Arkansas, into northern Mississippi and east to Georgia.

Hardiness: USDA Zones 3–8.

Garden site: Full sun.

Garden maintenance: Do not overcrowd. Remove spent flowers and choose mildew-resistant cultivars or the species itself if mildew is a problem.

Phlox pilosa

Phlox pilosa   **downy phlox**

A wonderful plant, and one whose wonder you'd better enjoy, as you will have it for a while. Plants differ from others in that the stems are about 2' tall and covered in short stiff hairs, thus accounting for its common name. In fact, all parts of the plant are downy, even the corolla tube. The leaves are narrow, sharply pointed, and yes, downy. On the base of each of the five rose-pink petals is characteristic violet spotting, resulting in a ring at the base of the flowers. Plants start off erect but often lean over in partial shade, even sitting on the ground if placed in too little sun. Plants tolerate shade, but not heavy shade. In the Armitage garden, they sneak through the deep shade and find a comfortable place where there is sufficient light to grow well. An excellent garden plant, but beware of its aggressive tendencies.

'Eco Happy Traveler' has lovely deep pink flowers in the spring. Plants spread well but not so much as the species; this is more of a clump-former.

'Joy Parsons' produces bicolored flowers, pink with a little white. Plants did well in trials at the University of Georgia.

Habitat: In prairies and woodlands from Connecticut to Manitoba south to Texas and east to Florida.
Hardiness: USDA Zones 3–8.
Garden site: Full sun to partial shade is preferred.
Garden maintenance: Very little. Cut back hard in the spring to enhance branching.

Phlox stolonifera 'Bruce's White'

Phlox stolonifera   **creeping phlox**

An American treasure and a perfect plant for the woodland garden or anywhere shade is more prevalent than direct sun. Plants thrive in moist, cool soils and tolerate the shade of deciduous trees but are also at home in areas with morning sun. The leaves are in the shape of a spatula and are usually light green. Plants grow only 3–4" tall when not in bloom and no more than 1' when the flowers are produced in the spring. They spread by runners (aboveground stems called stolons) but are not invasive; in a few years, the area will be a mat of lilac-blue flowers. The species is wonderful, but several excellent cultivars are also offered.

'Blue Ridge' and 'Pink Ridge' are about 6" tall and have blue-lilac and mauve-pink flowers, respectively.

'Bruce's White' has clean white flowers with a yellow eye.

'Homefires' has showy pink flowers.

'Sherwood Purple', the 1980 Perennial Plant of the Year and still one of the most popular cultivars, has mauve-purple flowers.

Habitat: In woods, mostly in mountains, from Pennsylvania to Ohio and south to Tennessee and Georgia.
Hardiness: USDA Zones 2–8.
Garden site: Moist shade is best.
Garden maintenance: None.

Phlox subulata 'Candy Stripe'

Phlox subulata
moss phlox, moss pink

Phlox subulata

Where this plant is successful—and that includes much of the eastern half of the country and the West Coast—it can be seen everywhere in early spring. It is so common in many eastern states, it is affectionately known as the gas station plant, because even gas station attendants, not well known for their love of landscaping, succeed with the thing. Its success can be attributed to its very small narrow leaves, which withstand drought, and its low-growing habit, which tolerates snow, wind, hail, and other abusive weather thrown at it. The flowers, which literally cover the plant, are among the earliest in the genus, occurring in February to early May. Pink is the most common color, but dozens of cultivars can be found in many hues, and even bicolors.

'Apple Blossom' is 3–6" tall with light pink flowers.

'Candy Stripe' is one of my favorites, with flowers of white with a pink stripe.

'Coral Eye' bears pink flowers with a coral eye.

'Emerald Cushion Blue' and 'Emerald Cushion Pink' are compact, producing lavender-blue and pink flowers, respectively.

'Maiden's Blush' bears pink flowers, each with a red eye.

'Millstream Daphne' produces deep pink flowers with a darker pink eye.

'Red Wings' has rose-red flowers with a dark red eye.

'Scarlet Flame' has scarlet-red flowers.

Habitat: In sandy or rocky soil from Maine to Michigan south to Tennessee and east to North Carolina.

Hardiness: USDA Zones 3–8.

Phlox amoena 'Cabot Blue'   *Phlox douglasii* 'Crackerjack'

Garden site: Full sun, excellent drainage. Plants look their best dripping from banks or walls.

Garden maintenance: None.

Other species for the garden

Nearly every phlox that grows wild in this country is sufficiently ornamental for the garden. The only limitation is finding a reputable source.

Phlox amoena (hairy phlox) is native to gravelly sunny areas in the Southeast. Flowers vary greatly in color; the easiest form to find is 'Cabot Blue', which bears many lavender-blue flowers on a 6–8" tall plant. Zones 6–9.

Phlox carolina (Carolina phlox) is similar to *P. maculata* but without the spots. The best selection is 'Miss Lingard', known as the wedding phlox, for the beautiful white flowers in early summer. Mildew susceptible. Zones 5–8.

Phlox douglasii (*P. caespitosa*) is a fine dwarf western plant that enjoys cool nights and warm days. 'Crackerjack' has brilliant crimson-red flowers in spring on 6–9" compact plants.

Phlox nivalis (trailing phlox) is closely related to *P. subulata* and often confused with it. Plants tend to flower later than *P. subulata*. 'Eco Flirtie Eyes' is a gorgeous off-white selection with a pink eye; 'Snowdrift' has clean white flowers over dark green compact foliage. Zones 5–8.

Phlox ovata (*P. latifolia*; mountain phlox) is 10–20" tall and bears mostly red-purple flowers. Not easily available, but a good performer in sun. Zones 4–8.

Hybrids

As would be expected, significant hybridization has occurred with our native material. While some are better than others to be sure, most are no better than their parents.

Phlox ×*arendsii* is a cross between *P. divaricata* and *P. paniculata*. Older cultivars include 'Anja', 'Hilda', and 'Suzanne'; all have been quite mildew sensitive

Phlox ×*arendsii* 'Baby Face'   *Phlox* ×*procumbens* 'Millstream Jupiter'

and have not lived up to the billing. 'Baby Face', a relatively new introduction, has rose-pink flowers.

'Chattahoochee' has marvelous deep blue flowers with a striking purple eye. Probably a hybrid between *Phlox divaricata* var. *laphamii* and *P. pilosa*. First discovered by the Chattahoochee River and introduced by the grande dame of American horticulture, Mary Gibson Henry. Plants are short-lived but extraordinary.

'Minnie Pearl', a handsome white-flowered form, brings a little of the Grand Ole Opry to the garden. She appears to be a naturally occurring hybrid between *Phlox maculata* and *P. glaberrima* found in Mississippi. Plants tolerate heat and humidity and are touted (I have not trialed them) to be mildew resistant, with flowers appearing earlier than the parents.

Phlox ×*procumbens* (*P. stolonifera* × *P. subulata*) is commonly sold. 'Millstream Jupiter' is one of the better choices. 'Variegata', with green and white leaves and purple-mauve flowers, is also well known; however, the leaves are more handsome than the flowers.

Recommended propagation

Seed: Most species can be raised from seed; *Phlox drummondii* is nearly always raised that way.

Cuttings: All phlox are easily propagated from terminal cuttings.

Division: The clump-formers (*Phlox maculata*, *P. paniculata*) can eventually be carefully divided, but division is not recommended for *P. subulata* and other mat-formers.

Etymology

Genus: From the Greek, *phlox* ("flame"), for the color of the flowers.

Specific epithet: *amoena* ("pleasant," "delightful"); *arendsii* honors German nurseryman Georg Arends (1863–1952); *carolina* ("of the Carolinas"); *divaricata* ("spreading," "straggly"); *drummondii* honors Thomas Drummond (1790–1831), who collected in Canada and the United States; *glaberrima* ("completely without hairs"); *maculata* ("spotted"); *ovata* ("egg-shaped leaf"); *paniculata* ("with flowers arranged in panicles"); *pilosa* ("covered with long soft hairs"); *procumbens* ("prostrate"); *stolonifera* ("having stolons or runners that root"); *subulata* ("awl-shaped").

Common name: Most names reflect habitat (Carolina), characteristics (downy, hairy), or habit (creeping, prostrate). Moss phlox and moss pink suggest a likeness to moss (habit) and pinks, *Dianthus* (flower color).

Physostegia virginiana　　obedient plant, false dragonhead　　Lamiaceae

I don't believe I have ever seen obedient plant in the wild, but then again, I am somewhat hiking challenged. That it is native to this country would be news to most gardeners who had overlooked the hint its epithet provides. I have always enjoyed the upright habit, the handsome pink flowers (which are about as obedient as my dog), and the dark green leaves. They fill in areas nicely, and the flowers can be cut and brought indoors with great success. What I didn't enjoy was their roaming tendencies, which result in shovelfuls of plants lying prostrate on the compost pile. Pink is the common color even among cultivars, several of which are quite easy to obtain.

'Alba', with white flowers, tends to be shorter and flowers earlier than the species.

'Bouquet Rose' is wonderful but aggressive. The bright pink flowers cover the 3–4' plants in early summer.

'Crown Rose' bears rosy pink flowers on 2–3' tall stems.

'Miss Manners' is a great name for a clump-forming cultivar that doesn't spread nearly as rapidly as the species. Plants have white flowers and stand about 2' tall.

'Olympus Gold' has green and golden yellow variegated foliage over which appear pink flowers. Plants are about 2½' tall, and are not as invasive as many others.

'Summer Snow' is similar to 'Alba', bearing white flowers earlier than the pink forms.

'Variegata', with green foliage edged in white, is not as aggressive as the species. Quite handsome, more for the foliage than the flowers.

'Vivid' is a compact form with excellent pink color.

Habitat: In wet woods and moist prairies from Vermont to Ohio, south to Oklahoma and Missouri and east to South Carolina.

Hardiness: USDA Zones 2–9.

Garden site: Full sun, moist soils. Not recommended for a small area: they can soon become bullies and downright invasive.

Garden maintenance: Ruthless comes to mind when dealing with this plant, unless nonaggressive cultivars are planted.

Physostegia virginiana 'Bouquet Rose'

Physostegia virginiana 'Summer Snow'

Other species for the garden

Physostegia purpurea, a southern species, is occasionally offered. It differs in the shape of its leaves and their toothed margins. Harder to find and no better than *P. virginiana*. Zones 5–9.

Recommended propagation

Seed: The species and several cultivars can be raised from seed quite easily.
Cuttings: Terminal cuttings taken in summer root easily.
Division: The preferred method, because it is so obvious.

Etymology

Genus: From the Greek, *physa* ("bladder") and *stege* ("roof-covering"), referring to the fruit being covered by the inflated calyx.
Specific epithet: *purpurea* ("tending to purple"); *virginiana* ("of Virginia").
Common name: Known as obedient plants because each individual flower will, upon being pushed in any one direction, temporarily remain in the new position as if it were hinged (see earlier comments about my dog). They also look like a dragonhead (which is reserved for *Dracocephalum*), thus they are false dragonheads.

Podophyllum peltatum with leucojum

Podophyllum peltatum | mayapple | Berberidaceae

To see mayapples growing wild in the spring makes my heart sing, not just because they are neat plants, but because I know I can easily find plants to purchase for Heather's and Laura's gardens. To eastern gardeners, these are as American as apple pie; to westerners, perhaps not quite so, but marvelous nevertheless. Their habit of growth is fun to share with students: I point out that when only a single stem arises, there will be but one leaf but no flowers; however, when the stem splits into a V and two leaves form, they are sure to see the six- to nine-petaled white flowers where the stems split. The reason some split and others don't is usually a question of juvenility (that is to say, young plants don't split). The plum-sized yellowish fruit is not uncommon, but fruit set is usually minimal because plants are self-incompatible. Reports on the fruit's toxicity range from mild to none. If your neighbor gives you some mayapple jelly, however, she may be trying to tell you something.

These are tough, aggressive plants and easy to work into mixed beds in a small garden. I love how colonies form, running by rhizomes to produce a blanket of dark green leaves through spring and early summer. Plants go dormant later in the season. Unfortunately, in some areas, particularly the Northeast, diseases such as rust can disfigure the leaves. There is little to be done except removing the spent leaves as plants go dormant in the summer, hence removing the inoculum, which may help reduce the occurrence of rust in subsequent years.

Habitat: In woods, hillsides, and meadows from Quebec to Minnesota south to Texas and east to Georgia.
Hardiness: USDA Zones 3–8.

Garden site: Shade and moisture are beneficial. Too much sun and drought result in rapid dormancy.

Garden maintenance: If gaps in the garden after dormancy are a problem, think about planting these among other plants that remain active all season. Mayapples are aggressive and will eat up ground (and perhaps their neighbors as well); some thinning may be needed. Rust fungus can be a problem; see earlier comments.

Recommended propagation

Seed: Seeds are not often present in the fruit, but if they are, separate them from the fruit and wash them well to remove inhibitory chemicals. Plants may take at least two years before being ready to transplant.

Division: By far the easiest way. Dig out the rhizomes as the plants go dormant, replant with an eye to another location, and get out of the way.

Etymology

Genus: From the Greek, *podos* ("foot") and *phyllon* ("leaf"). Apparently the similarity of the leaf to a duck's foot resulted in this contraction of *Anapodophyllum* (*anas*, "duck").

Specific epithet: *peltatum* ("shield-shaped"), for the way the leaf is attached to the stem (on the lower surface, away from the margin).

Common name: The fruit suggests a small apple; the month is when it flowers in the North.

Polemonium	Jacob's ladder	Polemoniaceae

America is home to over a dozen species of Jacob's ladders; most reside in the West, only a couple are in the East. As usual, one must travel abroad to see some of our wonderful plants and their hybrids in English, Irish, and German landscapes. I was very taken with *Polemonium foliosissimum* (leafy Jacob's ladder) in gardens in the United Kingdom. Once I realized it was ours, I tried to buy some plants here, and what a struggle that was; I searched and searched, and finally found some seed sources and one live plant source. That was ten years ago, and things have not improved much.

All have foliage that supposedly looks like the rungs of the ladder, filled with angels coming and going, that the biblical Jacob saw in his dream. The flowers are generally light to dark blue, often with a yellow center. Some species are native to alpine areas and do best in rock gardens and cool climates, while others are woodlanders, preferring cool, moist, shady areas to be at their best. All tend to be short-lived.

Polemonium carneum   salmon Jacob's ladder

I am pleased to say that this beautiful species is more readily available than it was a few years ago, but don't expect to find it at the local box store. These clump-formers are only 1–1½' tall and produce dozens of soft salmon and other pastel-colored flowers in the spring. It is short-lived, but if you can get it established in the woodland area of the garden, it will be worth every moment.

Plants are native to cool areas of the Northwest; eastern and midwestern gardeners can expect challenges in trying to establish them.

'Apricot Delight' has both lilac and apricot flowers.

Habitat: From Oregon to British Columbia and to the western Cascades.
Hardiness: USDA Zones 6–8.
Garden site: Moist, shaded woodland area is best.
Garden maintenance: They may go summer-dormant under dry conditions.
Allow seed to be released, then shear back to clean them up a little.

Polemonium foliosissimum   leafy Jacob's ladder

This is one of the more gardenworthy of the ladders, growing strongly to a height of 2–3' and producing wonderful and highly visible blue flowers with bright yellow stamens in spring and early summer. Plants will not succeed with everyone, true, but why this is not offered more is beyond me. I guess it is all part of the common gardeners' lament: "How will we know what will fail if we cannot find the plant to buy?" Plants need excellent drainage but will tolerate

Polemonium foliosissimum

consistent moisture and some afternoon shade; however, they are quite drought-tolerant once established. They are available through seed and occasionally on the Internet. Give them a go.

Habitat: In moist soil along streams from New Mexico and eastern Arizona and north to Wyoming, Nevada and Idaho.
Hardiness: USDA Zones 4–8.
Garden site: A well-drained area in partial sun. Too much shade will result in lanky stems and poor flowering.
Garden maintenance: Shear after seed release.

Polemonium reptans   spreading Jacob's ladder

This is by far the easiest species to find, and for most gardeners the easiest to establish, equaling the others in vigor. It is a woodland species, and the combination of consistent moisture and afternoon shade is its stock-in-trade. The foliage is handsome throughout the season; the slate-blue flowers are wonderfully beautiful in the spring. Plants also can produce a great deal of fruit, and they are almost as handsome in fruit as in flower; certainly fruit are the dominant features in the fall in the shade garden of the New York Botanical Garden. Plants are usually 8–18" tall but can get taller in heavy shade and rich soils. Additional plants will be produced over time by seed.

'Blue Pearl' appears to be a bit more vigorous than the species and produces many light blue flowers with white eyes in late spring.

'Stairway to Heaven' owes its selection to the sharp eyes of Bill Cullina, of the New England Wild Flower Society. When plants mature, each leaflet is a blend of white, pink, light green, and dark green. Similar blue flowers are produced in spring.

Polemonium reptans in fruit

Polemonium reptans 'Blue Pearl'

Habitat: In moist woods from New York to Minnesota south to Oklahoma and
Mississippi and east to Georgia.
Hardiness: USDA Zones 2–8.
Garden site: Moist, cool climates are best. Avoid full sun and drought.
Garden maintenance: Shear back after seed release.

Recommended propagation

Seed: Sow seeds immediately. They can be sown directly in a prepared garden
soil or in a prepared container.
Division: Plants can be divided when the clumps are sufficiently large.

Etymology

Genus: From the Greek, likely applied to a medical plant used by Greek orator
Polemon (c. 117–138) of Cappadocia (Cappadocia is part of present-day
Turkey). *Polemonium caeruleum* is native to southern Europe and has been
given many medicinal uses.
Specific epithet: *carneum* ("flesh-colored"); *foliosissimum* ("full of leaves," "leafy");
reptans ("creeping").
Common name: The pinnate leaves are opposite each other, suggesting the
rungs of a ladder.

Polygonatum **Solomon's seal** **Liliaceae**

North America is blessed with a couple of wonderful species of Solomon's seal.
Both produce pendulous white flowers in the spring and may be found in
shaded woodland locales. I love watching the stems emerge through the soils
in the spring, each bud enveloped by a helmet of overlapping pointed leaves.
Several of the more popular garden selections are native to Europe and Asia,
but there is not one of our own I would not welcome to my garden. They grow
from weird rhizomes that kind of look like they have been sitting around too
long, a little deformed and dried up. All bear tall, arching stems that are unmis-
takable in the landscape.

Polygonatum biflorum small Solomon's seal

This species has been inflated and deflated as additional species become part of
this complex or are taken away. In general, stems are about 18" tall with two or
three (sometimes only one) white flowers edged in green hanging from the
upper nodes. They are marvelous plants and will form large colonies where
properly sited.

A much larger form, likely tetraploid in nature, provides arching stems that
can easily grow 6–7' tall, with larger (and up to four) flowers produced at the

Polygonatum biflorum var. *commutatum*

upper nodes. This has been called *Polygonatum biflorum* var. *commutatum,* *P. commutatum,* or *P. biflorum* var. *canaliculatum.* Some respected sources simply call all the names synonyms, but it is hard to buy that when they are so obviously different. For me, I prefer either *P. biflorum* var. *commutatum* or *P. commutatum* for the larger one.

Habitat: From New Hampshire to Manitoba, south to Texas and east to Florida.
Hardiness: USDA Zones 3–8.
Garden site: Shade with consistent moisture.
Garden maintenance: None.

Polygonatum pubescens   hairy Solomon's seal

This is the least known of our native seals but for no particular reason. It is also our most northerly. The arching stems rise up 1½–2' and bear ten to twelve leaves up the stem. The underside of the midribs is softly hairy, accounting for its name. The spring flowers are held in pairs at each upper node and are white edged in green. Black fruit is not uncommon. Colonies will form in the garden, providing for a nice grouping without being invasive.

Habitat: In woods from Quebec to Manitoba south to Iowa and east to Maryland, Kentucky and the Appalachian Mountains of South Carolina and Georgia.
Hardiness: USDA Zones 3–8.
Garden site: Shade with consistent moisture.
Garden maintenance: None.

Recommended propagation

Seed: Seed is slow, taking two years to produce transplantable plants. Sow the seeds as soon as they ripen (turn white), and let them go through the winter in a cold frame.

Division: Dig your colonies when they are sufficiently large. They may be broken into pieces with eyes or simply transplanted as is.

Etymology

Genus: From the Greek, *polys* ("many") and *gony* ("knee-joint"), referring to the many-jointed rhizome.

Specific epithet: *biflorum* ("twin-flowered"); *canaliculatum* ("channeled"); *commutatum* ("changing"), used for a species close to one already known; *pubescens* ("downy").

Common name: One of the many wonderful explanations is that the shape of the leaf scars along the rhizome somewhat resemble the five-pointed star that became a religious symbol in the Middle Ages. Another suggests that the scars resemble a seal impressed on wax in former (King Solomon's) times. According to English herbalist John Gerard (1545–1612), plants sealed wounds. Pick your story and spread the word!

Pycnanthemum	mountain mint	Lamiaceae

The mountain mint is one of those plants that reminds me of an open bag of potato chips. As hard as it is not to grab a chip as you pass and put it to your mouth, it is just as difficult to pass by this plant and not grab a leaf and put it to your nose. And just like you can't eat just one chip, your nose will demand another sniff every time you see a mountain mint. The fragrance is not sweet like a rose or heavy like a sage, but tangy and refreshing.

The many species of mountain mints are mostly grown for their foliage, in particular the peculiar silvery color of their upper leaves and bracts. One or two are grown for the densely crowded flowers. Some species are clump-formers, but beware: many can be highly aggressive. They are not a good choice for a small garden, but where room allows, their aggressiveness is welcome, and they look far better as a large stand than as a single plant. In general, they are deer-resistant but attract butterflies by the swarm.

By the way, most species are lowland plants and have nothing to do with the mountains.

Pycnanthemum incanum

Pycnanthemum incanum hoary mountain mint

This was the first species I encountered, and immediately I had to have it for my garden. Plants persisted for about five years before the encroaching shade did them in. But in those five years, I never walked by it without giving a leaf or two a gentle rub between thumb and forefinger. Nor did any visitors to the garden escape un-minted.

Plants grow 2–3' tall, with pink flowers and gray-white bracts. The leaves are covered with whitish, curly hairs, which gives a dull cast, and although the plants may not be deemed "beautiful," they are quietly handsome. They are wanderers, but as the garden became shadier, they became a bit more forlorn and needed cutting back; eventually I replaced them with more shade-tolerant material.

Habitat: In woods and thickets from southern New Hampshire to Illinois, south to Alabama and east to Florida.
Hardiness: USDA Zones 3–8.
Garden site: Full sun and moist, but not wet, soils.
Garden maintenance: In full sun, plants should stand upright, and the fragrance and look will be fine. They can run, but I did not find that a problem. Plants can tolerate xeric conditions; if planted in too much moisture, plants will need cutting back at least once. Too much shade and soils that are too rich are kisses of death.

Pycnanthemum muticum blunt mountain mint

With its upright habit and silver-topped plants, this is the species that everyone is talking about (at least all six people who even talk about mountain mint). The leaves are ovate, somewhat blunt and toothed. In a grouping, they are absolutely beautiful and are almost as fragrant as *Pycnanthemum incanum*. In late summer and fall, the silvery tops almost glisten. To see an extraordinary planting, visit the Chicago Botanic Garden, whose Main Island puts one of our most overlooked natives to fabulous use. These are aggressive, as that planting attests, but exceptional if space allows.

Habitat: In woods and thickets from Maine to Michigan south to Texas and Florida.
Hardiness: USDA Zones 5–8.
Garden site: Full sun, adequate moisture.
Garden maintenance: Similar to *Pycnanthemum incanum*, but needs consistent moisture.

Pycnanthemum tenuifolium   slender mountain mint

This is among the more popular species in nursery circles—I don't think it holds a candle to *Pycnanthemum incanum* or *P. muticum*, but the narrow sessile leaves combined with clusters of relatively large white flowers make for an interesting combination. The small flowers, spotted with pink or violet, occur at the tops of the plants. Flowering begins in late spring and continues through the summer. Plants are clump-formers and not as aggressive as others; still, they can move about. Plants grow 1–3' tall, and the leaves are spicy but not as yummy as the others.

'Cat Springs' was found by Tony Avent of Plant Delights Nursery near Cat Springs, Texas. According to Tony, its narrow green leaves "have a strong fragrance of spicy peppermint." In mid June, the clumps are topped with large, pure white flower clusters, a dramatic improvement over the typical offered forms.

Habitat: From Massachusetts to Minnesota, south to Texas and east to Georgia.
Hardiness: USDA Zones 5–8.
Garden site: Full sun, moist but not wet soils.
Garden maintenance: As with *Pycnanthemum muticum*.

Other species for the garden
Pycnanthemum virginianum (common mountain mint) is occasionally offered. It has narrow leaves and white flowers like *P. tenuifolium* but is taller and tends to move around a little too much.

Hybrids
'Eagle Rock' is another Plant Delights offering, a clump-former with pink flowers. Native to rocky areas in Virginia, so excellent drainage is recommended. It is fortunate that plant people like Tony at Plant Delights are taking an interest in

this wonderful genus. Now let's make all his climbs up mountains and through snake-infested territory worth his while—go buy some of his mountain mints.

Recommended propagation

Seed: Seeds germinate readily.

Cuttings: Two- to three-node terminal cuttings root readily.

Division: Divide mature populations to your heart's content.

Etymology

Genus: From the Greek, *pyknos* ("dense") and *anthos* ("flower"), referring to the densely crowded flowers.

Specific epithet: *incanum* ("gray"); *muticum* ("blunt," "without a point"); *tenuifolium* ("slender-leaved"); *virginianum* ("of Virginia").

Common name: Mountain mints are not true mints (*Mentha*), nor are they native to the mountains. Oh well.

Ratibida	prairie coneflower	Asteraceae

The ratibidas are to the prairie as cheese is to apple pie. One just expects to see it with rudbeckias, liatris, and monarda, waving in the breeze with big bluestem and switch grass. This is an indispensable group of plants for the meadow garden or other informal planting. In general, ratibidas survive heat, drought, flooding, and winter cold, and thrive on most any soil.

Ratibida columnifera	Mexican hat

An easy plant to distinguish and not an easy plant to forget, with its narrow columnar disk, at least four times as long as it is wide. The ray flowers are only about 1" long and droop down from the base of the disk. Plants grow about 3' tall and produce handsome leaves that are pinnately divided into five to nine narrow segments. It attracts hordes of butterflies, reseeds but is not invasive, and works wonderfully well in combination with other natives flowering during summer and fall.

var. *pulcherrima* has mahogany or purple ray flowers and is significantly shorter than the species.

Habitat: From Montana to Colorado east to Minnesota, south to New Mexico and Texas.

Hardiness: USDA Zones 3–9.

Garden site: Full sun, dry soils. Wet feet are death.

Garden maintenance: Little is necessary, particularly if sited properly.

Ratibida pinnata gray coneflower

Plants are similar to *Ratibida columnifera* but do not produce the sombrero cone. They are handsome but more subdued, with a flatter disk that starts out gray and matures to brown then black. In summer, the flowers, which consist of the disk and yellow to gold drooping rays, open for weeks on end. Durability is its middle name.

Habitat: Ontario to South Dakota, south to Oklahoma, Louisiana and east to Florida.
Hardiness: USDA Zones 3–9.
Garden site: Full sun, well-drained soils.
Garden maintenance: A little lime sometimes helps get this species established; otherwise, treat it as you would *Ratibida columnifera*.

Recommended propagation
Seed: Seed is the easiest means of propagation.

Ratibida pinnata

Etymology
Genus: Derivation unknown.
Specific epithet: *columnifera* ("columnar"); *pinnata* ("feather-like"), pinnate, with leaflets arranged on each side of a common stalk.
Common name: A sombrero, a Mexican hat, is somewhat reminiscent of the flower shape of *Ratibida columnifera*.

Rudbeckia yellow coneflower Asteraceae

Rudbeckias, along with echinaceas and gaillardias, are so common they don't even need a common name. Approximately fifteen species have been described, all native to this country, from the eastern seaboard to the prairie states; perhaps fewer than six are known by gardeners, but at least a couple of those are known very, very well. The wonderful old-fashioned black-eyed Susan (*Rudbeckia hirta*) has been so bred and wed it is scarcely recognizable; and then there's that little-known variant (var. *sullivantii*) of a formerly little-known species (*R. fulgida*) that exploded on the garden scene when the Germans discovered it and called it 'Goldsturm'—no landscape is safe from its yellow and black flowers.

That rudbeckias are so common is testament to their toughness and their success and the reason we (or at least landscapers) keep planting these darn daisies. To be honest, I love most of them, and it is nice to know that, rather than scour the Internet, we can stroll up to almost any retail outlet, put our money down, and walk out with a native plant that was part of Lewis and Clark's journey.

Rudbeckia fulgida   orange coneflower

I was surprised that so many nurseries still offer the species or the more compact form, var. *sullivantii*. The species is 2–4' tall; the variety is only 1½–2' in height and a better choice for gardeners. With the takeover by 'Goldsturm', it seemed that the market for var. *sullivantii* had dried up; however, as it became clear that 'Goldsturm' was not easily distinguished from the variety, plant and seed sales increased. Another variety, var. *newmannii*, has smaller leaves and flowers is also useful and quite floriferous. Both var. *sullivantii* and var. *newmannii* are excellent, long-lasting summer daisies, outstanding in any full sun area.

Habitat: In woodlands and meadows from New Jersey to Missouri, south to Mississippi and east to Florida.
Hardiness: USDA Zones 3–8.
Garden site: Full sun, well-drained soils.
Garden maintenance: Plants will need cutting back hard once flowering has finished. They make so many flowers that when they begin to disintegrate in late summer and fall, they turn brown and are perfect for fungal infestation. Clean up plants by removing dead foliage in fall.

Rudbeckia fulgida var. *sullivantii* 'Goldsturm'

Rudbeckia hirta   black-eyed Susan

These plants can be so wonderful, I consider them one of the few that can give sunflowers a run for their money. The people of Maryland, who adopted the black-eyed Susan as their state flower in 1918, feel the same. Plants are 1–3' tall and bear rough, hairy alternate leaves, which may be divided, cleft, lobed, or entire; the flowers consist of yellow to orange ray flowers and a black cone. Unfortunately, plants are susceptible to many foliar diseases, especially botrytis, a fungal disease that turns the leaves black; this is a major problem when plants are crowded, or when a combination of humidity and rain occurs. Plants persist much longer in the North than in the South.

Plants are considered either annuals or biennials—regardless, they are short-lived at best. They all overwinter as basal rosettes, flowering from late spring into late summer. In areas of hot, humid summers with afternoon showers, they generally perish by August. It is highly unlikely that you will see plants of the actual species in garden centers; however, seeds are available, and these can be direct sown in a meadow or other informal garden setting. Many years of breeding have yielded many, many cultivars. Here are a few of my favorites.

'Becky' has long been a favorite for excellent outdoor performance, and landscapers opt for her above other single yellows. She is shorter than many cultivars and, in rain or wind, does not fall over as badly as the taller forms.

'Cherokee Sunset' has handsome bicolored flowers.

'Gloriosa' ('Gloriosa Double Flowered', 'Double Orange') is an old-fashioned semi-double or double, with large flowers up to 6" across in shades of orange and rust. Plants are 3–5' tall. An All-America Selection (AAS) award winner in 1981.

'Goldilocks' is a semi-double to double-flowered daisy, 18–24" tall. The 3–4" wide flowers are golden yellow. The doubleness is quite attractive, if you like double daisies, but flowers are even more susceptible to disease from summer rain and humidity.

'Green Eyes' features narrow yellow ray flowers surrounding a greenish disk.

'Indian Summer' is one of the finest black-eyed Susans I have seen. Plants are about 3' tall, compact not gangly, and seldom need support; when in flower, they are absolutely smothered in 6" wide, clean yellow singles. An All-America award winner in 1995. If I had but one choice, this would be it.

'Irish Eyes' is a handsome form, with yellow-orange ray flowers around a green eye.

'Marmalade' is an old standard, providing large golden yellow flowers with a contrasting dark disk. Plants grow 2½–3' tall.

'Prairie Sun', with two shades of yellow around the green eye, was an All-America award winner in 2002.

'Rustic Colors' are just that, a mix of bronze, gold, mahogany, and yellow with contrasting black centers. Plants range from 2' (sometimes called 'Rustic Dwarf') to 3½' tall.

Rudbeckia hirta 'Sonora'

Rudbeckia hirta 'Toto'

'Sonora' is the best of the bicolors, bearing 5" wide flowers with a mahogany-red center zone on the ray petals, then golden yellow beyond. Plants are only 15–20" tall.

'Toto' is my choice for a dwarf selection, with clean single gold-yellow rays surrounding a dark center. At 8–10" tall, they are useful anywhere good, persistent color is needed and are the least maintenance-needy of any cultivar. The Toto series offers different colors.

Habitat: In open fields from Massachusetts to Illinois, south to Alabama and east to Georgia.

Hardiness: USDA Zones 9–11.

Garden site: Full sun, moderate moisture.

Garden maintenance: Plants can be direct-sown and planted about 1' apart. Spray with fungicides if needed.

Rudbeckia laciniata	cutleaf coneflower

The dull green lower leaves are obviously three- to seven-lobed and toothed. The upper leaves are far less cut than the lower. The stems branch at the top and have short, stiff sandpaper-like hairs. Plants grow at least 3' tall (cultivars can get much taller) and equally wide, and in late summer they bear 2–3" wide heads consisting of drooping yellow ray flowers around a green cylindrical disk. Plants are long-lived; a ten-year performance is not uncommon. Beware, plants can be aggressive. Plants and seeds are available, but as with most rudbeckias, cultivars are far more common.

'Golden Glow' (var. *hortensia*) is 3–5' tall and produces fully double lemon-yellow flowers.

'Goldquelle' is a double yellow.

Rudbeckia laciniata 'Goldquelle'

Rudbeckia maxima

'Herbstsonne' ('Autumn Sun'), one of the most popular, features sulphur-yellow ray flowers around a green disk. Plants are 7' tall and flower in mid to late summer. This may be a hybrid with *Rudbeckia nitida*. Hardy to zone 5.

Habitat: In wet fields and ditches from Quebec to Montana and south to Arizona, northeastern Texas, east to Louisiana and Florida.
Hardiness: USDA Zones 3–9, although cultivars may be less cold hardy.
Garden site: Full sun, consistent moisture.
Garden maintenance: If placed in full sun, plants should not need staking; however, if plants are too dry or under too much shade, they will fall over. Aphids are usually present, and when they are, sprays of water knock them off without problem.

Rudbeckia maxima   **great coneflower**

The tallest of all the daisies, this thing can easily reach 8' in height, although in nature, plants are generally no more than 4' tall. Plants form basal clumps of large, wide leaves, which are blue-green in color. The long, leafless flower stems rise straight up from the basal rosette; the yellow ray flowers droop from the disk, which is much like that of prairie coneflower (*Ratibida*), that is, long and narrow. Plants are overrated as garden purchases, although the leaves are good-looking, and the stature is certainly impressive.

Habitat: In prairies throughout the central and southern United States.
Hardiness: USDA Zones 5–9.
Garden site: Full sun.

Garden maintenance: Provide plenty of room. Too much love (water, nutrients) will result in too-tall plants. They may need staking when in flower anyway but definitely will fall over if tough love is not provided.

Rudbeckia subtomentosa   sweet coneflower

This is a somewhat unknown coneflower in the East and West but well used in the Midwest and prairie states. Plants bear hairy gray-green leaves that, if crushed, provide a fleeting but ever so sweet perfume. The flower heads also produce a faint odor of anise. Plants can grow to 5' in height, but 3' is more common; and if they are pinched in late spring, they will form rather nice 2–2½' tall clumps. They do not do well in wet soils but tolerate more moisture than *Rudbeckia hirta*. Plants tend to be at their best in mid summer and fall, and perform particularly well in the Plains states, making a beautiful combination with liatris at Powell Gardens in Kingsville, Missouri.

Habitat: Michigan to Wisconsin, south to Oklahoma, Kansas, Louisiana and east to Tennessee.
Hardiness: USDA Zones 3–9.
Garden site: Full soil, consistent moisture levels.
Garden maintenance: A single pinch in late spring helps keep the plants in check.

Rudbeckia subtomentosa

Rudbeckia triloba

Rudbeckia triloba   **three-leaved coneflower**

Of all the coneflowers, I admit to liking this one the most. It doesn't match the flower power of 'Goldsturm', or the stature of *Rudbeckia maxima* or the fragrance of *R. subtomentosa*—it is simply a doer. They are short-lived to be sure but seed around sufficiently to always provide a plant or two. The leaves are three-lobed mainly at the base, losing the lobes as they ascend the stems. The yellow flowers are small and surround a black disk. Literally hundreds of small flowers can cover a single plant in mid to late summer.

Plants may bloom the first year from seed but often act as a biennial, waiting for the next summer to hold forth. After flowering, don't be surprised to see it start to fall apart. This is a cottage garden rudbeckia and looks at home in any informal garden, including a meadow.

Habitat: Connecticut to Michigan west to Nebraska, south to Texas and east to Florida.
Hardiness: USDA Zones 3–9.
Garden site: Full sun. In a mixed border it looks stunning; by itself, it may be too lax.
Garden maintenance: Cut back hard after flowering if seedlings are not wanted. Keep away from wet soils.

Other species for the garden
Most rudbeckias make fine garden plants, depending on who is defining "fine."

Rudbeckia grandiflora grows 3–4' tall and has golden daisies with a dark eye. They are robust and quickly becoming popular. Zones 5–8.

Rudbeckia missouriensis has flowers similar to common *R. hirta* but with narrower leaves. Zones 5–8.

Rudbeckia occidentalis is a western species with unusual rayless flower heads. They consist of disks that look like pinecones atop tall, naked green stems. Interesting, if not particularly ornamental. Zones 5–8.

Recommended propagation

Seed: Seed is the best method for all species, even for 'Goldsturm'.

Cuttings: Terminal cuttings can be taken and rooted with relative ease.

Division: On mature plantings, carefully dislodge some plants.

Etymology

Genus: For anatomist, botanist, wood carver, and writer Olof Rudbeck and his son, Olof Rudbeck the Younger, of Uppsala, Sweden. The elder founded Uppsala Botanic Garden; his son befriended Carl Linnaeus when Linnaeus was a student.

Specific epithet: *fulgida* ("shining, glistening"); *grandiflora* ("large-flowered") *hirta* ("hairy"); *maxima* ("largest"); *missouriensis* ("of Missouri"); *occidentalis* ("western"); *subtomentosa* (*sub*, "under"; *tomentosa*, "densely woolly"), for hairs on the underside of leaves; *triloba* ("three lobes"), on the basal leaves.

Common name: These make sense.

Ruellia	wild petunia	Acanthaceae

It may be argued that most useful species of *Ruellia* are escapees from Mexico, native to our continent only but not to the United States. In fact, the best and worst species for gardens is probably *R. brittoniana* (Britton's Mexican petunia), native to South America and Mexico and now found in Texas and much of the Southeast. The 3–4' tall blue-flowered species is handsome and eye-catching in

Ruellia brittoniana

Ruellia brittoniana 'Chi Chi'

its own right but is also available in shorter cultivars ranging from pink ('Chi-Chi') to white ('Alba') and in dwarf forms as well ('Katie's Dwarf'). The worst part is that they can reseed everywhere and rapidly become weeds. They are cold hardy only to zone 7b, so areas north of that have few reasons to be concerned; even in the Horticulture Gardens at the University of Georgia, where they perennialize, they have not been a weed problem. They can become an awful nuisance further south, however; and, where hardy, the Mexican petunia excels at invading wetlands. The Florida Exotic Pest Plant Council has classified it as a Category I invasive species, meaning that it "[alters] native plant communities by displacing native species, changing community structures or ecological functions, or hybridizing with natives."

All ruellias flower when temperatures are hot, all prefer full sun, and all have the reputation of being aggressive to invasive, some deservedly so, some not. Here are a couple of our own.

Ruellia humilis	fringed petunia

This is an easy-to-naturalize species for hot, sunny areas, particularly useful in meadows or in rock gardens. Plants are low-growing (less than 12" tall) and produce many light blue flowers throughout the summer. The sessile leaves are crowded at the base, alternate on the hairy stem, and hairy underneath and on the margins. Flowers last only a day, but they keep on opening as long as temperatures remain above 70F.

Habitat: From Pennsylvania west to Iowa, south to Texas and east to northern Florida.
Hardiness: USDA Zones 6–9.
Garden site: Full sun is preferable, but afternoon shade is tolerated. Soils are of little consequence.
Garden maintenance: Deadhead if seedlings become a problem. You will be giving plants away within three years.

Other species for the garden
Ruellia caroliniensis is similar to *R. humilis* except that the leaves have petioles. They do not extend as far north or west.

Recommended propagation
Seed: Easily grown from seed.
Cuttings: Terminal cuttings may be rooted without problem.
Division: Plants that have formed mature colonies can be divided.

Ruellia humilis

Etymology

Genus: For Jean Ruel (1474–1537), herbalist to Francois I of France.

Specific epithet: *brittoniana*, for Nathaniel Lord Britton, who studied the floras of the West Indies and the eastern United States; *caroliniensis* ("of the Carolinas"); *humilis* ("low-growing").

Common name: Flowers do look much like a petunia. Fringed petunia is a reference to the hairy leaves, not the petals.

Salvia	sage	Lamiaceae

Where does one start when discussing salvias? There's a green one and a pink one, "and a blue one and a yellow one / And they're all made out of ticky-tacky / And they all look just the same." Stop—I don't think Pete Seeger was singing about salvias in the 1962 folk song "Little Boxes." And of course, as any salvite will tell you, they are not all the same!

Salvias are part of the currency of plant geeks like myself, with collectors all over the country vying to acquire even the ugliest salvia for their garden. I believe that my readers are more intelligent than this, so we shall discuss this affliction no longer. Of the 700 or so species of *Salvia*, approximately fifty are native to the continental United States, but an additional twenty may now be found in the wild, having escaped from gardens or other growing areas. Of those fifty natives, you will be lucky to find more than six for sale without really searching far and wide.

All salvias have four-sided stems, opposite leaves, and a whorled arrangement of flowers. Most have a "sagey" smell, some more so than others. Salvias are often distinguished from other members of this large family by their foliar fragrance and by the ease with which the corolla is pulled away from the calyx. Try it, you will see. Their native habitats are so diverse one would be shocked if there was a single garden area that suited them all; however, wet areas and shade should be avoided.

Salvia azurea	azure sage

The azure sage is just that, boasting two-lipped azure-blue flowers, usually with a white center. Flowers open in mid to late summer and continue until frost. The hairy foliage is reasonably handsome, being gray-green and long and narrow. Plants tolerate heat and humidity (they look great in Savannah, Georgia), but the normally 3–5' tall plants can get ugly-lanky without some serious cutting back in the spring and early summer.

var. *grandiflora* (subsp. *pitcheri*) has larger, often paler blue flowers.

Salvia azurea

'Nekan', named by Bluebird Nursery for a seed strain that grows in Nebraska and Kansas (get it?), seems to be less prone to falling over.

Habitat: Michigan to Utah, south to Texas and east to Florida.
Hardiness: USDA Zones (4)5–9.
Garden site: Full sun, well-drained soils.
Garden maintenance: Cut back in early spring to reduce mature height and increase branching, or cut back after flowering. Adding some dolomitic lime to the planting area appears to enhance stem strength.

Salvia coccinea **scarlet sage**

This is one of the finest and most floriferous sages on the market. Plants are blessed with shiny green leaves and handsome scarlet flowers. Some people think it is too similar to the bedding sage, *Salvia splendens*; while they are both annuals and both have red flowers, they differ in many ways. The foliage of *S. coccinea* is thin and more or less translucent, easily seen if a leaf is plucked off and held to the sun; its whorled flowers are held quite distant from each other on many-flowered racemes, another departure from the crowded flowers of *S. splendens*. All in all, this species is more refined and elegant than other red salvias. Unlike many sages, plants flower all season and need a cut-back only if they become too tall. They are susceptible to whiteflies, but that is more of a greenhouse than a landscape problem. I think they perform a little better in the North than in the South; however, I have seen great plantings almost everywhere I have traveled. The several available cultivars offer scarlet sages that are not always scarlet.

Salvia coccinea 'Scarlet Nymph'

'Cherry Blossom' has lovely salmon and white bicolored flowers on 15–24" tall plants.

'Lactea', the precursor of 'Snow Nymph', has white flowers.

'Lady in Red', one of the first introductions, bears scarlet flowers on 2–2½' tall plants. Excellent for containers and still very popular.

Nymph series is an outstanding and eye-catching group, producing flowers in white ('Snow Nymph'), white and red bicolor ('Coral Nymph'), salmon ('Salmon Nymph'), deep red ('Scarlet Nymph'), and pink ('Pink Nymph').

Habitat: From Texas to Florida, north to South Carolina.
Hardiness: USDA Zones 8–11; treat as an annual in most parts of the country.
Garden site: Full sun. Allow for good air movement.
Garden maintenance: Cut back if needed. Fertilize lightly with a complete fertilizer in early spring and early summer.

Salvia farinacea   mealy-cup sage

Some common names for plants are pragmatic, some are romantic, and some express something about a local culture or area. And then there are those that pique your curiosity and leave you scratching your head. The first thing that came to mind when I saw the term "mealy-cup" was that maybe it was related to "mealy-mouth"; however, in sleuthing further, I determined that poor old salvia couldn't talk, so its unwillingness to state anything, directly or not, was moot. Turns out plants have a kind of whitish tinge to the stems and flowers (actually soft hairs) which looks a bit like meal, in the floury, farina, cornmeal sense. So, as Professor Higgins almost said, "I think I've got it!"

Salvia farinacea

These are considered annuals in most parts of the country and are sold as bedding plants for the handsome blue color of the flowers. The leaves are dull green, with that mealy look on the stems and sepals. As may be expected, the breeders got at this and bred plants to be compact, to about 12" tall in the garden. They are best when planted in large drifts; one or two plants is simply not sufficient.

'Argent' is an older form with silver-white flowers. Plants do not stand out from other plantings as well as the blue and violet forms.

'Cirrus' is about 15" tall with white flowers on silver-white flower stems. More compact and slightly whiter flowers than 'Argent'.

'Reference' has bicolor flowers, similar to but not as well known as 'Strata'.

'Rhea' is a compact form (12") with dark blue to violet flowers.

'Strata' bears bicolored blue and white flowers. I find it rather washed-out, not knowing whether it wants to be blue or white, but I am in the minority for sure: it earned a Fleuroselect award in Europe and an All-America award in the United States (1996).

'Victoria', the most common cultivar, has violet-blue flowers, bigger and more vivid than 'Rhea'. Still as good as any!

Habitat: Through New Mexico, most of Texas and into Louisiana, east to Florida.
Hardiness: USDA Zones 9–11.
Garden site: Full sun, well-drained soils.
Garden maintenance: Fertilize lightly with a complete fertilizer in early spring and early summer.

Salvia greggii

Salvia greggii 'Coral'

Salvia greggii   Texas sage

This species is an emerging star in the salvia world, not only for its handsome large flowers on strong plants but because it disdains the abusive heat and humidity common to many gardens. The two-lipped flowers, which may be red, pink, violet, or white, are held in whorls of two or three and have a wide lower lip and smaller upper lip. When I teach Texas sage to my students, I call it the "pouting" salvia, because the flattened lower lip reminds me of my daughter pouting when she was told no. My students may forget the name *Salvia greggii*, but they always remember the pouting salvia.

Essentially they are woody shrubs, not much different from a spirea or forsythia, except that in most parts of the country they die over the winter, so they never attain a shrubby appearance; however, even in a single season, you will notice how rapidly the stems become woody. While plants are native to the American South, primarily the Southwest, hybridization and selection have provided outstanding choices for gardeners across the country. Most selections of the species are sold as bedding plants or as small transplants and are seldom winter hardy below zone 8; hybrids, however, may overwinter in zone 7. All cultivars are alive with hummingbirds and butterflies.

'Alba' has white flowers with a green calyx. Also sold as 'White'.

'Big Pink' produces deep pink and lavender flowers with an obviously larger lower lip.

'Cherry Queen' (*Salvia greggii* × *S. blepharophylla*) is one of the many hybrids produced by the incomparable Richard Dufresne of North Carolina. We have had this sage in the Horticulture Gardens at Georgia for eight years, and every year it starts flowering in May and continues until frost. An absolutely outstanding plant for southern gardens.

'Chiffon' produces light yellow flowers on 2–3' tall plants.

'Coral' has purple—no, no, sorry—coral-colored flowers.

Salvia greggii 'Desert Blaze'

Salvia microphylla

'Dark Dancer' bears fuchsia flowers.

'Desert Blaze' has green and white variegated leaves with narrow white edges. Plants are only about 18" tall and bear red flowers in spring and fall.

'Keter's Red' has orange-red flowers.

'Maraschino' is an excellent maraschino-cherry sage, a cross between *Salvia greggii* and *S. microphylla*, a native of southern North America (southeastern Arizona through Mexico). Usually not winter hardy north of zone 7b.

'Pale Yellow' is likely a hybrid, bearing pale yellow flowers on 18" tall plants.

'Peach La Encantada' ('La Encantada') produces handsome peach-colored flowers on 15–18" tall plants.

'Purple Haze', introduced by Pat McNeal of Austin, Texas, has deep violet-blue flowers.

'Raspberry Royale' (*Salvia greggii* × *S. microphylla*) bears magenta flowers in late summer and fall. Easily available and the recipient of many accolades. Similar to 'Red Velvet'.

'Red Velvet' (*Salvia greggii* × *S. microphylla*) is about 3' tall and has velvety red flowers.

Habitat: Texas and New Mexico, extending south to Mexico.
Hardiness: USDA Zones 7b–10.
Garden site: Full sun, good drainage.
Garden maintenance: For most gardeners, plants are annuals, and little mainte-
nance is necessary. Trim and cut back in late spring if perennial.

Salvia lyrata   **lyre-leaf sage**

This eastern native has been overlooked entirely by gardeners; even salvia aficionados turn their noses up when this species is mentioned. That it is a weed

over half the country may have something to do with it; and worse, the leaves—lyre-shaped as they are—sort of look like dandelions. The foliage has dark mid-veins and a distinct purple hue in the spring, not at all unattractive; and the 1' long lavender-blue inflorescence is upright and handsome. Plants are less than 15" tall in the wild, a little taller in cultivation. This is an up-and-comer, and I expect to see it much more widely planted in the future.

Speaking of lyres, I had not seen one in a while, so I thought I should do an image search on Google to see what this epithet was really all about. Lyres have two curved arms, connected at the upper end by a crossbar. Mmm, I'll have to take a closer look at that leaf—I don't remember any crossbar.

'Purple Knockout' produces burgundy leaves in the spring and fall, deeper than those that normally occur on the species. A nice darker representative of the species.

Habitat: In woodlands from Connecticut to Missouri, south to Texas and east to Florida.
Hardiness: USDA Zones 4–9.
Garden site: Partially shaded open area is best. Plants form large colonies if allowed to reseed.
Garden maintenance: None.

Salvia regla   **mountain sage, Hildago sage**

This is a terrific sage (a) if you like your colors bright and (b) if you can wait long enough for those colors to appear. This southwestern native is an annual in most

Salvia regla

of the country, but it grows well wherever summers are warm. The flowers are rich orange-scarlet and show up a football field away. Unfortunately, the football-field glimpse does not occur until fall, and in the Northeast and Midwest, it is likely that frost will appear before the flowers. Even in Athens (zone 7b), it seems like a race against the coming cold. Most gardeners shouldn't bother, but those with late frosts should give this shrub a try.

'Mount Emory' has 2" red flowers and may be a little more cold hardy; 'Warnock's Choice' is 3–4' tall—both dimensions representative of the species.

Habitat: In open areas of Texas, into the Hildago province of Mexico.
Hardiness: USDA Zones 8–10.
Garden site: Full sun, well-drained soil.
Garden maintenance: None.

Recommended propagation
Seed: Most salvias can be grown readily from seed and will flower the first year.
Cuttings: Take two- to three-node softwood cuttings in late spring and early summer.

Etymology
Genus: From the Latin, *salvus* ("safe"), for its supposed medicinal values.
Specific epithet: *azurea* ("azure"); *coccinea* ("scarlet"); *farinacea* ("powdery"); *greggii*, for Josiah Gregg (1806–1850), frontier trader and author; *lyrata* ("lyre-shaped"), referring to the leaves; *regla* ("royal").

Sanguinaria canadensis	bloodroot	Papaveraceae

I seldom visit a woodland garden in the spring, particularly in the East, without seeing patches of white—bloodroot, sometimes extensive, sometimes just a few plants. Few vistas are more inviting than bloodroots shimmering in the early spring sunshine, but where do people get all this shimmer? As with our other woodlanders, like Virginia bluebells, wood poppies, or trilliums, a single plant does little to elicit oohs and ahs. A colony is what's wanted, and have you tried to buy a dozen bloodroots lately? They are not sold in the box stores, certainly, and seldom in plant stores; even if price were not a problem, they simply haven't transcended colony to retail bench. On the Internet, plants are available, but if they are cheap, they are probably being dug from the wild, and if they are nursery grown, be prepared (and be thankful to have the opportunity) to pay a hefty price. So this shimmer thing may take a little more time than you planned. That is why it is good to join garden clubs, master gardener groups, and the like: you may just meet others who are willing to share some of their colonies.

Bloodroots often flower before their dull green leaves pop out of the ground in the spring. Plants multiply by rhizomes, which push up the symmetrical flowers;

Sanguinaria canadensis

flowers often bear four narrow petals, alternating with four wider ones, although there is a great deal of variability. The two sepals are rarely seen except on the flower bud. After flowering, thin capsules form and throw seed out, quickly increasing the population. These are woodland creatures, but deciduous shade is excellent because they can soak in that early sunshine to build powerful roots for the next year, making more plants for that fantasy colony you lust for.

I have loads of fun breaking apart the root to show the blood-red sap—gets kids and grandparents alike hooked on the fun of gardening every time. A little "face painting" goes a long way in the battle to overcome the appeal of PlayStation and X-Box disease, which has paralyzed Generation Y. Find some, buy some, and enjoy your colony of three. I promise, they will go forth and multiply!

'Multiplex', a double-flowered form of the species, is sought-after because flowers tend to stay on the plant a little longer. I enjoy them, but I enjoy the simplicity of the singles even more.

Habitat: On dry, rocky slopes from Quebec to Manitoba, south to Oklahoma and east to Alabama and over to Florida.

Hardiness: USDA Zones 3–8.

Garden site: A partially shaded, moist area is best, although plants tolerate drought well. They go dormant in summer, but if drought or lack of shade is a problem, dormancy will occur sooner. Deciduous shade is preferable to coniferous shade.

Garden maintenance: None.

Recommended propagation

Seed: Collect seeds from the capsules when the seeds begin to turn brown. Be vigilant, or they will have already been dispersed. Sow immediately in other areas of the garden or in seed trays. Transplant at the beginning of the second season.

Cuttings: Softwood cuttings can be taken before flowers appear, but often flower buds occur before the foliage appears. Seed and natural rhizome movement are better.

Division: Only in the sense that members of a colony can be moved around.

Etymology

Genus: From the Latin, *sanguis* ("blood"), referring to the red sap in the rhizome.

Specific epithet: *canadensis* ("of Canada"), see *Cornus*.

Common name: A perfectly wonderful name.

Sanguisorba canadensis	Canadian burnet	Rosaceae

Many burnets are used in American gardens, but this is the only native that enjoys anything close to popularity. Essentially, these are bog plants, but they also grow in normal garden soils as long as moisture can be maintained. The foliage is pinnately compound, consisting of seven to fifteen toothed leaflets, and the young leaves are a useful addition to soups, drinks, and salads. Dozens of small white flowers are arranged in a 6–8" long spike, each flower consisting of four sepals but no petals.

They are handsome enough plants, but they can get large and leggy. The best reason for including the plant in a garden setting is to be able to cut the bottle-brush spikes of flowers and enjoy them inside. If a bog needs planting or a meadow needs populating, go at it. Plants are useless south of zone 6, but are terrific even as far north as Alaska, where they are known as Sitka burnet.

Habitat: In swamps, wet meadows, and bogs from Newfoundland to Labrador south to New England and west to Illinois and Michigan.

Hardiness: USDA Zones 2–6.

Garden site: Moist soils and full sun are preferable.

Sanguisorba menziesii

Sanguisorba canadensis

Garden maintenance: They can be aggressive in moist soils, so be careful: you may be removing some in a few years.

Other species for the garden
Sanguisorba menziesii (Menzies' burnet) is native to the Northwest, including Alaska. The foliage is bluish green, and the flower spikes are rosy to dark red. There is more foliage than flowers, and where I have seen it, it has been somewhat floppy; however, the further north one gardens, the better the chances of the plant looking good. Zones 2–6.

Recommended propagation
Seed: Stratify seeds by sowing in trays and keeping in a cold frame over the winter.
Cuttings: Two- to three-node softwood cuttings can be taken in early summer.

Etymology
Genus: From the Latin, *sanguis* ("blood") and *sorbeo* ("to soak up"), a reference to the rootstock's styptic properties.
Specific epithet: *canadensis* ("of Canada"), see *Cornus*; *menziesii*, for Archibald Menzies (1754–1842), a Scottish naval surgeon and botanist who accompanied Vancouver on his voyage of Pacific exploration.
Common name: Burnet means brownish, but I don't know how that relates to the genus.

Saururus cernuus	lizard's tail	Saururaceae

It is nice to be able to talk about waterways without talking about some foreign plant or fish or mussel wreaking havoc. Seems no swamp, stream, or lake is safe from aliens anymore, and planting something in a water setting can fill one with guilt. Give lizard's tail a try. I have always liked the 1–2' tall plants, if for no other reason than the great name, but I also appreciate the handsome heart-shaped leaves and the 4–6" long lizard-like spikes of white flowers. The flowers are interesting (at least to a plant nut like me) because they lack both petals and sepals; the white color comes from the long stamens. Add to that the pleasant fragrance of citrus from all parts of the plant and, well, I'm hooked.

For water gardens, place potted plants in about 6" of water. For natural ponds, plant along the edges under shallow water or in moist, boggy soils. Unrestrained rhizomes will spread to form nice-sized colonies.

Habitat: In shallow water and swamps from New England to southwestern Quebec, west to Minnesota, south to Texas and east to Florida.
Hardiness: USDA Zones 3–8.
Garden site: Find a pond or bog.

*Saururus
cernuus*

Garden maintenance: None, except that if the colony becomes too large, some
sharing with friends may have to be arranged.

Recommended propagation
Seed: Seeds should be stratified in a cold frame or cooler, and then planted in
warm conditions; keep germination medium moist. Germination rates of
80 percent are not uncommon.
Division: Divide the rhizomes when plants emerge in the spring.

Etymology
Genus: From the Greek, *sauros* ("lizard") and *oura* ("tail"), referring to the tail-
like inflorescence.
Specific epithet: *cernuus* ("inclining the head"), referring to the drooping tips of
the flower spikes.
Common name: A great choice.

Schizachyrium scoparium   little bluestem   **Poaceae**

Little bluestem is one of the dominant grasses of the tallgrass prairie. It was
once part of the big bluestem genus *Andropogon* (*A. scoparius*), and thus there is
a good deal of confusion among nursery people and gardeners when they are
looking for bluestems (hint: just ask for 'The Blues', see below).

I have opted not to use a pronunciation guide in this book (because my edi-
tor won't let me); however, if ever help was needed, it is now. After me now:
skits-ah-KEER-ee-um skoh-PAIR-ee-um. Leaves are blue-green on the flattened
bases of stems and are particularly beautiful when planted in drifts. The foliage

and flowers turn a handsome reddish to yellowish orange in the fall and look quite nice throughout the winter. The seed heads, when viewed in a mass, give the appearance of an old man's beard. Flowers are terrific in bouquets. Their easy establishment has made plants a favorite for landscaping greenways and restoring damaged wilderness or recreation areas. Plants are 1–3' tall.

'The Blues' is a far more popular garden choice than the species, mainly because it is much more readily available in garden stores; with its striking blue foliage and handsome russet winter color, it is worth the extra money. Great in containers, outstanding en masse.

Habitat: Throughout the country, except Oregon and Utah.
Hardiness: USDA Zones 4–9.
Garden site: Full sun.
Garden maintenance: Cut back to the ground in the spring.

Recommended propagation
Seed: Plants may self-sow.
Division: Anytime.

Etymology
Genus: Perhaps from the Greek, *schizo* ("divided"), for the divided rachis on the flowers, which gives the broom-like effect.
Specific epithet: *scoparium* ("broom-like").

Scutellaria	skullcap	Lamiaceae

Seems the skullcaps are one of the "in" plants these days—I'm amazed by the number of species being sold out there. To be honest, I could ask most people to describe coreopsis or echinacea, even gaura, and they would likely tell me something close to factual. Try that with scutellaria, and all you'll get is blank stares. And if people can't tell me anything about the entire genus, I wonder whence all this interest—in species that even experts are hard put to distinguish one from the other. Could it be that they propagate like weeds?

I am not complaining—so few natives are easily available, I think this is a great thing. I just hope gardeners catch up with the producers. In all species, the corolla forms an upward-curving tube, with two lips, much like a salvia. The upper lip is hood-like; the lower one is flat. All plants tolerate partial shade to full sun, and all have flowers in shades of blue, white, and pink. Most are low-growing, and some can become quite aggressive.

Scutellaria incana   **downy skullcap**

This is one of the more available species as well as one of the showiest, resulting in more converts every year. Plants are clump-formers and can grow up to 3' high, but 2' is more common. The bluntly toothed ovate leaves have minute white hairs on the underside and are up to 5" long and nearly 3" across. The blue flowers are held in whorls on branched inflorescences. This is one skullcap worth donning.

Habitat: In woods and thickets from New Jersey and western New York west to
    Iowa and Kansas, and south through Arkansas and Alabama, east to Florida.
Hardiness: USDA Zones 3–9.
Garden site: Partial shade to full sun in the North, afternoon shade in the
    South.
Garden maintenance: Cut back if they get a little too tall; otherwise, leave them
    alone.

Scutellaria serrata   **showy skullcap, Allegheny skullcap**

I spend money on this plant simply because it works well in my shaded garden. The leaf margins are cut like a blunt saw, a scalloped effect, and have a wonderful reddish tint, particularly in the spring and early summer. The dark lavender to purple flowers, 1–2" long, appear in spring and early summer. After pollination, tan-colored fruit are formed, which are not at all unattractive. Plants grow 15–18" tall. You should join me in purchasing them, especially all you Pennsylvania gardeners, since it is now an endangered species in your state.

343

Habitat: In woods from New York to West Virginia south to Missouri, Alabama and east to South Carolina.
Hardiness: USDA Zones 4–9.
Garden site: Partial shade suits them best.
Garden maintenance: Do not allow to dry out. Cut back if they become excessively tall.

Scutellaria suffrutescens	pink skullcap

This is a relative newcomer to the gardening world, introduced from nurseries in Texas. Whether this is even native to the United States is debatable: some say it is native to Arizona and New Mexico and skipped to Texas from there; others believe it crossed the border from Mexico. Putting borders aside for moment, I can tell you I have been impressed with its performance, even though it is an annual for most of the country. Plants are shrubby but grow only 6–8" tall. They are best in rocky areas or containers where drainage can be controlled. The small, narrow leaves have rounded tips and are slightly hairy, and the pink flowers, like little snapdragons, continue to open through most of the growing season.

Habitat: Semixeric areas in southwest to south central Texas.
Hardiness: USDA Zones 8–10.
Garden site: Full sun, well-drained soils.
Garden maintenance: Prune out dead stems if plants overwinter; otherwise, little needs doing.

Other species for the garden
Scutellaria integrifolia (hyssop skullcap) is 12–20" tall with entire leaves and blue (sometimes pink) flowers in late spring and early summer. It is a prolific self-sower and can be quite weedy. Said to be a good naturalizer. Zones 4–9.

Scutellaria ovata (heart-leaved skullcap) can be aggressive and, although quite handsome, should be used with some caution. Violet-blue flowers appear over soft leaves in early summer. Drought- and shade-tolerant. Zones 4–9.

Scutellaria resinosa (shrubby skullcap) has woody stems like *S. suffrutescens*. Plants are only 8–12" tall and produce entire leaves with many tiny glands on the underside. Violet-blue flowers are produced in late spring and continue for a long period of time. Zones 5–9.

Recommended propagation
Seed: Provide a cold treatment by planting in a tray and placing in a cold frame or cooler through the winter. Plants will often flower the next season.
Cuttings: Two- to three-node cuttings taken in spring or early summer should root if provided with a mild rooting hormone.
Division: The clump-formers can be divided, preferably in early spring.

Etymology

Genus: From the Latin, *scutella* ("small dish"), referring to the pouch on the calyx.

Specific epithet: *incana* ("hoary, gray"); *integrifolia* ("with entire or uncut leaves"); *ovata* ("ovate"), the broad end at the leaf's base; *resinosa* ("resinous"); *serrata* ("saw-toothed"); *suffrutescens* ("somewhat shrubby").

Common name: An extension of the calyx (sepals) protects the developing seeds; it is convex and looks a little like a yarmulke or skullcap.

Sedum	stonecrop	Crassulaceae

Sedums are the darlings of gardening and the epitome of the expression "plants that work," thanks to upright forms like 'Autumn Joy' and low-growing taxa like 'Angelina'. Not only are they pretty, easy to grow, and available, they have also been at the forefront of the green roof movement and other ecologically sound horticultural practices. The majority of sedums in our gardens are from other lands; our natives are far less known, therefore far less available. Can they compete? The short answer is yes, the long answer depends on what you are looking for. All are drought-tolerant, but none are tolerant of deep shade. Most of the low-growers flower in the spring; the upright forms, in summer and fall. I recommend these American natives, of the 300 or so species in the genus, to round out any collection.

Sedum spathulifolium	broad-leaf stonecrop

The tightness of growth seen in this species is quite amazing and wonderfully ornamental. The stems are short, and the spatula-like leaves are bunched together at the stem tips, making rosettes like hens and chicks. Plants are only 3–4" tall but have wonderful blue-gray leaves, each with a burgundy tint to the margins—really the best part of the plant. They are evergreen (although when under snow, no one much notices). Plants spread to 18" in a couple of years if properly sited. They can be placed in full sun and are especially useful for rock outcrops and crevices. In mid to late spring, yellow flowers occur on a three-forked inflorescence. Plants are native to West Coast and tend to grow only in the spring and fall.

'Cape Blanco', from Cape Blanco on the Oregon coast, is a popular selection, producing mats of silvery white foliage on 3" tall plants.

'Purpureum' has leaves with a flush of purple.

Habitat: On coastal cliffs and rocky ledges from the southern Coast Ranges of California east to the Sierra Nevada, through western Oregon and north to British Columbia.

Hardiness: USDA Zones 5–8.

Garden site: Rocks and gravel are good media to plant this in, although any well-drained material will suffice. Summer rain is not welcome, so be sure plants are placed where the rain can drain away quickly. Plants tolerate full sun on the West Coast but perform fine with some afternoon shade in the East and South.

Garden maintenance: None if properly sited.

Sedum ternatum   wild stonecrop, whorled stonecrop

I suppose any one of the plants in this book could be called wild something, and this is no more wild a stonecrop than any other. The leaves are scattered along the stems in whorls, generally in threes, thus the other common name. Plants grow 6–8" tall in the Armitage garden. They are not the most dramatic of sedums; however, they are tough as nails, tolerating drought, tree roots, shade, and humidity. They are so easy to grow that I tend to neglect them, and if I placed them in more sun, extricated them from the dogwood roots, and actually fertilized them once in ten years, they would probably be far more noticeable.

The rounded leaves are silvery green, and plants sprawl with creeping stems, being far less tightly wound than *Sedum spathulifolium*. The starry white flowers are produced in late spring and summer on a three-branched inflorescence. This is a shade-tolerant sedum, but morning sun helps performance immensely.

'Larinem Park', offered by creative nurseries, seems to be more compact than the species, and perhaps a bit more floriferous.

Sedum ternatum

Habitat: In damp places from New York to Michigan, south to Tennessee and east to Georgia.

Hardiness: USDA Zones 4–9.

Garden site: Site in area of morning sun and afternoon shade. Plants tolerate drought but perform better with irrigation every now and then.

Garden maintenance: Irrigate as needed.

Other species for the garden

Sedum nevii (Nevius' stonecrop) is offered online, I'm pleased to say. Plants are threatened in Georgia and endangered in Tennessee, confined to a small area in the southeastern corner of the state. Plants grow only about 3" tall and bear white flowers above the small blue-green leaves. Zones 5–9.

Sedum telephioides (tall stonecrop) looks a bit like 'Autumn Joy' and bears pale pink flowers in late summer and fall. Plants grow 12–15" tall. Native to the southern Appalachians and into Indiana and Illinois. Zones 4–9.

Recommended propagation

Seed: Can be done, but cuttings are easiest.

Cuttings: Two- to three-node terminal cuttings are easily rooted at almost any time.

Etymology

Genus: From the Latin, *sedo* ("to sit"), from the manner in which some species grow on rocks and walls.

Specific epithet: *nevii*, perhaps for Ruben Denton Nevius (1827–1913) of Alabama, who also discovered snow wreath, *Neviusia*; *spathulifolium* ("leaves shaped like a spatula"); *telephioides* ("similar to *Telephium*"), possibly connected with Telephus, a king of Mysia, an ancient region in northwest Asia Minor; *ternatum* ("in clusters of three").

Common name: Stonecrop refers to the preferred habitat of many species.

Senecio aureus	golden ragwort	Asteraceae

Senecio is an enormous (perhaps less so lately: many species have been split off into *Packera*) and diverse genus with about 1000 species, most of which have no value as ornamentals and many of which have proven to be noxious weeds. Of those native to this country, this is the only one I would invite to my home, and then only as a filler in shady woodlands, never into a civilized garden. *Senecio aureus* (*Packera aurea*) is my kind of plant—an ornamental weed. It has

Senecio aureus

Senecio aureus, seed heads

dandelion-like flowers, and its leaves are, well, leafy; the plant looks kind of shaggy by the time it throws its seeds (most of which will come up the next day) all over the place.

In colonies, however, the 1–3' tall plants make a bright and colorful show. The species is also interesting in that the yellow flowers arise from purple buds, and its basal and cauline (stem) leaves are totally different from each other. Do I recommend it for my daughters? Not really, but then I don't try to get rid of it either.

Habitat: In meadows and swamps from Quebec to North Dakota, south to Arkansas and east to Florida.

Hardiness: USDA Zones 4–9.

Garden site: Partial shade and moist soils seem to suit it well.

Garden maintenance: Remove spent flowers before they go to seed if you wish to control the population.

Recommended propagation

Seed: Easily grown from seed.

Division: Cull out plants from a colony and move them around if desired.

Etymology

Genus: From the Latin, *senex* ("old man"), referring to copious white hairs in the flowers.

Specific epithet: *aureus* ("golden").

Common name: Plants resemble ragwort (*Senecio jacobaea*), another member that is still firmly in the genus.

Shortia galacifolia	Oconee bells	Diapensiaceae

This species is as marvelous as ever and still as difficult to purchase. I was able to come up with only three sources on the Internet, but perhaps that is three more sources than a couple of years ago. People truly love this plant, likely because it is so hard to find, but I agree wholeheartedly with Charlie Johnson of Waincliffe Garden Nursery in Yorkshire, England: it is "difficult to obtain and difficult to cultivate but worth trading your right arm for." If you can find some nursery-raised plants, don't complain about the price—give thanks someone is making them available to you.

The pendulous five-lobed flowers are white, bell-shaped, and beautifully fringed, rising over leathery rounded leaves in the spring. Plants are always a source of pride and interest in anyone's garden. They are difficult to site, performing in peaty areas of moist shade. They need some acidification with acid mulches and should not be fertilized with organic fertilizers as this will surely burn the thin roots. If you live in the flatlands of the South, save your money: they do poorly in heat and humidity.

Shortia galacifolia

Shortia galacifolia

Habitat: In moist banks along streams in the Appalachian Mountains of North and South Carolina.

Hardiness: USDA Zones 4–8.

Garden site: Consistently moist, acid soils and shade.

Garden maintenance: If sited well, no maintenance is needed.

Recommended propagation

Seed: Seed germinates reasonably quickly, but seedlings are very slow to grow on.

Cuttings: Cuttings that incorporate a little bit of the stem work better than tip cuttings.

Division: This is the easiest means of propagation, if a colony is established.

Etymology

Genus: For Kentucky biologist Charles W. Short (1794–1863).

Specific epithet: galacifolia ("with leaves like *Galax*").

Common name: Plants were thought to have originated in Oconee County, South Carolina.

Silene	campion	Caryophyllaceae

There is no shortage of great campions for the garden; some are perfect for rock gardens and well-drained areas, others for the meadow garden, and others are tolerant of heat and humidity. Most of our native campions, however, perform better with cool nights and warm days, and do poorly in hot, humid weather (the Armitage garden has been a burial ground for the few poor silenes who involuntarily wandered in). Plants have opposite leaves; flowers consist of five notched petals and an inflated calyx, sometimes obvious, most times not. Many silenes are best described as weeds, but a few of our natives are like Fourth of July fireworks and well worth trying to establish.

Silene caroliniana	wild pink

This has become more and more available, both from seed and started plants. Plants form 5–9" tall mounds of foliage and are covered with starry pink flowers in spring (and sometimes later in the season). The calyx is not obviously inflated. Plants look good even when not in flower but can decline in poorly drained soils or if weather becomes hot and dry. In the South, try planting them in the fall and enjoy the flowers in early spring. Various subspecies, including subsp. *pensylvanica*, may be found, but they do not differ markedly from the species itself.

Habitat: In dry, sandy areas from New Hampshire west to Kentucky and east to Georgia.
Hardiness: USDA Zones 4–9.
Garden site: Sun in the North, afternoon shade in the South.
Garden maintenance: Removing spent flowers helps in the persistence of the plants.

Silene regia	royal catchfly

This brilliant prairie plant is the tallest of the useful garden species, growing up to 3' in height. The late spring and summer scarlet flowers are truly star-shaped, and truly brilliant. Unfortunately, its lanky growth and the poor persistence of its lower leaves make it a better meadow plant than an up-front-and-personal garden subject. It will not go unnoticed, however, no matter what is surrounding it.

Silene caroliniana subsp. *pensylvanica*

Silene regia

Habitat: In dry woods and prairies in Kansas and Oklahoma.
Hardiness: USDA Zones 4–9.
Garden site: Full sun and well-drained soils are best.
Garden maintenance: None if planted in a meadow; otherwise, smaller plants should be planted around it to diminish problems of habit.

Silene virginica   **fire pink**

My guess would be that this is the brightest fireball in the genus and, unfortunately, among the shortest lived. When seen from a distance, these plants draw you to them like a magnet—and they have the same effect on the dozens of butterflies and hummingbirds that are charging their way. Plants and flowers are similar to *Silene regia*, but fire pink is only 12–18" tall. Native to rocky outcrops, they do best in well-drained areas and make magnificent mounds in the rock garden or container. So many flowers and seed are produced, the plant simply wears out, which explains its lack of longevity. Removing some of the flowers might help plants persist a little longer, and with luck, new seedlings will appear. As with other silenes, hot, humid, and dry to a fire pink is like a heater to Frosty.

Habitat: In open plains and rocky slopes from western New York to southern Ontario, west to Minnesota, south to Ohio and Alabama and east to Georgia.
Hardiness: USDA Zones 4–9.
Garden site: Full sun to partial shade, well-drained soils.
Garden maintenance: Removing some of the flowering stems, thus reducing the amount of seed set, may help with perenniality.

Silene virginica

Silene polypetala

Other species for the garden

Silene polypetala is not seen in too many retail centers, being on the endangered list in several states. That is a shame, as its magnificent fringed pink flowers and compact stature make it a beautiful plant for the shade garden. Short-lived but spectacular. Zones 7–9.

Silene stellata (starry campion) has frilly white flowers; each petal is cut into three to four lobes. Zones 4–9.

Recommended propagation

Seed: Stratify the seed for about three months, then transfer to warmer conditions for germination.

Cuttings: New growth (stolons) can be rooted.

Division: As with cuttings.

Etymology

Genus: From the Greek for *Viscaria*; the name is now applied to this genus.

Specific epithet: caroliniana ("of the Carolinas"); polypetala ("many petals"); regia ("royal"); stellata ("star-like"); virginica ("of Virginia").

Common name: Campion is believed to be derived from "champion," because some species were used to make garlands for victors in public games or tournaments. Much of the older literature still refers to plants in the genus as "champions." Catchfly probably dates to when *Viscaria*, a very sticky herb, was part of the genus. Pink refers not to the color but to the notched flowers, which appear to have been cut with pinking shears.

Silphium	rosinweed	Asteraceae

I have been asked on many occasions to name plants I think are ready to take center stage in American gardening. *Echinacea purpurea* (purple coneflower) came out of hiding in the mid 1990s; wonderful cultivars have since been introduced and continue to become available. Similar breakout stories concern salvias, sedums, and heucheras, for example. Perhaps silphiums will be next—after all, they are tough; at least ten species are presently grown and available for breeding; they attract birds and butterflies by the dozens; and already a legion of people love them. The biggest drawbacks to their becoming the next star are size (most are huge); lack of flower colors (all are yellow to gold); and the tendency of some species to fall apart quickly after flowering (they can look particularly gruesome in late summer or fall). I may be in la-la land, but I am still convinced this group of daisies will become more popular.

Broken stems exude a bitter resin (rosin) that Native Americans used as a mouth-cleansing chewing gum. Do not fertilize these plants; otherwise, they will be even bigger—not necessarily stronger—and may fall over in a strong wind.

Silphium gracile   **slender rosinweed**

We tried a bunch of silphiums in the Horticulture Gardens recently, and this one caught my eye. By its second year, it threw up five strong flowering stems and filled out well. It is not as impressive as *Silphium laciniatum* or *S. perfoliatum*, but its stature was reasonable (4' tall), its foliage handsome, and the ray flowers were broader than most, making the flowers more full. I want to observe it for another year or so before I recommend it to my daughters, but I think it may be a winner.

Habitat: In open fields from Texas to Florida.
Hardiness: USDA Zones 5–9.
Garden site: Full sun.
Garden maintenance: None.

Silphium integrifolium   **wholeleaf rosinweed**

This may emerge as a garden star simply because it is not as monstrous as many of the others. It is not a dwarf, but heights of 3–4' are more in keeping with what gardeners can easily handle. The rough, paired leaves are entire and sessile; the yellow flowers are 2–3" across, with narrow, almost star-like ray flowers.

Habitat: In prairies and roadsides from Ohio to Minnesota, west to Nebraska,
    south to Oklahoma and east to Alabama.
Hardiness: USDA Zones 4–8.
Garden site: Full sun.
Garden maintenance: None; do not fertilize.

Silphium laciniatum   **compass plant**

This entire plant is bristly hairy and should not be embraced too lovingly. Its well-developed rough leaves are scattered up the stem, starting with large (up to 18" long) deeply pinnately lobed basal leaves that are similar to those of pin oak. Each lobe is pointed and often lobed itself. Leaves become progressively smaller as they ascend the rough stem. The flower stalk can grow up to 8' in height (4' is more common); the size often keeps it from the front of the garden. Flowers appear in mid season and are about 4" across, with long narrow ray flowers and a brown to black disk. According to Midwest garden expert Natalia Hamill, the foliage turns brown after flowering, and then to "black toast . . . so you need to plant something in front of it to cover the black hole that's left in the garden." After flowering, birds seek out the nutritious seeds. Plants put down a long taproot, which breaks up even the worst clay soils.

For years botanists and gardeners have been intrigued by the way in which the basal leaves are arranged: they tend to stand in a vertical plane, orienting themselves north and south, perhaps to minimize exposure to the sun, thus the common name. Early settlers ingested compass plant to treat rheumatism. Dried leaves were considered useful as an antispasmodic, diuretic, and expectorant, and parts of the plant were used to treat coughs and fevers.

Habitat: In roadside ditches and prairies from Quebec, west to Montana, south to Arizona, east to Louisiana and Florida. Common in Kansas and Oklahoma.
Hardiness: USDA Zones 3–9.
Garden site: Full sun.
Garden maintenance: With their deep taproot, plants are not easily moved, so get the spot right the first time.

Silphium perfoliatum cup plant

If you are a rookie to rosinweeds, this might be the one to try first. Yet more yellow daisies but plants are fun to look at—big (at least 4–5') and imposing, to be sure. The smooth four-angled stem (purple in the handsome var. *connatum*) appears to perforate the large leaves, forming two "cups" at the stem, which act as catch basins for water; occasionally birds find them useful to drink from. To be honest, the leaves and plant cups are more ornamental than the flowers, which are average as far as yellow daisies go. In mid to late summer, however, lots of flowers are produced, each 3–4" across with 1" or longer ray flowers.

Silphium perfoliatum

Habitat: From Ontario west to South Dakota, south to Oklahoma and east to Georgia.
Hardiness: USDA Zones 3–9.
Garden site: Full sun.
Garden maintenance: None.

Silphium terebinthinaceum　　　prairie dock

The first time I saw this plant was in the garden of Ann Wakeman in Fulton, Missouri (see *Blephilia ciliata*). She was showing her prairie planting and mentioned the prairie dock in passing, which at the time looked just like an ugly old burdock, truly belonging in an abandoned field, although there is nothing wrong with bold. Later at the Chicago Botanic Garden, I came upon a wonderful planting of yellow daisies labeled with an entirely unpronounceable botanical name—it was prairie dock, again. What a transformation!

All vegetative parts of the plant are basal, making a huge rosette of 16–20" long paddle-like leaves. Just when I think nothing could be uglier, they shoot up 4–5' naked bristly stalks bearing 3" wide sunflowers. This is a plant just waiting to be incorporated into a meadow or prairie planting, but I don't expect to see any soon in my daughters' gardens.

Habitat: In fields and open roadsides from southern Ontario to Minnesota, south to Missouri, Louisiana and east to Georgia.
Hardiness: USDA Zones 3–9.
Garden site: Open site, full sun.
Garden maintenance: Flower stems can be removed after flowering, as they tend to fall apart quite rapidly.

Other species for the garden
Midwest gardeners seem to be the most knowledgeable about the many silphiums out there. The rest of us are catching up, and perhaps we can get these plants spread out a little more.

Silphium dentatum (*S. asteriscus*), a southeastern native, is another on the goody list. It grows 4–6' tall and produces an abundance of excellent yellow daisies. Zones 5–9.

Silphium simpsonii (*S. gracile* var. *simpsonii*; Simpson's rosinweed) is new to the trade. I have seen it in only a few places, including our own trials at UGA. It has a great deal of potential: it flowers early (late May in Georgia), is floriferous, and stays in flower for nearly three months. About 5' tall. Native to the South. Zones 6–9.

Recommended propagation
Seed: Seed germinates readily if stratified for three months at 40F, then transferred to 70F.

Silphium terebinthinaceum

Silphium dentatum

Etymology

Genus: Thought to have come from the Greek *silphion*, used by Hippocrates for another plant entirely (possibly *Cachrys ferulacea*, a southern European plant in the Apiaceae family), which produced gum-resin.

Specific epithet: *dentatum* ("toothed," having dentate margins); *gracile* ("graceful, slender"); *integrifolium* ("with entire or uncut leaves"); *laciniatum* ("slashed or torn into narrow divisions"); *perfoliatum* ("perfoliate"); *simpsonii*, after Joseph Herman Simpson (1841–1918), who collected plants in Florida, primarily Manatee and Sarasota counties.

Common name: Rosin refers to the sticky resin that is common to most species.

Sisyrinchium	blue-eyed grass	Iridaceae

Have you talked to anyone about blue-eyed grass lately? "Oh, sure—I think my lawn is blue grass," he said. "Not blue grass, but blue-eyed grass," I rejoined, slowly. "What have you been smoking?" he mumbled as he walked away. "Damn gardeners, always high on something." So went a real conversation, typical of ones I've had with many a nongardening person, who appear to be normal in every other way.

Of the ninety or so species of blue-eyed grasses, about forty are native to the United States, but only a handful, at most, are useful garden plants. Of that handful, you will be hard-pressed to purchase more than a species or two—and a few hybrids whose parentage is suspect. They all tend to have short, narrow leaves and flowers in a small cluster. All but one of our natives have blue flowers.

Sisyrinchium angustifolium common blue-eyed grass

Plants are about 1' tall and can easily be mistaken for clumps of grass. The flat stems and leaves are about ¼" wide. There is little to recommend this plant for the garden except that seeing small blue flowers with yellow centers on a tuft of grass in spring and early summer is kind of neat. Of course, you may see a lot more, as the plant produces many dark brown fruits containing lots of viable seed, resulting in blue-eyeds everywhere. Cute, and fun, but not something you will miss after a few years.

'Lucerne' bears bigger flowers, up to ¾" across, with bright yellow centers. Plants have dramatically more eye appeal and are worth seeking out.

Habitat: In meadows and damp woods from Newfoundland to Minnesota, south to east Texas and east to Florida.
Hardiness: USDA Zones 4–9.
Garden site: Full sun in the North, afternoon shade in the South.
Garden maintenance: Plants may reseed vigorously; cutting them back after flowering is hardly an option.

Other species for the garden
Sisyrinchium idahoense (Idaho blue-eyed grass) and *S. bellum* (California blue-eyed grass) are western natives, both with intense blue flowers; *S. idahoense* 'Album' is the white-flowered exception. *Sisyrinchium californicum* (golden blue-eyed grass) is readily available from western nurseries, and it is fun to try the only native yellow-flowered species; it is the least cold hardy of the group. All

Sisyrinchium angustifolium with columbines

Sisyrinchium angustifolium 'Lucerne'

Sisyrinchium idahoense 'Album'　　　　*Sisyrinchium californicum*

require excellent drainage and are best used in well-drained troughs or rock-eries. The hybrids are easier to find than these.

Hybrids

I am not certain, but it appears that some of the hybrids include at least one of our native blue-eyeds. For native purists, however, they may be too tainted, so stay away.

'California Skies' and 'Suwanee' are both showier and not as weedy, and I suspect that there is a good deal of native blood within. 'Devon Skies' and 'Quaint and Queer' are also handsome—well, 'Devon Skies' is, anyway—but they seem to have more European DNA. Just my guesses.

Recommended propagation

Seed: Provide a cold treatment in the cold frame or cooler for three months, then germinate in warmer temperatures.

Division: Easy at any time.

Etymology

Genus: No good explanation.

Specific epithet: *angustifolium* ("narrow-leaved"); *bellum* ("beautiful"); *californicum* ("of California"); *idahoense* ("of Idaho").

Common name: Blue flowers with an eye, borne on a plant that looks like grass—I'd say the name fits.

Smilacina	false Solomon's seal	Convallariaceae

This well-known spring-flowering plant has been a favorite of native plant enthusiasts and gardeners alike for years. A great choice for woodland gardens with light to dense shade. Plants spread by rhizomes but will not become invasive. The off-white terminal flowers are formed in late spring and form handsome fruit later in the season. Many taxonomists have moved the genus into *Maianthemum* (which see), and out of the lily family into the closely related lily-of-the-valley family, Convallariaceae.

Smilacina racemosa	false Solomon's seal

On this most common species the plants grow 1–3' tall with three to four unbranched stems bearing twelve to twenty entire alternate leaves like those of Solomon's seal, *Polygonatum*. The leaves are quite handsome on their own, arranged alternately up the pendulous stem, each leaf being smooth, entire, and with parallel veins. The white flowers are held in dense clusters at the end of the stem, usually resulting in the stem bending down even further. Put your nose in the flowers—you will be pleasantly surprised.

Later, the small berries start out green, and if the birds or other critters don't get them, they ripen to bright red. I love seeing them in late fall when the leaves have turned a tan color and papery and the red fruit are still clinging. Great with ferns and hostas or lining woodland trails.

Birds aren't the only animals who sometimes find the plant useful. The rhizomes were known to be cooked for food but were also utilized as a poultice. The berries were eaten raw, though you might want to practice first before you offer them to respectable people.

Habitat: Essentially ranging all over the continent, except for the Gulf states,
from Quebec to British Columbia, as far south as the mountains of Georgia.
Hardiness: USDA Zones 3–8.
Garden site: Moist, partially shaded areas.
Garden maintenance: None.

Smilacina racemosa

Smilacina racemosa, fruit

Smilacina stellata	starry false Solomon's seal

Although smaller in every way and not nearly as in-your-face as its bigger cousin, it is still a terrific plant for the woodland garden. Leaves are fewer and less obviously veined, and the star-shaped fragrant white flowers are also quite different from the clusters of small flowers found in *Smilacina racemosa*. This may be a small plant, but it is not to be outdone. Even the red fruit put on a terrific show.

It is not as easy to purchase simply because it is not as showy or as big as common false Solomon's seal. It will not knock your socks off, but that is no reason not to give it a go.

Habitat: Newfoundland to British Columbia, south to California, east through
   Arizona to the mountains of Georgia.
Hardiness: USDA Zones 3–8.
Garden site: Moist, partially shaded area.
Garden maintenance: None.

Recommended propagation
Seed: Quite slow, requiring about two years for transplanting.
Division: Easy—cut and transplant at any time.

Etymology
Genus: From *Smilax*, the greenbriar vine. Plants are not even remotely similar,
   so the reason for this genus being associated with *Smilax* is unclear.
Specific epithet: *racemosa* ("with flowers in racemes"); *stellata* ("star-like").
Common name: Plants closely resemble Solomon's seal (*Polygonatum*),
   especially when not in flower.

Solidago	goldenrod	Asteraceae

So many goldenrods, so few takers. It is interesting that goldenrod, which we have blamed for various ailments like hay fever, was once thought of as a cure-all, and even today holistic practitioners are high on the medicinal attributes of goldenrod. It is used to treat urinary tract infections and kidney stones and pain caused by arthritis and osteoarthritis; it is even reputed to ease back pain. Perhaps this reputation is one of the reasons species of goldenrod were adopted as the state flowers of Kentucky and Nebraska.

And among gardeners, the reputation of this fine American genus is also on the upswing as so many more gardeners tolerate so many more weeds, diseases, and bugs. Our poor old goldenrod, which was forever blamed for numerous maladies, is no longer tossed in the rubbish heap and forgotten; now we have native gardeners, meadow gardeners, and reclamation gardeners, all working to redress former wrongs. And it is working: town crews no longer spray or even cut gold-enrod on the roadsides in the fall, and native plant nurseries are offering many more home-boys, allowing gardeners to purchase more than the Barbie-dolled-up cultivars that have become acceptable to mainstream gardeners.

Goldenrods are weeds—let's get that straight. I have nothing against orna-mental weeds, and the fact they are hosts for butterflies and hummingbirds is terrific, but they also harbor aphids, powdery mildew spores, rust, and many other goodies not quite so welcome. I understand that all creatures on this Earth are part of a plan and are here for a reason; I just don't want all those creatures in my garden.

A handful of species are easily found in retail and mail-order outlets, but after all is said and done, it is those Barbie cultivars that will help save the species from garden oblivion. They have shown gardeners and landscapers that goldenrod, with a tweak here and there, is much more than a weed, and growers are willing to produce plants that would not have sold in sufficient numbers before.

Solidago caesia   blue-stem goldenrod, wreath goldenrod

This is a favorite for its purplish stems and sessile, sharply serrated leaves. The clusters of golden flowers are held closely to the leafy flowering stem, which arches out and grows more or less horizontally. This habit allows plants to grow vigorously but not get too tall. Flowers occur in late summer and fall.

The interesting way in which the flowers are held and the handsome bluish leaves and stems make this a favorite for cut flowers as well. Cut the stems just as the flowers are about ready to open. Plants tolerate full sun and afternoon shade and normal soils as well as wet places.

Solidago caesia

361

Habitat: In woods from Nova Scotia to Wisconsin, south to Texas and east to Florida.

Hardiness: USDA Zones 3–9.

Garden site: In general, full sun and consistently moist soils are recommended; however, a little afternoon shade, particularly if soils are not consistently moist, will make the planting more successful.

Garden maintenance: Plants can become shrubby; if desired, cut back in early spring.

Solidago rugosa	**rough-stem goldenrod**

An extremely variable plant in nature, growing 2–7' in height. Some specimens have rough leaves, some less so; some have branched inflorescences above the foliage, others yet have inflorescences tucked into the axils. The only thing that seems to be agreed upon is the rough stem and that additional taxonomic work needs to be done; however, for meadows and conservation areas, this is a tough, reasonably handsome plant that will do what is expected: grow, flower, and establish a population.

For the majority of gardeners and landscapers, however, that is simply not going to wash. Fortunately, the North Carolina Botanical Garden and Niche Gardens introduced a more compact and more floriferous form, 'Fireworks'; the plantings at Chicago Botanic Garden must be seen to get an appreciation of this outstanding selection, which schedules its fireworks for early fall.

Habitat: From Newfoundland to Ontario and Michigan, south to Texas and east to Florida.

Solidago rugosa 'Fireworks' with miscanthus

Hardiness: USDA Zones 3–9.
Garden site: Full sun.
Garden maintenance: Cut back hard in spring, or plants will become too tall
and naked at the base.

Solidago speciosa   showy goldenrod

This species is on the Top Ten list of those who enjoy meadow and prairie gardens, seldom disappointing in its display in late summer and fall. Tiny flowers
belie the ornamental beauty of this showy plant: hundreds of small individual
flowers are carried on each 12" long inflorescence, and a dozen or so inflorescences are open at the same time. Plants are best in full sun and grow vigorously; while they can get quite tall, in general they attain a mature height of only
2–3'. Excellent for birds, butterflies, and cut flowers.

Plants put down deep roots and once established are excellent for dry garden
sites. In fact, conditions on the dry side are necessary for superior performance.

Habitat: In open prairies from Massachusetts to Wyoming, through the
Midwest, south to Texas and east to Georgia.
Hardiness: USDA Zones 3–8.
Garden site: Full sun, well-drained soils. Rocky outcrops also work.
Garden maintenance: Cut back hard after flowering if reseeding is a problem.
Rust and other foliar diseases can be a problem, but if sited in a sunny
meadow, these will be minor.

Solidago sphacelata   autumn goldenrod

This is another species that is on the dwarf side, generally growing 2–3' in
height. Plants are naturally well-branched without having to be cut back. Many
thin stems are produced, each carrying heart-shaped leaves in the spring
through late summer. In the fall, dozens of small golden flowers are formed at
the ends; their weight causes stems to bend toward the ground. This is a good
plant in its own right, but in gardening, a a named selection always elicits more
interest than a species.

'Golden Fleece', introduced by Dick Lighty from Mt. Cuba Center in
Delaware, is a more compact and better-behaved plant for the garden and landscape. Growing only about 15" tall with a 2' spread, it is an example of a good
native plant being selected so that mainstreamers will take notice of it.

Habitat: In open fields from Virginia to Illinois, south to Alabama and east to
Georgia.

Solidago
'Crown of
Rays'

Hardiness: USDA Zones 4–9.

Garden site: Full sun.

Garden maintenance: Plants often occur in areas of basic soils. A light application of dolomitic lime in the fall might improve the vigor of the plants.

Other species for the garden

Many goldenrods are being sold, particularly through Internet and mail-order sources, including several hybrids. These are still more popular in Europe than here, but give us time.

Solidago flexicaulis is appearing more and more in catalogs and online, possibly because of the interesting zigzag flowering stems. Plants tolerate partial shade conditions. Zones 3–9.

I am also seeing *Solidago nemoralis* (gray goldenrod) more as producers and gardeners come to appreciate its compact habit and gray-green foliage. Plants are shade- and drought-tolerant and do well in poor soils. Zones 3–9.

Solidago odora (sweet goldenrod), with its anise-flavored foliage and early flowering habit, has been gaining in popularity. Zones 3–9.

Solidago sempervirens (seaside goldenrod) is being sold by more growers because of its good compact habit and its tough constitution. Plants tolerate even the abuse of Atlantic Ocean salt spray, a useful trait for seaside gardens. Zones 3–9.

Hybrids

Many of these have native parentage, and all may be more gardenesque to mainstream gardeners.

'Baby Gold' stands 2–2½' tall with large racemes of bright yellow flowers.

'Cloth of Gold' is a dwarf (18–24" tall) but vigorous grower with dense, deep yellow flowers.

'Crown of Rays' ('Strahlenkrone'), which came to me many years ago as a potential cut flower cultivar, has to be one of the best goldenrods I've ever trialed. Plants grow 2–3' tall without falling over and are covered with bright yellow plumes of flowers in mid to late summer.

'Golden Thumb' ('Tom Thumb', 'Queenie') grows about 1' tall with yellow flowers and yellowish green foliage. My choice as the most ornamental cultivar.

'Goldstrahl' ('Golden Rays', 'Peter Pan') has canary-yellow flowers and stands 2–3' tall. Flowering continues through October.

'Lightning Rod', which originated at Collector's Nursery in Battle Ground, Washington, appears to be a variegated form of *Solidago canadensis*, with green leaves streaked with gold. Interesting.

'Super' bears wonderful sulphur-yellow flowers in mid summer.

Recommended propagation
Seed: Provide a three-month period of stratification, then bring the tray into warmer conditions for germination.

Cuttings: Three- to four-node cuttings taken in spring and early summer root well.

Division: All plants that grow through spreading rhizomes may be divided any time.

Etymology
Genus: From *solido* ("to make whole"), from the reputed healing properties of the plants.

Specific epithet: *caesia* ("light blue"), in reference to the stem color; *flexicaulis* ("having a pliant stem"), in reference to the zigzag stem; *nemoralis* ("growing in groves or woods"); *odora* ("fragrant"); *rugosa* ("rugose"), in reference to the rough stems; *sempervirens* ("evergreen"); *speciosa* ("showy"); *sphacelata* ("withered"), in reference to the thin stems.

Common name: The flowering stems do indeed suggest rods of gold.

| *Spigelia marilandica* | indian pink, worm grass | Loganiaceae |

Here is one plant simply waiting for a cheerleader! Wherever it is seen, gardeners want some, yet it is still not mainstream, and I continue to wonder why. If I am honest with myself, it reflects the average American consumer's lack of vision: plants that don't flower in the spring do not compete well beside early perennials, bulky shrubs, and colorful annuals. As green plants, they are overlooked, declining on the retail shelf, thus orders are not renewed the next year, therefore growers don't grow them . . . ad nauseam. That mail-order sales have proliferated in recent years reflects a more sophisticated gardener, people who will spend money on plants unseen because they can't find them at retail.

I buy every plant of indian pink I can lay my hands on. I love the color of the flowers, and when they make a reasonable colony in the Armitage garden, I am one happy fellow. Plants bear glossy opposite leaves directly attached to the stems and grow 12–18" tall. The flowers appear at the top of the stem; crimson and red flower buds open to reveal a yellow center. Absolutely striking. They are best in moist woodland or along shady paths. And if hummingbirds are your thing, this is a hummingbird magnet.

Another reason indian pinks are not as common as they should be is that propagation is slow and difficult. For gardeners, however, that is simply a challenge. Barry Glick of Sunshine Farm and Gardens in West Virginia wrote a nice article on indian pink that will inspire you to rise to the challenge: www.bbg.org/gar2/topics/wildlife/2002sp_spigelia.html.

Plants in this family contain poisonous alkaloids (including strychnine); in the case of *Spigelia*, spigeline proved useful to Native Americans for destroying parasitic worms.

Habitat: In moist woods from Maryland to Indiana, west to Missouri and
   Oklahoma, south to Texas and east to Florida.
Hardiness: USDA Zones 4–8.
Garden site: Plants can tolerate more sun the further north one gardens, but
   afternoon shade and consistent moisture result in faster growth.
Garden maintenance: None.

Spigelia marilandica

Other species for the garden

Spigelia gentianoides (gentian pinkroot) is a gorgeous pink-flowered species from western Florida. Its beauty far outstrips its availability, and since it is on the Federal Endangered Species List, it is time to be working on obtaining some nursery-grown pots. Unfortunately, I don't think we will see it as a common garden plant any time soon.

Recommended propagation

Seed: Hard to find commercially; must
   be collected before it is dispersed.
   Plants germinate reasonably quickly
   in containers left outdoors or overwintered in cool cold frames.
Cuttings: Difficult. Use rooting hormone (KIBA is useful).

Division: Possible from well-established colonies. Be careful to include some rootstock, and transplant immediately.

Etymology

Genus: For Adrian van der Spiegel (1578–1625), a professor of anatomy at Padua, Italy.

Specific epithet: *gentianoides* ("resembling a gentian"); *marilandica* ("of Maryland").

Common name: Indian pink is a reference to Native Americans, worm grass to its anthelmintic properties.

Spiranthes cernua var. *odorata*	nodding lady's tresses	Orchidaceae

Here is a good trivia challenge for your next carpool ride to a master gardener conference: "Name three orchids we grow as garden plants in this country." This will stump most of your friends. Obviously, one correct answer is lady's tresses. It will probably surprise you that there are over 150 species in the genus, but what won't surprise you is that you will be lucky to find more than one for sale even after extensive research. Most other species are small and, although cute, are simply unavailable commercially.

In this species, a rosette of narrow leaves arises from thick roots. Flower stems bear spikes of small white or greenish flowers, often arranged in spirals around the flowering stem. When we put these plants in the Horticulture Gardens at UGA, I was not terribly hopeful. After all, how many orchids would really be at home in our heat, humidity, and extraordinarily poor soils? I had seen them in Pennsylvania and the Midwest, but they were still difficult to locate, and I was a bit of a skeptic. They are native to bogs and moist areas, but since we didn't have a bog, I simply planted them where space was available.

They surprised me by coming up strong for three to four years and producing handsome white flowers in late summer and fall, on 10–15" tall plants. Unfortunately, they were eaten by a crinum lily before we could rescue them. The flowers have a distinct perfume of vanilla and can be cut and brought indoors to enjoy as well. I recommend them highly, particularly in moist, reasonably rich soils. Plants may also be called *Spiranthes odorata*, but most taxonomists agree plants are a variety of the nodding form, not a distinct species.

'Chadds Ford', a selection from the Brandywine Valley in Pennsylvania, is a little more compact, with excellent flowers.

Habitat: In moist areas from Tennessee to Pennsylvania, south to Louisiana and east to Florida.

Hardiness: USDA Zones 5–9.

Garden site: Moist soils with afternoon shade seem to suit plants well. They appear to perform poorly in alkaline soils.

Spiranthes cernua var. *odorata* 'Chadds Ford'

Garden maintenance: Place plants where consistent moisture can be maintained. Stay away from alkaline soils.

Recommended propagation
Seed: Easier than most orchids. Plant seedlings into composted soil or mature mixes.
Division: Mature clumps can be divided.

Etymology
Genus: From the Greek, *speira* ("spiral") and *anthos* ("flowers"), referring to the spiral inflorescence.
Specific epithet: *cernua* ("inclining the head"), hence nodding; *odorata* ("fragrant").
Common name: The spiral inflorescences resemble locks of braided hair.

Sporobolus heterolepis	prairie dropseed	Poaceae

This ornamental grass is being used more and more by landscapers and native plant gardeners, gaining popularity for its narrow, glossy, fine-textured leaves and terrific mounding habit. It is an excellent meadow plant but can also be used as an edger (set 18" apart) or as a border grouping when planted in three or more. It seldom gets taller than 18", and in the fall, the entire plant turns a nice orange color. The fragrant (kind of like Juicy Fruit gum) flowers are silvery and produce lots of round fruit, drooping to the ground in the fall and winter. Plants are drought-tolerant, can handle full sun, are not invasive, and never need staking. What's keeping you? A little better in the North than in the South.

Habitat: From Connecticut to Quebec west to Saskatchewan, south to Colorado and Texas.
Hardiness: USDA Zones 3–8.
Garden site: Full sun, well-drained soil.
Garden maintenance: Cut off flowers if reseeding becomes a problem.

Other species for the garden
Sporobolus airoides (alkali dropseed) is certainly different from prairie dropseed. Plants have much more obvious and bigger flowers, each flowering stem look-

Sporobolus heterolepis, winter

Sporobolus heterolepis

ing like a bronze pine tree after a fire. Plants grow 3' in foliage, topping out at 6' in flower. Very impressive, little known. Zones 4–8.

Recommended propagation

Seed: Seeds are reasonably easy to grow. Provide a cool treatment in a cold frame and germinate in a warmer area after about three months' cold.

Division: With effort.

Etymology

Genus: From the Greek, *spora* ("seed") and *ballein* ("to throw"), referring to the way in which the seed drops from the plant.

Specific epithet: *airoides* ("resembling *Aira*," hairgrass); *heterolepis* ("diversely scaled"), referring to the various lengths of the flower plumes.

Common name: Occurs in the prairies, drops its seeds. Perfect.

Stokesia laevis	Stokes' aster	Asteraceae

The native daisies have had the most success obtaining mainstream status— witness the popularity of coreopsis, echinacea, gaillardia, and helianthus. Similarly, Stokes' aster is produced by growers who may not have a clue the plant is even native, and purchased by gardeners simply for its toughness and ornamental value. I have traversed many a trail in this country, but I don't recall seeing a single Stokes' aster along the way. I guess that could be said for many of our native plants, but I know I would recognize this one. The fact that it is rare in nature has made the selections all that more important.

Stokesia laevis 'Blue Danube'

Stokesia laevis 'Mary Gregory'

The flowers are generally lavender to purple and consist of five-lobed spreading ray flowers around a central disk. The alternate leaves clasp the stem, and the entire plant is smooth, almost entirely without hairs. Plants are skinny and tall, growing 3' and prone to falling over in wind or abusive weather. It is difficult to find the species for sale, even from seed; however, there is no end to cultivars from which to choose. Some are indistinguishable from others, but it is nice to read the accolades, each one better than the one before. You be the judge.

'Alba' has white flowers, and although not as floriferous as the blue cultivars, the flowers contrast well with the foliage.

'Blue Danube' produces lavender-blue flowers up to 4" in diameter. The most popular of the named forms.

'Blue Moon' has dark blue flowers on 2' tall plants.

'Blue Star', with a little less lavender in the flowers, is almost a Spode-blue.

'Colorwheel' is supposed to provide "flower colors ranging from white to dark purple and everything in between" simultaneously. I have not been impressed with the plants in our trial gardens, but judging from the testimonials of others, it must just be me.

'Honeysong Purple' has large purple flowers around a contrasting center.

'Klaus Jelitto', named for the great German seedsman, bears lavender flowers that are a little larger than the species.

'Mary Gregory' was introduced by Niche Gardens in Chapel Hill, North Carolina. The flowers are yellow rather than lavender and persist for a long time. A big change!

'Omega Skyrocket' was discovered by Ron and Susan Dieterman of the Atlanta Botanical Garden. Seeds were grown on and plants then introduced by Saul's Nursery in Atlanta. It is unique in that plants grow 3–4' tall and bear almost white to pale blue flowers. It is the most robust stokesia I have seen. Plants do not require support and are more easily used as long-stemmed cut flowers than others.

'Peachie's Pick' is the best of the bunch, with compact plants and persistent lavender flowers. Named for Peachie Saxon of Mississippi.

'Silver Moon' bears creamy white flowers. They are larger than those of 'Alba' and equally handsome.

'Wyoming' bears many flowers of rich deep blue.

Habitat: In moist areas from South Carolina west to Louisiana and south to Florida.
Hardiness: USDA Zones 5–9.
Garden site: In well-drained, sunny areas.
Garden maintenance: Plants abhor wet feet. Plant on high ground, and in colder areas, cover with an open type of mulch that will provide some warmth but won't remain wet.

Stokesia laevis 'Peachie's Pick'

Recommended propagation

Seed: Seeds of the species and a few cultivars are available and relatively easy to germinate and grow on. No cold treatment is necessary.
Cuttings: Root cuttings may be used in the winter.
Division: If a colony is sufficiently large, divisions may be attempted. Be sure to cut the division with root attached.

Etymology

Genus: For Jonathan Stokes (1755–1831) of England, a botanical author.
Specific epithet: *laevis* ("smooth").

| ***Streptopus roseus*** | twisted stalk, rose mandarin | Liliaceae |

I scratched my head, I tugged at my chin, I walked in circles—I could not figure these plants out when I was looking at them in eastern Canada. They looked like a cross between *Disporum* and *Polygonatum*, but they had the fattest, reddest berries I had ever seen. It turns out I had not forgotten (at my age, that is always a kind revelation); I simply never knew that the plants belonged to the genus *Streptopus*, in this case *S. roseus*.

I hesitate, for the usual reason, to include this wonderful woodland plant: it is nearly impossible to purchase. Interestingly but not surprisingly, I came across more sources in the United Kingdom than in the United States. Hello??

The foliage is common-looking enough, but the 1" wide solitary fairybell-like flowers are flared and pink, an unusual color for a woodland plant. They are held on long stalks, which are really interesting. They arise from the stem itself,

*Streptopus
amplexifolius*

which, at about halfway along the stalk, takes a sharp bend, directing the flower downward. Weird, but fun to look at. The flowers may not jump out at you immediately, but the large red fruit that occurs in July will, and it is as pretty as and more noticeable than the flowers. This is a plant for northern gardeners, perhaps useful as far south as the southern Appalachians, but better in zones 3–5 than in zones 6–8. They also do well in the coastal Northwest, where heat is seldom an issue.

Habitat: From Labrador to Ontario and Minnesota, south to the mountains of
 New Jersey, Kentucky and down into Georgia.
Hardiness: USDA Zones 2–6.
Garden site: Shaded, moist, cool.
Garden maintenance: None.

Other species for the garden

Streptopus amplexifolius (white mandarin) is similar but with leaves that clasp the stem and greenish flowers with white veins. Similar fruit. Zones 2–5.

Recommended propagation

Seed: Gather when the fruit is red. Seeds germinate after a cold treatment but
 are very slow to grow after germination. Take care that seedlings do not succumb to overwatering or animal browsing.
Division: Divide carefully in the spring.

Etymology

Genus: From the Greek, *streptos* ("twisted") and *pous* ("foot"), in reference to the
 twisted flower stalks.
Specific epithet: *amplexifolius* ("leaf-clasping"); *roseus* ("rose-colored").

Common name: Mandarin is a common name for *Disporum*, which these plants closely resemble.

Stylophorum diphyllum   wood poppy, celandine poppy   Papaveraceae

This plant should be as common in nurseries as columbines, but with only one flower color and little genetic diversity to fiddle with, it never will be. Where these plants do well, they really do well, seeding themselves all over the place. In a woodland setting, where they belong, this is a plus and not at all a problem. These are spring-flowerers, but flowers can be seen on and off all summer, and the plants themselves do not go dormant, unless drought or other abuse is omnipresent.

Fuzzy buds produce the four-petaled 2" wide yellow flowers in early spring; flowering continues for six to eight weeks. The flowers have about twenty obvious stamens and one large pistil. The two paired leaves are hairy and green on top, grayish on the underside. When the plant is broken, yellow sap is apparent. Again, plants seed with abandon, so colonies pop up here and there. They are poor choices for formal gardens, but where "higgly-piggly" design reigns, these are the hig-pig kings.

Habitat: From the Northeast to Wisconsin, south to Arkansas and east to Tennessee.
Hardiness: USDA Zones 4–8.
Garden site: A shaded, moist area enhances performance.
Garden maintenance: None to speak of, unless too many plants are a problem. In that case remove as much fruit as possible before the seed matures.

Stylophorum diphyllum

Recommended propagation

Seed: Easy to let Mother Nature do the germination; however, if a few fruit from your neighbors happen to blow into your pocket, sow them immediately in a seed tray. They will flower the next spring.

Division: Only in the sense that entire plants can be removed from a colony and started elsewhere.

Etymology

Genus: From the Greek, *stylos* ("style") and *phoros* ("bearing"), referring to the long columnar style.

Specific epithet: *diphyllum* ("two-leaved").

Common name: These members of the poppy family are denizens of the woodland, and they also resemble the greater celandine, *Chelidonium*.

Symplocarpus foetidus	skunk cabbage	Araceae

This thing is said to stink like a skunk, but that is not being fair to skunks. A number of plants are called skunk cabbages; the prettiest is *Lysichiton americanum*. This one is wonderful, but I wouldn't call it pretty. Plants are generally the first to flower no matter where it grows. Flowers emerge, amazingly, from the snow and ice and muck in late winter or very early spring. The blooms have been the subject of much research; studies confirm they manufacture their own heat and can raise the air temperature around them by five to ten degrees Fahrenheit. Snow is a pushover for this skunk.

The flowers are surrounded by a spotted maroon-colored dome (spathe); after that withers, the cabbage-like leaves appear, their vein-laden blades growing up

Symplocarpus foetidus

to 3' in length. Plants are wonderfully architectural, and their fragrance is exaggerated. It is only on a still day that the fetid odor becomes obvious—unless, of course, you enjoy playing in the muck, and then you too will smell like a skunk. Plants go dormant in the summer or as soon as the water recedes.

Habitat: In shallow water, swampy woods from Quebec to Manitoba, from Illinois west to Iowa and south to Tennessee and east to Georgia.
Hardiness: USDA Zones 3–7.
Garden site: Moisture, deciduous shade.
Garden maintenance: None. Plants are difficult to remove once established.

Recommended propagation

Seed: The seeds are large and should be soaked in water for about a week, then planted in a container where moisture can be controlled. Two years is required before plants are large enough to transplant.

Etymology

Genus: From the Greek, *symploke* ("connection," "embrace") and *karpos* ("fruit"). The ovaries coalesce to form one fruit.
Specific epithet: *foetidus* ("fetid").
Common name: Smells like a skunk, looks like a cabbage—an apropos name, I'd say.

Tagetes lemmonii   copper canyon daisy, Mt. Lemmon marigold   Asteraceae

How many marigolds do native plant people put in their gardens? A better question is, how many marigolds does anyone put in their garden anymore? Bedding marigolds have been a mainstay of retailers and seed companies for years, but their day in the sun is waning as newer plants hit the retail aisles. But wait, don't give up on marigolds quite yet, not until you have tried this wonderful Southwest gem.

Plants can grow vigorously, but they will grow over and on each other; so, although they may have 4–5' long stems, they will be only about 3' in height. The brilliant yellow-gold flowers are visible across the garden and almost smother the plants all summer. The foliage is also interesting, in that it is not marigold-stinky but rather a cross between anise and lemon. Some of you will not like it, but some of you don't like the smell of roses either. If you are in the wonderful San Antonio Botanical Garden or on spectacular Mt. Lemmon, north of Tucson, stop and smell the daisies.

Habitat: Mainly in southwestern Arizona and into Texas and Mexico.
Hardiness: USDA Zones 7–10.
Garden site: Dry soils, somewhat basic in pH, and full sun.
Garden maintenance: They can reseed; move as needed. Cut back spent flowers if they become a nuisance. Apply dolomitic lime in the fall.

*Tagetes
lemmonii*

Recommended propagation
Seed: Easy from seed.
Cuttings: Root easily.
Division: Plants can be divided once a colony is established.

Etymology
Genus: For Tages, an Etruscan deity.
Specific epithet: *lemmonii*, after John Gill Lemmon (1832–1908), who with his wife, Sara Plummer Lemmon (1836–1923), collected plants throughout the American West.
Common name: Plants are also native to the Sierra Madre mountains of Mexico, where the famous copper canyon can be found. Plants may be found in the canyon as well.

Talinum calycinum	**fame flower**	**Portulacaceae**

I know talinum by the great weed, *Talinum paniculatum*, otherwise known as jewels of Opar. It has escaped to America and is the easiest species to purchase, sold alongside petunias in retail plant shops. As far as our natives are concerned, only this very succulent-leaved, purple-flowered species is reasonably attainable. That it is closely related to purslane (*Portulaca*) is obvious by the thick 2" long leaves, their similar flowers, and by the fact that, like purslane, flowers typically open at noon and remain open only until mid afternoon. Fame is fleeting!

The 1" wide, five- to eight-petaled flowers are handsome, usually pinkish rose and with thirty or more obvious yellow stamens. The 6–9" tall plants often occur in rocky soils; most people who have tried to grow this confirm what this tells us:

plants need excellent drainage in order to succeed. They are probably best in sandy soil and make excellent trough plants. Plants will reseed in gritty soil.

Habitat: On cliffs, sand, and dry barrens from Nebraska to Utah, and south to Oklahoma.
Hardiness: USDA Zones 5–9.
Garden site: Excellent drainage a must. Full sun.
Garden maintenance: None. If reseeding is a problem, remove flowers.

Recommended propagation
Seed: Easy from seed. Light is required for germination, so don't bury deeply.
Cuttings: Cuttings may be taken, but seed is the best means.

Etymology
Genus: Derivation unknown.
Specific epithet: *calycinum* ("calyx-like").
Common name: Fame, like the flowers, is fleeting? Possibly a corruption of the word "flame."

Tellima grandiflora	fringe cups	Saxifragaceae

You must enjoy subtlety and detail to enjoy fringe cups in the garden. Those characteristics are commonplace in many of our shade-tolerant natives, but because *Tellima* is so similar to more perky members of the family like *Tiarella* and *Heuchera*, fringe cups often get overlooked. After all, there is only so much subtlety a gardener can stand.

Nevertheless, the column of cup-shaped flowers—best viewed on hands and knees—is really quite beautiful; each flower consists of five deeply cut petals in shades of white to pink. This western native is also wonderfully fragrant—not teenage-daughter overpowering, but classy-wife subtle. The hairy, rounded leaves consist of numerous toothed lobes and are reasonably handsome but won't win any Top Ten foliar awards. They are found basally as well as up the stem.

Plants are native to the West Coast but also range significantly further north and on high elevations. As would

Tellima grandiflora

be expected, they struggle in the heat and humidity common in the southern half of the country.

Habitat: In damp woods and along streams from southern California through the Coast Ranges, into northern Sierra Nevada north to Oregon, Washington, and Alaska.

Hardiness: USDA Zones 3–7.

Garden site: Moist shade is best.

Garden maintenance: None, other than irrigating in times of drought.

Recommended propagation

Seed: Seed will germinate readily if sown in trays and placed at 70F.

Division: Plants within colonies can be easily moved, but avoid dividing individual plants.

Etymology

Genus: Plants were originally placed under *Mitella* (which see), and a sense of playfulness accompanied their move: *Tellima* is an anagram of the former genus.

Specific epithet: *grandiflora* ("large-flowered"). When plants were in *Mitella*, the flowers were large compared to other species there.

Common name: Based on the appearance of the flowers.

Thalia dealbata	powdery thalia	Marantaceae

If you have a sunny pond, this is an excellent plant, providing large leaves that appear to be a cross between those of canna lilies and birds-of-paradise. You will notice that they are neither of those, however, when you note the fine white powder-like substance on the plant, particularly on the foliage. Plants can easily grow to 6' tall when in flower, so this is not for the whiskey barrel pond, but rather for the statement pond. The spikes of purple flowers, held on slender stems in late summer and fall, sway gracefully in the breeze—not something you would normally expect of such a monster plant.

Plants require damp to boggy soil and can be submerged up to 18"; when grown in the North, they should be submerged in the winter below the freeze line. In rich soil, they will spread rapidly and likely will outgrow containers in a year or two.

Habitat: In ponds and swamps from Texas north into Arkansas and Missouri, occasionally into Illinois (where it is endangered) and east to South Carolina.

Hardiness: USDA Zones 6–9.

Garden site: Wet, full sun.

Garden maintenance: Plants on stream banks can become aggressive, if not downright obnoxious. In containers, they may simply have to be repotted after a year or so.

Other species for the garden

Thalia geniculata (alligator flag) is offered by several nurseries on the Internet. Plants are much taller (10–12') and bear the largest leaves of any native species except palms. The small violet flowers are held on tall zigzag branches. Plants are not powdery. Zones 9–11.

Recommended propagation

Seed: The hard seeds can be soaked and stratified, but division is much easier.

Division: Dig and divide the rhizome in spring through summer.

Thalia dealbata

Etymology

Genus: For German physician and botanist Johannes Thal (1542–1583), who died too young.

Specific epithet: *dealbata* ("covered with white powder"); *geniculata* ("bent sharply like a knee"), in reference to the zigzag flower stems.

Common name: Grows in swamps, flowers are like flags—alligator flag seems good to me.

Thalictrum meadow rue **Ranunculaceae**

Dozens of exceptional species are used in gardens, but few of the popular ones are from this country. That is not to say our children are not just like those of Lake Wobegon (above average), it is just that they aren't as good-looking as the men from there. All the thalictrums from our shores are excellent in leaf and ornamental in flower.

Thalictrum dasycarpum purple meadow rue

Plants are dioecious, meaning that male and female flowers occur on different plants. This generally sounds more exciting than it really is; however, in this plant's case—where petals are missing from all the flowers, and the most ornamental parts are the stamens—well, the female inflorescences are simply not as big, not as full, and not as showy. The color of the flowers is off-white, thanks to the broad, flat-stalked stamens. It is probably best to buy them in flower if possible, or ask specifically for males. Salespeople will look at you like you are crazy—be proud of it!

The foliage is hairy beneath and quite handsome, regardless of gender. The leaves are cut once, then each segment is cut again, and each of those cut yet again (ternately compound). Each final segment is generally three-lobed. All this hacking and cutting results in a fine-leaved plant that is almost ferny in appearance. The basal leaves are attached with long petioles but become sessile near the top of the plant.

Female plants can reseed, if males are present, and the seeds have been used to produce thalicarpine, a promising cancer drug. Plants are 4–5' tall, often with purple-tinged branches toward the top.

Habitat: In meadows and by streams from North Dakota to Oklahoma and Colorado, and occasionally as far west as Washington.
Hardiness: USDA Zones 3–8.
Garden site: Partial shade in consistently moist but not boggy soils.
Garden maintenance: These plants can get tall and may need some support, even when grown through other plants. After flowering, plants may turn yellow; cut back if they become unsightly.

Thalictrum dioicum early meadow rue

Thalictrum dioicum

This is a more easterly species and one that always flowers earlier than *Thalictrum dasycarpum*. Leaves are similarly feathery, but the flowers may be opening even before all the foliage has formed, usually when the deciduous tree canopy is forming. The flowers of the male plants are yellow tinged with orange, the result of the thin, dangling stamens. The female flowers are hardly showy at all. Plants grow 2–3' tall, and both the foliage and the flowers are somewhat pendulous.

Habitat: In woods from Quebec to Manitoba and south to North Dakota, Missouri, east to Alabama and Georgia.
Hardiness: USDA Zones 3–8.

Garden site: Partial shade.

Garden maintenance: Little is necessary. Plants can decline after flowering; cut back if necessary.

Thalictrum pubescens
tall meadow rue

Thalictrum pubescens

This species, also known as *Thalictrum polygamum*, may be the best-looking of all the native forms and is as little appreciated as the others. Plants often bear perfect flowers (those with stamens and pistils), but some will be only male or female. The flowers are not pendulous like the others mentioned; rather, they are upright, carried in obvious plumes in the summer, resulting in another of its common names, king-of-the-meadow. As with the other species, there are no petals, and the greenish sepals fall off shortly after flowering. The broad white stamens provide the flower color. The foliage is much like that of a columbine.

This is a big plant, growing up to 8' in a single season. Plants thrive in moist, open areas.

Habitat: In meadows, along streams and ditches from Newfoundland and Labrador to Ontario, south to Tennessee and east to Georgia.

Hardiness: USDA Zones 3–9.

Garden site: Moist to wet is best, partial shade.

Garden maintenance: May need support in a garden setting.

Recommended propagation

Seed: Generally easy from seed. Ripe seeds germinate if placed in a seed tray and kept at 40F for at least three months, or overwintered in a cold frame.

Etymology

Genus: Derivation unknown.

Specific epithet: *dasycarpum* ("hairy fruit"); *dioicum* ("dioecious"), having male and female flowers on separate plants; *pubescens* ("downy").

Common name: Plants resemble the common rue (*Ruta*) and often occur in meadows and other open places.

Thermopsis	false lupine	Fabaceae

These spectacular plants certainly do look a little like lupines but are even more easily confused with yellow-flowered baptisias. All the native *Thermopsis* species are yellow and early to flower. Unfortunately, plants are not long-lived, which has limited their popularity. Even so, they are used far too infrequently.

Thermopsis villosa	Carolina false lupine

I have grown this species (also known as *Thermopsis caroliniana*) for years. Other than their disappearing too soon for my liking, I find these lupines beautiful and appropriate for gardens. In my experience, plants grow about 3' tall, but I have seen reports of up to 5'. The lupine-like, gray-green leaves consist of three segments, and both the petioles and the veins beneath the leaves are hairy. At the base of the petiole is a leaf-like structure called a stipule, and its 2" length and 1" width, among the largest in the genus, helps to distinguish *T. villosa* from other species.

The inflorescence appears in spring or early summer; each bright yellow flower is held on a small flower stalk close to the flower axis. The foliage tends to decline after flowering if there is a lot of summer rain; the seed pods, like beans covered with shaggy hairs, follow. Perhaps the short garden life experienced in Athens may have to do with the clay soils, warm temperatures, and high humidity during the summer, but wherever you live, don't expect full-season glory.

Habitat: In open places in North Carolina west to Tennessee, south to Alabama and east to Georgia.

Thermopsis villosa

Hardiness: USDA Zones 4–8.

Garden site: Full sun, well-drained soils.

Garden maintenance: If plants look to be declining after flowering, fungicides for foliar diseases can help. Once fruit is formed, they will probably decline anyway.

Other species for the garden

Thermopsis montana (golden pea) is the western equivalent of *T. villosa* and quite similar in habit and flower color. The leaves are more narrow, and the fruit is not as hairy. Plants are equally pretty and more useful for western gardeners. Zones 4–8.

Recommended propagation

Seed: Plants are easiest to raise from fresh seeds. Seeds may need to be scarified by rubbing between sandpaper.

Etymology

Genus: From the Greek, *thermos* ("lupin") and *opsis* ("like"), because the flowers are similar to lupines.

Specific epithet: *montana* ("pertaining to mountains"); *villosa* ("covered with soft hairs").

Common name: False lupine and golden pea are based on similarities to those better known plants.

Tiarella	foamflower	Saxifragaceae

Walk through wildflower areas in the spring in almost every part of this country, and you will find foamflowers. Powell Gardens, Chicago Botanic Garden, Atlanta Botanical Garden, and other public gardens use foamflowers not only to teach visitors about our rich native history, but also because they are an easy plant to grow and, with recent breeding, provide enormous diversity. If you garden with shade, you have probably welcomed in a few foamflowers already.

Many cultivars appear in catalogs and at the nursery, but few species are used in gardens. All flower in the spring, usually with white flowers but occasionally with obvious tinges of pink, and all are less than 1' tall. Most differences in cultivars have to do with the appearance of the leaves, not the usual variations of habit, or flower color or form.

Tiarella cordifolia	Allegheny foamflower

The unimproved, unvarnished species (var. *cordifolia*) of this common foamflower is a gem in itself and the foundation for the many available cultivars.

Plants are stoloniferous, meaning they will spread around the garden, and for most gardens, this is a definite improvement. To see how they spread, visit Peirce's Woods at Longwood Gardens or Mt. Cuba in Delaware in May and wander the shaded paths away from the hustle and bustle of the more formal gardens. The flowers are held tightly on terminal inflorescences above the basal rosettes of heart-shaped leaves. The leaves may have obvious pink or reddened midribs. Plants thrive in moist soils and shady areas.

I can't count the number of new cultivars that have appeared in the last five years, and just when I think I have a handle on what is out there, another half-dozen appear. Most of the newer entries are hybrids crossing *Tiarella cordifolia* var. *cordifolia* with *T. c.* var. *collina* (*T. wherryi*), *T. trifoliata*, *T. t.* var. *laciniata*, and perhaps other species. Nearly all the breeding has concentrated on the foliar aspects, and just when one dissected black-centered leaf appears to be unique, another cultivar with a lime-green, mottled leaf appears. I have trialed over thirty different cultivars in the gardens in Athens, and I have a few favorites, to be sure. They are all impressive in the container; the true test is how they look three years later. Here are more than you want.

'Arpeggio', from the breeders at Primrose Path Nursery, provides deeply lobed leaves with a central maroon blotch. The light pink flower are carried on 12" stems.

'Black Snowflake' has highly dissected foliage with dark markings in the center and white flowers in the spring.

'Black Velvet' from Dan Heims of Terra Nova Nurseries has black-centered cut leaves and white flowers with a pink blush.

'Brandywine' is a mainstay, a large-leaved (3–4" wide) form with light green heart-shaped leaves, each with bold red venation.

'Butterfly Wings' has highly dissected leaves, often with purple midribs and white to pink flowers. Quite unique foliage. From Primrose Path.

Tiarella cordifolia

Tiarella cordifolia var. *collina*

Tiarella cordifolia 'Oakleaf'

Tiarella 'Spring Symphony'

var. *collina* (*Tiarella wherryi*) is a clump-former. The leaves are more sharply pointed and sometimes appear to be more glossy, but so many forms are being sold, that may not always be so. Zones 4–9.

'Dark Eyes' is a vigorous grower and fills in rapidly. The burgundy center of the heart-shaped leaves accounts for its name.

'Eco Red Heart' is one of the many new plants from American icon Don Jacobs. Plants have deep red centers in the leaves and pink to white flowers.

'Heronswood Mist' is beautiful—cream mottling on lime-green foliage and handsome flowers to boot. I have not been able to keep this growing for more than a couple of years, but that is probably just me.

'Ink Blot' is a medium to small selection with dark green leaves and blotches of red, particularly near the center.

'Iron Butterfly' has large divided leaves adorned with purple to black stripes in the center. The flowers are white with a hint of pink.

'Jeepers Creepers' is a ground cover form, spreading rapidly. The rounded leaves have dark stripes in the middle. White flowers in the spring.

'Neon Lights' is an excellent example of the breeding for bright, visible foliage that made tiarellas more gardenesque. The leaves are deeply cut and wonderfully patterned.

'Oakleaf' was a pioneer foamflower selection, and its excellent foliar markings and shape keep it popular.

'Pink Brushes' has obviously pink flowers and attractively quilted leaves with a central dark splotch.

'Pink Skyrocket' flowers heavily with pink flowers over dissected leaves. Very handsome.

'Pirates's Patch' bears large uncut leaves with a large patch of black (hey, I don't name them!). Many white flowers with a hint of pink.

'Sea Foam' has white flowers that persist for a long time. Foliage is deeply cut.

'Skeleton Key' bears dozens of white flowers and light green lobed leaves.

Tiarella trifoliata

'Spring Symphony' is the best foam-flower and the one I recommend to my daughters. Good-looking foliage, astounding numbers of flowers, and the longest flowering time of any I have tried. Add to that its tough nature and long garden life, and this hybrid is a no-brainer.

'Winterglow' has large leaves flecked with red throughout and white flowers. The fall color is golden yellow, better than most others at that time of year.

Habitat: In moist woods from Nova Scotia to Michigan, south to Alabama and east to Georgia.
Hardiness: USDA Zones 3–8.
Garden site: Moist shade.
Garden maintenance: Often plants want to heave out of the soil, and the stems at the base of the plant become exposed to the elements. If this occurs, mound soil to the first set of basal leaves.

Other species for the garden

Tiarella trifoliata, with fuzzy three-lobed leaves, is occasionally offered, but you will have it with you every time a hybrid is purchased: its deeply cut var. *laciniata* is one of the taxa reshaping the dissected leaves of the hybrids. Zones 4–8.

Recommended propagation

Seed: Plant seeds outdoors in a cold frame.
Cuttings: Treat the stolons as cuttings, being sure some leaves come away with each piece.
Division: Carefully dig the stolons, being sure that roots are actively growing.

Etymology

Genus: A diminutive of the Greek, *tiara* ("small crown"), in reference to the shape of the fruit.
Specific epithet: *collina* ("pertaining to hills"); *cordifolia* ("heart-shaped leaves"); *laciniata* ("slashed or torn into narrow segments"); *trifoliata* ("three-leaved").
Common name: The flowers are somewhat foamy in their appearance.

Tradescantia	spiderwort	Commelinaceae

The spiderworts are easy to identify: they have linear leaves, leaf bases that curl around the stem, and dozens of flower buds waiting to open into unusual three-petaled flowers. The cluster of flower buds is surrounded by leafy bracts; at any given time, two or three flowers will pop open through the bracts, but many more appear over time. Plants handle full sun but are equally at home in partial shade. At least three species are of interest, and all are available if you look diligently; however, unless you are a hard-core spiderman, you are more likely to come across selections and hybrids, of which there is no shortage. Most offer different flower colors; a few provide interesting foliage as well.

Tradescantia ohiensis   Ohio spiderwort, blue jacket

If you only looked at catalogs or retail offerings, you would be surprised to learn that species other than *Tradescantia virginiana* (which see) do exist. Unfortunately, the only easy way to incorporate them in your garden is to understand that they are often parents of the hybrid you just purchased. Sometimes, however, plants of this native species can be located, and it is worth the effort to find them. They do not differ dramatically from the more common Virginia spiderwort, but they have a whitish bloom on the leaves and stems. The leaves are narrow, and the petals are smaller. Plants can grow up to 4' in height, but 2–3' is more common.

The best cultivar, and perhaps the only one, is 'Mrs. Loewer'. Her thin, grassy leaves, somewhat blue-green all season, are kind of unkempt, particularly at the end of a warm day (sounds like me); but she flowers seemingly forever, and if you hide her behind a shrub or other plant, she will pop her flowers out wherever she spots daylight. Cut her back if she gets too ragged; she will return.

Habitat: In open areas from Massachusetts to Minnesota, west to Nebraska, south to Texas and east to Georgia.
Hardiness: USDA Zones 5–8.

Tradescantia ohiensis 'Mrs. Loewer'

Garden site: Full sun, although afternoon shade results in a less disheveled appearance.

Garden maintenance: Cut back hard when plants look ragged.

Tradescantia virginiana   Virginia spiderwort

By far the most common species in nature as well as the garden center. Of course at most garden centers, it is the hybrids that are for sale, sometimes under the (invalid) name *Tradescantia ×andersonii*. Regardless, the species and its hybrids are remarkable plants, growing in full sun if the soil is moist and in rather deep shade as well. The leaves are smooth or nearly so, but the sepals and flower stalks are hairy. The flower petals are nearly 1" long and are always blue to purple. Although the individual flowers remain only for a day, there are so many buds-in-waiting that flowering persists for a long time; in our trials, twenty weeks of flowering is not uncommon. Look out, however, as they can also reseed vigorously, becoming something of a pest.

Most of the following are hybrids and will either be listed as such or under this species. There are far too many of them. Here are but a few to catch your fancy; some have graced our gardens for dozens of years.

'Bilberry Ice' has white flowers with a blue tint on the margins and a dark purple stripe along the center of the petal.

'Bluestone' bears mid blue flowers.

'Carmine Glow' has deep carmine flowers.

'Concord Grape' bears grape-colored flowers in mid to late summer.

'Innocence' has large creamy white flowers.

'Isis' has Oxford-blue flowers 3" in diameter. Among the best of the blues.

'J. C. Weguelin' is an excellent, vigorous cultivar with 2" wide China-blue flowers.

Tradescantia virginiana 'Pauline'

Tradescantia virginiana 'Sweet Kate'

'Joy' is a relatively new cultivar with purple flowers held close to the large dome-like plant. Plants grow about 2' tall.

'Little Doll' is a dwarf form, growing only about 8" tall, with lavender flowers. An interesting selection for the front of the garden or even for edging.

'Osprey' has large blue feathery stamens that contrast well with the large white flowers.

'Pauline' bears lilac-pink flowers 2–2½" wide.

'Purple Dome' stands about 2' tall and is laden with flowers of rich purple.

'Purple Profusion' is nearly 2' tall and bears *Tradescantia virginiana* 'Sylvana'
many puple flowers throughout the season.

'Red Cloud' has rosy red blooms on 2' tall plants. One of the best cultivars available.

'Snowcap' is probably the purest white form, with 2–3" wide flowers.

'Sweet Kate' is a knockout, with her chartreuse leaves and deep blue flowers.

'Sylvana' has proven itself in our trials at Georgia, providing a season-long display of rosy purple flowers.

Habitat: In woods, meadows, and roadsides from Maine to Minnesota, south to Missouri, east to Tennessee and Georgia.

Hardiness: USDA Zones 3–9.

Garden site: Consistent moisture will help plants grow almost anywhere; if soils remain dry, site in a partially shaded (afternoon shade) area. Plants in the North handle full-sun conditions better than those in the South.

Garden maintenance: Plants can be cut back later in the season if they appear bedraggled. The foliage will be far more pleasant to look at, and they will likely flower again.

Other species for the garden

Tradescantia hirsuticaulis (hairystem spiderwort) is a dwarf (less than 2' tall) form with pale blue flowers. Occasionally offered; not as vigorous as others but quite pretty.

Tradescantia rosea (*Callisia rosea*; rosy spiderwort) is finding its way to gardeners thanks to progressive nursery people, and this is a good thing. Plants are only 8–10" tall but bear many pink to purple flowers all season. Zones 6–10.

Recommended propagation

Seed: Seed should be sown immediately, although germination is seldom much above 50 percent.

Cuttings: Cuttings are easy.

Division: Easiest method of propagation. Divide in early spring for best success.

Etymology

Genus: For John Tradescant senior and his son, John Tradescant junior, gardeners to King Charles I.

Specific epithet: *hirsuticaulis* ("with a hairy stem"); *ohiensis* ("of Ohio"); *virginiana* ("of Virginia").

Common name: Spiderwort may have come from the belief that plants would help with spider bites, or from the spider-like veins on the flowers.

Trillium   Liliaceae

If ever a genus was an American icon, it is *Trillium*. Like the American elm, or the sunflower, trilliums are as American as motherhood and apple pie. Found throughout the country, they are all early spring ephemerals. Everyone wants trilliums in their garden, but difficulties in propagation (many take up to seven years from seed) have limited their appearance on retail benches and catalogs. That is not to say there are not many species and even cultivars offered; it is simply that if you want them, you must pay for them (one catalog offering listed a 4" pot of *Trillium grandiflorum* 'Plenum' at $75.00). You will often find that your best nurseries, even those dealing with native plants, will not be selling trilliums because of the difficulty in providing reasonably priced nursery-grown plants. Price is important because, let's face it, one trillium really doesn't do it. Do not despair, however: more nurseries than ever before are doing it right, and if you support them, they will continue to propagate—and prices will fall.

Unfortunately, trilliums are still being harvested from the wild, and if you are tempted by a deal that looks too good to be true, you are close to joining the dark side. The destruction of habitats and the wholesale gathering of wildflowers are topics impossible to avoid when discussing native plants. I am very upset with, even disgusted by, individuals and companies that engage in these practices—and a near-vigilante in my unofficial campaign against them. Trilliums have been abused for years, and that there are still marvelous populations from Michigan to Georgia says something about the tenacity of this genus in the face of . . . Enough said.

Speaking of which, what can I say about this large group of plants that hasn't already been said? Two of my favorite books—*American Treasures* by Rob and Don Jacobs, and *Trilliums* by Frederick and Roberta Case (both published in 1997)—tell it all. But the fact that there are books, catalogs, and Internet sites at your disposal has never stopped me before. Here are but a few of the trilliums I would recommend to my daughters. Some, the sessile trilliums, have flowers sitting directly atop the trifoliate leaves, which are usually mottled with white. Others have flowers attached with a flower stem called a pedicel; these pediceled trilliums carry their flowers either above or nodding below the leaves, which are usually green.

Trillium catesbaei   *Trillium cernuum*

All species are essentially maintenance-free. The most important ingredient for success is proper siting—shade, moisture, and as little disturbance as possible.

Trillium catesbaei   rose trillium, Catesby's trillium

One of the prettiest and easiest-to-grow of the pediceled forms, but not one of the easiest flowers to view. The rosy flowers with their upturned petals are held beneath the leaves, requiring a hands-and-knees viewing. The leaves are green on this 12" tall plant. Plants work well in much of the country, being quite tolerant of heat and cold.

Habitat: In woods from North Carolina and Tennessee, south to Alabama and east to Georgia.
Hardiness: USDA Zones 4–9.

Trillium cernuum   nodding trillium

Another pediceled species, it is similar to *Trillium catesbaei* in that flowers are hidden beneath the foliage, making it a difficult trillium to love. The blooms are almost entirely white with recurved petals. The leaves are glossy green and sessile. This is a northern species and should not be expected to thrive in the Deep South.

Trillium rugelii (southern nodding trillium) is a little better choice for southern gardeners. It is still a mountain species, but I have grown it successfully in my Athens garden for years. Plants are similar to *T. cernuum* but the petals are more curved back and the anthers are obviously dark purple. Found in the mountains of the Carolinas and Georgia, and into eastern Tennessee. Zones 4–8.

Habitat: From Newfoundland to Ontario into Michigan and east to
   Pennsylvania.
Hardiness: USDA Zones 3–7.

Trillium cuneatum   toad trillium, sweet Betsy

For me, this sessile species is one of the most difficult to distinguish from other similar species. The leaves vary from only slightly to extensively mottled, and the flowers range from brown to purple. It is distributed over a huge area and, without doubt, natural hybridization has resulted in numerous intermediate forms. It is a large plant, with great ovate leaves up to 6" long and 4" wide and maroon petals. The petals are widest above the middle and taper to the base (cuneate). Of trilliums, it is among the earliest to flower and easiest to grow, and will establish itself well in temperate gardens.

Trillium cuneatum

Other closely related species are *Trillium decumbens* (decumbent trillium), whose leaves essentially hug the ground and whose petals are much narrower and longer; *T. sessile* (sessile trillium), whose flowers are much smaller and whose leaves are usually less mottled; and the little-known but extraordinary *T. underwoodii* (Underwood's trillium), native into Florida, with a short stem and smaller flowers than *T. cuneatum*. A wonderful plant—if you can find it, buy it, particularly if you garden in the South.

Habitat: From North Carolina west to
   Tennessee, south to Mississippi and east to
   north Georgia.
Hardiness: USDA Zones 4–8.

Trillium erectum   stinking Benjamin

This pediceled species is highly variable, but then, most trilliums are. The relatively large maroon flowers reside above the leaves, often to one side. Maroon, off-white, and even greenish are not uncommon colors. Put your nose into the flower, and you may catch a whiff of the "wet dog" smell that gives the common name. The leaves are sessile and pointed at the tips. Plants

Trillium erectum

are better adapted to the northern half of the country; they struggle a little in warm, humid climates.

Trillium vaseyi (sweet Beth) has a similar flower color and habit, but the flowers are significantly larger and are rather sweet-smelling. One of my favorites, but difficult to find. Also a mountain species. Zones 3–7.

Habitat: From Quebec to Ontario and Michigan into Delaware and the mountains of Tennessee and Georgia.
Hardiness: USDA Zones 3–7.

Trillium grandiflorum   great white trillium

This pediceled species is by far the best-known trillium. Plants have blanketed entire hillsides and valleys. The bad news is that have been harvested to smithereens; the good news is that they are becoming more and more available

Trillium grandiflorum

Trillium grandiflorum, aging flowers

Trillium grandiflorum var. *roseum*

Trillium grandiflorum 'Multiplex'

through reputable sources. That it is Ohio's state flower as well as the provincial flower of Ontario says volumes about the intelligence of those northerners. It should also hint that this great white is better suited to the great white North, although the Armitage garden is becoming whiter every year.

The flowers typically have pointed 2" long white petals with wavy edges, although rose, pink, and double-flowered forms are also documented. The flowers are held on a 3" long stalk above the leaves. Plants are often found in calcareous soils, and application of dolomitic lime in fall may help. The flowers usually turn pink as they decline.

var. *roseum* has a wonderful pink flower and 'Multiplex' ('Flore Pleno', 'Plenum') bears fully double flowers. All the trilliums are spectacular at the Garden in the Woods in Framingham, Massachusetts, but this species and all its forms are worth a visit alone.

Habitat: From Quebec to Minnesota, to Pennsylvania and Arkansas and east to the mountains of Georgia.
Hardiness: USDA Zones 3–7.

Trillium luteum	**yellow trillium**

Trillium luteum

Trillium discolor

The bright, long, narrow petals of this sessile trillium make it the easiest species to identify. The color is variable, but the petals range from pale to bright lemon-yellow, while the sessile leaves are beautifully mottled in silver. Plants have been harvested aggressively and continue to be so. While a few other species produce yellow flowers, this is by far the most commonly grown and gardened.

Another yellow-flowered form that I enjoy is *Trillium discolor* (pale yellow trillium). The soft yellow petals are much shorter than those of *T. luteum*, and the plant itself is shorter. It is more subtle but more ornamental than *T. luteum*. Native to the northern border of Alabama and Georgia. Zones 5–9.

Habitat: Western North Carolina and north Georgia, mainly into eastern Tennessee and southern Kentucky.
Hardiness: USDA Zones 4–8.

Trillium stamineum

Other species for the garden

I can't imagine there is a single bad trillium out there. Some are very demanding in their soil, moisture, and other environmental needs (don't even try *Trillium chloropetalum* in the East, or *T. undulatum* anywhere—it just does not assimilate well). With most others, it is simply a matter of finding them for sale and parting with the money needed to start your hillside.

Trillium lanceolatum (*T. lancifolium*), more and more nursery-grown, provides handsome burgundy flowers over mottled narrow lanceolate leaves.

Trillium stamineum (twisted trillium) is a fun plant with twisted petals and mottled foliage.

Recommended propagation

Seed: If you have seven years, go for it. Help Mother Nature by preparing soil around the plant, the more easily to receive any seed that falls. Seedlings can be carefully transplanted in a couple of years.

Division: Divide in winter or very early spring.

Etymology

Genus: From the Latin, *tri* ("three"), in reference to all parts of the plant being in threes.

Specific epithet: *catesbaei*, for Mark Catesby, who explored the Carolinas in the early 1700s; *cernuum* ("inclining the head"), hence nodding; *chloropetalum*, from the Greek, *chloros* ("green") and *petalon* ("petal"), in reference to the greenish petal color; *cuneatum* ("wedge-shaped"), generally with the narrow end down; *decumbens* ("trailing with the tips upright"); *discolor* ("pale"); *erectum* ("erect"), referring to the stiff pedicel; *grandiflorum* ("large-flowered"); *lanceolatum* ("spear-shaped"), referring to the shape of the leaves; *sessile* ("without a stalk"); *stamineum* ("with prominent stamens"); *underwoodii*, after botanist L. M. Underwood (1853–1907); *undulatum* ("wavy"), referring to the margins of the petals; *vaseyi* honors American botanist George Vasey (1822–1893).

Trollius laxus	globeflower	Ranunculaceae

Talk about an overlooked plant. People are always going on and on about globe-flowers when they return from the United Kingdom or the Continent. Then they forget about them or kill some expensive alien they rushed out to acquire, and never know that their own is beautiful in its own right. Like all globeflowers, our native species thrives in moist, cool areas and is no more likely to do well in Baton Rouge than the overseas forms; however, in large areas of the Northeast and running north across the country to the West Coast, gardeners should be trying our native on for size. Plants have five-lobed or divided anemone-like leaves and stand only 12–15" tall. They bear wonderful pale yellow single flowers with vibrant bright yellow anthers in the spring and early summer. The flowers, which are 1–1½" wide, have no petals and consist of sepals only. Plants will reseed well if sited properly.

The eastern form, var. *laxus*, is easier to grow in most areas of the country. The white-flowered western form, var. *albiflorus*, needs to be cool and moist and grows in zones 4–8.

Habitat: var. *laxus* is distributed from Connecticut to Ohio south to Delaware and Pennsylvania, var. *albiflorus* is distributed from Manitoba to British Columbia south to Washington, Idaho and east to Colorado.

Hardiness: USDA Zones 3–7.

Garden site: Moist soils are necessary. If soils are consistently moist, then full sun is appropriate. Calcareous soils are recommended to everyone but southern gardeners.

Garden maintenance: None, excepting the occasional addition of dolomitic lime.

Trollius laxus

Recommended propagation
Seed: Sow seeds in a container and place in a cold frame. Plants will germinate in the spring after temperatures warm up.

Etymology
Genus: From the German, *trollblume* ("globeflower").
Specific epithet: *laxus* ("loose"), referring to the open arrangement of flowers; *albiflorus* ("white-flowered").

Uvularia	bellwort, merry bells	Convallariaceae

Join me in the Armitage garden in the spring and revel in the epimediums, trilliums, and some of my favorites, the merry bells. They are subtle, not even close to eye-popping, and are easily overlooked, so what's the deal? That they are all of the above makes them special, to say nothing of the light green leaves and the nodding yellow lily-like flowers. They are similar to fairy bells (*Disporum*) and a little like a small Solomon's seal.

Uvularia perfoliata	perforated bellwort

This plant is worth growing in the garden if for no other reason than to admire the way its leaves appear to be pierced by the stem and live to tell about it. Every time I look at this arrangement, I cannot help but think about how diverse and fascinating plants are; it is just so neat—like leaves at war, and losing. You can imagine the stares I get from my students when I teach the term "perfoliate."

Uvularia perfoliata

Plants pop out of the ground in early spring, with gray-green leaves and the main stem forking into two about 8" up from the ground. The terminal flowers are already formed and ready to open. The yellow flowers hang down and are twisted; they are not overpowering but make a nice contrast to the foliage. After flowering, a three-sided fruit forms (the easiest way to distinguish perforated bellwort from Solomon's seal and fairy bells). Plants move around the garden with abandon. They will not be invasive, but your neighbor might enjoy a shovelful if they become too numerous.

Habitat: In open woods from Massachusetts to Ontario, south to Louisiana and east to Florida.
Hardiness: USDA Zones 3–8.
Garden site: Moist shade to open shade. Acid soil is necessary for best performance.
Garden maintenance: None.

Uvularia sessilifolia   **wild-oats, sessile bellwort**

This species is not at all different from *Uvularia perfoliata* as far as what it provides the garden and the gardener; however, as the name implies, the leaves are sessile. The pale yellow flowers are about 1" long, a little smaller but otherwise similar to other merry bells. The plants are quite skinny and actually do look like oats coming out of the ground.

Habitat: From Quebec and New England to North Dakota and South Dakota, Oklahoma, and east to Alabama and the mountains of Georgia.
Hardiness: USDA Zones 3–8.
Garden site: Shaded area with some moisture.
Garden maintenance: None.

Uvularia sessilifolia

Uvularia grandiflora

Other species for the garden

Uvularia grandiflora (large-flowered bellwort) is similar to *U. perfoliata* but has leaves that are slightly hairy on the underside and flowers that are a little bigger. I have grown 'Sunbonnet' in my garden, and it is bigger and bolder in every way.

Recommended propagation

Seed: Seed is slow but effective. Germination is rapid, but about two additional years is required for mature plants.

Division: Plants can be divided carefully. Top growth may be very slow the first year after division, but the rhizomes should grow fine.

Etymology

Genus: From the anatomical term "uvula" (the lobe hanging from the back of the soft palate in humans), in reference to the hanging flowers.

Specific epithet: grandiflora ("large-flowered"); *perfoliata* ("perfoliate"), that is, the leaf embraces or surrounds the stem; *sessilifolia* ("with sessile leaves").

Common name: Merry bells is perhaps for the bell-shaped flowers, which heralded the end to winter. Bellwort includes the term "wort," which often signals a medicinal or culinary herb but also just means "plant."

| *Veratrum viride* | false hellebore, itchroot | Melanthiaceae |

I keep looking and looking to see if anyone is growing this plant for sale, and there are slim pickings indeed. Plants are beautiful with their large ovate pleated leaves and upright stature, growing 4–6' in height. But to expect flowers the first year (or fifth) is to court disappointment. Flowering takes many years, and when the flowers do finally appear, they are from another planet: lime-green and waxy, on upright flowering stems at the top of the plant and on drooping flower stems beneath. Plants do well in the same environment enjoyed by skunk cabbage, that is, wet and mucky.

The difficulty in finding commercially produced plants may be that they may go dormant in mid summer. Additionally, even though they are poisonous (the roots particularly so), all parts of the plant have been used for medicinal purposes for years.

Habitat: In swamps and wet meadows from Quebec to Minnesota, south to Missouri, east to Maryland and south to the mountains of Tennessee and North Carolina. Plants are also found on the West Coast.

Hardiness: USDA Zones 3–8.

Garden site: Plants can tolerate full sun if placed in a wet environment.

Garden maintenance: If plants go dormant later in the season, there will be a gap to contend with. Plant them in and among other wet-tolerant plants.

Veratrum viride

Other species for the garden

Veratrum californicum (western false hellebore) is native to California, Washington, and west to Montana. It is occasionally offered by western mail-order sources. Similar to but not as green a flower as *V. viride*, nor as poisonous. Zones 5–8.

Recommended propagation

Seed: Provide a cold treatment for the seeds, preferably in a seed tray that spends the winter in a cold frame. Plants will germinate the next year, but it may take two years before they grow vigorously and will take six to seven years until they flower.

Etymology

Genus: From the Latin, *vere* ("truly") and *ater* ("black"), referring to the color of the rhizome.

Specific epithet: *californicum* ("of California"), *viride* ("green").

Common name: True hellebores (*Helleborus*) were called veratrums at one time, hence false hellebore for *Veratrum*—an excellent example of the futility of employing common plant names and expecting to be understood.

Verbena	vervain	Verbenaceae

Verbenas are everywhere in American gardens, mostly as bedding plants and colorful additions to hanging baskets and containers. Nearly all put to such uses are classified as *Verbena* ×*hybrida*, and while among these there may be some of our native *V. canadensis*, the hybrids can hardly be counted as natives (even by me), as most of the parentage is provided by three or four South American and Mexican species. And many of our popular garden verbenas (*V. bonariensis*, *V. tenuisecta* [*Glandularia pulchella*], *V. rigida*) are from elsewhere and have escaped to gardens and roadsides.

But the popularity of overseas vervains means dedicated marketing campaigns, and some of our natives are getting a second look. Most are best for meadows, often being rather tall and somewhat weedy in appearance, but then some of our best daisies could also be described that way.

Verbena canadensis rose verbena

Plants are quite diverse, thus it is difficult to determine where the species leaves off and *Verbena* ×*hybrida* begins: you may think you are purchasing rose verbena but wind up with a hybrid rather than the real thing. The stems of this species trail along the ground, usually with the tips pointing up (decumbent). The more or less triangular leaves are lobed or divided, the lobes themselves often toothed. Often the vegetative parts of the plant are hairy, but not rough to the touch. The flowers are held in many-flowered inflorescences and are usually rose to pink.

Plants are excellent for the garden, but perenniality is always a question mark, certainly north of zone 7. Excellent drainage and full-sun conditions go a long way toward helping plants survive winter conditions. Cultivars of rose verbena are few; the purple-flowered 'Homestead Purple' is the one-and-only cultivar for many producers.

Habitat: In rocky and open places from Pennsylvania to Colorado, south to Texas and east to Florida.

Hardiness: USDA Zones 7–10.

Garden site: Full sun, well-drained soils are essential.

Garden maintenance: Cut back hard in mid summer if plants are looking a little bedraggled; they will come back well. Do not water during the night. Be on the lookout for spider mites.

Verbena canadensis 'Homestead Purple'

Verbena canadensis with *V. bonariensis*

Verbena stricta	hoary vervain

There are a number of sprawling vervains (*Verbena canadensis, V. bipinnatifida*); however, the upright forms are equally interesting, if not equally ornamental. Hoary vervain grows 2–3' tall and consists of stiff gray-green leaves, 2–2½" long and toothed. The leaves are sessile and their underside is covered with whitish hairs. The flowers are held in spiky spear-like inflorescences atop the plants, almost like rockets ready to take off. Each rocket consists of many violet flowers opening from bottom to top. The upright habit and deep flower color lends the plants to a meadow planting, but they also look reasonable in a normal garden setting. They need to be tried more.

Habitat: In fields and prairies from Ontario to Montana and south to Arkansas, New Mexico and east to Tennessee. Also occurs in New England to North Carolina.
Hardiness: USDA Zones 3–9.
Garden site: Full sun, well-drained soils.
Garden maintenance: Cut back if needed.

Other species for the garden
A few other native verbenas are being offered by more enterprising nursery people, who need to have us support their efforts.

Verbena bipinnatifida (*Glandularia bipinnatifida*; Dakota verbena) is similar to *V. canadensis* but with deeper cut leaves and fewer flowers; however, its hardiness (zone 5) may help place this trailing species in more midwestern and prairie gardens.

Verbena hastata (blue vervain) is upright like *V. stricta* and has similar rocketing inflorescences, but of dark blue to violet flowers. It is not as useful for normal settings but fits well into meadow gardens. Zones 3–8.

Recommended propagation
Seed: Seed germinates rapidly if sown when ripe.
Cuttings: Trailing forms are easy from cuttings, upright forms not quite so.

Etymology
Genus: From the Latin name for plants of ceremonial value, likely including laurel, myrtle, and *Verbena officinalis*.
Specific epithet: *bipinnatifida* ("almost [*-ifida*] twice-pinnate"), a reference to the leaves; *canadensis* ("of Canada"), see *Cornus* (*Verbena canadensis* is not found in what we know as Canada); *hastata* ("spear-shaped"), probably referring to the shape of the flower stems; *stricta* ("erect," "upright").
Common name: From the Celtic, *fer* ("to remove") and *faen* ("stone"), referring to its use in treating bladder stones.

Vernonia	ironweed	Asteraceae

The ironweeds have been old-fashioned favorites for years. Ok, so not necessarily favorites, but they have been in gardens for a long time. Ok, so they are weeds and people didn't really plant them there. Native plant enthusiasts gush over their ironweeds because of the butterflies they attract, and probably because they were free (native plant enthusiasts are not known for their liberal spending habits). A few ironweeds are available; one is easily found, and a couple deserve more respect. Most are over 4' tall, and all have clusters of purple flowers, each flower surrounded by a circle of grayish bracts. They are all tough as nails—as one nurseryman wrote, "The common name could refer to ironweed's constitution."

Vernonia lettermannii	threadleaf ironweed

As soon as you read this, put down the book and purchase this plant. Perhaps because its native habitat is limited, this species is hardly known at all; several enterprising producers offer it but not as many as should do. Plants are only about 3' tall, which is a welcome relief from the giant *Vernonia noveboracensis*, and have wonderful thin leaves that remind me of *Amsonia hubrichtii* (both of which see). Not only are the leaves handsome, but they are so numerous on the many stems that they lend a bushy, compact look—that is, a plant that would be loved even if it were not native. Add to that its drought-tolerant constitution, and this species seems to have it all. The flowers are similar to other ironweeds (small blobs of purple), and unfortunately they don't fill the plant with flowers. Many of the late summer flowers are not held above the foliage and get lost, so

Vernonia lettermannii (dwarf form)

I guess they don't have it all quite yet. Even so, having taken this into consideration, I wrote the first sentence in this paragraph, the one dictating your subsequent actions.

I have trialed this species for a few years, and a more dwarf form we have selected is soon to be released. So far, it has not spread; and other than on some basal foliage, it has not been disfigured with mildew, at least not in Athens.

Habitat: In open fields in Oklahoma and Arkansas.
Hardiness: USDA Zones 4–9.
Garden site: Full sun.
Garden maintenance: Plants grow very thickly, which makes their appearance outstanding but also reduces air movement. Diseases such as mildew could become a problem. Thin out the stand after two to three years. Plants do not need a lot of water; do not irrigate heavily.

Vernonia noveboracensis   New York ironweed

This is the ironweed of prairie plantings, meadow plantings, and plain purple plantings. Its most obvious attribute is its 4–7' height, but when it produces those deep purple flowers in the fall, it can be a knockout. That the flowers may be 7' off the ground simply makes it an architectural feature. Butterflies flock to the plants, and if room is available, it may be fun to have. It is more at home in an informal setting.

Mildew can be a problem but is less of one where air circulation is good. Don't lean the plant against the garage wall.

Vernonia noveboracensis

Habitat: In fields and marshy areas
from Massachusetts to West
Virginia and Ohio south to
Mississippi and east to Georgia.

Hardiness: USDA Zones 3–9.

Garden site: Full sun. Too much shade
will result in taller plants.

Garden maintenance: Don't overwater.
Plants can tolerate wet feet, but they
will be significantly shorter under
dry conditions (which is a good
thing).

Other species for the garden

The dozens of native ironweeds all
attract wildlife and bring wild America
into suburbia, but as usual, finding
them for sale is a challenge.

Vernonia glauca

 Vernonia glauca (gray ironweed) is
similar to New York ironweed, a little shorter but with gray-green undersurface
to the leaves. Zones 4–8.

 Vernonia missurica (Missouri ironweed) grows only 3–5' tall and bears stiff
stems and clusters of purple flowers in late summer. Zones 3–8.

Recommended propagation

Seed: Seeds germinate readily.

Cuttings: Root three-node cuttings in late spring; plant in the ground by mid
summer.

Division: Divide when the clump gets sufficiently wide.

Etymology

Genus: For William Vernon, an English botanist who explored what is now
Maryland in the late 17th century.

Specific epithet: *glauca* ("glaucous"), in reference to the bloom on the leaves; *let-termannii*, for G. W. Lettermann, who wrote about Southwest plants in the
1800s; *missurica* ("of Missouri"); *noveboracensis* ("of New York").

Common name: Ironweed refers to the rusty color of the fruit.

Veronicastrum virginicum   culver's root   Scrophulariaceae

I remember first planting this as a potential cut flower during our specialty cut
research days in the mid 1980s. I knew little about this little-known plant at the
time, other than that it was related to *Veronica* and had a brilliant common name

Veronicastrum virginicum 'Album'

(even if I didn't know what it meant). I quickly learned a great deal about this fine native: not only was it an excellent cut flower, it also turned out to be a great garden plant, one that has since earned a place in mainstream American gardens and is now far easier to find, both as the species and in several cultivars.

Plants are easily distinguished from *Veronica* by their olive-green whorled leaves and upright architectural habit; and while veronicas occur in many colors, *Veronicastrum virginicum* is most commonly white ('Album'), occasionally lavender, and rarely pink. The flowers are held in a long raceme and open over two to four weeks. The flower stems branch at the top of the plant into the dominant raceme and two others, one on each side.

'Apollo' is a lavender-blue form.

'Fascination' is a seed-grown form in shades of rose.

'Pink Glow' has reasonably good pink flowers.

Habitat: In meadows and prairies from Massachusetts and Vermont to Manitoba south to Texas, western Florida and Georgia.

Hardiness: USDA Zones 3–8.

Garden site: Full sun.

Veronicastrum virginicum 'Pink Glow'

Garden maintenance: No bugs, no disease, just a good plant. For the best and
biggest flowers, snip off the side flower buds when they are less than 1"
long. In too much shade or with too much fertilizer applied, plants can get
floppy.

Recommended propagation
Seed: Seeds germinate well.
Cuttings: Two- to three-node cuttings root if taken in early summer.
Division: The roots are large, but division may be accomplished as plants
emerge in the spring.

Etymology
Genus: *astrum* ("resembling"), thus resembling *Veronica*.
Specific epithet: *virginicum* ("of Virginia").
Common name: The root was used by Native Americans and later by Europeans
as an emetic. Culver may have been an 18th-century doctor who recom-
mended its use.

Viola	violet	Violaceae

This is one of the world's most successful genera, whose species have been
established almost everywhere in the temperate world. Of the 500-plus species,
at least ninety-six are native to the continental United States, and Illinois, New
Jersey, Rhode Island, and Wisconsin have adopted the violet as their state flower.
But try to buy something other than Johnny-jump-ups, pansies, and bedding violas at any retail outlet—it won't happen. Even mainstream mail-order nurseries,
for the most part, have left violets to the breeders of pansies and violas. Now, I
love all those colorful plants—no natives can touch them for flower power and
persistence of bloom—but there must be some useful garden violets available.
And there are, any number of them: it just takes a little digging, but America
lives on. Find sources for some native violets, and give them a try.

Many gardeners are frightened of violets; some species are known to shed
their seeds far and wide, quickly becoming violet weeds. I would like to tell you
that most of the bad guys come from other lands, but that's just not so. Some of
our natives, such as the dooryard or confederate violet (*Viola sororia*) and marsh
violet (*V. cucullata*), are also aggressive. It is their nature; they evolved to throw
seeds and colonize, and even if the state of Kansas tells us we shouldn't be teaching evolution, the "intelligent design" of violets tells us otherwise.

Viola labradorica   **Labrador violet**

There are some plants that no matter how easy they are, you still love them and don't get upset if they take root on the back of your cat. If they appear where they shouldn't, then they can be moved, no troubles. Such are the Labrador violets. Without a doubt, these are doers.

The blue flowers appear early and often, but even when not in flower, the foliage is outstanding: the small heart-shaped leaves are dark green in the summer and almost black in the cold weather. Plants mostly reproduce by seed. I have them beneath a dogwood, and between the shade and the root competition, a lesser plant might not make it. No sweat for this one. If I am this successful in Georgia, light years away from Labrador, think of the success you'll have if you are in, say, Dover, Delaware.

Habitat: In shaded areas from Labrador to Ontario and south to Maine.
Hardiness: USDA Zones 2–8.
Garden site: Shady, moist conditions suit it well.
Garden maintenance: None.

Viola pedata   **bird's foot violet**

Isn't it always the way? The plants you don't want spew seed and run like chickens all over the garden, and those you cherish die if you look at them the wrong way. Of course, an analyst would tell me that is why I cherish them, and if they were easy, I wouldn't care for them. Bad argument—I love and cherish my bluebells, wood poppies, and columbines, and they are spewers and runners, for sure. Oh well, running be damned. All I know is that I can't grow bird's foot violets to save my life. But I certainly admire them in other people's gardens.

Plants send out a rosette of beautifully divided leaves from a fat crown in the spring, somewhat like the foot of a bird, I guess. The violet flowers are spectacular, and var. *bicolor* (*Viola bicolor*; 'Bicolor') is even prettier, with its dark and light blue color. They are best grown in grit where the soil dries out rapidly, so the crown never stays wet. Full sun, uncommon for most violets, is also useful. Of the several cultivars, the one I particularly love is from the talented Don Jacobs of Eco Gardens, 'Eco Artist's Palette', with purple and white

Viola pedata

flowers. Get your pots of grit ready and buy whatever you can find; they are all wonderful.

Habitat: In dry soil in open areas from Maine to Minnesota, south to Kansas and Texas and east to Florida.
Hardiness: USDA Zones 3–9.
Garden site: Full sun (although afternoon shade is tolerated in the South) and gritty soil. Often containers work best.
Garden maintenance: Keep the grit gritty.

Viola pubescens hairy yellow violet

I had trouble finding a commercial source of this plant, but it is too pretty not to point out, with the hope that perhaps a neighbor will share some with you. Most violets are, well, violet in color, so when I find a nice yellow like this, I like to try it out.

The stems and heart-shaped leaves are hairy and dwarf the small flowers. The bright yellow flowers, which have brown stripes in the center, are produced in a flush in the spring. Large clumps can form, but beware of powdery mildew. Its close relative *Viola hastata* (halberd-leaved violet) has similar flowers but with long, triangular leaves, and is equally wonderful.

Habitat: In woods from Maine to North Dakota and south to Nebraska and Oklahoma and east to Mississippi and Georgia.
Hardiness: USDA Zones 3–9.

Garden site: Partial shade, moist soils.

Garden maintenance: None. If mildew becomes a problem, rip them out and try others—there are many yet to grow.

Viola striata	creamy violet

Another subtle, easy, no-care plant for along a pathway or tucked away near a rock. Plants have bushy stems and heart-shaped leaves, and move around by seed and stolons. The flowers, which are held on a 6" tall stem, appear later than most but are worth waiting for, especially if you don't mind getting up close. They are off-white with obvious stripes of violet.

There is nothing spectacular or even showy about these violets; as with many other marvelous garden plants, you must slow down to enjoy them. After all, if we want to rush around and not see anything, we can go shopping at the mall.

Habitat: In woods and meadows from New York to southern Ontario, west to Minnesota and south to Missouri and eastward to Alabama and Georgia.

Hardiness: USDA Zones 3–9.

Garden site: Partial shade, some moisture.

Garden maintenance: None.

Recommended propagation

Seed: Collecting the explosive seeds is a challenge; it is sometimes easier to buy some. Sow them in the ground or in trays in a cold frame.

Cuttings: *Viola pedata* can be propagated by root cuttings.

Division: Only in the sense that seedlings can be moved easily.

Viola striata

410

Etymology

Genus: From the Latin for sweet-smelling flowers. The name was also used for sweet violets, stocks, and wallflowers.

Specific epithet: *hastata* ("spear-shaped"); *labradorica* ("of Labrador"); *pedata* ("cut like a bird's foot"); *pubescens* ("downy"); *striata* ("striped").

Waldsteinia	barren strawberry	Rosaceae

Most species of this underused evergreen ground cover are native to the United States; however the one that is most commonly sold (*Waldsteinia ternata*) is native to Asia. Figures! The half-dozen species do not differ a great deal from each other, minor differences occurring in leaf and flower morphology, and in nativity. They all have strawberry-like leaves (they are closely related to the cultivated strawberry, *Fragaria*, which is also a member of the rose family) but with handsome yellow flowers.

Waldsteinia fragarioides	barren strawberry

This species has several leaves at the tip of the running rhizome, each glossy leaf divided into three serrated segments. The ½" wide yellow flowers open on 6–8" stalks in spring. The fruit is small and inedible. Plants are more vigorous in the North and should be avoided where hot, humid summers are common. Plants perform well in sunny areas, a welcome departure from the many ground covers used in the shade.

Waldsteinia fragarioides

Habitat: In woods and open areas from New Brunswick to Quebec, west to Minnesota and south to Missouri and Tennessee and east to Georgia.
Hardiness: USDA Zones 4–7.
Garden site: Full sun to partial shade.
Garden maintenance: None.

Waldsteinia lobata	lobed barren strawberry

Similar to *Waldsteinia fragarioides*, with equally brilliant and glossy foliage, but the petals are smaller and the leaves are lobed rather than divided. Its claim to fame is its increased tolerance to heat and humidity.

Habitat: On river banks from North Carolina to Georgia.
Hardiness: USDA Zones 7–9.
Garden site: Full sun if soils are moist, partial shade otherwise.
Garden maintenance: None.

Other species for the garden

Waldsteinia parviflora, an excellent choice for warm-summer gardens, is occasionally offered. Small yellow nodding flowers and three-lobed leaves characterize this species, which some consider synonymous with *W. fragarioides*. Zones 6–8.

Recommended propagation

Seed: Germination is usually low and can be disappointing.
Division: Easy. Divide in the spring.

Etymology

Genus: For Count Franz Adam Waldstein-Wahlenberg (1759–1823), an Austrian botanist.
Specific epithet: *fragarioides* ("resembling *Fragaria*," strawberry); *lobata* ("lobed"); *parviflora* ("small-flowered").
Common name: Inspired by the strawberry-like appearance of a plant that is barren of good fruit to eat.

Woodwardia areolata	netted chain fern	Blechnaceae

Netted chain fern is at home under drought conditions and yet is equally happy in high-rainfall years. It is eating up the entire garden at the Armitage residence, gulp by giant gulp; I have been pleased, more or less, because it is an easy weed to enjoy. Although plants are a little smaller, the glossy green fronds are similar in appearance to the equally aggressive sensitive fern (*Onoclea sensibilis*, which see); they are both winged, unlike most other ferns, but the fertile frond (where

*Woodwardia
areolata*

the spores are produced) of *Woodwardia areolata* is thin and contracted, unlike the bead-like stalks of sensitive fern.

Netted chain ferns run like crazy by rhizomes, fall apart around 28F, and pop up quickly in the spring. I like them better than sensitive fern because they are more compact, fill in rapidly, don't need wet soils, and, if necessary, can be removed more easily. Just a good doer for the partially shaded garden.

Habitat: From Nova Scotia into southern Maine and south from New Hampshire to Florida, west to Texas.

Hardiness: USDA Zones 4–9.

Garden site: Partial shade; does better with morning sun than deep all-day shade. High moisture levels are tolerated but not necessary.

Garden maintenance: None, except to share with your neighbor.

Other species for the garden

Woodwardia fimbriata (giant chain fern) is quite impressive, growing 6–8' in height, especially if planted in moist soils. Plants are native to the West, including Arizona, California, Nevada, Oregon, Washington, and British Columbia. Give them plenty of room to grow.

Recommended propagation

Seed: Spores are viable, but division is too easy to be fooling with spores.

Division: Easy, best in the spring.

Etymology

Genus: For English botanist Thomas Jenkinson Woodward (1745–1820).

Specific epithet: *areolata* ("marked in small areas"), perhaps referring to the netted venation; *fimbriata* ("with a small fringe"), perhaps referring to the deeply cut pinnae.

Common name: The veins are netted, and the spores on the fertile frond are in the shape of chains.

Yucca	Adam's needle	Agavaceae

The yuccas in front of our Mexican food-and-beer joint in Athens are impressive, in fact, a lot more impressive than the food or the beer—ok, at least the food. They are impressive in their absolute disdain for abuse, enduring rain and drought, exhaust fumes from passing cars, college students in passing cars, and the 100 percent lack of maintenance. Yep, much more impressive than the burritos. Yuccas by nature are tough, from the deserts of the Southwest to the taquerias of the Southeast. And good grief, they have been discovered. A few wonderful nurseries like Ty Ty Nursery in south Georgia and Yucca Do Nursery in Hampstead, Texas, have been trumpeting the benefits of yuccas for years; now there are a bunch of nouveaux yucca-come-lately nurseries, but all that means is that there are more places and more choices.

Yuccas are native in almost every state (the exceptions are Maine, Vermont, New Hampshire, Wisconsin, Idaho, Washington, and Oregon), and any number of species will work in most gardens (see the specialist nurseries in "Sources and Resources" for more information). They go under such wonderful names as banana yucca (*Yucca baccata*), Joshua tree (*Y. brevifolia*), soaptree (*Y. elata*), Our Lord's candle (*Y. whipplei*), and the wonderfully literary Don Quixote's lace (*Y. treculeana*). Other common names (Spanish bayonet, Spanish dagger for *Y. gloriosa*; Adam's needle for *Y. filamentosa*) give a hint as to the sharpness of most of the leaf tips. I removed my yuccas when we became grandparents—didn't need Mary Grace exploring those daggers.

Speaking of states, did you know that the yucca is New Mexico's state flower? There its white flowers have earned it the name *Lamparas de Dios* ("Lamps of the Lord"). Not only is it attractive, its roots and palm-like leaves provided residents of the Southwest with the raw materials for making soap and baskets.

In general, the garden forms are grown for their architectural habit and interesting (and sharp!) foliage. The white bell-shaped flowers can tower over the plants, but they are short-lived. With the introduction of variegated forms, the foliage can be enjoyed all year. There are dozens of species; go to one of the finer establishments if you want something out of the ordinary, but I must say, even the ordinary is not all that familiar.

Yucca filamentosa	Adam's needle

An exceptional garden plant, this species is the one to try first if you are not really sure about this yucca thing. The plants have no stems; instead they form clumps, thus won't grow like trees. The white bellflowers can rise 10' above the crown. Twisted threads on the margins of the leaves are characteristic of the species, which has become very popular with landscapers for that characteristic they all love—toughness. And with the good-looking foliage of new selections

Yucca 'Bright Edge'

Yucca 'Gold Band'

Yucca 'Golden Sword'

Yucca 'Golden Sword'

and hybrids, yuccas are being used more and more. Without doubt, if they make a Mexican food joint look better, think what they will do for your garden.

No one seems to be exactly sure to which species some of the named varieties belong, or if they are hybrids. They may be offered as cultivars of *Yucca filamentosa, Y. filifera, Y. flaccida,* or *Y. smalliana.*

'Bright Edge' is a bit smaller than many others and bears leaves with broad, dull golden margins.

'Color Guard' is one of the better variegated forms. The leaves have a broad gold center surrounded by deep green margins.

'Garland's Gold' has long leaves that fold down about halfway down the length.

'Gold Band' has a wide golden yellow band in the center of the green leaves.

'Golden Sword' is similar to 'Color Guard', but it is at its best in cool weather, fading somewhat in the heat.

'Variegata' is mixed up. The selection of *Yucca filamentosa* has leaves with white margins, which often turn pink; the center of the leaf is dark blue-green. 'Variegata' also occurs with *Y. smalliana*, which is similar to but not as cold hardy as *Y. filamentosa*; in this selection, the margins are yellow.

Habitat: From Michigan west to Nebraska, south to Texas and east to Florida.
Hardiness: USDA Zones 5–10.
Garden site: Full sun, good drainage.
Garden maintenance: Be careful of the needles around kids.

Yucca glauca	soapweed

Plants have narrow gray-green to blue-green leaves with grayish margins, and flowers that stand up just above the needles. Some people say this species is more refined, with its narrower foliage and short stature (1–3'); others say it is messy because both dead leaves and green leaves are interspersed on the plant. Regardless, it is probably the hardiest of the yuccas, growing all the way into the prairies of Canada. Plants contain saponin glycosides, which were used by Native Americans and settlers as a soap called amole.

Habitat: From Saskatchewan south to New Mexico, east to Texas and north to Alberta.
Hardiness: USDA Zones 3–9.
Garden site: Full sun, well-drained soils.
Garden maintenance: None, but be careful of the tips of the leaves around children.

Recommended propagation
Seed: Seeds germinate reasonably easily; a cold treatment usually helps speed and rate of germination. Seedlings should be transplanted early, before the taproot gets established.
Cuttings: Root cuttings are sometimes used commercially.

Yucca glauca

Division: Only with a backhoe.

Etymology

Genus: Plants were originally mistaken for cassava, whose native name was *yuca*.

Specific epithet: *filamentosa* ("bearing filaments"); *glauca* ("glaucous"), in reference to the bloom on the leaves.

Common name: Most names have to do with the appearance of the sharp leaves (needle, bayonet), or their use (soapweed, soaptree), or the appearance of the rigid upright flowers (Our Lord's candle).

| *Zephyranthes atamasca* | atamasco lily | Amaryllidaceae |

The genus consists of over seventy species of bulbs and provides gorgeous white, pink, and yellow flowers. Some of the favorites, such as *Zephyranthes candida*, *Z. citrina*, and *Z. grandiflora*, are native to Argentina, Guyana, and Guatemala, respectively, and are lovely in their own right; but recently, hybridizers have added a wonderful cacophony of color, and they are being noticed by more gardeners every year. We have a few of our own growing near streams and rivers, including *Z. refugiensis* and *Z. pulchella* (Texas) and *Z. simpsonii* (Florida). Any of the natives you can find are well worth trying—there is not a dog among them, as every southern boy who walked barefoot near river banks will attest. Unfortunately, there are few enough river banks spouting anything more than kudzu and privet these days.

The best known of this unknown group is the atamasco lily, which produces bright, strap-shaped leaves in the spring, and then in early summer throws out

Zephyranthes atamasca

wonderful 2½–3" wide flowers, white tinged with pink. They reside on 12" stems, and although they persist for but a short period of time, what a time it is. After flowering, they go dormant in mid to late summer. In general, they prefer moist conditions but can be seen on roadsides in south Georgia and Alabama, having escaped from the tentacles of privet. If you live in an area where atamascos do well, get some!

Habitat: From Virginia to Mississippi and east to Florida.
Hardiness: USDA Zones 7–10.
Garden site: Moist areas, full sun to partial shade.
Garden maintenance: None.

Recommended propagation
Seed: Seeds can be germinated if placed in moist trays and left undisturbed. Fresh seeds are best. From seed to planting in the ground is about two years.
Division: Offset bulbs can be divided when the colony is sufficiently large.

Etymology
Genus: From the Greek, *zephyros* ("of the west wind") and *anthos* ("flower"), referring to the origin of the genus in the Western Hemisphere.
Specific epithet: Another noun in apposition, from the Native American word for this lily.
Common name: A reiteration of the specific epithet.

Zinnia grandiflora	prairie zinnia	Asteraceae

We think of zinnias as greenhouse plants (in the garden, they often succumb to leaf diseases), but some of the toughest daisies can be found here. Few of the zinnias we plant in our gardens are native to the United States (and many have escaped), but the prairie zinnia is, to the Southwest, where it is just as at home in the dry conditions as the cacti and salamanders are. Plants are only 4–6" tall and bear much-branched stems from a woody base. The tiny, needle-like leaves have evolved to reduce water loss, and when not in flower, plants make a mossy mat. They are best suited to rock gardens or rock paths.

Habitat: Kansas to Nevada, into Texas, Arizona and northern New Mexico.
Hardiness: USDA Zones 7–10.
Garden site: Full sun, very well-drained soils.
Garden maintenance: None.

Recommended propagation
Seed: Not difficult from seed.
Cuttings: Terminal cuttings root easily.

Etymology

Genus: For Johann Gottfried Zinn (1727–1759), a professor of botany in
　　Gottingen, Germany.
Specific epithet: *grandiflora* ("large-flowered").
Common name: Native to dry prairie sites, thus its common name.

Zizia	golden alexanders	Apiaceae

Zizia differs from other members of the family in that there is no stalk on the
central inflorescence. I look forward to writing about this genus for two reasons.
One is that when I get here, the end is near; the other is that I have come to
appreciate these plants, and more than for just their interesting name. Two
species of these yellow-flowering perennials are found reasonably easily in nurseries and on the Internet; both tolerate a good deal of abuse and keep on coming back. Plants attract butterflies in abundance and are a primary host for the
Missouri woodland swallowtail butterfly. They are spectacular at Chanticleer in
Pennsylvania, and at Mt. Cuba in Delaware.

Zizia aptera	heart-leaved meadow parsnip

With a common name like that, I don't know whether to love it or eat it. The
leaves differ from *Zizia aurea* in that the basal leaves are simple (not divided)
and ovate in shape. The few stem leaves are small and often divided into three
to five leaflets. The yellow flowers, which occur in late spring, are held well
above the foliage. They are tough plants, tolerating full sun but also performing
well in partial shade, but I don't think they are as good a plant as *Zizia aurea*.

Zizia aptera

Zizia aptera

Zizia aurea

Habitat: In fields and prairies from Quebec to British Columbia down to Oregon, east to Utah and Missouri and south to Georgia.
Hardiness: USDA Zones 3–8.
Garden site: Full sun to afternoon shade. Consistent moisture helps performance.
Garden maintenance: None.

Zizia aurea	**golden alexanders**

Where plants are properly sited, they are fuller than *Zizia aptera*, with more numerous, larger leaves, and grow more vigorously. Their vigor provides more stems, which in turn provide more flowers at any one time. The leaves are usually divided into three to five segments all the way up the stem. Plants grow 1–2' tall and maintain reasonably tight clumps; they do not move all over the garden, at least not quickly. The flowers are held above the foliage, and their eye-catching bright yellow is seen from a long way off. Flowers bloom in late spring, after most of the ephemerals have disappeared.

Habitat: In meadows and damp woods from Quebec to Saskatchewan, south to Texas, east to Florida.
Hardiness: USDA Zones 3–8.
Garden site: Full sun or partial shade (afternoon shade is ideal). Plants are said to grow in heavy shade, but I would not recommend that much shade.
Garden maintenance: None.

Recommended propagation
Seed: The easiest method; seeds germinate readily. Sow the dark brown seeds in containers, allow to go through a winter or a chilling period of 40F for about three months.
Division: Easy once the colony has expanded sufficiently.

Etymology
Genus: For German botanist Johann Baptist Ziz (1779–1829).
Specific epithet: *aptera* ("wingless"), in reference to the fruit; *aurea* ("golden").
Common name: Alexanders refers to other European plants similar to this. The foliage somewhat resembles the foliage of parsnips.

SOURCES AND RESOURCES

Nurseries

With so many nurseries now carrying native plants, there is no excuse for not including a few species in the garden. Not all the state and provincial nurseries listed carry an extensive array of native plants and seeds, but they all carry some. Many excellent nurseries have no Web presence, and I likely missed them. No slight intended; apologies to those I neglected.

American Meadows
223 Ave. D #30
Williston, VT 05495
Tel 802.951.5812
Fax 802.951.9089
www.americanmeadows.com

American Ornamental Perennials
P.O. Box 489
Eagle Creek, OR 97022
Tel 503.637.3095
Fax 503.637.3096
www.graminae.com

Annie's Annuals
P.O. Box 5053
Richmond, CA 94805
Tel 510.215.1326
www.anniesannuals.com

Arrowhead Alpines
1310 N Gregory Rd.
Fowlerville, MI 48836
Tel 517.223.3581
Fax 517.223.8750
www.arrowhead-alpines.com

Avant Gardens
710 High Hill Rd.
Dartmouth, MA 02747
www.avantgardensne.com

Big Dipper Farm
26130 SE Green Valley Rd.
Black Diamond, WA 98010
Tel 360.886.8133
www.bigdipperfarm.com

Blanchette Gardens
267 Rutland St.
Carlisle, MA 01741
www.blanchettegardens.com

Bluebird Nursery
Box 460, 519 Bryan St.
Clarkson, NE 68629
Tel 800.356.9164
Fax 402.892.3738
www.bluebirdnursery.com

Bluestem Nursery
1946 Fife Rd.
Christina Lake, BC V0H 1E3
P.O. Box 239
Laurier, WA 99146
Tel/fax 250.447.6363
www.bluestem.ca

Bluestem Nursery
4101 Curry Rd.
Arlington, TX 76001
Tel 817.478.6202
Fax 817.563.7763
www.bluestemnursery.com

Bluestone Perennial Nursery
7211 Middle Ridge Rd.
Madison, OH 44057-3096
Tel 800.852.5243
Fax 440.428.7198
www.bluestoneperennials.com

Canyon Creek Nursery
3527 Dry Creek Rd.
Oroville, CA 95965
Tel 530.533.2166
www.canyoncreek.com

Carolina Wild
314 Camellia Dr.
Anderson, SC 29625
www.carolinawild.com

Carroll Gardens
444 East Main St.
Westminster, MD 21157-5540
www.carrollgardens.com

Catskill Native Nursery
607 Samsonville Rd.
Kerhonkson, NY 12446
Tel 845.626.2758
www.catskillnativenursery.com

Chalk Hill Clematis
Box 1847, 11720 Chalk Hill Rd.
Healdsburg, CA 95448
Tel 707.433.8416
Fax 707.433.8963
www.chalkhillclematis.com

Cistus Nursery
22711 Gillihan Rd.
Sauvie Island, OR 97231
Tel 503.621.2233
www.cistus.com

Cusheon Creek Nursery
175 Stewart Rd.
Salt Spring Island, BC V8K 2C4
Tel 250.537.9334
Fax 250.537.9354
www.theamateursdigest.com

Cypripedium Garden
17 Ready Way
Nepean, ON K2J 2R7
www.infonet.ca/cypr

Digging Dog Nursery
P.O. Box 471
Albion, CA 95410
Tel 707.937.1130
Fax 707.937.2480
www.diggingdog.com

Doyle Farm Nursery
158 Norris Rd.
Delta, PA 17314
Tel/fax 717.862.3134
www.doylefarm.com

Earthskin Nursery
9331 NCR 3800E
Mason City, IL 62664
Tel 217.482.3524
www.earthskinnursery.com

East Bay Nursery
2332 San Pablo Ave.
Berkeley, CA 94702
Tel 510.845.6490
www.eastbaynursery.com

Eastern Plant Specialties
P.O. Box 5692
Clark, NJ 07066
www.easternplant.com

Easyliving Wildflowers
P.O. Box 522
Willow Springs, MO 65793
Tel/fax 417.469.2611
www.easywildflowers.com

Elkhorn Nursery
P.O. Box 270
Moss Landing, CA 95039
Tel 831.763.1207
Fax 831.763.1659
www.elkhorn.wildwestdesign.com

Forest Farm
990 Tetherow Rd.
Williams, OR 97544-9599
www.forestfarm.com

Gardens of the Blue Ridge
P.O. Box 10
Pineola, NC 28662
Tel 828.733.2417
Fax 828.733.8894
www.gardensoftheblueridge.com

Garden Makers
P.O. Box 65
Rowley, MA 01969-0165
Tel 978.948.8481
Fax 978.948.8481
www.gardenmakers.com

Goodwin Creek Gardens
P.O. Box 83
Williams, OR 97544
www.goodwincreekgardens.com

Grass Roots Nursery
24765 Bell Rd.
New Boston, MI 48164
Tel 734.753.9200
Fax 734.654.2405
www.grassrootsnursery.com

Herbs Roots & Barks LLC
977 Daws Ridge Rd.
Nancy, KY 42544
Tel 606.871.9711
www.shadeflower.com

Heronswood Nursery
7530 NE 288th St.
Kingston, WA 98346
Tel 360.297.4172
www.heronswood.com

High Country Gardens
202 Rufina St.
Santa Fe, NM 87057-2929
Tel 800.925.9387
Fax 800.925.0097
www.highcountrygardens.com

Horsford Nursery
2111 Greenbush Rd.
Charlotte, VT 05445
Tel 802.425.2811
Fax 802.425.2797
www.horsfordnursery.com

Ion Exchange Nursery
1878 Old Mission Dr.
Harpers Ferry, IA 52146
Tel 800.291.2143
Fax 563.535.7362
www.ionexchange.com

Iris City Gardens
7675 Younger Creek Rd.
Primm Springs, TN 38476
www.iriscitygardens.com

JFNew Native Plant Nursery
128 Sunset Dr.
Walkerton, IN 46574
Tel 574.586.2412
Fax 574.586.2718
www.jfnewnursery.com

Joy Creek Nursery
20300 NW Watson Rd.
Scappoose, OR 97056
Tel 503.543.7474
Fax 503.543.6933
www.joycreek.com

Las Pilitas Nursery
3232 Las Pilitas Rd.
Santa Margarita, CA 93453
Tel 805.438.5992
www.laspilitas.com

Lazy S'S Farm Nursery
2360 Spotswood Trail
Barboursville, VA 22923
Fax 540.832.0869
www.lazyssfarm.com

Loco Valley Plant Farm
Rt. 8, Box 3386-B
Nacogdoches, TX 75964
Tel 409.715.9468

Magnolia Gardens Nursery
1980 Bowler Rd.
Waller, TX 77484
www.magnoliagardens.com

Missouri Wildflowers Nursery
9814 Pleasant Hill Rd.
Jefferson City, MO 65109
Tel 573.496.3492
Fax 573.496.3003
www.mowildflowers.net

Mountain Rose Herbs
P.O. Box 50220
Eugene, OR 97405
Tel 800.879.3337
Fax 510.217.4012
www.mountainroseherbs.com

Mountain Valley Growers
38325 Pepperweed Rd.
Squaw Valley, CA 93675
Tel 559.338.2775
Fax 559.338.0075
www.mountainvalleygrowers.com

Morning Sky Greenery
44804 E Hwy. 28
Morris, MN 56267
Tel/fax 320.795.6234
www.morningskygreenery.com

Mostly Natives Nursery
Box 258, 27235 Hwy. 1
Tomales, CA 94971
Tel 707.878.2009
Fax 707.878.2079
www.mostlynatives.com

Munchkin Nursery & Gardens
323 Woodside Dr. NW
Depauw, IN 47115-9039
Tel 812.633.4858
www.munchkinnursery.com

Native Plant Nursery
P.O. Box 7841
Ann Arbor, MI 48107
Tel 734.677.3260
www.nativeplant.com

Native Plant Nursery & Gardens
2158 Bower Ct. SE
Salem, OR 97301
Tel 503.581.2638
Fax 503.581.9957

Native Plant Source
318 Misty Crescent
Kitchener, ON N2B 3V5
Tel 519.748.4021
Fax 519.748.2788
www.nativeplantsource.com

Natural Garden
38W443 Hwy. 64
St Charles, IL 60175
Tel 630.584.0150
Fax 630.584.9185
www.thenaturalgardeninc.com

Nature Hills Nursery
3334 N 88th Plaza
Omaha, NE 68134
Tel 888.864.7663
Fax 866.550.9556
www.naturehills.com

North Haven Gardens
7700 Northaven Rd.
Dallas, TX 75230
Tel 214.363.5316
www.nhg.com

Ohio Prairie Nursery
P.O. Box 174
Hiram, OH 44234
Tel 866.569.3380
Fax 330.569.7090
www.ohioprairienursery.com

Overhill Gardens
1404 Citico Rd.
Vonore, TN 37885
Tel/fax 423.295.2288
www.overhillgardens.com

Pacific Rim Native Plant Nursery
44305 Old Orchard Rd.
Chilliwack, BC V2R 1A9
Tel 604.792.9279
Fax 604.792.1891
www.hillkeep.ca

Peaceful Valley Farm Supply
P.O. Box 2209
Grass Valley, CA 95945
Tel 530.272 4769
www.groworganic.com

Perennial Garden
13139 224th St.
Maple Ridge, BC V4R 2P6
www.perennialgardener.com

Phoenix Perennials
3380 6th Rd.
Richmond, BC V6V 1P3
Tel/fax 604.270.4133
www.phoenixperennials.com

Pine Ridge Gardens
832 Sycamore Rd.
London, AR 72847
Tel 501.293.4359
www.pineridgegardens.com

Plants of the Southwest
3095 Agua Fria St.
Santa Fe, NM 87507
Tel 800.788.7333
Fax 505.438.8800
www.plantsofthesouthwest.com

Prairie Frontier
Waukesha, WI 53189
Tel 262.544.6708
www.prairiefrontier.com

Prairie Moon Nursery
P.O. Box 163
Winona, MN 55987
Tel 507.452.1362
Fax 507.454.5238
www.prairiemoonnursery.com

Prairie Nursery
P.O. Box 306
Westfield, WI 53964
Tel 800.476.9453
Fax 608.296.2741
www.prairienursery.com

Rice Creek Gardens
11506 Hwy. 65
Blaine, MN 55434
Tel 763.754.8090
www.ricecreekgardens.com

Santa Rosa Nursery
P.O. Box 1187
Gulf Breeze, FL 32562
Tel 866.681.0856
www.santarosagardens.com

Shooting Star Nursery
160 Soards Rd.
Georgetown, KY 40324
Tel 502.223.1679
Fax 502.227.5700
www.shootingstarnursery.com

Singing Springs Nursery
8802 Wilkerson Rd.
Cedar Grove, NC 27231
www.singingspringsnursery.com

Specialty Perennials
481 Reflection Rd.
Apple Valley, MN 55124
Tel/fax 952.432.8673
www.hardyplants.com

Stecks Nursery
100 Putnam Park Rd., Rt. 58
Bethel, CT 06801
Tel 800.800.9732
Fax 203.792.1936
www.atstecks.com

Sugar Creek Gardens
1011 North Woodlawn
Kirkwood, MO 63122
Tel 314.965.3070
www.sugarcreekgardens.com

Sunlight Gardens
174 Golden Ln.
Andersonville, TN 37705
Tel 800.272.7396
Fax 865.494.7086
www.sunlightgardens.com

Sunny Border Nursery
www.sunnyborder.com

Sunshine Nursery
Rt. 1, Box 4030
Clinton, OK 73601
Tel 580.323.6259
Fax 580.323.3759
www.sunshinenursery.com

T's Flowers and Things
9181 W 300 N
Delphi, IN 46923
www.tsflowers.com

Terrapin Gardens
13825 162nd Ave. NE
Woodinville, WA 98072-9036
www.terrapin-gardens.com

Thompson and Morgan Seed Co.
www.thompson-morgan.com

Toadshade Wildflower Farm
53 Everittstown Rd.
Frenchtown, NJ 08825
Fax 908.996.7500
www.toadshade.com

Triple Brook Farm
37 Middle Rd.
Southampton, MA 01073
www.triplebrookfarm.com

Ty Ty Nursery
4723 Hwy. 82 W, Box 130
TyTy, GA 31795
Tel 800.972.2101
www.tytyga.com

Walters Gardens
1992 96th Ave., Box 137
Zeeland, MI 49464
Tel 888.925.8377
Fax 800.752.1879
www.waltersgardens.com

Wildflower Farm
RR 3
Schomberg, ON L0G 1T0
Tel 866.476.9453
Fax 905.859.4809
www.wildflower.com

Wild Seed Farms
425 Wildflower Hills
Fredericksburg, TX 78624
Tel 800.848.0078
Fax 830.990.8090

Wrightman Alpine Nursery
1503 Napperton Dr., RR 3
Kerwood, ON N0M 2B0
Tel/fax 519.247.3751
www.wrightmanalpines.com

Yucca Do Nursery
P.O. Box 907
Hempstead, TX 77445
Fax 979.826.4571
www.yuccado.com

Plant societies

State and provincial societies

Many thanks to Jack Sanders and the North American Native Plant Society (see under "National societies") for compiling these data. Note that addresses for state and provincial societies may change from year to year.

Alabama
Alabama Wildflower Society
11120 Ben Clements Rd.
Northport, AL 35475

Alaska
Alaska Native Plant Society
P.O. Box 141613
Anchorage, AK 99514-1613

Alberta
Alberta Native Plant Council
52099, Garneau Postal Outlet
Edmonton, AB T6G 2T5
www.anpc.ab.ca

Arizona
Arizona Native Plant Society
P.O. Box 41206, Sun Station
Tucson, AZ 85717-1206
aznps.org

Arkansas
Arkansas Native Plant Society
P.O. Box 250250
Little Rock, AR 72225

British Columbia
Garry Oak Meadow Preservation
    Society
A-954 Queens Avenue
Victoria, BC V8T 1M6

Native Plant Society of British
    Columbia
2012 William St.
Vancouver, BC V5L 2X6
www.npsbc.org

Victoria Horticultural Society
Native Plant Study Group
P.O. Box 5081, Postal Stn. B
Victoria, BC V8R 6N3

California
California Native Plant Society
1722 J St. #17
Sacramento, CA 95814-2931
www.cnps.org

Colorado
Colorado Native Plant Society
P.O. Box 200
Fort Collins, CO 80522-0200

Connecticut
Connecticut Botanical Society
P.O. Box 9004
New Haven, CT 06532-0004
www.ct-botanical-society.org

Delaware
Delaware Native Plant Society
P.O. Box 369
Dover, DE 19903
www.delawarenativeplants.org

Mt. Cuba Center for the Study of
    Piedmont Flora
Box 3570
Greenville, DE 19807

District of Columbia
Botanical Society of Washington
Dept. of Botany, NHB 166
Smithsonian Institution
Washington, DC 20560

Florida
Florida Native Plant Society
P.O. Box 690278
Vero Beach, FL 32969-0278
www.fnps.org

Georgia
Georgia Native Plant Society
P.O. Box 422085
Atlanta, GA 30342-2085
www.gnps.org

Idaho
Idaho Native Plant Society
P.O. Box 9451
Boise, ID 83707-3451

Illinois
Illinois Native Plant Society
Forest Glen Preserve
20301 E 900 North Rd.
Westville, IL 61883
www.il-inps.org

Indiana
Indiana Native Plant and Wildflower
    Society
16508 Oak Rd.
Westfield, IN 46074-9436

Iowa
Iowa Native Plant Society
Ada Hayden Herbarium
Iowa State University
Ames, IA 50011-1020
www.public.iastate.edu/~herbarium/
    inps/inpshome.htm

Kansas
Kansas Wildflower Society
R. L. McGregor Herbarium,
    University of Kansas
2045 Constant Ave.
Lawrence, KS 66047-3729
www.cs.hesston.edu/kws

Kentucky
Kentucky Native Plant Society
Dept. of Biological Science
Eastern Kentucky University
Richmond, KY 40475
www.knps.org

Louisiana
Louisiana Native Plant Society
216 Caroline Dormon Rd.
Saline, LA 71070
www.lnps.org

Maine
Josselyn Botanical Society
566 N. Auburn Rd.
Auburn, ME 04210

Maryland
Maryland Native Plant Society
P.O. Box 4877
Silver Spring, MD 20914
mdflora.org

Massachusetts
New England Wild Flower Society
180 Hemenway Rd.
Framingham, MA 01701-2699
www.newfs.org

Michigan
Michigan Botanical Club
7951 Walnut Ave.
Newaygo, MI 49337
michbotclub.org

Minnesota
Minnesota Native Plant Society
250 Bio. Sci. Center, University of
    Minnesota
1445 Gortner Ave.
St. Paul, MN 55108-1020
www.mnnps.org/

Mississippi
Mississippi Native Plant Society
Crosby Arboretum, Box 190
Picayune, MS 29466
www.msstate.edu/dept/crec/
    camnps.html

Missouri
Missouri Native Plant Society
P.O. Box 20073
St. Louis, MO 63144-0073
www.missouri.edu/~umo_herb/
    monps

Montana
Montana Native Plant Society
P.O. Box 8783
Missoula, MT 59807-8782

Nevada
Northern Nevada Native Plant Society
Box 8965
Reno, NV 89507-8965

New Jersey
Native Plant Society of New Jersey
Office of Continuing Professional
    Education
Cook College, 102 Ryders Ln.
New Brunswick, NJ 08901-8519
www.npsnj.org

Newfoundland
Wildflower Society of
    Newfoundland/Labrador
Botanical Garden, Memorial
    University
St. Johns, NF A1C 5S7
www.chem.mun.ca/~hclase/wf/
    index.html

New Mexico
Native Plant Society of New Mexico
P.O. Box 5917
Santa Fe, NM 87502

New York
Finger Lakes Native Plant Society of
    Ithaca
532 Cayuga Heights Rd.
Ithaca, NY 14850

New York Flora Association
New York State Museum
3132 CEC
Albany, NY 12230
www.nyflora.org/

Niagara Frontier Botanical Society
Buffalo Museum of Science
1020 Humboldt Pkwy.
Buffalo, NY 14211
www.nfwhc.org/nfbs.htm

North Carolina

North Carolina Native Plant Society
North Carolina Botanical Garden
Totten Garden Center 3375
University of North Carolina
Chapel Hill, NC 27599-3375
www.ncwildflower.org

Yellow Creek Botanical Institute
P.O. Box 1757
Robbinsville, NC 28771

Nova Scotia

Nova Scotia Wild Flora Society
Nova Scotia Museum
1747 Summer St.
Halifax, NS B3H 3A6

Ohio

Cincinnati Wild Flower Preservation
   Society
9005 Decima St.
Cincinnati, OH 45242

Native Plant Society of Northeastern
   Ohio
640 Cherry Park Oval
Aurora, OH 44202
communities.msn.com/NativePlant
   SocietyofNortheastOhio

Ohio Native Plant Society
6 Louise Dr.
Chagrin Falls, OH 44022

Ontario

Canadian Wildflower Society,
   Dogtooth-Wellington
Botany Dept., University of Guelph
Guelph, ON N1G 2W1

Canadian Wildflower Society, East
   Toronto
43 Anaconda Ave.
Scarborough, ON M1L 4M1

Canadian Wildflower Society, London
1 Windsor Crescent
London, ON N6C 1V6

Field Botanists of Ontario
c/o W. D. McIlveen
RR 1
Acton, ON L7J 2L7
www.trentu.ca/fbo/

Oklahoma

Oklahoma Native Plant Society
Tulsa Garden Center
2435 S. Peoria
Tulsa, OK 74114-1350

Oregon

Native Plant Society of Oregon
P.O. Box 902
Eugene, OR 97440
www.npsoregon.org

Pennsylvania

Botanical Society of Western
   Pennsylvania
5837 Nicholson St.
Pittsburgh, PA 15217

Delaware Valley Fern Wildflower
   Society
263 Hillcrest Rd.
Wayne, PA 19087
www.dvfws.org

Pennsylvania Native Plant Society
P.O. Box 281
State College, PA 16804-0281
www.pawildflower.org

Quebec
FloraQuebeca
445 rue du Portage
Mont-Laurier, QC J9L 2A1
www.floraquebeca.qc.ca

Rhode Island
Rhode Island Wild Plant Society
P.O. Box 114
Peace Dale, RI 02883-0114

South Carolina
South Carolina Native Plant Society
P.O. Box 759
Pickens, SC 29671
www.scnps.org

Southern Appalachian Botanical
    Society
Newberry College
2100 College St.
Newberry, SC 29108

South Dakota
Great Plains Native Plant Society
P.O. Box 461
Hot Springs, SD 57747

Tennessee
Tennessee Native Plant Society
c/o Dept. of Botany
University of Tennessee
Knoxville, TN 37996-1100

The Wildflower Society
Goldsmith Civic Garden Center
750 Cherry Rd.
Memphis, TN 38119-4699

Texas
Native Plant Society of Texas
P.O. Box 891
Georgetown, TX 78627-0891
www.npsot.org

Utah
Utah Native Plant Society
P.O. Box 520041
Salt Lake City, UT 84152-0041
www.xmission.com/~unps/
    index.html

Virginia
Virginia Native Plant Society
400 Blandy Farm Lane #2
Boyce, VA 22620
www.vnps.org

Washington
Washington Native Plant Society
6310 NE 74th St. #215E
Seattle, WA 98115
Tel 888-288-8022
www.wnps.org

West Virginia
West Virginia Native Plant Society
P.O. Box 808
New Haven, WV 25265-0808

Wisconsin
Botanical Club of Wisconsin
Wisconsin Academy of Arts, Sciences
    and Letters
1922 University Ave.
Madison, WI 53705

Wyoming
Wyoming Native Plant Society
1604 Grand Ave. #2
Laramie, WY 82070

National societies

Many of these societies are educational in nature: some are "global"; others, more specific.

American Association of Field
    Botanists
P.O. Box 23542
Chattanooga, TN 37422

American Penstemon Society
1569 South Holland Ct.
Lakewood, CO 80226

Center for Plant Conservation
Missouri Botanical Garden
P.O. Box 299
St. Louis, MO 63166

Lady Bird Johnson Wildflower Center
4801 La Crosse Blvd.
Austin, TX 78739
www.wildflower.org

Natural Areas Association
320 South Third St.
Rockford, IL 61104

North American Native Orchid
    Alliance
84 Etna St.
Brighton, MA 02135

North American Native Plant Society
Box 84, Postal Station D
Etobicoke, ON M9A 4X1
www.nanps.org

Society for Ecological Restoration
University of Wisconsin Arboretum
1207 Seminole Hwy.
Madison, WI 53711

The Wild Ones Natural Landscapers
    Ltd.
P.O. Box 1274
Appleton, WI 54912-1274
www.for-wild.org

Internet sites

So many sites on the Internet offer information concerning native plants. Here is a short list of Web sites I found useful and have not yet mentioned in the other lists. They are in alphabetical order, after www or http; contact your state extension service for recommended sites for your region. Again, apologies ahead of time for those I have missed.

www.davesgarden.com
    One of the better "private" sites I visited—extensive and devoted to gardeners.

www.efloras.org
    Flora of North America, among others. Excellent information.

www.ext.colostate.edu/psel
    Plant Select, a cooperative program between the Denver Botanic Gardens and Colorado State University "designed to seek out and distribute the very best plants for gardens from the high plains to the intermountain region."

www.fs.fed.us/database
> Federal government (USDA Forest Service) "data and information systems" links.

www.grownative.org
> An excellent site for Midwest natives, in the wild and in the landscape.

www.hardyfernlibrary.com
> Makes identifying hardy ferns "as easy as falling off a *Dryopteris celsa.*"

www.hortsource.com
> A horticultural resource site for gardeners.

www.missouriplants.com
> In-depth descriptions of many plants native to the Plains states.

www.mobot.org/hort/gardens/kemper/intro/index.shtml
> Kemper Center for Home Gardening at the Missouri Botanical Garden.

www.nazflora.org
> A photographic, annotated catalog of northern Arizona vascular plants.

www.nearctica.com
> Excellent coverage of eastern wildflowers.

www.plantnative.org
> Native plant nurseries directory.

http://plants.usda.gov
> USDA Web site, excellent for habitat information.

www.serpin.org
> Southeastern rare plant information network.

www.swcoloradowildflowers.com
> Southwestern Colorado wildflowers, ferns, and trees, covering the Four Corners area of Colorado, New Mexico, Arizona, and Utah.

http://2bnthewild.com
> An excellent site for native plants of the Southeast.

www.uga.edu/ugatrial
> The University of Georgia trials mentioned throughout the book.

www.wildflower2.org
> The Native Plant Information Network of the Lady Bird Johnson Wildflower Center.

www.winternet.com/~chuckg/dictionary.html
> A listing of the meaning of botanical names.

Books

I have not included a huge bibliography: there are dozens of books about local wildflowers (the cooperative extension office in nearly every state has publications on native plants) and an assortment of well-illustrated guides to wildflowers for various regions of the country. I myself referred to dozens of field guides for native plants around this country and works by such wonderful authors as Wilber Duncan, Jan Midgely, Harry Phillips, Bebe Miles, and Peter Loewer. I used several books all the time, however—Internet be damned—because they provided essential, sound information. It would take me a decade or so to come close to doing what they did.

The New England Wild Flower Society Guide to Growing and Propagating Wildflowers of the United States and Canada by William Cullina, 2000.
334 pages. Houghton Mifflin.
Bill Cullina is the nursery manager at the Garden in the Woods, the wonderful botanic garden of the New England Wild Flower Society in Framingham, Massachusetts. He is this country's best resource for practical information about wildflowers. His wit and writing style make the book highly readable, and his information on propagation is by far the best I have come across. I used it, along with what little I know and the knowledge of others, in my brief descriptions of propagation.

Stearn's Dictionary of Plant Names for Gardeners by William T. Stearn, 1996.
373 pages. Timber Press.
An excellent reference for the inquisitive and curious among us. Dr. Stearn has researched the origin and meaning of hundreds of botanical names. I referred to it all the time in researching the etymology of the plant names.

Wildflowers of the United States by Harold William Rickett, 1966–73.
6 vols. New York Botanical Garden.
If I could keep but one set of books of wildflowers, it would be this. I can only imagine the time, energy, and frustration expended by Rickett and the staff at the New York Botanical Garden in putting this massive collection together. The country is divided into six regions (Northeast, Southeast, Texas, Southwest, Northwest, and Central Mountains and Plains), each region consisting of two or three volumes. Descriptions, photos, and distribution for thousands of wildflowers can be found in these texts; with no apologies, I referred to them constantly and found them particularly useful for their information on habitat. Books are out of print but can be found in specialist book stores (I obtained mine from The Captain's Bookshelf in Asheville, North Carolina) and on the Internet.

USEFUL LISTS

The lists presented here are simple references for gardeners or professionals searching for native plants to fulfill a specific need. In general, only the genus has been provided (with any exclusions noted); additional information may be found in the text. Some genera appear but once, others many times. The lists are guidelines only and are not meant to be taken as gospel.

Drought-tolerant plants

Plants in this category tend to wilt more slowly under drought conditions. They may be more efficient in the use of water or have root systems that "mine" water. Many drought-tolerant plants have small leaves (like grasses) to reduce the loss of water through transpiration. That they tolerate drought does not mean they will not perform better when irrigated: in this category, the important word is "tolerate." Refer to extension publications and other texts on xeric gardening for additional information.

Agastache (cana, rupestris)
Andropogon
Antennaria
Asarum
Asclepias (sullivantii, tuberosa)
Aster (oblongifolius)
Baptisia
Berlandiera
Bouteloua
Buchloe
Callirhoe
Chasmanthium
Chrysopsis
Conoclinium
Coreopsis
Echinacea (pallida, paradoxa, simulata)
Epilobium
Eragrostis
Eryngium
Eupatorium (all but fistulosum, subsp. maculatum)
Gaillardia
Gaura
Helianthus (maximiliani, occidentalis)
Mitella
Muhlenbergia
Nassella
Oenothera
Pachysandra
Panicum
Parthenium
Penstemon
Phacelia
Schizachyrium
Scutellaria
Sedum
Silene
Sporobolus
Tagetes
Talinum
Thermopsis
Zinnia

Water lovers

These plants perform better when their roots are consistently wet and may be perfectly at home in a bog, pond, or swamp.

Darmera	*Iris*	*Thalia*
Geum	*Lysichiton*	*Trollius*
Hibiscus	*Saururus*	

Plants that attract butterflies

Butterflies are not only attractive, they are the "in" creatures these days. I am not sure when these flitting little things became the royals of the garden, but they have attracted societies, books, and studies as to why they flit where they do. Butterfly conservatories have sprung up like zoos, with netting replacing the bars. I too enjoy butterflies, although I am not crazy about the caterpillars from which they must come. However, native gardens—especially meadow and prairie gardens—come alive when butterflies are invited in. Here are a few genera that can be counted on to attract these insects—have fun.

Agastache	*Dicentra*	*Phlox*
Amsonia	*Echinacea*	*Physostegia*
Antennaria	*Eupatorium*	*Pycnanthemum*
Aquilegia	*Gaillardia*	*Rudbeckia* (hirta)
Asclepias	*Helenium*	*Salvia* (greggii, lyrata)
Aster	*Helianthus*	*Senecio*
Baptisia	*Heliopsis*	*Solidago*
Boltonia	*Hibiscus*	*Spigelia*
Centaurea	*Liatris*	*Stokesia*
Chelone	*Lilium*	*Verbena*
Clematis	*Marshallia*	*Vernonia*
Conoclinium	*Monarda*	*Viola*
Coreopsis	*Penstemon*	*Zinnia*

Plants that attract hummingbirds

It is amazing what the sight of a tiny, flittering bird does to a grown-up. Just one visit gets everyone in the flight path hooked, and plants that attract hummingbirds become the holy grail. There are many hummingbird-magnets, some more magnetic than others; here are a few that seem to work.

Agastache	*Liatris*	*Physostegia*
Aquilegia	*Lilium*	*Salvia*
Asclepias	*Lobelia*	*Silene*
Epilobium	*Monarda*	*Silphium*
Hibiscus	*Penstemon*	*Spigelia*
Impatiens	*Phlox*	*Verbena*

Plants that are less palatable to deer

Regardless of where I speak or the make-up of the audience, one of the first questions I can count on will be about deer (or rabbits or . . .). Guaranteed! That deer are such a widespread problem suggests that predators are almost nonexistent and that population control has failed miserably. Not only are our gardens being decimated, but far more importantly, so are our woodlands and prairies. In the garden, everything from homemade recipes to commercial products sold at the garden center have been used with varying degrees of success. Hunting season has been extended in some areas, but the populations are still out of control in many counties and states.

If the deer are hungry enough, there seems to be little they will not eat; however, here are a few plants that seem to pop up consistently on those ubiquitous deer lists.

Aconitum	*Dicentra*	*Penstemon*
Actaea	*Echinacea*	*Polemonium*
Amsonia (*hubrichtii,* *tabernaemontana*)	*Equisetum*	*Ratibida*
	Eryngium	*Rudbeckia*
Andropogon	*Eupatorium*	*Salvia* (most)
Aquilegia	*Gaillardia*	*Sedum*
Asclepias	*Geranium*	*Senecio*
Aster	*Helianthus*	*Silene*
Baptisia (*australis,* *sphaerocarpa*)	*Heuchera*	*Smilacina*
	Hibiscus	*Solidago*
Berlandiera	*Liatris*	*Spigelia*
Boltonia (*asteroides*)	*Lobelia* (*siphilitica*)	*Stylophorum*
Bouteloua	*Mertensia*	*Tiarella*
Chasmanthium	*Monarda*	*Veronicastrum*
Chelone	*Oenothera*	*Viola*
Coreopsis (*auriculata*)	*Pachysandra*	*Zinnia*
Delphinium		

Rabbit-resistant plants

Rabbits are less visible than deer; when our vehicle hits them as they cross the road, the car usually wins. That they are so numerous is as much a tribute to their reproductivity as to the lack of predators. Similar to deer, concoctions are useful, and also similar, if rabbits are numerous and hungry enough, their palate seems to tolerate almost anything. Here are a few genera that may be less palatable. The list is smaller than that for deer, but this likely reflects less rabbit-interest: less attention has been paid to plants that may be ignored by rabbits.

Agastache	*Eryngium*	*Salvia*
Aquilegia	*Gaillardia*	*Silene*
Coreopsis	*Geranium*	*Zinnia*
Equisetum	*Penstemon*	

Plants for full sun

These sun-tolerant plants may be chosen for areas in "the back forty"—that is, sites with more than six hours of direct sun a day. Most plants listed here do not perform as well if placed in areas of afternoon shade.

Agastache
Amsonia
Andropogon
Anemone (*canadensis*)
Asclepias
Aster
Baptisia
Bidens
Boltonia
Bouteloua
Buchloe
Callirhoe
Camassia
Centaurea
Chasmanthium
Chelone (*obliqua*)
Chrysopsis
Conoclinium (if moist soil)
Coreopsis
Delphinium
Echinacea
Elymus
Epilobium
Equisetum
Eryngium

Eupatorium
Euphorbia
Gaillardia
Gentianopsis
Geum
Helenium
Helianthus
Heliopsis
Iris (all but *cristata*, *fulva*, *versicolor*)
Marshallia
Monarda
Muhlenbergia
Nassella
Nemophila
Oenothera
Panicum
Parthenium
Penstemon
Phlox (all but *divaricata*, *pilosa*, *stolonifera*)
Physostegia
Pycnanthemum
Ratibida
Rudbeckia
Ruellia (*humilis*)

Salvia
Sanguisorba
Schizachyrium
Scutellaria
Sedum
Silene
Silphium
Sisyrinchium
Solidago (all but *caesia*, *flexicaulis*)
Sporobolus
Stokesia
Tagetes
Talinum
Thalia
Thalictrum
Thermopsis
Tradescantia
Trollius
Verbena
Vernonia
Veronicastrum
Yucca
Zephyranthes
Zinnia

Plants for partial shade

The definition of shade is confusing. Does the area have all-day shade, or shade only in the morning or afternoon? Is the shade from deciduous or coniferous trees, or from buildings? Plants in this category are best sited where they receive morning sun and afternoon shade; all will tolerate morning sun.

Actaea
Adiantum
Adlumia
Agastache
Anemone (*canadensis*)
Antennaria
Aquilegia

Arisaema
Asarum
Athyrium
Blephilia
Cardamine
Caulophyllum
Chelone (all but *obliqua*)

Chrysogonum
Claytonia
Clintonia
Conoclinium
Corydalis
Cypripedium
Darmera

Dicentra
Diphylleia
Disporum
Dryopteris
Elymus
Equisetum
Erythronium
Gentiana
Geranium
Geum
Gillenia
Hepatica
Heuchera
Hydrastis
Hydrophyllum
Hymenocallis
Impatiens
Iris (cristata, fulva,

versicolor)
Isopyrum
Jeffersonia
Lobelia (cardinalis)
Mertensia
Mitella
Monarda
Onoclea
Osmunda
Pachysandra
Phlox (divaricata, pilosa, stolonifera)
Polygonatum
Pycnanthemum (all but virginianum)
Sanguinaria
Scutellaria

Sedum (ternatum)
Senecio
Shortia
Smilacina
Spigelia
Spiranthes
Stylophorum
Tellima
Thalictrum
Tiarella
Tradescantia
Trillium
Uvularia
Viola (labradorica)
Waldsteinia
Woodwardia
Zizia

Plants for heavy shade

Plants in this list can be sited in areas that receive shade all day. One would expect to see some ephemeral woodlanders (especially if shade is deciduous), ferns, and forest-floor plants. That they tolerate all-day shade does not mean they will not perform better in partial shade: in this category, once again, the important word is "tolerate."

Arisaema
Asarum
Athyrium
Chrysogonum
Darmera
Disporum

Dryopteris
Onoclea
Osmunda
Pachysandra
Podophyllum

Polygonatum
Shortia
Stylophorum
Viola (labradorica)
Woodwardia

Ephemerals

The characteristic of summer dormancy is a protective mechanism. When conditions are not favorable, the plant goes dormant and returns the next spring. Lack of rain, unseasonably hot or cold temperatures, or other environmental anomalies can result in earlier dormancy and even cause some species that otherwise would not do so to enter into dormancy. The genera listed here contain species that are often dormant by mid to late summer.

Cardamine
Claytonia
Clintonia
Delphinium

Dicentra
Dodecatheon
Erythronium
Mertensia

Podophyllum
Stylophorum
Trillium

Annuals

The botanical definition of "annual" is a plant that grows, flowers, fruits, and dies in one season—a definition rebutted by the longevity of so-called annuals in a greenhouse. In gardening circles, an annual is simply a plant that will not tolerate winter. What is an annual in Minnesota may be a perennial in Texas and Florida. The following genera have what we refer to as annual species throughout most of the country.

Coreopsis	*Monarda*	*Phacelia*
Euphorbia	*Nemophila*	
Helianthus		

Bulbs or corms

The following genera contain species that come back from an underground structure, such as a bulb or corm. The many genera with rhizomes are not included here.

Camassia	*Erythronium*	*Lilium*
Claytonia	*Hymenocallis*	*Zephyranthes*
Crinum	*Hypoxis*	

INDEX OF BOTANICAL NAMES

INDEX OF COMMON NAMES